AN EARLY MYSTIC OF BAGHDAD

A Study of the Life and Teaching of Ḥārith B. Asad al-Muḥāsibī A.D. 781–857

MARGARET SMITH

SHELDON PRESS
LONDON

By the same author

An Introduction to Mysticism
The Way of Mystics
The Sufi Path of Love

First published in Great Britain in 1935

Reprinted in 1977 by Sheldon Press
Marylebone Road, London NW1 4DU

Printed in Great Britain by
Billing & Sons Ltd, Guildford, London and Worcester

ISBN 0 85969 131 4

PREFACE

Ḥārith b. Asad al-Muḥāsibī, whose life and teaching form the subject of this study, was born at Baṣra about A.D. 781, and lived and taught at Baghdad. He has long been recognised by Islāmic scholars as the real master of primitive Islāmic mysticism, and his writings prove him to be one of the greatest mystic theologians of Islām. Although he was a prolific writer, none of his works have as yet been published or edited, and this study is based almost entirely on unpublished MS. sources to be found in the libraries of Europe and the East.

A study of al-Muḥāsibī's writings proves conclusively that he was the precursor of al-Ghazālī in giving to Ṣūfī mysticism an assured place in orthodox Islām, and that al-Muḥāsibī's teaching formed the basis of much of the teaching of the greatest of the Muslim mystics, both Arab and Persian, who succeeded him, and especially of those who, in their turn, influenced the Christian scholastics.

al-Muḥāsibī's most important work, the *Ri'āya liḥuqūq Allāh*, well known to Orientalists in both East and West, is, perhaps, the finest manual on the interior life which Islām has produced : an edition of the Arabic text is long overdue, and I have already begun the work of collating the existing MSS.

My thanks are due to Dr. A. Guillaume, of Culham, for valuable suggestions ; to Mr. A. J. Arberry, of the India Office, for the generous loan of his own MSS., and to Professor R. A. Nicholson, of Cambridge, for constant and invaluable help while I was engaged upon this study. I have to express my gratitude also to all those who gave me assistance while I was travelling in the Near East, in the spring of 1933, in search of material. These included the Director of the Royal Library at Cairo and his assistants ; Dr. Bergmann and Dr. Billig, of the Hebrew University Library at Jerusalem, where I spent many profitable hours ;

Shaykh al-Maghibi, of the Zahiriyya Library at Damascus; and Dr. H. Ritter, of Constantinople, who gave me valuable material and references to assist me in my work.

Like others who had the privilege of his friendship, I owe much to the late Professor F. C. Burkitt, of Cambridge, whose unfailing kindness and willingness to give of his time and help, to those who sought it in the pursuit of their own studies, will remain in the memory of all who knew him.

Finally, most grateful thanks are due to my College, which, by electing me to a Research Fellowship, enabled me to carry out this study, to secure the necessary material, and to undertake the travels which were essential to its completion.

MARGARET SMITH.

CAMBRIDGE,
July, 1935.

TABLE OF CONTENTS

CHAPTER I

ENVIRONMENT AND EARLY LIFE—THE CITY OF PEACE

It was the accession of the 'Abbāsid Dynasty to power (A.D. 750-1258) which led to the transference of the capital of the Muslim Empire from Damascus, which had been the headquarters of the Umayyad rule, to the Middle East, since the new rulers found their chief supporters among the non-Arab peoples of Persia and Khurāsān, and there, on the site of a Christian village on the west bank of the Tigris, the Caliph al-Manṣūr (A.D. 750-775) laid the foundations of his new city of Baghdad (the Gift of God), the "Abode of Peace," the earthly Paradise, in A.D. 762, and for five hundred years it remained the seat of the 'Abbāsid government, and the centre of a Muslim civilisation and culture of very wide extent.

Situated where it was, the new Muslim capital could not fail to be also a world-centre, a mart for trade not only between all the provinces of the Empire, but for traders from the Far East and from Africa and the West. To Baghdad came the products of India and the Malay Archipelago, of China and Turkistān and Russia, the ivory and slaves of East Africa, and these were brought long distances by land and sea by traders and navigators from all parts.[1] But it was not only as an international trade-centre that Baghdad came into contact with the civilised world of the time; of greater importance and value were the contacts made between the "House of Islām" and the ideas and culture of far older and more advanced civilisations than that from which it had had its rise. Persians, and especially the natives of Khurāsān, were employed in a variety of important posts by the 'Abbāsid rulers, who found that in 'Irāq and Syria they needed the help of those members of the tolerated sects who had an expert knowledge of book-keeping and secretarial work, and especially of the system of land taxation prevailing in Persia. Many of the govern-

[1] *Cf.* R. Levy, *A Baghdad Chronicle*, pp. 32 *ff*.

ment clerks were Christians, and under the Caliph al-Mu'taṣim (A.D. 833-842) there was a Christian Secretary of State, and a Christian in charge of the Treasury, and others of the Caliphs employed Christian physicians, interpreters and scribes.[1]

Such contacts meant that Islamic faith and culture at this period were subject to influences from outside, which included not only those of Christianity, represented by the Nestorian and Jacobite Churches, but also those of Judaism, from the many and influential Jewish communities in 'Irāq and the two great academies of Jewish learning which had been established at Punbeditha and Sora. There was in addition the influence of Zoroastrianism, from the Magians of Persia—not only those who maintained their own faith, but also those converted to Islām—and of paganism, from the inhabitants of such centres of intellectual life as Ḥarrān or Charræ, near Edessa. So the learning and philosophy of Greece and Rome from the West, and of Persia and of India from the East, were brought to the knowledge of Muslims. Literature, history, medicine and astronomy began to be studied from the reign of al-Manṣūr onwards, and the contributions of poets, philosophers, historians, mathematicians, and savants of many schools of thought served to make the Arabic language the instrument of a world-literature of rich and varied content. The Caliph al-Mahdī (A.D. 775-785) was a patron of music and poetry, and a new school of poetry arose, which differed greatly from that of the early Arab writers, who were concerned with the expression of Beduin life and interests, while the new poetry was clearly affected by Persian and Hellenistic culture. Abu'l-'Aṭāhiya (*ob.* A.D. 828), one of the early exponents of this new school, wrote poetry marked by a spirit of philosophic asceticism, which is akin to the teaching of the earliest ascetic mystics of Islām.[2] That he was accused of unorthodoxy was no bar to the appreciation of his work, for at the court of the earlier 'Abbāsids a certain amount of free-thinking, resulting from the general

[1] J. Zaydan, *History of Islamic Civilisation*, pp. 166 *ff*.

[2] *Diwān* (Beyrout, 1886). For specimens of his poetry translated *cf*. R. A. Nicholson, *Literary History of the Arabs*, pp. 298 *ff*.

enlightenment and the new knowledge of other faiths, was the fashion, and so long as these innovators conducted themselves with discretion and gave no trouble to those in authority, they were encouraged in their efforts by rulers who wished to be considered as patrons of learning and progress.[1]

It was the reign of al-Mahdī's son, Hārūn al-Rashīd (A.D. 786-809), which represented the beginning of the greatest age of Islāmic culture, for Hārūn was a great patron of the arts, and spared neither trouble nor expense to bring to his court the most distinguished men of the day. Schools were established in large numbers, and practically everyone was literate; books were cheap, and booksellers' shops were numerous, and then, as now, in the East, were a meeting-place for scholars. The next Caliph, al-Ma'mūn (A.D. 813-833), went further still in his zeal for learning, and in Constantinople, Armenia, Syria and Egypt, and in Ḥarrān also, the works of the Greek and Syriac writers were collected, in many cases from the monasteries. The "House of Wisdom" (*Bayt al-Ḥikma*), with a library and astronomical observatory attached, was established in Baghdad, and the most skilful translators available, mainly Christians, with a knowledge of Arabic and Greek as well as Syriac, were employed to translate foreign books into Arabic, including books of history and travel as well as science and philosophy. Any educated resident in Baghdad, therefore, from this time onward, could make acquaintance with the ideas and the principles of the great civilisations which had preceded him, and the city became a centre for the study of Roman law, Greek medicine and philosophy, Indian mysticism, and the subtleties of Persian thought, while the Semitic genius for religion found full scope, and there were set up rival schools of grammarians, poets, and religious commentators.

The 'Abbāsid period included the development of the four great orthodox schools of Muslim theology, under the leadership of the four Imāms. Abū Ḥanīfa (*ob.* 150/767) relied on analogy from the Qur'ānic texts rather than tradition (*ḥadīth*) and laid down the principle of expediency

[1] *Cf.* D. B. Macdonald, *Development of Muslim Theology*, III., p. 133.

(*istiḥsān*); Mālik b. Anas (*ob.* 179/795) relied on tradition, and also accepted the principles of consideration of the public advantage (*istiṣlāḥ*), and of the general consensus (*ijmā'*); al-Shāfi'i (*ob.* 204/820) rejected the *istiḥsān* and the *istiṣlāḥ* and relied entirely upon the Qur'ān, the *ḥadīth* and the principle of consensus; Aḥmad b. Ḥanbal (*ob.* 241/855) was strictly orthodox and opposed to any innovations.

Al-Ma'mūn's reign also included the rise of two great tendencies in religious thought, one being that of the Mu'tazilites (separatists), including the *Qadariyya* (upholders of free will), who maintained that man had freedom of will, and they upheld the sovereignty of reason, calling themselves "the Supporters of Unity and Justice" (*ahl al-Tawḥīd wa'l-'Adl*), because they denied the existence of the Divine attributes as being destructive to the Unity of God, and held that God was not the author of evil, and would not punish men unless they were morally responsible for their own acts. The Mu'tazilites employed the methods of the Alexandrian-Jewish philosophers and adopted an allegorical interpretation of the sacred text, in order to reconcile their own rationalistic idea of God with the irrational idea presented in the Qur'ān. This view gained many adherents, and al-Ma'mūn himself accepted it. The other great tendency was towards mysticism, and it was at this period that Ṣūfism had its rise and development, though at this time it still took the form of asceticism and quietism, rather than of any general pursuit of a mystic theosophy.

al-Ma'mūn himself encouraged freedom of discussion on religious subjects and permitted the holding of debates at his court between Muslims and those of other faiths, and it was during his reign that the famous apology for Christianity by al-Kindī, and its refutation by the Muslim al-Hāshimī, was issued.[1] At this period also Muslims were accustomed to celebrate with the Christians such feasts as those of Christmas and Palm Sunday, and were not averse to being present at Christian services.[2] It was small won-

[1] *Risālat 'A. b. al-Hāshimī ila 'A. al-M. b. Isḥāq al-Kindī wa Risālat al-Kindī ila'l-Hāshimī.*

[2] *Cf.* J. Zaydan, *op cit.*, p. 178; Abū Ṣāliḥ, *Churches and Monasteries of Egypt,* fols. 40*b ff.*, 102*b ff.*

der that a Caliph so tolerant of other faiths should have been known as Amīr al-Kāfirīn (the Commander of the Infidels). Both the *Kitāb al-Dīn wa'l-Dawlat* (written in A.D. 867) of 'A. b. R. al-Tabarī, a Christian converted to Islām, and the *Refutation of the Christians*[1] of al-Jāḥiz (*ob.* A.D. 869) shew the toleration of the Caliphs at Baghdad and the influential position of the Christians up to the time of al-Mutawakkil (A.D. 847-861), a position shared also by the Jews.

Second only in importance to Baghdad was Baṣra, the capital of Khurāsān, which attained an equally high level of prosperity and culture under the 'Abbāsids, being the chief port of the Arab sea-trade, and also a centre of intellectual life, famed for its mosques, which served as schools of learning, and its libraries. Baṣra was famous alike for its theological learning and for its development of Arab philology.

It was at this period, during the 'Abbāsid rule, in the Golden Age of Islām, when Islāmic literature and culture had reached their highest development, and in the region which was the centre of this culture, where the most brilliant and distinguished scholars of the age, writers, poets, grammarians and theologians, were to be found, teaching, writing, and offering the best they had to give to the new generation, that Abū 'Abdallah Ḥārith b. Asad 'Anazī, known later as al-Muḥāsibī, was born, towards A.H. 165 (A.D. 781), at Baṣra. His name of 'Anazī may indicate that he was an Arab of the Beduin tribe of 'Anaza. At an early age he seems to have come to Baghdad and there to have received a very thorough education of the best type available. His writings reveal a complete acquaintance with the theological teaching of the time, and his education plainly included a knowledge of the works and the methods of the philosophers, and those of the unorthodox schools of thought, especially that of the Mu'tazilites, for his teaching witnesses not only to his wide and varied knowledge of Muslim traditions and orthodox Muslim theology, but also shews an acquaintance with exact philosophic definitions and a knowledge of the dialectic methods

[1] Ed. J. Finkel. Cairo, A.H. 1344.

used by the Rationalists of the day.[1] Further, his education most evidently did not exclude contact with Christian and Jewish teaching, from which he draws illustrations and examples for his own purpose, and to which also it may be that he owed his keen sense of the essential need for moral, rather than external, purification.

Very little is known of al-Muḥāsibī's life beyond a few anecdotes, but his biographers agree that his father was a heretic, a *Wāqifī* or *Rāfiḍī*, while another writer states that he was a Qadarī and a Magian. In this connection the Qāḍī Abū 'Ali b. Khayrān related that he saw Ḥārith b. Asad at the gate of al-Ṭāq—the great arched gate at the eastern head of the main bridge over the Tigris—in the middle of the road, clinging to his father, with the people gathered round them, and he was saying to his father, " Divorce my mother, for you are of one faith and she is of another."[2] When the father of Ḥārith al-Muḥāsibī died, he left his son a fortune of thirty thousand dinars ; though Ḥārith was in great poverty, not possessing a single *dāniq*, he refused to take any particle of it, and gave instructions that it should be taken to the Treasury and given to the Government. When asked the reason for this action, he replied that the Prophet had forbidden members of two different sects to inherit from one another. The Prophet had laid it down, he said, and the statement was authentic, that the *Qadarī* was the Magian (the Fireworshipper) of Islām, and since his father was a *Qadarī* and the prophet had forbidden Muslims to inherit from Magians, he could not, being a Muslim, inherit from one who was reckoned a Magian. So he renounced it all, and appears to have lived in poverty until his death.[3]

He was given his title of al-Muḥāsibī because of his practice of frequent self-examination : he used to examine (*ḥasab*) himself when in a state of recollection of God. It was said also, in explanation of his name, that he did not pronounce a single word without having reflected thoroughly on it.

[1] *Cf.* de Boer, *History of Philosophy in Islam*, pp. 42 *ff*.

[2] Abū Nu'aym " Ḥilyat al-Awliyā," fol. 5*a* (Damas.) ; Dhahabī, " Ta'rīkh al-Islām," fol. 23*a*.

[3] Abū Nu'aym, *op cit. loc. cit.* : 'Aṭṭār, *Tadhkirat al-Awliyā*, I., p. 225.

We are told that he was the chief of the Ṣūfī Shaykhs of Baghdad, "a Ṣūfī," says one of his biographers, "whose arrow attained its mark." He was obviously an acceptable teacher and preacher, whose preaching "gave fresh life to men's hearts."[1] He belonged to the Shāfi'ī school of canon law, having studied under the Imām Shāfi'ī himself, and he did not hesitate to recommend his hearers to make use of the reason (*'aql*); he himself, as we have seen, employed the dialectic methods and terminology of the Mu'tazilites, though he was in opposition to their doctrines, and taught and wrote against them and against the *Rāfiḍiyya* (Shī'ites) and heretics in general. His authority was undisputed as a teacher well versed in Ḥadīth and in knowledge of the outward and inward law of conduct (*al-ẓāhir wa'l-bāṭin*). While avoiding the investigation of what did not concern him, he did not hesitate to rebuke the heretical and contentious and was always ready to give sincere advice to novices and those who were travellers on the mystic Way. 'Aṭṭār speaks of him as "that lord of the saints, that pillar among the devout, that great and revered leader, that man of eminent qualities, who was among the most learned of the Shaykhs in regard to things material and spiritual, and in conduct and counsel was an approved spiritual influence unto men, so that the saints of his time accepted his authority in regard to every branch of knowledge."[2]

He is spoken of as a contemplative (*mushāhid*), given to meditation (*murāqib*), but always ready to help others, and a good and loyal friend.[3] His asceticism and his attainment of the mystic "states" (*aḥwāl*) were equally well known, and he was accredited, like other Muslim saints, with the power to work miracles. It was noted as a mark of the Divine favour towards him that he was given a sign whereby he might know if food was of doubtful origin—that is, obtained by means counted unlawful by the Ṣūfīs, who would eat only what was earned by their own labour, or given by friends who had acquired it lawfully. When al-Muḥāsibī stretched out his hand to any doubtful food, a vein in his

[1] al-Munāwī, "al-Kawākib al-Durriya," fol. 107*a*.
[2] Aṭṭār, *Tadhkirat al-Awliyā*, I., p. 225.
[3] Abū Nu'aym, *op. cit.*, fol. 4*a*.

finger throbbed, so that his finger would not obey his will, and he knew that the morsel was unlawful. A similar account is that given by most of his biographers on the authority of al-Junayd,[1] who said: "Ḥārith was very emaciated, and as he passed by one day, when I was seated at my door, I saw that his face was still more shrunken through want of food. So I said to him, 'O my uncle, will you not enter our house and partake of something with us?' and he said, 'Do you desire that?' and I replied, 'Yes, and you will please me by that and do me a kindness.' Then we entered in together, and I went straightway to my uncle's house, which was more spacious than ours, with no lack of excellent food, such as we did not possess in our own house, and I came back with many different kinds of food, and set it before him. Then he stretched out his hand and took a morsel and raised it to his mouth, and I saw him chew it, but he did not swallow it; then he sprang up and went out, without speaking to me. And on the morrow I met him and said, 'O my uncle, you gave me pleasure and then you filled me with distress.' And he said, 'O my son, I was in great need, and I made every effort to swallow the food which you set before me, but between myself and God there is a sign, and if the food is not acceptable to Him, there arises a pungent odour from it to my nostrils and I cannot swallow it, and I cast forth that morsel in your porch, and went my way.'" Then he went again into the house of al-Junayd, and al-Junayd brought him a piece of dry bread and al-Muḥāsibī ate that, saying, "When you offer anything to a dervish, then offer such as this."[2]

There are other stories related of al-Muḥāsibī on the authority of al-Junayd, among them one to the effect that Ḥārith came to his house and said, "Come out with us, we are going into the desert." And al-Junayd continues: "I said to him, 'Will you drag me forth from my life of retirement, in which I feel safe about myself, out on to the highroads, with their risks, and with exposure to what

[1] al-Junayd b. Muḥammad of Baghdad (*ob.* 298/910), a disciple of al-Muḥāsibī.

[2] Abū Nu'aym, *op. cit.*, *loc. cit.* *Cf.* also Sarrāj, *Kitāb al-Luma*, p. 331, and Ṣibt Ibn al-Jawzī, "Mir'āt al-Zamān," fol. 121*b*.

attracts the sensual desires ?' He said, 'Come out with us, there is nothing for you to fear.' So I went forth with him, and the road seemed to be completely deserted; we saw nothing to be avoided. And when we arrived at the place where he was accustomed to sit with his friends and discuss with them, he bade me question him and I said, 'I have no questions to ask you.' Then he said, 'Ask me about anything that comes into your mind,' and questions crowded in upon me, and I asked him about them and he gave me answers to them on the spot. Then he departed to his house and set them down in writing."

al-Junayd also related that he used often to say to Ḥārith, "'My solitude has become my fellowship, but you drag me out to the desert and into the sight of men and the public highroads.' And then he would say to me, 'How often will you speak to me of your "fellowship" and your "solitude"? Though half of mankind were to draw near to me, I should not find any fellowship with them, and though the other half were to keep far away from me, I should not feel lonely because of their distance from me.' "[1]

There is a story said to have been related by al-Muḥāsibī concerning al-Ma'mūn, which would seem more appropriate to the bigoted and cruel al-Mutawakkil than to his much more tolerant and humane uncle. Al-Muḥāsibī says: "I had spent the night in my *miḥrāb* (prayer-niche), and behold there appeared a youth of most handsome mien and sweet fragrance, who saluted me and sat down in my presence, and I said to him, 'Who art thou ?' and he replied, 'A pilgrim, and I seek out the devout in their *miḥrābs*,' and he continued, 'I see no effort displayed by you, and where are your good works ?' I said, 'They are the concealment of afflictions and the proclamation of benefits received.' Then he uttered a loud cry and said, 'I did not suppose there was anyone of this description to be found between the boundaries of East and West, though it was my desire to seek him out.' I said, 'But you knew that those to whom the mystic "states" are granted bear heavy burdens and conceal those Divine mysteries.' He gave another cry and became unconscious, and when he recovered consciousness he rose and went in

[1] Abū Nu'aym, fols. *4b*, *5a*.

to the presence of al-Ma'mūn, who said, 'Who are you?' He replied, 'I am a pilgrim and I do not consider any admonition to be more excellent than the admonition of an unjust tyrant, and you, by God, are unjust and I should be unjust if I did not call you unjust.' Then al-Ma'mūn gave orders concerning him, and he was put to death. 'I was grieved about him,' said Ḥārith, 'and I saw him in a dream, and he said, "O Ḥārith, I have brought those who conceal the mystic states granted to them, and who hide what is within their breasts," and I said, "Where are they?" and he said, "Now they are coming to meet you," and lo, there appeared riders, who said, "O Ḥārith, as regards the pilgrim, he offered himself to God, in warfare for His sake, and God has accepted him, but as regards him who put him to death, God is wroth with him." ' "[1]

Of al-Muḥāsibī's sense of humility before God, there is a story related by Jāmī to the effect that Ḥārith al-Muḥāsibī for four years stood night and day with his back against a wall, and never rested except on his two knees. He was asked why he wearied himself in this manner, and replied, "In the presence of the King's Majesty I am ashamed to deport myself otherwise than as a slave."[2]

There is an illustration of his constant sense that this world was only a temporary abiding place and a place of preparation for the next, in his declaration that the best of the nation were those who were not distracted from the duties of this present life by the thought of the next life, not from the thought of the next life by concern for this present life, and in this connection it is related that a certain improviser recited these verses in al-Muḥāsibī's presence:

"I weep in exile, as the eye of a stranger weeps,
I shall not grieve on the day when I depart from this abode,
For strange it is that I should have deserted
My native land, the home of my Beloved."

When al-Muḥāsibī heard these lines, he rose and was moved to tears, and displayed such grief that all who were

[1] Ṣibt Ibn al-Jawzī, "Mir'āt al-Zamān," fol. 122*b*.
[2] Jāmī, *Nafaḥāt al-Uns*, p. 56.

present felt compassion for him. Then we are told that Ḥārith himself recited :

" Fear is most fitting for the sinner, and grief, when he calls upon God,
But love is seemly for the obedient, and him who is pure from defilement,
While strong yearning belongs to the elect and the saints, according to those who are wise,"

verses which had been recited to him by 'Abd al-'Azīz b. 'Abd Allah.[1]

There is another anecdote shewing how he learned humility, perhaps in early manhood, from one less learned than himself, but possessed of greater spiritual insight. According to this story, as related by himself, al-Muḥāsibī had written a book on Gnosis (*ma'rifa*, the intuitive knowledge of God). He was much pleased with the book, and while he was considering it with approval, there was a knock at the door, and a young dervish came in and greeted him, and then asked him, " Is Gnosis a duty towards God, incumbent upon man, or is it a right which man can claim from God ?" al-Muḥāsibī replied, " It is a duty towards God, which is incumbent upon man." The dervish said, " It would be unjust of Him to veil it from him, whose duty it is," and al-Muḥāsibī rejoined, " Yes, it is a right which man can claim from God." Then the dervish said, " He is too just to do men wrong," and rose and saluted al-Muḥāsibī and took his departure. Then al-Muḥāsibī, feeling his lack of qualifications for dealing with the subject, burnt the book, and abandoned his intention of writing on the subject, saying, " After this, I am not prepared to speak of Gnosis." 'Aṭṭār comments on the dilemma thus presented and says that the reason why he destroyed the book and gave up his intention was that if it is asserted that the servant gains Gnosis by himself, and by his own effort can attain to it, and then it can be claimed from him by God, this is not lawful (since it is a gift and

[1] al-Khaṭīb, *Ta'rīkh Baghdād*, VIII., p. 212 ; Ṣibt Ibn al-Jawzī, *op. cit.*, fol. 122*b*.

grace from God and no man can secure it by his own unaided striving). On the other hand, to say that the servant has a right to Gnosis, and that it is due to him, is equally unlawful, for man can have no claim upon God. 'Aṭṭār feels that al-Muḥāsibī was so perplexed by the dilemma that he abandoned the writing of the book, and 'Aṭṭār goes on to state that what God requires from His servant He will bestow upon him of His grace, but the servant cannot demand it as a right. 'Aṭṭār suggests further that Gnosis is a duty incumbent upon the servant, in the sense that since God gives him that grace, it is for him also to do his part; of the illumination given him, he must make the fullest use, and being granted the knowledge of God, must act in accordance with that knowledge. 'Aṭṭār adds, "God knows which explanation is right."[1] al-Muḥāsibī, perhaps out of more mature experience, did write a book on this subject, which is extant.[2]

It is related of al-Muḥāsibī that he said one day to a dervish, "Be God's or be nothing"—that is, unless a man belongs to God and lives for His sake, his life will be useless and of no account. So 'Aṭṭār explains the saying, and expresses his admiration for it, but Hujwīrī takes it somewhat differently: "Be one who strives for spiritual perfection, or be quiescent. Either be subsistent through God, or perish to thine own existence; either be united through Purity or separated by Poverty; either in the state described by the words, 'Bow ye down to Adam' (Sūra 2 : 32, representing man in a state of perfection and purity, made in the image of God and partaking of the Divine), or in the state described by the words, 'Did there not come over man a time when he was not worthy of mention?' (Sūra 76 : 1). If thou wilt offer thyself to God of thine own free choice, thy resurrection will be through thyself, but if thou wilt not, then thy resurrection will be through God."[3]

There is a story told which reveals al-Muḥāsibī's dislike of emotionalism, which is given as an example of his teaching to his pupils, whom he had warned against indulging in

[1] 'Aṭṭār, *op. cit.*, I., p. 228; Ṣibt Ibn al-Jawzī, *op. cit.*, fol. 122*a*.
[2] *Cf.* p. 53 below.
[3] Hujwīrī, *Kashf al-Maḥjūb*, p. 109.

expressions and actions which, even though they were sound in principle, might give a wrong impression, and be thought evil. He possessed a blackbird, which used to utter a loud note. One day Abū Ḥamza, a pupil of his and a man given to ecstasy, came in, and when the bird piped he cried out. Ḥārith thereupon rose and seized a knife, saying, "Thou art an infidel," and but for the intervention of his disciples would have killed Abū Ḥamza, to whom he said, "Become a Muslim, O miscreant." The disciples exclaimed, "O Shaykh, we all know him to be one of the elect saints and believers in the Unity of God; why does the Shaykh regard him with suspicion?" Ḥārith answered, "I do not suspect him; his opinions are sound and I know that he is a convinced believer in the Divine Unity, but why should he do something which resembles the actions of those who believe in Incarnation, and has the appearance of being derived from their doctrine? If a senseless bird pipes, after its fashion, capriciously, why should he behave as though its note were the voice of God? God is indivisible, and the Eternal does not become incarnate, or united with phenomena, nor commingled with them." When Abū Ḥamza perceived the Shaykh's insight, he said, "O Shaykh, although I am right in theory, yet, since my action resembled the action of heretics, I repent and withdraw."[1]

As we have seen, al-Ma'mūn and his immediate successors supported the Mu'tazilite rationalism and encouraged liberal theology and the expression of free thought, but with the accession of the Caliph Mutawakkil (A.D. 847-861) a blind reaction set in. The Mu'tazilite doctrines were declared to be heretical; there was a general return to the traditional doctrine of Islām, and a ruthless persecution of the unorthodox. All theological speculation (*kalām*) was proscribed, and though al-Muḥāsibī had made use of the logical and dialectic methods of the Mu'tazilites only to oppose them, for certain of his writings are definitely directed towards the refutation of Mu'tazilite doctrines, yet his originality and the mystical tendencies of his teaching made him suspect, and from this time onwards he can no longer have been free to teach openly in Baghdad.

[1] Hujwīrī, *op. cit.*, p. 182. *Cf.* also 'Aṭṭār, II., pp. 259, 260.

Aḥmad b. Ḥanbal,[1] founder of the narrowest and least spiritual of the four orthodox schools of Sunnī doctrine, had suffered much harsh treatment at the hands of the Mu'tazilites, while their doctrines were accepted as the religion of the State, and now when his influence predominated in religious affairs, he took his revenge upon his adversaries and all who came under any suspicion of unorthodoxy, and among these was Ḥārith al-Muḥāsibī. We are told, on the authority of the Ṣūfī Abu'l-Qāsim al-Naṣrabādhī (*ob.* 372/982), that Ḥārith was reputed to engage in the discussion of speculative matters, and wrote books on scholastic theology, and Aḥmad b. Ḥanbal hated him on this account. Ibn Ḥanbal was told that al-Muḥāsibī was an adherent of Ṣūfī doctrines and constantly made use of such doctrines as proofs to support his arguments, and by way of examples, and being asked if he had heard al-Muḥāsibī's teaching, Ibn Ḥanbal admitted that he had heard him, had indeed been present at one of al-Muḥāsibī's assemblies, when he met with his disciples and discoursed with them, and Ibn Ḥanbal had remained all night within hearing, and did not deny the sincerity of his " states " and those of his companions.[2]

There are several accounts given of this incident. It appears that Aḥmad b. Ḥanbal said to Ismā'īl b. Isḥāq al-Sarrāj, one of al-Muḥāsibī's disciples, " I have heard that Ḥārith comes frequently to your house ; could you not send for him to come to you, and give me a seat which would not be seen by Ḥārith, but which would give me a view of him and enable me to hear his discourse ?" Ismā'īl b. Isḥāq willingly agreed, for this initiative on the part of Ibn Ḥanbal pleased him, and he went forthwith to seek out al-Muḥāsibī, and asked him to come that night, and his friends with him. Ḥārith agreed, but said, " They have abundance (of food) ; do not provide for them anything to eat save the dregs of oil and dry dates, for more than this you cannot manage." Ismā'īl did as he was bidden, and went off to tell Aḥmad b. Ḥanbal. The latter came after sunset, and seated himself in an upper chamber, where he occupied himself with the

[1] *Cf.* p. 4 above.

[2] Sha'rānī, *al-Ṭabaqāt al-kubrā* (*Lawāqiḥ*), I., p. 64. *Cf.* also al-Ghazālī, *Munbidh min al-Ḍalāl*, p. 15.

recitation of the Qur'ān till he had finished what was incumbent upon him.

Meanwhile Ḥārith al-Muḥāsibī came with his disciples, and they ate their meal and then stood for the prayer of nightfall, after which they sat down round Ḥārith and were silent; not one of them spoke until nearly midnight. Then one of them began and asked Ḥārith a question, and he began to speak, and his companions listened, remaining motionless; then some began to weep and others to cry out, while al-Muḥāsibī continued to speak. Then Ismā'īl b. Isḥāq went to the upper chamber to see how Ibn Ḥanbal fared, and found that he had wept until he became unconscious. Ismā'īl went back to the assembly, and they continued in that state until morning dawned, and they rose up and went their several ways. Then Ismā'īl went up to Aḥmad b. Ḥanbal again and found that he had recovered, and Ismā'īl asked him what he thought of these men, and he replied, "I do not know that I have ever seen any men like these, nor have I heard the like of this man's words concerning mystical theology (*'ilm al-Ḥaqā'iq*)"; and one version states that he added, "I have listened to Ṣūfī doctrines very different from these; I ask forgiveness from God." But in spite of what he had seen and heard, Ibn Ḥanbal warned Ismā'īl b. Isḥāq against associating with such people, and so rose up and departed.[1]

Ibn Ḥanbal carried his persecution of al-Muḥāsibī to the point of banning his writings and banishing him.[2] Al-Ḥusayn b. 'Abdallah al-Kharqī[3] related that he had asked someone what Ibn Ḥanbal disapproved of in al-Muḥāsibī, and the other replied, "I told Abū 'Abdallah (Ibn Ḥanbal) that al-Muḥāsibī had gone to Kūfa and was writing down traditions, and had declared that he repented of all that Ibn Ḥanbal disapproved of in him, and Aḥmad b. Ḥanbal rejoined, 'There is no penitence on the part of Ḥārith. When evidence is brought against him on some count he denies it; repentance is only on the part of him who acknow-

[1] Khaṭīb, *op. cit.*, VIII., pp. 214 *ff.* *Cf.* also Dhahabī; *I'Tidal*, I., p. 173, Ṣibt Ibn al-Jawzī, *op. cit.*, fols. 122*a*, 122*b*.

[2] *Cf.* Ibn Khallikān, *Biographical Dictionary*, I., p. 365.

[3] *Ob.* A.H. 299. *Cf.* Khaṭīb, *op. cit.*, VIII., pp. 59 *ff.*

ledges his error, but that one who is accused and denies his fault is not repentant.' Then he continued, 'Be on your guard against Ḥārith, for there is none more pernicious in his influence than Ḥārith.' "[1]

Though al-Muḥāsibī returned to Baghdad, the fanatical adherence of the people to Aḥmad b. Ḥanbal was such that he was forced to live in retirement, keeping in seclusion and living in great poverty, in his own house. Ja'far b. Akhī Abū Thawr (al-Kalbī) related that he was present at the death of Ḥārith al-Muḥāsibī, and he said, "If I see what I desire, I will smile at you, and if what I see is otherwise, you will perceive it in my face." An hour later Ja'far looked at him, and al-Muḥāsibī smiled and passed away.[2] Nearly all his biographers relate that, owing to the hostility of the Ḥanbalites, only four persons attended the funeral of al-Muḥāsibī to offer the ritual prayers over his body. He died in the year A.H. 243 (A.D. 857), a year after the death of his persecutor Aḥmad b. Ḥanbal.[3]

[1] Dhahabī, "Ta'rīkh al-Islām," fol. 23*b*.
[2] Khaṭīb, *op. cit.*, VIII., p. 215; Ṣibt Ibn al-Jawzī, *op. cit.*, fol. 122*b*.
[3] Jāmī, *op. cit.*, p. 56.

CHAPTER II

THE INNER LIFE OF THE MYSTIC

SUCH were the outward events of the life of Ḥārith al-Muḥāsibī, fragmentary, unimportant, linked up with legends and trivial anecdotes. But the outward life of the saint and mystic has frequently been uneventful, providing little authentic material for the biographer and historian, more especially when, as in this case, his latter days have been spent in seclusion, overshadowed by bitter hostility and persecution. The fact that the saint has so often been obscure in his generation was well known to the Ṣūfīs themselves. Abū Sa'īd b. Abi'l-Khayr, the Persian mystic poet (*ob.* A.D. 1094), placed the hidden and unrecognised saint above the saint manifest and known to the people. The former, he says, is he whom God loves and the latter he who loves God.[1] The marks of the saints of God, says that " God-intoxicated " mystic, Ma'rūf Karkhī (*ob.* 200/815), are three, " Their thought is of God, their dwelling is with God, and their business is in God." It is therefore in what can be learnt from the teaching and writings of al-Muḥāsibī, of his own inner life, that we should expect to find the key to his real character and personality, and to discover that he was a true saint and mystic, a gnostic (*'ārif*) of the Ṣūfīs, if we accept the definition of Ṣūfism set forth by al-Junayd of Baghdad, the pupil of al-Muḥāsibī, on whose life and character, indeed, he may well have based his definition. " Ṣūfism," said al-Junayd, " means that God makes thee to die to thyself and to become alive in Him. It is to purify the heart from the recurrence of creaturely temptations, to bid farewell to all natural inclinations, to subdue the qualities which belong to human nature, to keep far from the claims of the senses, to adhere to spiritual qualities, to ascend by means of Divine knowledge, to be occupied with that which is eternally the best, to give wise counsel to all people, faithfully to observe the Truth, and to follow the Prophet in respect of the re-

[1] M. b. al-Munawwar, *Asrār al-Tawḥīd*, p. 381.

ligious Law."[1] A study of al-Muḥāsibī's writings and teaching will shew how closely he adhered to this ideal.

In his book of the *Waṣāya* or *Naṣā'iḥ* (Book of Precepts or Counsels) al-Muḥāsibī gives an account of his own spiritual struggles in the endeavour to find the way of salvation, and the means by which he found peace and attained to his goal. "For a long period of my life," he writes, "I did not cease to consider the schisms in the community (of Islām) and to seek the right road and the way to be followed, knowledge supported by the general consensus and a practical rule of life, and I sought for guidance on spiritual things from the theologians. I studied the Word of God long and thoughtfully, with the allegorical interpretation (*ta'wīl*) of the jurisconsults, and I considered the different sects of the community and their sayings, and selected therefrom what I could, and I saw their controversies to be like a deep sea, in which many have been overwhelmed, and from which only a few chosen ones have been delivered. I observed that every section of them asserted that salvation consisted in following them, and that perdition was the result of differing from them. Among all those belonging to these sects, it is rare to meet with one who has real knowledge of spiritual things.

"Among their adherents is the ignorant man, and to be far from him is good fortune. Another is the man who apes the theologians, but is really a worldling. Then there is that one who relies upon knowledge of religion without possessing religious convictions, who seeks to be highly esteemed because of his knowledge, and to have the status of a religious man in this world. Another is the one who is possessed of knowledge, but is unable to interpret it, and another is he who imitates the devout (*nussāk*), seeking benefit for himself, but he has no independence and no power of insight and his opinion is not to be relied upon. Another type is the man who depends upon reason and worldly wisdom, but is lacking in piety and the fear of God. Then there are those who follow after lust and agree thereto, and these care only for this world and for the power it gives. There are also those Satans among mankind who shrink

[1] 'Aṭṭār, *op. cit.*, II., p. 32.

from the thought of the next life and attach themselves to this world and seek to gain all they can from it, and in truth they are alive unto this present world and dead unto the heavenly places; indeed, they know nothing of Heaven, but with Hell they are well acquainted.[1]

"So I searched among these types to find myself, and I was unable to do so; therefore I betook myself to those who were rightly guided, and sought guidance from learning, and made use of meditation, and after long consideration it was made clear to me, through the Word of God, and the Sunna of His Prophet, and the consensus of opinion of the faithful, that following after passion makes a man blind to the true path, and leads him astray from the Truth, and through his blindness he is long delayed. So I began by casting passion out of my heart, and I considered the schisms in the community, desiring to seek that sect which would shew me the way to salvation, while avoiding destructive lusts and that sect which leads to perdition, and I was careful not to come to a hasty conclusion without proof, and thus I sought the way of salvation for my own soul. Then I found that the way of salvation consists in cleaving to the fear of God, and the fulfilment of what He has ordained (*farā'iḍ*), and scrupulous observance (*wara'*) of what He has made lawful and unlawful, and all His canonical sanctions (*ḥudūd*) and the service of God for His own sake alone (*ikhlāṣ*), and in taking His Apostle as a model.[2] So I sought for knowledge of these things from those who held fast to God's command and the Sunna, and I found that those who were worthy of imitation were rare, and my difficulties were increased by the lack of God-fearing guides, and I feared greatly lest death should cut short my life, through my anguish on account of the schisms among the faithful, and I exerted myself in the search for what I had not found for myself of Divine knowledge, and the All-Compassionate gave me guidance from those in whom I found indications of devoted piety, of abstinence, and of preference for the next world over this. I found that their directions and their maxims were in agreement with the advice of the Imāms of the Way of Salvation, that they were

[1] *Cf.* Philippians iii. 19, 20.
[2] *Cf.* al-Junayd's definition of Ṣūfism given above.

agreed upon giving good advice to the community, not giving to any freedom to sin, yet not despairing of the Divine mercy towards any sinner, recommending patience in misfortune and adversities, and acquiescence in the Divine Will, and gratitude for favours received. They seek to make God loved by His servants, in reminding them of His favours and His loving-kindness and in calling upon the faithful to repent unto God. Such persons are wise in knowledge of the Majesty of God, and the greatness of His power, learned in His word and in His law, well acquainted with the true faith, knowing well what is to be loved and what hated, scrupulous in the matter of heresies and sensual desires, avoiding prolixity and exaggeration and all personal faults, relying upon themselves, without having recourse to others, wise in their knowledge of the next life and of what is to be feared at the resurrection from the dead, of God's generosity in reward and His severity in punishment. God has made them to grieve continually with a special concern, by means of which they are kept from preoccupation with the pleasures of this world, and guard their piety by the canonical sanctions. And I realised that the cult of the true faith and sincerity in God's service were as a deep sea, and one like myself could not be saved from sinking therein, and could not abide within those sanctions; but these men I knew to be treading the way of salvation, imitators of the Apostles and Prophets, being lanterns to those who seek illumination, and leaders for those who need guidance.

"Desirous of following their rule of life, and having learned much from their gifts, being full of admiration for their obedience to the law of God, I saw that no further proof was needed for one who had grasped the argument. I realised that to adopt this way of life and to act in accordance with it was incumbent upon me. I pledged myself to it in my inmost self, and I concentrated on it with my spiritual vision. I made it the foundation of my faith, and I based my acts upon it in all circumstances while asking God to incite me to gratitude for what He had bestowed on me, and to strengthen me to observe the sanctions which He had made known to me."[1]

[1] "Waṣāya" (Naṣā'iḥ), fols. 1*b ff.*

Such is al-Muḥāsibī's own *apologia pro vita sua* and his account of his conversion to the whole-hearted service of God, to which his life was henceforth devoted. "For thirty years," he says of himself, "my ear listened to nothing but my own conscience, but for thirty years since then my state has been such that my conscience has listened to none but God."[1] His sayings, especially those collected by his biographers as being representative of his teaching, throw much light on his character, and also on his capacity for expressing profound truths in a terse and vivid fashion, and with a pithiness which must have driven home his teaching to his own immediate circle of adherents, and to those of the Muslim community who were in contact with him, and these qualities account for the preservation of so many of his works up to the present day.

The root-principle of service to God, he states, is scrupulous abstinence (*wara'*), and the basis of this is godliness (*taqwā*). This in its turn is based on self-examination, and self-examination is due to fear and hope. Fear and hope arise from knowledge of the promises and warnings of God, and this understanding of the promises and warnings of God comes from remembrance of the greatness of His recompense, and that is the result of reflection and consideration (*fikra wa 'ibra*).[2] This teaching that the outward life of obedience to God depends upon, and arises from, a state of inward purification is borne out by a much-quoted saying of al-Muḥāsibī: "When a man purifies his inmost self by meditation (*murāqaba*)," which is the heart's knowledge of the proximity of God,[3] "and perfect sincerity (*ikhlāṣ*)," which he defines as the withdrawal of the creatures from "bargaining" with God, and since the self is the first of the creatures, it means the disinterested search for God alone[4]—"then God makes his outward conduct to be distinguished by earnest endeavour and faithful observance of the Sunna." Those whose outward life is blameless and who are inwardly striving after perfection, God will guide unto Himself according to His Word, "Those who strive after

[1] 'Aṭṭār, *op. cit.*, I., p. 226. [2] Abū Nu'aym, *op. cit.*, fol. 6*a*.
[3] 'Aṭṭār, *op. cit.*, I., p. 227.
[4] Sarrāj, *Kitāb al-Luma'*, pp. 55, 218.

Us, We will guide in Our paths."[1] This is linked by one of his biographers with the saying, "He who does not purify himself by self-discipline (*riyāḍāt*) will not have opened unto him the way to the 'stations' (of the Mystic Path)."[2]

Character, in al-Muḥāsibī's view, is the most important thing in life, and he quotes a tradition of the Prophet which states, "The heaviest thing which is put into the scales —*i.e.*, that which counts for most on the Day of Judgment, is a fine character,"[3] and he had found by his own experience that character depended upon the cleansing of the soul from sins, and, above all, from anything that savoured of insincerity. To that end were asceticism and self-discipline required, and his sayings are plainly based on his own experience of the struggle necessary to attain to inward peace and complete acquiescence in the Will of God, and this meant humility of a kind not easy to a man conscious of his own unusual capacities, and, through education and study, well equipped with all the knowledge that could be acquired by human endeavour. We see how he came to realise that knowledge of God and knowledge of himself were the means, and the only means, by which to attain to spiritual perfection, and that mere knowledge (*'ilm*), without the understanding (*ma'rifa*) that could be acquired by no human effort, but only by the grace of God, was useless, and worse than useless, since it could lead a man into sin. He himself had chosen to be the bondservant of God, and the characteristic of that state of servantship (*'ubudiyya*) is that God's servant counts nothing as his own, and knows that he has no power to determine good or ill for himself, and knowing therefore that all is the gift of God, he has learnt that the true acceptance of His Will means to remain steadfast when misfortune comes, without being affected by it, either outwardly or inwardly.[4] Such acquiescence in the Divine Will means also dependence upon God, for the one who is anxious about the future or about his daily sustenance is

[1] al-Sulamī, "Ṭabaqāt al-Ṣūfiyya," fol. 11*b*; Abū Nu'aym, *op. cit.*, fol. 6*a*.

[2] Jāmī, *op. cit.*, p. 56.

[3] al-Sulamī, *op. cit.*, *loc. cit.*

[4] al-Sulamī, *op. cit.*, fol. 12*a*.

despising the power of God. "The best provision," he says, "is that which is enough, our daily bread, accepted without anxiety for the needs of the morrow."[1] Anecdotes related of al-Muḥāsibī's life shew that he himself was satisfied with bare subsistence, and had learnt, in whatever state he was, therewith to be content, though he knew what it was to suffer from the temptations of Satan to covet this world's goods.[2]

Contentment and patience he reckoned to be the chief qualities in a fine character, and he is perhaps throwing light upon his own personality when he counsels men to the patient endurance of injury, to be slow to wrath, of smiling countenance (or, as one writer has it, compassionate), and to speak good words. The value al-Muḥāsibī set upon patience is shewn by his saying, "To exercise patience is to know how to serve as a target for the arrows of adversity," and by his statement that everything has an essence, and the essence of man is the Reason, and the essence of Reason is patience, which, as opposed to passion, gives Reason an opportunity to direct the actions of men.[3] al-Muḥāsibī had learnt, by bitter experience, to suffer injury with patience, but he had also learnt that a good conscience was a better thing than outward triumph. "The wrong-doer," he says, "will be put to shame, even though men praise him now, and the one who is wronged will be safe in the hereafter, though men blame him now, and the contented man is rich, though he be hungry, and the covetous man is poor, though he possess the whole world," and he adds that the man who has gained most mastery over himself is that one who has learnt to be satisfied with God's Will for him.[4] His own moral progress from concern with the trivial and transient, to concern for that which is essential, is indicated by his statement that a man's grief is of different types: grief for the loss of a thing which is loved; grief due to fear of the future; grief arising from the desire to get possession of something which is slow to arrive, and lastly, grief at the

[1] Abū Nu'aym, *op. cit.*, fol. 5*b*. [2] al-Munāwī, *op. cit.*, fol. 107*a*.

[3] al-Sulamī, *op. cit.*, fol. 12.*b* *Cf.* Halifax: "He who is master of patience is master of his soul."

[4] al-Sulamī, *op. cit.*, *loc. cit.*

soul's remembrance of its disobedience to God, over which he sorrows. At the end of life, remorse is only for the years wasted in opposition to, and separation from, God.[1]

Failure to find any real satisfaction in the creatures is revealed in the cynical statement made that three things are so rare that a whole lifetime is hardly long enough to ensure finding them: "A beautiful face combined with chastity, fair words with honesty, and outward friendship with loyalty."[2]

His own habit of thorough reflection, before either acting or speaking, indicated by his name of al-Muḥāsibī, is recommended to a disciple who asked his advice, and to whom he gave a code of ten commandments, embodying a man's duty to God and to his neighbour and, incidentally, to his own soul for the promotion of its spiritual welfare, a code which he would be enabled to carry out by means of self-examination, by subjugation of the lower self, by strong determination and perseverance, aided by the grace of God.

Firstly, do not call to witness the name of God in an oath, whether it be true or false, broken or fulfilled.

Secondly, keep yourself from all falsehood.

Thirdly, undertake no obligation which you are unable to fulfil, and if you undertake an obligation, be faithful in fulfilling it.

Fourthly, curse no man, even though he do you wrong.

Fifthly, wish no evil to any creature, and seek no retribution when injured, for retribution is in the hands of God.

Sixthly, never give evidence in regard to any man's acts, whether it be infidelity, or polytheism or hypocrisy, for in refraining from this you display compassion towards man, and thus you keep far from presumption in regard to God, and keep near to His mercy.

Seventhly, do not premeditate any sinful act, whether secret or open, and preserve your members from all such acts, and you will have your reward in this world and the next.

Eighthly, do not inflict upon anyone else that which would mean pain to yourself and would be a burden to you, whether it be for something you need or something which

[1] al-Sulamī, *op. cit.*, fol. 12*a*. [2] Abū Nu'aym, *op. cit.*, fol. 5*b*.

you can do without, for if you act thus, you will fulfil what is due to others.

Ninthly, withdraw your confidence from the creatures, desire naught of what they possess and depend upon God alone, for He can give you all things.

Tenthly, do not consider yourself to be better than your fellow-men, but rather as of less value than all others, for it is such who are counted great in the sight of God.[1]

al-Muḥāsibī evidently knew the temptation to relax in the effort to attain to moral purification and the danger of falling back, for he warns his followers in all circumstances to beware of weakening of intention, because at such a time the Adversary is sure to gain the victory, and therefore whenever the purpose is seen to be growing weak, then is the time to give oneself no rest, but to seek refuge in God.[2] Satan, whom he constantly calls "the Adversary," is to al-Muḥāsibī a real and constant danger, always lying in wait to entice the soul, never weary, never to be caught napping, but always ready to seize his opportunity and to lead man into sin, whenever he is off his guard or neglectful of the means of salvation.[3]

al-Muḥāsibī's own rule of life was the practice of asceticism, and by self-mortification of body and spirit he believed that he had found the road that led to God, but asceticism to him was only a means to an end. The renunciation of this world, while still mindful of it and aware of its attractions, he held, was the characteristic of the ascetic; but the renunciation of it, together with complete forgetfulness of it, being oblivious to all it offered, was the characteristic of the gnostic.[4] The gnostic (*'ārif*) is the one who has attained to understanding and to a direct knowledge of God, and of the mystic union al-Muḥāsibī writes as one who has passed through that great and indescribable experience. Merely human learning produces fear, asceticism brings peace of mind, but gnosis leads to salvation in and with

[1] "al-Muḥāsaba," fols. 80*b*, 81*a* (Berlin 2814). *Cf.* "Sharḥ al-ma'rifa" and Aṭṭār, *op. cit.*, I., pp. 226, 227.

[2] 'Aṭṭār, *op. cit.*, I., p. 227.

[3] *Cf.* p. 121 below.

[4] Khaṭīb, *op. cit.*, I., p. 227.

God, and he whose company is with the gnostics will find therein the joy of the Blessed in Paradise, who contemplate God face to face and dwell for ever in His presence. "The gnostics are those who plunge into the waters of Satisfaction (*riḍā'*)[1] and are submerged in the sea of purity, seeking to bring forth the pearl of attainment, until they are united with God in their inmost selves."[2] Of that state of mystic communion al-Muḥāsibī tells us that the joy of fellowship with his Lord so takes possession of his heart and mind that he can no longer be concerned with this world and what is therein, or with aught save God alone.

So from his own writings we learn something of al-Muḥāsibī's inner self and the means by which he was enabled to make progress in the spiritual life until he felt that he was indeed "a new creature" and had attained to that for which he had been created. By relentless and unceasing self-examination he had come to know his own soul and its besetting sins; by self-discipline he had learnt to be master of his soul, to cope with its temptations and to get the better of its tendency to sin, and so, by his own ceasing striving, aided by the grace of God, without which his own efforts would have been in vain, to attain to self-purification and a state in which he had ceased to depend upon himself or the creatures, and had given himself entirely into the hands of God, merging his own personal will in the Divine Will, becoming empty of self in order that his soul might be open to the revelation and indwelling of God. Through the way of Purgation he had attained to Illumination and thence to the Unitive life, lived with and in God.

[1] "*Riḍā'*," says the Ṣūfī Ibn 'Aṭā', "is the contemplation by the heart of the Eternal Will of God for His servant, for he knows that His will for him is best and is satisfied therewith." Sarrāj, *op. cit.*, pp. 53, 54.

[2] 'Aṭṭār, *op. cit.*, I., p. 228, Ṣibt Ibn al-Jawzī, *op. cit.*, fol. 122*a*.

CHAPTER III

THE DISCIPLES AND ASSOCIATES OF AL-MUḤĀSIBĪ

THE most celebrated of the disciples of al-Muḥāsibī and the man who appears to have been his closest friend was Abu'l-Qāsim b. Muḥammad al-Junayd al-Khazzāz al-Qawārirī of Baghdad, one of the best known of all the Ṣūfī teachers, who died in A.H. 298 (A.D. 910). His knowledge earned him the title of the " Peacock of the Learned " (*Ṭāwwūs al-'Ulamā*) in his own lifetime, and his wisdom and spiritual insight made his teaching acceptable to succeeding generations of Ṣūfīs and orthodox theologians alike. He was a pupil of Abū Thawr al-Kalbī (*ob.* 240/854), and was the nephew and also the pupil of Sarī Saqaṭī (*ob.* 235/866). He relates of himself that when he left his uncle, Sarī asked him to whose assembly he would go, and he replied, " To Ḥārith al-Muḥāsibī." Sarī then said, " Yes, go and acquire his doctrine (*'ilm*) and his method of self-training (*adab*), but leave his splitting of words in speculation (*tashqīq lil-kalām*) and his refutation of the Mu'tazilites alone." " And when I had turned my back," adds al-Junayd, " I heard Sarī say, ' May God make you a traditionist who is a Ṣūfī and not a Ṣūfī who is a traditionist "—that is, that knowledge of the traditions and the Sunna should come first, and then by practising asceticism and devotion he might advance in knowledge of Ṣūfism and become a Ṣūfī gnostic, but that the reverse process of trying to attain to the higher degrees of Ṣūfism without being well grounded in orthodox theology was dangerous.[1] al-Junayd criticised his master al-Muḥāsibī for his use of dialectic in refuting the doctrines of the Mu'tazilites, but otherwise supported al-Muḥāsibī's teaching. al-Junayd was the author of a considerable number of works, and these include not only writings which deal with ascetical and mystical subjects, but also a number of personal epistles to friends or disciples, which have come down to us.[2]

[1] al-Makkī, *Qūt al-Qulūb*, I., p. 158.

[2] For a list of these *cf.* L. Massignon, *Essai*, p. 276. *Cf.* also *J.R.A.S.*, July, 1935, pp. 499 *ff.*

Of Ṣūfism al-Junayd says, "We did not derive it from discussion, but from fasting and renunciation of this world and the abandonment of that to which we are accustomed and which is reckoned to be good."[1] Ṣūfism, in his view, was death to self and life in God. "The best and highest companionship," he said, "is reflection concerning the Unity of God." Again he said, "Concern yourself with God alone, and beware lest, with the eye that has looked upon God, you contemplate anything but Him, and so fall from His regard."[2] The common people, he held, were veiled from the knowledge of God by the three veils of the creatures, this present world, and the self, while the elect were veiled by the consideration of their own good works, of the reward to be gained for them, and of the joys of Paradise.[3] This teaching that the knowledge of God could be gained only through serving Him for Himself alone is entirely in accordance with that of al-Muḥāsibī.[4]

al-Junayd deals fully with the problem of the mystic union, which to him represented the return of the soul to its original home in God. He therefore goes back to the Primæval Covenant—when the souls of men, before they were joined to the earthly bodies of their existence in time and space, accepted God as their Lord—and he regards it as a declaration of love and devotion to God, made to Him in anticipation, on behalf of the whole of humanity to come. Therefore the concern of all who seek to recover this state of complete acquiescence in the Divine Will is so to purify the whole being, including the inmost self, as to be fit to attain to annihilation within the Divine Essence (*fanā' fi'l-Madhkūr*). Of the unification which is the preliminary to complete union, al-Junayd says that it means the separation of the eternal from that which was originated in time, the passing out from the narrow limitations of temporal form into the limitless spaces of the mansions of Eternity.[5] He teaches that the saint who desires to attain to this unification should be as a dead body in the hands of God, acquiescing in all the vicissitudes which come to pass through His

[1] Qushayrī, *Risāla*, p. 19.
[2] Jāmī, *op. cit.*, p. 91.
[3] *Ibid.*, p. 92.
[4] *Cf.* p. 161 below.
[5] Hujwīrī, *op. cit.*, p. 281.

decree and all that is brought about by the might of His power, being submerged in the depths of the ocean of Unity. So the mystic passes away from himself and from the demands of the creatures upon him, and from all response to them, into the realisation of the existence of the Unicity of God, into the direct experience of His presence, leaving behind him his own feelings and actions, as he passes into the life with God, and so becomes that which God desired for him, that the servant at the last should return to the state in which he was at the first, and should become as he was before he began to be.[1] So the creature returns to the ideal which the Creator had of it at the beginning, and in order to enter upon that new life it must be " reborn " through Love, whereby the attributes of the lover are changed into those of the Beloved. Now it is no longer the mystic who lives, but God who lives in him and acts through him, in accordance with His promise, " When I love him, I will be his eye by which he sees, and his hearing by which he hears, and his hand by which he reaches out."[2] al-Junayd was conscious within himself of this Divine indwelling, and of the power of God working through the " new creature." For thirty years," he says, " God spake by the tongue of Junayd and Junayd was not there, and men knew it not."[3] The supreme acknowledgment of the Divine Unity, he declared, is the denial of the Divine Unity, for God, to the Ṣūfī, is no longer One but All, the Real beyond Reality.[4]

Another well-known disciple of al-Muḥāsibī was the celebrated Shaykh Abū Ḥamza Muḥammad b. Ibrāhīm al-Baghdādī al-Bazzāz (*ob.* 269/883), an associate of al-Junayd, of the ascetic Bishr al-Ḥāfī, of Sarī Saqaṭī and al-Nūrī, and in his travels he was a companion of Abū Turāb al-Nakhshabī al-Nasafī. There is a story related by al-Junayd of how Abū Ḥamza arrived at Baghdad from Mecca, shewing signs of great emaciation as a result of the journey, and al-Junayd asked him what he would like to eat. Abū Ḥamza said, " Stew cooked with vinegar, and sweet cake." al-

[1] Sarrāj, *op. cit.*, p. 29. [2] *Ibid.*, p. 59.

[3] 'Aṭṭār, *op. cit.*, II., p. 10.

[4] *Ibid.*, p. 29. *Cf.* Horten, *Indische Strömungen in der Islamischen Mystik*, pp. 26 *ff.*, and al-Muḥāsibī, pp. 250 *ff.* below.

Junayd took half a raṭl (one pound) of flour and ten raṭls of meat and egg-plants and vinegar, and ten raṭls of syrup, and made the sweet cake and the stew for him, and placed the two before him, and left Abū Ḥamza alone. When al-Junayd entered later, he found that Abū Ḥamza had consumed it all, and the latter, noting al-Junayd's astonishment, said, " O Abu'l-Qāsim, do not be surprised, for this is only my third meal since I left Mecca."[1]

Abū Ḥamza visited Baṣra several times, and at one period he used to discourse in the mosque at Tarsus. His teaching was well received there, until one day a crow uttered a shrill cry from the roof of the mosque,[2] and Abū Ḥamza cried out, saying, " Here am I, at thy service." He was accused of heresy and of being a believer in the doctrine of incarnation (*ḥulūl*) and was cast forth from the mosque as a heretic.[3] Yet it is also related that Abū Ḥamza used to attend the assemblies of Aḥmad b. Ḥanbal, the persecutor of al-Muḥāsibī, and whenever any question concerning Ṣūfism came up, Ibn Ḥanbal would turn to him and ask his opinion on it. In the persecution instigated by Ghulām al-Khalīl during the caliphate of al-Mu'tamid (A.D. 870-893), Abū Ḥamza was arrested as a Ṣūfī and a heretic, and was condemned to death, but later set free.

Abū Ḥamza is said to have been the first to hold a regular position and to occupy a " chair " for the exposition of the Ṣūfī doctrines in Baghdad. We are told that he was the first to discourse on the perfect form of Recollection (*ṣafā' al-dhikr*), on the concentration of the attention (*jama' al-himma*), on love to God (*maḥabba*), on yearning for Him (*shawq*), on drawing near to Him (*qurb*) and on fellowship with Him (*uns*). His doctrines were acceptable to the people and his reputation was high among them.[4] His teaching was given in the Rusāfa mosque in Baghdad, and it is said that afterwards he taught in the chief mosque at Medina, and, while engaged in teaching there, died suddenly.[5]

Among Abū Ḥamza's sayings is one to the effect that he

[1] al-Sulamī, *op. cit.*, fol. 66*b*.
[2] *Cf.* p. 13 above.
[3] al-Dhahabī, " Ta'rikh al-Islām," fol. 104*a*. *Cf.* Ibn al-Jawzī, *Talbīs Iblīs*, p. 180.
[4] al-Khaṭīb, *op. cit.*, I., p. 393.
[5] al-Sulamī, *op. cit.*, fol. 66*a*.

who has escaped from all affliction is provided with three things: "An empty stomach with a contented heart, continuous poverty with present asceticism, and perfect patience with constant remembrance of God." Of that intuitive knowledge which is the Divine gift he said, "He who knows the path of God through that intuition will find it easy to walk therein, for God Himself gave him the knowledge thereof, without intermediary, but he who has learnt it by means of demonstration and proof sometimes goes astray, and only occasionally goes direct."[1] Of the lover of God who walks in that path, Abū Ḥamza said, "It is impossible to love Him without remembering Him, and impossible to remember Him without finding satisfaction in that experience, and impossible to find that satisfaction and then concern yourself with any but Him."[2]

Abū Ḥamza differed from al-Muḥāsibī on the question of "absence"—that is, the heart's absence from all save God—and "presence," the heart's consciousness of the presence of the self and its own attributes. Abū Ḥamza held that "absence" was to be preferred to "presence" because the self is the greatest of all veils between the creature and God. When the heart is absent from self, the evils inherent in the self are annihilated. "Thine eye is closed to thyself and to all that is other than God, and thy human attributes are consumed by the flame of proximity to God." In contemplation the soul enters into unification and, being "absent" from the self, is present with God, and looks upon Him face to face.

Another pupil and disciple of al-Muḥāsibī who became famous was Aḥmad b. Muḥammad Abu'l-Ḥasan al-Baghawī, known as Nūrī (*ob.* 295/907), a pupil also of Sarī Saqaṭī, a friend of al-Junayd, and the companion in adversity of Abū Ḥamza. His biographer tells us that he was called Nūrī because, when he was speaking after nightfall, a light (*nūr*) used to issue forth from his mouth, so that the whole house was illuminated by it. Others said that he was called Nūrī because by the light of intuition he used to read the inmost thoughts of his disciples, so that al-Junayd said of him, "Abu'l-Ḥasan is a spy on the hearts of men

[1] al-Sulamī, *op. cit.*, fol. 66*b*. [2] *Ibid.*, fol. 66a.

(*jāsūs al-qulūb*)." It was also related of him that he had a cell in the desert to which he repaired each night to engage in devotion, and people watching that spot used to see a light shining forth from his cell and streaming up to the heavens.[1] A saying of his is appropriate in this connection: "One day I looked upon a Light, and I did not cease to contemplate it until I became that Light."[2]

Nūrī was an ascetic of the ascetics, rejecting flattery and self-indulgence and practising mortification to an extreme degree. He held and carried into practice the doctrine of "preference" (*īthār*), the choice of another's interest rather than his own, and the principle of vicarious suffering, and several stories of his life shew how he carried this into practice. On one occasion Nūrī had fallen sick and al-Junayd came to visit him and brought him roses and fruit. Shortly afterwards al-Junayd himself was ill, and Nūrī, in his turn, came to visit him. On arriving, Nūrī bade his disciples, who had accompanied him, to take each one upon himself a part of al-Junayd's sickness, that he might be restored. They willingly agreed, and immediately al-Junayd rose up, fit and well. Then Nūrī said to him, "This was what you should have done when you came to visit me, instead of bringing flowers and fruit." Another anecdote displaying the same spirit on his part tells of a fire which broke out in the slave-market at Baghdad, in which many lives were lost. In one of the shops were two Greek slave-boys of great beauty, and the flames had surrounded them, so that they could not escape. Their master proclaimed that he would give a thousand pieces of gold to anyone who would bring them out, but no one had the courage to attempt it. Suddenly Nūrī arrived and heard those two slave-boys crying out in their distress. Saying, "In the Name of God, the Compassionate, the Merciful," he entered the burning building and brought both of them out to safety. The owner of the slaves offered the thousand pieces of gold to Nūrī, but he said, "Take them away, and give thanks to God, for He would not have bestowed upon me such a degree of His favour, if I had accepted gifts such as these

[1] ʿAṭṭār, *op. cit.*, II., p. 46; Hujwīrī, *op. cit.*, p. 194.
[2] Jāmī, *Nafaḥāt al-Uns*, p. 87.

dinars in exchange for the next world."[1] As related above, Nūrī was one of those arrested with Abū Ḥamza in the persecution of the Ṣūfīs instigated by Ghulām al-Khalīl, and both of them, together with a third Ṣūfī, Raqqām, were condemned to death as heretics. When the executioner approached Raqqām, Nūrī advanced and offered himself in place of Raqqām. The executioner was astonished that he should desire to meet the sword before his turn had come. Nūrī replied that life was the most precious thing in the world, and for his brethren's sake he wished to sacrifice the few moments of life that remained to him. "One moment in this world," he said, "is better than a thousand years in the next, for this is the place of service, and that is the place of proximity to God, and proximity to Him is gained by service." The Caliph received news of what had passed and postponed the execution, sending the Ṣūfīs to the house of the Chief Qāḍī Ismā'īl b. Isḥāq for further examination. When the Qāḍī had questioned them on the law and doctrinal matters, Nūrī said, "O Qāḍī, you have not yet asked any question to the point, for God has servants who eat through Him and drink through Him, and sit through Him and live through Him, who abide continually in the contemplation of Him. If they were cut off from that contemplation, they would cry out in anguish." The Qāḍī wrote to the Caliph, "If these Ṣūfīs are heretics, then who in the world are the true believers in the Unity of God?" The Caliph sent for the three Ṣūfīs and dismissed them with honour.[2]

Ja'far al-Khuldī, the biographer (*ob.* 348/959), related that he had heard Nūrī pray, "O Lord, in Thy eternal knowledge and power and will, Thou dost punish the inhabitants of Hell, whom Thou didst create: if it be Thine inexorable purpose to make Hell full of mankind, Thou art able to fill that Hell and all its limbos with me alone, and to send them to Paradise." Then Ja'far dreamt that one came and said to him, "God bids thee tell Abu'l-Ḥasan that his sins have been forgiven, because of his compassion towards God's creatures and his reverence for God."[3]

1 'Aṭṭār, *op. cit.*, II., pp. 52, 53.

2 Hujwīrī, *op. cit.*, pp. 190, 191.

3 *Ibid.*, p. 193.

Nūrī's teaching was in accordance with his practice and his life. "The mark of the true *faqīr*," he said, "is that when he receives nothing he is content, and when he receives something he regards another person as better entitled to it than himself and so he gives it away."[1] "Ṣūfism," he said, "is enmity to this world and friendship with the Lord." Again he said, "Ṣūfism means the renunciation of what belongs to the self, for the sake of what belongs to God—the Ṣūfīs are those whose spirits have been freed from the defilement of human nature, purified from carnal taint, and delivered from the lusts of the flesh, so that they have found rest with God in the first rank and the highest degree, and have fled from all save Him."[2] Worship, he said, was contemplation of the Divine. When asked about the mystic ecstasy, he said, "It is a flame kindled in the heart by longing for the Beloved, and whether it rises up from joy or grief it brings remembrance of Him."[3] Of the love which leads the mystic into the unitive life he said, "It is the rending of veils and the revealing of what is hidden from the eyes of men."[4]

A pupil and disciple of al-Muḥāsibī who gained a considerable reputation as a Ṣūfī was Aḥmad b. Masrūq Abu'l-'Abbās al-Ṭūsī (*ob.* 298/910), who was reckoned to be one of the *awtād* (supports), four saints who were of those "who have power to loose and to bind and are the officers of the Divine court," from amongst whom the successor to the *Quṭb* (Pole) or chief of the Ṣūfī hierarchy was elected. Though originally from Ṭūs, Aḥmad b. Masrūq lived and died in Baghdad. He was a friend and one who related (*rāwī*) of Sarī Saqaṭī and one of the teachers of Abū 'Ali Rudhbārī (*ob.* A.D. 933). He relates that he dreamt of the Day of Resurrection and saw tables set out for a feast and was about to sit down when he was told that these were for the Ṣūfīs. He protested that he was one of their number, but an angel said to him that he had indeed been one of them, but much talk and his love for being distinguished above his fellows

[1] Hujwīrī, p. 26.
[2] *Ibid.*, pp. 36, 37.
[3] 'Aṭṭār, *op. cit.*, II., pp. 54, 55.
[4] Sarrāj, *op. cit.*, p. 59.

had distracted him from what was fitting for a Ṣūfī. He said, " I repent," and so awoke.[1]

Aḥmad b. Masrūq was well known for his humility and his asceticism. On the vexed question of whether the Ṣūfī should listen to music and song[2] he held the opinion that it was not fitting for the devout man to listen to love-poems unless he was firmly established in his devotion both outwardly and inwardly, strong in his spiritual state, and well versed in religious knowledge; but for such men as himself, he felt that it was unfitting, for they were not sufficiently attached to the service of God to be sure that such music might not lead them astray.[3] Like his master al-Muḥāsibī, he felt that spiritual perfection was a matter of slow growth, conversion was the first step and discipleship the next, and those who neglected these were ignorant of the way by which gnosis (*ma'rifa*) was to be sought. " The tree of the knowledge of God," he said, " is nourished by the water of reflection, and the tree of heedlessness by the water of ignorance, and the tree of conversion by the water of repentance, and the tree of love by the water of self-giving and preference of the Beloved to oneself."[4] That which the gnostics fear most, he said, is that they may lose God. Of the devotion of the true Ṣūfī to God, he said, " If anyone takes joy in aught save God, his joy brings only sorrow, and if anyone is not intimate with the service of his Lord, his intimacy produces loneliness"—that is, all save Him is perishable and whoever rejoices in what is perishable, when that perishes, becomes stricken with sorrow. Except His service all else is vain, hence the sorrow and loneliness of the entire universe consist in regarding that which is other than God.[5]

One of al-Muḥāsibī's closest friends and most devoted disciples was Abū Bakr Isma'īl b. Isḥāq Sarrāj (*ob.* 286/899), a native of Nīshāpūr, who spent forty years of his life in Baghdad, where, with his brothers, he lived a life of extreme asceticism, in spite of the possession of considerable wealth.

[1] Sha'rānī, *al-Ṭabaqāt al-kubrā*, p. 80.
[2] *Cf.* Hujwīrī, *op. cit.*, pp. 418 *ff.*
[3] Sha'rānī, *ibid.*
[4] al-Sulamī, *op. cit.*, fol. 53*a*; Qushayrī, *op. cit.*, p. 23.
[5] Hujwīrī, *op. cit.*, p. 147.

It was at his house that al-Muḥāsibī was accustomed to meet with his disciples, for meditation and for the teaching of Ṣūfī doctrines, and he seems also to have been on sufficiently friendly terms with Aḥmad b. Ḥanbal for the latter to ask leave of him to attend one of these assemblies (*cf.* p. 14 above), though at the end Ibn Ḥanbal warned Isma'īl against associating with such a man as al-Muḥāsibī.[1] Sarrāj did not become famous as a teacher, but he was responsible for handing down to us much of what we know of his master's life.

Another well-known disciple of al-Muḥāsibī was the jurisconsult Abū 'Alī al-Ḥusayn Ibn Ṣāliḥ Ibn Khayrān (*ob.* 310/923), a Shāfi'ite renowned for his scrupulous abstinence from anything unlawful, and also known as a teacher. The office of Chief Qāḍī was offered to him, but he refused to accept it, and the Wazīr 'Alī b. 'Īsā kept him under arrest in his house for a period of ten days. The Wazīr said that his purpose was that it should afterwards be said of that period, that in it lived one who was offered the post of Qāḍī of the East and the West, and who would not accept it.[2]

Among those who associated with al-Muḥāsibī and discussed theology with him one of the oldest was Abū 'Alī Ḥasan b. 'Alī al-Masūḥī,[3] who derived his teaching from Bishr b. al-Ḥārith al-Ḥāfī, and among his disciples or pupils were al-Junayd, Abū Ḥamza and Abu'l-'Abbās al-Masrūq, and he was also a great friend of Sarī. It was stated that he was one of the first to gather a group round him for the discussion of Ṣūfī doctrines and that he attracted to himself all those who had been Sarī's friends. His pupils al-Junayd and al-Masrūq related of him that he had no house of his own, but used to live at the *Bāb al-Kannās* (Gate of the Sweeper), in a mosque which sheltered him from the heat and cold. He was heard to say that one day he entered the mosque when he found the heat very oppressive and his eyes were weary and he fell asleep, and it seemed to him that the roof of the mosque opened and there

[1] Khaṭīb, *op. cit.*, VIII., p. 214; al-Dhahabī, *I'tidāl*, I., p. 173; Taghrībirdī, *op. cit.*, II., p. 167.

[2] Khaṭīb, *op. cit.*, VIII., p. 53; Jāmī, *op. cit.*, p. 229.

[3] Dhahabī, "Ta'rīkh," fol. 22*b*.

descended to him a radiant silver-clad celestial visitant, who encouraged him to continue in his life of devotion, for the joy that was set before him.[1] al-Junayd once spoke to Ḥasan al-Masūḥī about social intercourse and he said, " Woe be to you! Of what consequence is it? If every creature under the heavens were to die, I should not feel lonely." A friend of his related that at one time al-Ḥasan was living in seclusion in a solitary spot, and for a week he was forgotten, and when his friend asked his forgiveness for being unmindful of him, Ḥasan said, " Do not disturb yourself, for God removes the loneliness of solitude from His friends, as Sumnūn the Lover wrote:

' Beware, O soul, of being alone with thyself,
For there is joy in fellowship (with God) and consolation.' "[2]

This Sumnūn, quoted by Ḥasan al-Masūḥī, was a recluse famous for his teaching on Love, which he held was the foundation and chief principle of the road to God. All " states " and " stations " were stages of love, and all these may be destroyed, except the station of love itself. " The lovers of God," he said, " have borne away the glory of this world and the next, for they are with God, the Object of their love, in both worlds. The glory of this world is God's being with them, and the glory of the next world is their being with God."[3]

Among al-Muḥāsibī's less celebrated disciples was Abū Bakr Aḥmad b. al-Qāsim b. Naṣr, brother of Abū Layth al-Fara'iḍī (*ob.* 310/932), originally from Nīshāpūr, who was known as al-Sha'rānī, a recluse who lived in great asceticism. In certain lines ascribed to him he says, " Hold fast to your resolution in any matter with which you are concerned. Even if you are safe, there is no harm in being resolute. Weakness is injurious, and resolution can do no injury," lines which are doubtless based on al-Muḥāsibī's constant insistence on the importance of intention and resolution in carrying it out.[4]

[1] Khaṭīb, *op. cit.*, V., p. 266. [2] Jāmī, *op. cit.*, p. 104.
[3] Hujwīrī, *op. cit.*, pp. 308, 312; Kalābādhī, *Kitāb al-Ta'arruf*, p. 125.
[4] Khaṭīb, *op. cit.*, IV., p. 252; Dhahabī, " Ta'rīkh," fol. 22*b*; Jāmī, *op. cit.*, p. 265.

Another mentioned as a disciple, but one of whom comparatively little is known, was Abū 'Abdallah b. Ḥasan b. 'Abd al-Jabbār b. Rashīd, known as al-Ṣūfī al-Kabīr (*ob.* 306/918). He was not a native of Baghdad, but was resident there and was known as a traditionist as well as a Ṣūfī.[1]

Among those mentioned as associating with al-Muḥāsibī was Abū Ja'far Muḥammad b. Ya'qūb al-Farajī, the author of the *Kitāb al-Wara'* (Book of Abstinence), the *Kitāb Ṣifāt al-Murīdīn* (Book of the Characteristics of Novices), and other works, the titles of which suggest the influence of al-Muḥāsibī. Abū Ja'far was also a friend of Abū Turāb al-Nakhshabī. He said of himself that for twenty years he had asked no question unless he had settled the matter in his own mind before he spoke. He said also that for thirty years he had made no agreement with God—*i.e.*, had taken no vow upon himself, fearing lest it should not be fulfilled and he should become a liar.[2]

A faithful disciple who has handed down many of the sayings of al-Muḥāsibī was Abū 'Abdallah Aḥmad b. 'Abdallah b. Maymūn al-Khawwāṣ, an ascetic who associated also with Sarī Saqatī, and from him, through 'Uthmān b. M. al-'Uthmānī and others, Abū Nu'aym al-Isfahānī (*ob.* A.D. 1038) derived much of the material contained in his biographical notice of al-Muḥāsibī.[3]

Other friends of al-Muḥāsibī mentioned briefly by his biographers were Muḥammad b. Aḥmad b. Abī Sunḥ (perhaps to be identified with M. b. Aḥmad al-Zanjānī),[4] Abū Ḥafṣ al-Khaṣāf,[5] and Ja'far, the brother of Abū Thawr Kalbī, who was present with al-Muḥāsibī when he died.[6]

Among the famous Ṣūfīs of Baghdad who, though he is not stated to have been among the personal friends and disciples of al-Muḥāsibī, was contemporary with him, and with whom, owing to his relationship to al-Junayd, al-

[1] Khaṭīb, *op. cit.*, IV., p. 83; Dhahabī, *op. cit.*, fol. 22*b*. *Cf.* Sublkī, *Ṭab. al-Shāf*, II., p. 40.

[2] Sarrāj, *op. cit.*, XXV., pp. 179, 354. *Cf.* al-Muḥāsibī, "Kitāb al-Makāsib."

[3] Abū Nu'aym, "Ḥilya," fols. 231b, 235*a ff*.

[4] Khaṭīb, *op. cit.*, VIII., pp. 212, 213.

[5] Dhahabī, *op. cit.*, "Ta'rīkh," fol. 24*a*.

[6] Khaṭīb, *op. cit.*, VIII., p. 215.

Muḥāsibī must certainly have been brought into contact, was Abu'l-Ḥasan Sarī b. Mughallis al-Saqaṭī (*ob.* A.H. 253 or 257), a pupil of the great Ṣūfī Ma'rūf al-Karkhī, deriving his traditions, like al-Muḥāsibī, from Yazīd b. Hārūn. Sarī was a friend of Ḥasan al-Masūḥī, the disciple of al-Muḥāsibī, and included among his own disciples Abu'l-'Abbās b. Masrūq al-Ṭūsī, al-Junayd, his nephew, and Nūrī, all of them also pupils and disciples of al-Muḥāsibī. Sarī was one of the first to devote his attention to teaching on the " states " and " stations " of the traveller on the mystic path, and many of the Ṣūfī Shaykhs of Baghdad traced back the origin of their doctrines to his teaching. He was also well known as the writer of mystical verses.[1]

It was related of him that he had a shop in Baghdad, and when the bazaar caught fire, he heard that his shop was burnt and said, " Then I am set free from the care of it." Later, news came that his shop was safe, while those around had been destroyed. Sarī then gave all that he possessed to the poor and took the path of Ṣūfism.[2] Of the traveller along that path he said that his greatest strength lay in the conquest of self. " He who is too weak to train himself will be too weak to train another." Again he said, " The sign of persistent sin in a man is his blindness to his own faults and his observation of the faults of other men." On the same subject he said, " I have seen nothing so liable to make good works of none effect, or so likely to corrupt men's hearts and bring them to speedy destruction, or more productive of lasting sorrow, or more liable to incur the wrath of God, and induce the love of hypocrisy and arrogance and self-will, than a man's failure to know himself, while he observes the faults of others."[3] Ṣūfism, he said, meant three things for the Ṣūfī : that the light of his gnosis did not extinguish the light of his abstinence (*wara'*), that his inward speculations did not make him opposed to the outward conduct taught by the Qur'ān and the Sunna, and that the favours of God bestowed on him did not lead him to tear aside the veil from what God had made unlawful to him.[4]

[1] Khaṭīb, IX., p. 187.
[2] Hujwīrī, *op. cit.*, p. 110.
[3] Sha'rānī, *op. cit.*, pp. 63, 64.
[4] Qushayrī, *op. cit.*, p. 10.

Sárī knew the value of seclusion and solitude for the growth of the spiritual life. He who desired to safeguard his faith and to give rest to his body and to be free from what would grieve him, he said, should withdraw from the society of men, for the times required seclusion and solitude. "The beginning of gnosis," he said, "is the withdrawal of the soul that it may be alone with God." Only so could the loving soul attain the consummation of its love, for love, said Sarī, "is not perfected between two who love, until one says to the other, 'O thou (who art) I.'"[1] Concerning the true lovers of God, it is related that once, while al-Junayd was staying in his house, Sarī Saqatī dreamt that he was standing in the presence of God, and God said to him, "O Sarī, I created mankind, and all of them claimed to love Me. Then I created the world, and nine-tenths of them deserted Me, and there remained one-tenth. Then I created Paradise, and nine-tenths again deserted Me, and one-tenth of the tenth remained with Me. And I imposed upon them one particle of affliction, and nine-tenths of those who were left deserted Me, and I said to those who remained, 'Ye did not desire the world, nor seek after Paradise, nor flee from misfortune; what then do ye desire and what is it that ye seek?' They replied, 'It is Thou Thyself that we desire, and if Thou dost afflict us, yet will we not abandon our love and devotion to Thee.' And I said to them, 'I am He Who imposes upon you affliction and terrors which even the mountains cannot abide. Will ye have patience for such affliction?' They said, 'Yea, verily, if Thou art the One Who afflicts; do what Thou wilt with us.' These are indeed My servants and My true lovers."[2]

Saqatī was heard to pray, "O God, whatever punishment Thou dost inflict upon me, punish me not with the humiliation of being veiled from Thee," for if the soul is not veiled from God, its torment and affliction will be lightened by the remembrance and contemplation of Him, but if it

[1] Sha'rānī, *op. cit.*, p. 63; Jāmī, *Nafaḥāt al-Uns*, p. 54.

[2] al-Ḥurayfīsh, *al-Rawḍ al-Fā'iq*, p. 279. 'Aṭṭār relates a somewhat similar legend of Dhu'l-Nūn. The Christian mystic Raymond Lull (*ob.* A.D. 1315) quotes this legend in his *Book of the Lover and the Beloved*, p. 69.

is veiled, then even His grace may be deadly to it. No punishment in Hell is more painful or harder to bear than that of being veiled, for if God were revealed to the dwellers in Hell, then the sinful there would think no more of Paradise, since the vision of Him would so fill them with joy that they could think no more of bodily pain. And of the joys of Paradise none is more perfect than the removal of the veil, for if those who dwell there had all its pleasures and a hundredfold beside, but were veiled from the vision of God, their hearts would be utterly broken. Therefore God allows the hearts of His lovers to have the vision of Him always, so that the delights thereof may enable them to endure every tribulation, and they say, as Sarī said, in their prayers, "We count all torments more desirable than that of being veiled from Thee, for when Thy Beauty is revealed to our hearts, we reckon tribulation as nought."[1]

Another great Ṣūfī, contemporary with al-Muḥāsibī, of whom he must have known, for he was associated with his friends, and with whom he must at times have come into contact, was Abū Turāb al-Nakhshabī al-Nasafī (*ob.* 245/859), one of the chief Shaykhs of Khurāsān, celebrated for his piety, his asceticism, and his devoutness alike. He was a writer as well as teacher.[2] He was especially renowned among the Sūfīs for his extensive travels, but he condemned the journeys of novices not made in accordance with the instructions of their spiritual directors. Among his sayings was this: "Men hold three things dear and so bring themselves to nought—the self, and make that into a god, and ease, and make that into a god, and wealth, and make that into a god. Two things men seek after and do not find, joy and rest, for both of these belong to Paradise."[3] Of the true dervish he said that his food was what he found and his clothing what covered him and his dwelling-place wherever he alighted, while in the mystical sense the food of the dervish was ecstasy and his clothing piety and his dwelling-place the Unseen.[4] The Ṣūfī, he said, is that one whom nothing defiles and through whom all things are made pure. He is the one who entrusts himself completely to God, with a

[1] Hujwīrī, *op. cit.*, p. 110.
[2] Sarrāj, *op. cit.*, p. 205.
[3] 'Aṭṭār, *op. cit.*, p. 297.
[4] Hujwīrī, *op. cit.*, p. 121.

trust which hands over his body to the service of God, and attaches his heart to what is Divine and makes him content with what is sufficient. If God gives unto him, he offers thanks ; if He withholds, he is patient, being satisfied and conformed to the Will of God.[1]

It was related that Abū Turāb al-Nakhshabī was alone in the desert when death came to him, and he was found there by his friends, standing on his feet, his face turned towards the *Qibla*, his water-pot in front of him, and his staff still gripped in his hand, and no wild beast had ventured to touch him.[2]

Another of al-Muḥāsibī's contemporaries, with whom he was in close contact, was Abū Ja'far M. b. al-Ḥusayn Burjulānī (*ob.* 238/852), who lived in Baghdad and was the editor of many stories urging men to the life of prayer. Among his books were the *Kitāb al-Ruhbān* (The Book of Monks) and the *Kitāb al-Zuhd wa'l-Raqā'iq* (The Book of Asceticism and Subtilties). His disciples included Aḥmad b. M. b. Masrūq al-Ṭūsī, also a disciple of al-Muḥāsibī. He was apparently more fortunate than the latter, in meeting with the approval of Aḥmad b. Ḥanbal.[3]

Of the preaching of monks Burjulānī writes with much approval in verses included in the book above mentioned :

"The sermons of monks and the mention of their deeds,
News of what is true from souls that are infidel;
Sermons which bring us healing, and we take them for ourselves,
Even though the tidings comes from some infidel;
Sermons exhorting to righteousness, bringing warning to the soul,
Leaving her sorrowful, as she wanders among the tombs;
Sermons which the soul cannot bear to remember, which arouse to grief the heart they have affected—
Then beware, thou who dost understand, if thou canst restrain thyself,
And hasten, for death is the first who will visit you."[4]

[1] Sarrāj, *op. cit.*, pp. 35, 52.
[2] 'Aṭṭār, *op. cit.*, I., p. 297.
[3] Khaṭīb, *op. cit.*, II., p. 22.
[4] *Textes Inédits* (ed. L. Massignon), p. 14.

One of al-Muḥāsibī's contemporaries, whose assemblies he was accustomed to attend, was Abū Hamām al-Walīd b. Shaja' b. al-Walīd b. Qays al-Sakūnī (*ob.* 243/857), a pupil of 'Abd Allah b. al-Mubārak, and a Kūfī by origin, who lived in Baghdad, to whose veracity Aḥmad b. Ḥanbal paid tribute. He was seen after his death in a dream, with lamps suspended over his head, and was asked whence he had obtained them, and he replied, "This one through the Tradition of the Tank, this one through the Tradition of Intercession and this by such and such a tradition."[1] It was from discussion on mystical subjects with fellow-mystics in al-Walīd's group of followers that al-Muḥāsibī derived some of the teaching that he has handed down to us.[2]

Such were al-Muḥāsibī's friends and associates, with whom he spent his time, theologians, traditionists, devout men, ascetics, men who had travelled far and learnt much on their travels and, above all, mystics, who knew much of the doctrines of the Ṣūfīs and who knew also what it was to tread the mystic path, to experience the mystic "states" and to attain to the life in God of the saint. From such friends as these al-Muḥāsibī must have learnt much, and to many of them he also gave much.

[1] Khaṭīb, *op. cit.*, XIII., pp. 443 *ff*.
[2] Abū Nu'aym, *op. cit.* (Leyden), fol. 232*a*.

CHAPTER IV

THE WORKS OF AL-MUḤĀSIBĪ

THE writings of al-Muḥāsibī were based on his own spiritual experience and were inspired by the desire that others should be led to the way of salvation by the means which he had found effective in his own case. He was concerned with the refutation of error, especially the doctrines of the Mu'tazilites and others of unorthodox or heretical opinions, and the positive teaching of asceticism and the fundamental principles of the religious life, including the essential need of inner purification, which might lead to the gift of the Beatific Vision, for those fitted to receive it, and the attainment of the goal of the mystic and saint, the consciousness of life lived in union with God.

The Ṣūfīs asserted that the number of al-Muḥāsibī's works, original writings and commentaries, reached a total of two hundred;[1] but if so, only a small proportion of this total has come down to us, and of these the greatest and most comprehensive work, and that for which al-Muḥāsibī is most justly famed among Muslim writers, is his *Kitāb al-Ri'āya liḥuqūq Allāh wa'l-qiyām bihā* (Book of Observance of what is due to God and Abiding Therein),[2] which is called by Ḥājjī Khalīfa, the great Turkish bibliographer who died in A.D. 1658, the *Ri'āya fī Taṣawwuf* (Observance of the Principles of Ṣūfism). It was written to enable believers to find the way of life in which they could render to God what was due to Him, and is composed in the form of counsels given to a disciple in response to questions on his part. It consists of about sixty chapters, with many subsections.

In his introduction, al-Muḥāsibī impresses upon his readers the necessity for listening, if they are to hear the

[1] al-Subkī, *al-Ṭabaqāt al-Shāfi'īyya*, II., p. 37.

[2] MS. Oxford, Hunt. 611, fols. 1-151*b* (copied A.H. 539); Broussa, Jāmi' Kabīr, 1534; Angora, Diyānet isléri riyāséti, 403 (copied A.H. 739). Summarised by Abū Muḥammad al-Sulamī (660/1262) and Yūsuf Ṣafadī. *Cf.* MSS. Berlin 2812, 2813.

voice of God speaking to them and are to profit by what He has to say to them. Next he deals with self-examination and its rules, whereby a man may know what is the state of his soul and be led to repentance and to a state of preparedness for death, whenever it may come. Then he passes on to hypocrisy, its causes, and the temptations to it, and how these can be met, by thinking lightly of this world and by a thoroughly sincere intention (*ikhlāṣ*) in all action. He proceeds to shew how a man may hope to serve God, with no taint of self-interest, for His own sake alone, how the intention (*nīya*), which is the most important part of action, is to be formed, and how it is to be directed always towards God. al-Muḥāsibī deals at considerable length with the temptation to seek for popularity, and warns the sincere seeker that he must be prepared to accept the contempt of others rather than their esteem. From this he passes to the temptation to self-esteem (*'ujb*) and the necessity for fighting against this and against pride (*kibr*), by cultivating the virtue of humility. Then he writes of the different ways in which the servants of God may deceive themselves through delusion (*ghirra*). He gives detailed treatment to the qualities of emulation and jealousy and shews to what extent, and for what purposes, the former may be justified. Finally, he closes this great work by giving the rule of life by which the servant is to govern his conduct by day and by night, being always mindful of Him Whom he serves, and of the constant self-discipline necessary to maintain such a rule, and to guard against temptations which may assail him even after he has begun to serve God with his whole heart and mind.

This is al-Muḥāsibī's great treatise on the interior life, which reveals a profound knowledge of human nature and its weaknesses, while in the means which he suggests for combating these weaknesses and for attaining to the single-hearted service of God, he shews also the discerning wisdom and inspired insight of a true spiritual director and shepherd of souls.[1]

[1] The work attributed to al-Muḥāsibī entitled *al-Ri'āya fī taḥṣīl al-Maqāmāt—lil-sālikīn* (MS. Cairo 84) is apparently by a later writer, though much of it is in accordance with al-Muḥāsibī's teaching.

The second among al-Muḥāsibī's writings in respect of length and importance is his *Kitāb al-Waṣāyā* or *Naṣā'iḥ al-Dīniyya* (Book of Religious Precepts *or* Counsels)[1], consisting of forty-one chapters, written in order to give sincere counsel to the faithful and to serve as means of instruction to all novices (*murīdīn*). al-Muḥāsibī begins by expressing his concern at the schisms in the community, and his desire to find out which of the faithful had really found the way of salvation, and then he proceeds to the account of his search and conversion already given.[2] He maintains that the happiness of man, in this world and the next, consists in holding fast to the fear of God, and a man proves that he is Godfearing by his scrupulous abstinence from all that is unlawful (*wara'*), by abiding in the canonical sanctions (*ḥudūd*) and by purifying his heart from all that is abhorrent to God. Corruption of the true faith, on the other hand, arises from a presumptuous attitude towards God, due to the abandonment of this scrupulous abstinence, and the transgression of the Divine law, and obstinate persistence in sin against God. al-Muḥāsibī gives a dark picture of the schisms and the schismatics of the faith. Truth, he says, is not to be found, and those who followed after it have perished, while the wise man is bewildered by the dark clouds of temptation, and lust is predominant, and the souls of men seek only this transient life and what it offers for the satisfaction of sensual desire. It is the love of this world and the glory thereof which is the root of evil and is leading men astray from the path of God, which leads onwards and upwards to eternal life. Therefore he warns men against the love of wealth and the desire of accumulating it, and counsels them to be content with little, and to avoid amassing wealth on the plea of using it for the purpose of good works, exposing themselves to sin and especially to such preoccupation with worldly things that the heart cannot be set free for the remembrance and the worship of God. This leads him to advocate the virtue of contentment with what is sufficient for their needs, and he warns men to avoid

[1] MS. British Museum, Or. 7900; MS. Stambul, Baghdādī Wehbī 614; Cairo, Taṣ. 1416.

[2] See pp. 18 *ff*. above.

the vices of avarice and pride, and to do this, it is necessary to search the heart for secret sins. Control of the actions of the heart is equally necessary with control of the " members " responsible for the outward conduct, and therefore the motive of action is that which is of primary importance, and it is in accordance with the motive that action will be judged. al-Muḥāsibī deals next with the canonical obligations of Prayer and Fasting and works of supererogation, which, he holds, are not to take the place of what is prescribed by God, but only to complement it. He emphasises the duty of gratitude to God, which is the courtesy due to Him from His creatures for His gifts, and most of all, for the gift of the revelation and knowledge of Himself. He bids men to approach God in shame for their lack of gratitude, and in anxiety for their shortcomings, with deep awe of Him, mingled with real hope of His mercy, and joy in the recollection of Him and in their personal intercourse with Him through prayer, while they long for His coming and desire to be in His presence for evermore. Those who approach God thus, with assured faith and perfect trust and confidence in Him, will find peace and fellowship with Him, and their concern henceforth will be with Him alone. Such is the state of the righteous and the saints, and al-Muḥāsibī bids his readers strive earnestly that they may attain thereto.

A work of considerable interest is the *Kitāb al-Tawahhum wa'l-ahwāl* (Book of Supposition and the Terrors to Come)[1], an eschatological meditation on Paradise and Hell. In this, al-Muḥāsibī paints a vivid picture of the Last Day, when the number of the dead is completed, and the earth and the heavens are bereft of those who dwelt therein, and have become a still and silent void, and there remains only the One Reality, the All-Powerful, the All-Exalted, the Eternal Who does not cease to be, the Incomparable, alone in His Majesty and His Glory. By His call, all the creatures are summoned to appear before Him, and the dead arise and stand upon their feet, a mighty army from all the nations, king and beggar side by side; and not mankind only, but the beasts of prey, with their fierceness subdued, and the

[1] MS. Oxford, Hunt. 611, fols. 152*a*-171*a*. *Cf.* also Abū Bakr M. b. Khayr, *Biblioteca Arabico-Hispana*, Tom. IX., p. 272.

wild creatures from mountain and desert, with the cattle and reptiles and insects, in number as the stars of heaven, gather together, bowing their heads in humility and adoration, before the King of kings. Then the sun and the moon will be darkened and the heavens and the earth will be cleft asunder and pass away, and the celestial beings, who dwell in the Seven Heavens, will shepherd those risen from the dead, on the Plain of the Resurrection, and there, from the fierce blaze of the heavenly sun, no protection will be found save in the shadow of the Throne of the Most High. Then the records of men's deeds will be distributed, to be taken, by those who have done evil, in the left hand, and by those who have done good, in the right, and the balance will be set up, and he whose evil deeds outweigh the good will be condemned to eternal misery, and he whose good deeds outweigh the evil will be called to eternal happiness.

al-Muḥāsibī pictures the summons of the soul, trembling like a new-born camel, to come into the presence of God, to stand before Him, to be questioned upon its deeds, and, at the memory of His Compassion and His unfailing loving-kindness and its own disobedience and wilfulness, the soul is filled with unutterable shame. But when the soul learns that its sins are forgiven and it has found acceptance with its Lord, that shame is turned to joy, and its face is lightened and reflects the radiance of its Lord. The soul then passes on its way to Paradise, and there once more it looks upon the King in His Beauty and enters into the joys of the Blessed. Then al-Muḥāsibī imagines the final summons to His chosen saints to meet with their Lord, when all veils are drawn aside and they gaze upon God face to face, and contemplate Him in His Beauty and His Majesty, and hear the words of the One Incomparable, calling them to draw near unto Himself, and as lovers they rejoice in the consummation of their love, having entered into eternal communion with the Beloved.

Another eschatological work is the *Kitāb al-Ba'th wa'l-Nushūr* (Book of the Rising and the Resurrection from the Dead),[1] which shews points of resemblance to the last mentioned and has probably been modelled on it. This

[1] MS. Paris 1913, fols. 196*a*-202*b*.

work deals mainly with the Day of Resurrection, when, according to the traditions, each soul is clothed upon again with its body, and the risen souls go to seek the intercession of the saints and prophets for salvation in that day. al-Muḥāsibī here relates the legend that at the gate of Paradise is a mighty tree, with branches so many that none knows their number save God, and upon them sit the " infants of the faith," those who were born in the true faith, but whose span of life in the world was but a few months or less, or who did not live to reach adolescence. They are waiting for their mothers and fathers to enter Paradise, and those who are fortunate enough to find their parents among the righteous to whom it is appointed to dwell therein come joyfully to meet them, bearing vessels filled with the water of life, wherewith to quench their thirst, and children and parents pass into Paradise together. But those unhappy little ones, who do not see their mothers and fathers, weep bitterly and lament that they should be orphaned both in the lower world and in this. Then the angels tell them that their parents have been prevented from entering Paradise by the burden of their sins, and the children, weeping, sit down to await them, hoping and praying that God will forgive their parents and unite them once again. But those who have sinned against God and have entered the fires of Purgatory are not lost eternally, for in those purifying flames they remember their Lord and cry upon Him for deliverance, and He has mercy upon them, and having purified them, as by the fire, from the dross of sin, He bids the archangel Gabriel go with the Prophet and tell the angel of Purgatory that he in whose heart is the weight of one grain of faith is to be brought forth from those flames. Then those purified souls come forth and meet with their children and beg them to give them to drink after their long thirst, but the children do not recognise them, for their purifying discipline has changed them beyond recognition, so the Lord bids them to plunge into the river of the Water of Life, and they come out thence, having been changed from the terrestrial into the celestial. Then are they clad in the robes of the redeemed and enter into the realms of the Blessed, and the veil, which is pure Light, is taken away, and they look upon the face of God and hear His voice bidding them enter into the joy of their Lord.

The question of what is lawful and unlawful, and what is doubtful in the matter of earning a livelihood, and the scrupulous abstinence from all that is in any way dubious, which is to be observed by the righteous, is dealt with in the *Risālat al-Makāsib wa'l-Wara'wa'l-Shubuhāt* (Treatise on Earning a Livelihood and Abstinence and Doubtful Things).[1] In this work al-Muḥāsibī modifies the quietist tendencies of certain of his predecessors, and condemns excessive rigorism in the matter of what is dubious, while continuing to advocate the need for abstinence and asceticism. The basic principle in these matters, he teaches, should be reliance upon God (*tawakkul*), Who can be trusted to provide for His creatures, and therefore they have no excuse for recourse to what is unlawful or doubtful in origin. In this connection al-Muḥāsibī sets forth a fine conception of God as Creator, with discerning knowledge of, and care for, His creatures. Faith in God and the remembrance, with the lips as with the heart, that He is the Sole Provider, the Lord of life and death, and Sovereign over all things, will lead men to this complete trust in Him, and to the observance of His sanctions. But this does not mean that a man should refrain from taking lawful means to earn a livelihood, or live in idleness at the expense of others.[2] The right type of abstinence (*wara'*) is to abstain from what God has prohibited and what is abhorrent to Him of action, whether in word or in deed, and of thought and motive, and what this is can be known by self-examination before proceeding to action.

This work includes an interesting section on the practices of the ascetics and Ṣūfīs of al-Muḥāsibī's time and preceding times, shewing their scrupulous anxiety to refrain from anything including the least taint or possibility of what was unlawful. Some, he says, betook themselves to the mountains and the valleys, and gathered tamarisk leaves and what

[1] MS. Stambul, Jārallāh 1101, fols. 29*a*-51*b*.

[2] As a modern writer on Mysticism expresses it, "Entire dependence, yet effort is required, for it is a dependence which is active. God gives us the wheat, but we must reap and grind and bake" (E. Underhill).

could be picked up in the way of seeds and pulse and herbs, which had a value if stored, and these they collected in summer for use in winter. Others chose to exist on windfalls and fresh herbs and grass and such vegetation as was to be found growing wild, when hunger drove them to eat.[1] Some were content with what had been thrown away, while another group preferred to beg for food. Some ascetics living in the regions of Syria used to glean what they could of corn and barley, following the reapers, but this, al-Muḥāsibī notes, was not a practice in his time. He refers also to those who would not glean behind the reapers on land bought with money wrongfully acquired, or land bestowed by the Government upon its supporters, or consisting of estates of which the rightful owners had been despoiled. Others, again, chose to earn a living by manual labour, or by taking up the sword in the service of God, in preference to gleaning at the harvest, because the latter procedure had no precedent under the rule of the first four Imāms, and these were agreed upon fighting under the banner of every Commander of the Faithful, whether good or bad. Others chose to retire into a monastery and live there in seclusion, unless there was a call for the services of Muslims, on account of the advance or invasion of some enemy into the territory of Islām, and in these circumstances it was obligatory for them to wield the sword; but when the need had passed, and the community no longer required their services, they would retire once more into the monastery they had established, holding that it was the more excellent way. This group among the Ṣūfīs al-Muḥāsibī considers to be much in error.

He deals also with the question of buying and selling and what is to be considered lawful or unlawful for the servant of God in this respect, and quotes the case of those who considered that to buy a knife, or wood to serve as fuel for cooking, from the Government, was unlawful, and so also was the purchase of a leather whip or a whetstone from a Christian. Others disliked trading with women for thread (the twisting of thread being done by women), or for a

[1] *Cf.* the "grazers" (*βοσκοί*), Christian ascetics of Syria who ate only grass, herbs and roots (Evagrius, I., c. 21).

rosary, lest it should mean temptation to look upon what was unlawful.

al-Muḥāsibī deprecates bigotry and fanaticism and the attitude of those who would starve rather than partake of what did not seem to them lawful, and points out that this extremist view had brought some to the loss of reason and to suicide. The right road to follow, he thought, was that of scrupulous abstinence from what was known to be unlawful, after self-examination in order to be sure in the matter, and trust in God that He would not fail to provide all that was necessary for His creatures, who need not have recourse to what was unlawful or to extreme fanaticism in the search for the lawful, which was in itself unlawful.

A treatise dealing with self-discipline is the *Risālat ādāb al-Nufūs* (Treatise on the Training of Souls),[1] called also *Risāla fi'l-Akhlāq* (Treatise on Ethics).[2] The lower soul, the self (*nafs*), al-Muḥāsibī regards as needing constant watchfulness and care, in all times of activity or leisure, in silence and in speech, in its goings out and comings in, in its pleasure, in what it loves and what it hates, in its time of laughter and of weeping alike. The tongue, he considers, is to be feared more than a wild beast, it is the most dangerous of all the " members " and the chief cause of sin ;[3] " he who is silent is safe." The virtues to be cultivated for the training of the soul are singlemindedness in the service of God (*ikhlāṣ*), reliance on Him (*thiqa*), gratitude (*shukr*), humility, submission, the giving of faithful counsel (*naṣīḥa*) and the love of what God loves and hatred of what He hates. al-Muḥāsibī does not fear any neglect of good works on the part of the believer, or of abstinence, but he does fear that the soul may suffer from lack of " gnosis "—real understanding of the things that pertain to righteousness—and from weakness of will, for action is based on knowledge, and that is the gift of God, to be used with the help of the reason. The aim, therefore, of all soul-training is that the

[1] MS. Stambul, Jārallāh 1101, fols. 59*b*-103*b*.

[2] MS. Keuprūlū Zadeh 725.

[3] *Cf.* St. James : " The world of iniquity among our members is the tongue, which defileth the whole body. The tongue can no man tame ; it is a restless evil, it is full of deadly poison " (iii. 6, 8).

soul may attain to understanding (*ma'rifa*) of what God desires, and then, by resolution and an assured purpose based on that understanding, to a rightly directed will which is concerned to carry out only that which is in accordance with the eternal Will of God.

A very valuable treatise on the gnosis which is attained by means of self-examination and meditation, which enables the soul to receive that which is the gift of God, is the *Sharḥ al-Ma'rifa wa badhl al-Naṣīḥa* (Exposition of Gnosis and the Bestowal of Good Counsel), known also as the *Kitāb Muḥāsabat al-Nufūs* (Book of Self-Examination) and the *Risālat fi'l-Murāqaba wa inqiṣāmiha* (Treatise on Meditation and what it Includes).[1] In this treatise al-Muḥāsibī states that knowledge is of four types—knowledge of God; knowledge of the enemy of God, Iblīs; knowledge of the self; and knowledge of the work of God—and he develops these themes.

Knowledge of God, he holds, is attained by contemplation of Him and remembrance of His proximity and faith in His unfailing care. Knowledge of the enemy of God means the realisation that the servant is bidden to strive against him at all times, without weakening in the effort, for Iblīs has more power against him than any other creature, and to give way to him will bring a man to destruction. Knowledge of self is to realise that the self is headstrong in doing evil and must be placed where God has placed it, and kept in subjection by constant vigilance and self-examination (*muḥāsaba*). Knowledge of how God acts enables the servant to act in accordance with His Will and to follow the path which leads to salvation. In conclusion, al-Muḥāsibī urges his readers to use his book as a mirror to be set before their eyes in all circumstances, for there is no good counsel which has been revealed to him by God which he has not bestowed upon them, and his hope is that the book may lead them to give glory to God and seek His assistance and the grace of His favour.

Another work concerned with the training of the soul and self-discipline is the *Kitāb bad' man anāb ila Allāh* (Book of

[1] MS. Berlin 2815 (copied A.H. 1200); Br. Mus., Or. 4026, fols. 66*b ff.*; MS. Cairo, Taṣ. Sh. 3 (copied A.H. 1173).

the Beginning of Conversion unto God),[1] the tone of which suggests that it is autobiographical, representing the course of al-Muḥāsibī's own experience. He tells how at first he was hindered by the things which detached him from his Lord (*al-qawāṭi'*) and by everything which distracted him from His service, and how he did not attain to happiness and peace of mind except after toil and effort, and he makes it clear that all novices who seek for salvation must expect to take that path. The beginning of repentance, like the end, is due to the grace of God;[2] but when God has stirred the conscience, then it is for man to examine and discipline himself, and to keep continually before him the remembrance of death and the hereafter, and so, by attaining mastery over the lower soul, and keeping his eyes fixed upon higher things, he will make continual progress in the Path of God, and having relinquished the pleasures and temptations of all that would hinder him from the service of his Lord, will attain to fellowship with Him.

A treatise in which al-Muḥāsibī deals with a number of practical questions is the *Kitāb al-Masā'il fī A'māl al-Qulūb wa'l-Jawāriḥ* (Book of Questions concerning the Actions of the Heart and the Members—*i.e.*, the interior and the outward life),[3] in which he is concerned with the respective merits of concealing or displaying good works, and incidentally warns men against seeking notoriety by their habits, religious or otherwise. Connected with this is his warning against being concerned with the good opinions of others, when engaged in public prayer.[4] He discusses the question of works of supererogation and finds much in them to commend, as a completion of what is obligatory, and as a preventive of the waste of a man's life in what is useless or positively sinful, "for none occupy themselves with the recollection of God, but angels surround them and the glory

[1] MS. Stambul, Jārallāh 1101, fols. 18*b*-24*b*.

[2] *Cf.* St. Paul: "The goodness of God leadeth thee to repentance" (Romans ii. 4).

[3] MS. Stambul, Jārallāh 1101, fols. 114*a*-145*b* (copied A.H. 523).

[4] *Cf.* St. Matthew: "When ye pray, ye shall not be as the hypocrites, for they love to stand and pray in the synagogues and the corners of the streets, that they may be seen of men" (vi. 5).

of the Lord descends upon them." Such works are a means also, for the lovers of God, of securing preoccupation with Him, for they fear lest even the glance of an eye should come between them and their Lord, since a lover fears everything which may come between him and the Beloved.

The actions of the heart al-Muḥāsibī sums up under three heads; first, adherence to faith and avoidance of unbelief; second, adherence to the Sunna and avoidance of heresy; third, adherence to obedience (to God) and avoidance of stubborn persistence in what is abhorrent to Him. These actions include the exercise of many other virtues, especially constant vigilance and patience. al-Muḥāsibī also considers the respective merits of silence and speech, and concludes that silence is safer, but speech is more excellent if directed towards the praise of God and the furtherance of His purposes. He writes here of the nature and merits of acquiescence in the Will of God (*tafwīḍ*), that self-renunciation which is the fullness of freedom, leading to the perfect liberty of the children of God.

In the *Risālat al-ʿAẓama* (Treatise on the Divine Majesty),[1] al-Muḥāsibī is concerned to prove the existence and the unity of the Godhead. He uses the teleological argument, shewing that the interdependence of all creatures, one upon another, points to unity of purpose in the creation. After arguments to refute the possibility of any dual control of the universe, he brings forward the fact of the unfailing grace of God, shewn by His provision for the needs of His creatures from the moment when He brings them into existence. He shews by stories of the ancients what has been the fate of those who refused to believe, and concludes that the reader who reflects on these proofs cannot fail to believe in God, and that God will guide him by means of a faith which nothing can destroy, until he comes at last to Paradise and the perfect satisfaction of the Blessed.

Of the book entitled *Tanbīh ʿala Aʿmāl al-Qulūb* (Book of Admonition on the Works of the Heart) only a fragment is extant,[2] and this is a chapter on the Unicity of God, in

[1] MS. Stambul, Jārallāh 1101, fols. 24*a*-27*b*. This appears to be only an extract from a larger work.

[2] *Ibid.*, fol. 28*a*.

which the line of reasoning adopted corresponds to the arguments put forward in the work just considered.

The *Kitāb al-Masā'il fī Zuhd wa ghayriha* (Book of Questions concerning Asceticism and other subjects)[1] is concerned with the nature of Asceticism and the qualities which lead the servant to the renunciation of this world and its attractions, and all things, whether lawful or unlawful, which may hinder the soul in its progress towards spiritual perfection. al-Muḥāsibī deals here with the type of virtues which incite the servant to this asceticism, and the vices which are a hindrance to it. Other subjects dealt with are Worship and Prayer.

Prayer is also the subject of the *Kitāb Fahm al-Ṣalāt* (Book of the Comprehension of Prayer),[2] which is concerned mainly with the ritual prayer, but also, to some extent, with personal intercession.[3]

A short treatise of great importance because of the light it throws upon al-Muḥāsibī's ideas of psychology, and the relation of "natural" to "spiritual" gifts, is the *Kitāb Mā'iyyat al-'Aql wa ma'nāhu wa Ikhtilāf al-Nās fihī* (Book of the Essence of the Reason and its Significance and how Men differ in Opinion in Regard to It),[4] in which al-Muḥāsibī discusses the opinions of others and states his own view that the reason is a natural disposition bestowed by God upon His creatures.[5]

Another work on ascetic theology is that entitled *Kitāb Iḥkām al-Tawba wa radd maẓālim al-'ibād wa'l-Khalāṣ minha qabl al-Mi'ād* (Book of the Establishment of Repentance and the Restitution of Wrongs [done] to the Pious, and Deliver-

[1] MS. Stambul, Jārallāh 1101, fols. 1*a*-17*b*. Perhaps identical with the *Kitāb al-Zuhd* mentioned by al-Ghazālī in his *Iḥyā'*.

[2] *Ibid*., fols. 51*b*-58*b*. Called here *Mukhtaṣar Kitāb Fahm al-Ṣalāt* (Epitome of the Book of the Comprehension of Prayer) and therefore possibly an abridgment of the work as written by al-Muḥāsibī.

[3] For a fuller treatment of al-Muḥāsibī's teaching on Prayer *cf.* Chapter XI. below.

[4] MS. Stambul, Jārallāh 1101, fols. 104*b*-113*b*. Summarised by Mālīnī (409/1018) in his *Arbā'īn*, by Dhahabī in his *'Ibar*, and Ibn al-Jawzī in his *Dhamm ul-hawā*.

[5] For a further discussion of al-Muḥāsibī's psychological views *cf.* Chapter VI. below.

ance from them before the Resurrection),[1] in which al-Muḥāsibī regards repentance as a duty imposed by God upon His servants, and he deals here with the distinction between mortal and venial sins and the need for repentance from both.

A short treatise concerned with a practical view of life is the *Kitāb al-Mustarshid* (Book of the Traveller on the Right Road),[2] in which al-Muḥāsibī warns his reader that sin produces heedlessness, and heedlessness hardens the heart, and hardness of heart leads to alienation from God, and alienation from God leads to Hell. At the same time he gives an attractive picture of the rightly guided traveller on the road to God, who is humble-minded, friendly towards those whom he teaches, tractable when questioned, able to give a healing remedy to those who seek it, helping that one who needs guidance, and in all things practising what he preaches.

In the *Kitāb al-'Ilm* (Book of Knowledge)[3] al-Muḥāsibī classifies knowledge as being of three types: first, knowledge of what is lawful and unlawful, which is knowledge of what concerns this world and is outward knowledge; second, knowledge of what concerns the next world, which is inward knowledge; third, knowledge of God and His laws concerning His creatures in the two worlds, and this is a fathomless sea, and only the most learned of the faithful attain to it. al-Muḥāsibī proceeds to classify the religious as including those who are content with outward righteousness, renouncing visible defects in conduct only, whited sepulchres, whose " inward parts are a desolation," and on the other hand those who seek the purification of the inward self and renounce all secret sins. His conclusion is that it is impossible to be a lover of this world and a lover of God, for no man can serve two masters—he must choose between God and Mammon.

In his *Kitāb al-Ḥubb lillāh ta'āla wa marātib ahlihi* (Book of

[1] MS. Cairo, Taṣ. Shīn. 3 (copied A.H. 1173). This work appears to have been edited.

[2] *Ibid.* This also appears to have been edited.

[3] MS. Milan, Bib. Ambrosiana 460, fols. 18*a*-21*a* (copied in A.H. 1066).

Love to God and the Stages of His Lovers), to be identified with the *Faṣl fī'l-Maḥabba* (Chapter on Love), included by Abū Nu'aym in his *Ḥilyat al-Awliyā*,[1] we have the most mystical of all al-Muḥāsibī's writings, in which he tells of the love of God for His saints, and the signs by which these lovers of God may be known while they dwell in this world among men. To such lovers is granted the Vision of God and that communion with Him which is the aim of the mystic, the indwelling of the human by the Divine.[2]

Only a short fragment is extant of the *Kitāb al-Ṣabr wa'l-Riḍā'* (Book of Patience and Satisfaction),[3] which treats of the two complementary principles of bearing patiently, and accepting gladly, the decrees of God, whatever they may be. It is written in the form of a dialogue between master and disciple, like others of al-Muḥāsibī's works. al-Muḥāsibī's teaching on Satisfaction is given more fully in al-Hujwīrī's *Kashf al-Maḥjūb*, and al-Hujwīrī may have derived it from this treatise in its complete form. He gives it as representing a new point of view, which is much quoted by later writers.[4]

Among the works of al-Muḥāsibī of which no copy is known to exist is the *Kitāb al-Kaff 'ammā suḥira bayn al-Saḥāba* (Book on Abstaining from what was rejected among the Companions),[5] which is probably to be identified with a work of his referred to as the *Kitāb al-Dimā'* (Book of the Streams of Blood—*i.e.*, which were shed among the Companions without securing doctrinal unity).[6] Another work which is no longer known to exist is the *Kitāb al-Tafakkur wa'l-I'tibār* (Book of Reflection and Induction).[7] The latter process al-Muḥāsibī defines elsewhere as inferring one thing

[1] MS. Leyden, Or. 311*a*, fols. 231 *ff.*; MS. Damascus, Zah. Taṣ. 117 (XI.), fols. 4*a ff.* *Cf.* Abū Bakr M. b. Khayr, *Biblioteca Arabico-Hispana*, Tom. IX., p. 272.

[2] *Cf.* Chapter XII. below.

[3] MS. Bankipore 820, last three folios (copied A.H. 321). *Cf.* O. Spies, *Islamica*, VI. 3, 1934, pp. 283 *ff.*

[4] Hujwīrī, *op. cit.*, pp. 176 *ff.*

[5] Dhahabī, "Ta'rīkh al-Islām," MS. Leyden 843, fol. 24*a*.

[6] *Fihrist*, p. 184.

[7] *Ibid.* *Cf.* Sarrāj, *Kitāb al-Luma'*, p. 231.

from another, and reflection on the results is the completion of the process.

In his *Risālat al-'Aẓama* al-Muḥāsibī refers to a *Kitāb fahm al-Qur'ān* (Book of the Understanding of the Qur'ān), which is presumably his own work, but no copy of it is known to exist.[1]

There is further a *Kitāb al-Ghayba* (Book on Absence), mentioned by Abū Bakr M. b. Khayr,[2] which may represent a work now lost, or may be identified with a section included in some other work.[3]

[1] "Risālat al 'Azama," fol. 26*b*.

[2] *Op. cit.*, p. 272.

[3] *Cf. Ḥilya*, fol. 241*a*, and p. 31 above, and pp. 207, 208 *ff.* below.

CHAPTER V

AL-MUḤĀSIBĪ'S SOURCES

BAGHDAD, as we have seen, at the time when al-Muḥāsibī lived there, was a focus of world culture and refinement, where the most distinguished theologians and commentators of Islām, as well as many Jewish and Christian scholars, were to be found, teaching, discussing and writing. It was possible, therefore, for an earnest seeker after truth, such as al-Muḥāsibī—anxious to purify the true faith from abuses and heresies, and to establish a rule of life for the faithful which should bring them back into the strait way leading to salvation and enable them to know and to strive to fulfil what was due to God and to Him alone—to have every opportunity for gaining knowledge from those who were leaders in the spiritual life, and for discussion alike with those who differed from him and those who had similar desires with himself, and so to realise the difficulties and problems which beset the believer and the novice and, by long study and meditation, to come to a knowledge of their solution.

The translation into Arabic of the writings of classical and Syriac authors, under the 'Abbāsids, the freedom of intercourse between Muslim and Christian theologians which then prevailed, and the presence of a large and influential Jewish community in Baghdad, led to an increased knowledge not only of the Old and New Testaments, but of the Jewish Haggāda and Mishnah, and of mystical literature, both Christian and Jewish. So it came about that among the Muslim traditions (*ḥadīth*) reckoned as authentic and orthodox in al-Muḥāsibī's time, some were, in fact, borrowed directly from Talmudic and Christian literature, and al-Muḥāsibī's sources, therefore, include much material which, while nominally derived only from Islāmic teaching, actually owed its origin to Judaism and Christianity.

al-Muḥāsibī's authorities are, in most cases, quoted by name, and, according to the invariable custom of Muslim writers, his first and chief authority for any doctrine is the

Qur'ān, the Word of God, and his second the Sunna, the canonical law embodying the traditions of Muḥammad, supplementing the teaching of the Qur'ān and held to be of almost equal authority by all orthodox Muslims. al-Muḥāsibī's biographers state, and his own writings confirm the statement, that he derived his traditions in the first place from Abū Khālid Yazīd b. Hārūn al-Sulamī (*ob.* 206/821).[1] Yazīd b. Hārūn studied under Sa'īd al-Anṣārī and Sulaymān al-Taymī, and among his pupils was Aḥmad b. Ḥanbal. As a traditionist Yazīd b. Hārūn met with the criticism that he did not distinguish between traditions which were authentic and those that were doubtful, and that he was not sufficiently careful as to whose authority he quoted. That he had a reputation for orthodoxy and was fearless of the consequences in upholding his convictions is proved by the story told of the Caliph al-Ma'mūn, who stated that if it were not for Yazīd b. Hārūn, he would declare the Qur'ān to be created (in accordance with the views of the Mu'tazilites, to which al-Ma'mūn adhered). Asked why he should fear Yazīd b. Hārūn, the Caliph said he feared lest Yazīd should refute him, and there should be dissensions among the people, and a tumult be caused. Someone then went to Wāsiṭ, where Yazīd was living, and found him in the mosque there, and having repeated what al-Ma'mūn had said, was bidden to repeat his statement in front of the people. He did so, and Yazīd denied that the Caliph could have said such a thing, and swore by God that whoever said that the Qur'ān was created was an unbeliever. It is to be noted that al-Muḥāsibī later gave much attention to the refutation of Mu'tazilite teaching.

al-Muḥāsibī appears to have been a pupil also of Muḥammad b. Kathīr Abū Isḥāq al-Qurashī al-Kūfī, known as al-Ṣūfī,[2] who was criticised for the transmission of a tradition with mystical tendencies, according to which the Prophet was reputed to have said, "Fear the powers of discernment (*firāsa*) of the believer, for he sees by the light of God." Aḥmad b. Ḥanbal refused to accept his traditions and stated that though

[1] al-Sulamī, "Ṭabaqāt," fol. 11*b* A.H. 186 is given as the date of his death by L. Massignon, *Essai*, p. 212.

[2] Khaṭīb, *op. cit.*, VIII., p. 212.

he derived them from a trustworthy source, he had perverted them in the course of transmission. al-Bukhārī also rejected his authority.[1] But al-Muḥāsibī expressly states that the principle on which he has selected his authorities is that of the moral value of their life and teaching, and this he felt was the test of their spiritual authority, rather than the acceptance of their traditions as being unimpeachably orthodox.

In addition to these two, the long list of authorities, extending from the Prophet to writers and teachers of his own time, quoted by al-Muḥāsibī, not only shews the breadth of his researches, but is of great interest as an indication of the sources available for a writer of his early date. Among the earliest authorities cited are Ka'b al-Aḥbār (*ob.* 32/652) and 'Abdallah b. Salām (*ob.* 43/663), and it is noteworthy that both of these were Jews, natives of Yaman, who had been converted to Islām, and both were responsible for the introduction of Jewish teaching and legends into Islāmic *Ḥadīth*.[2]

Among the Companions of the Prophet cited is Muḥammad b. Naṣr al-Ḥāritha, one who had passed through the mystic experience and had been granted the vision of things invisible. He says that he had cut himself off, and turned away, from the things of this world, until its stones and its treasures of gold and silver and its clay had become of equal value in his sight, and he had passed his nights in vigils and his days in thirst until, at last, he says, "I was rapt away from this world and looked upon the Throne of God made manifest, and contemplated the Divine mysteries, having passed away from the temporal to the eternal, from the transient to the everlasting."[3] Another of the Companions quoted is Mu'ādh b. Jabal, who was reputed to be the most learned of all men of his time, in respect of what was lawful (*ḥalāl*) and unlawful (*ḥarām*), and as such, his opinion was likely to have weight with one so scrupulous as al-Muḥāsibī.[4] Yet another Companion cited is Tamīm al-Dārī, a devout ascetic, who would spend a whole night until daybreak reciting a single verse of the Qur'ān (Sūra 45: 20). He was the first who narrated (*qaṣṣa*) religious stories, with the leave of

[1] Khaṭīb, *op. cit.*, III., p. 191.
[2] Shar'āni, *Ṭab.*, I., p. 39.
[3] Kalābādhī, *Kitāb al-Ta'arruf*, pp. 98, 107. Hujwīrī, *op. cit.*, p. 227.
[4] Sarrāj, *Kitāb al-Luma'*, p. 120.

the Caliph 'Umar b. al-Khaṭṭāb, and that al-Muḥāsibī should select him as one of his authorities is a fact of especial interest, because he was formerly a Christian.[1]

al-Muḥāsibī cites also certain of the " People of the Bench or Verandah " (*Ahl al-Ṣuffa*), who were said to be poor devotees, whose custom it was to sit on stone benches outside the mosques and to live on the alms of the faithful, and the Prophet was reputed to have commended them as an example to his community, because of their poverty and self-mortification and their contentment with the state in which they were. Such as they, he said, would be his companions in Paradise.[2] Those of the *Ahl al-Ṣuffa* cited by al-Muḥāsibī include 'Abdallah b. Mas'ūd (*ob.* 32/652) and the famous Abū Darda 'Uwaymar b. Zayd, who held that one hour of reflection (*tafakkur*) was better than forty nights of prayer, and that one particle of righteousness, combined with godliness and assured faith, was preferable to unlimited ritual observance.[3] Both he and his wife Umm Darda, equally well known as a transmitter of traditions, are quoted by al-Muḥāsibī, together with another of this group, who was no less famed as a traditionist, Abū Hurayra (*ob.* 58/677). Of his habits of devotion it was said that he and his wife and their handmaiden used to divide the night between them, and each prayed in turn for one-third of the night.[4] To him are attributed many traditions of ascetical and even mystical tendencies—*e.g.*, " In truth God is glad at the repentance of His servants, when they repent and return unto Him " ; and again, " Fasting is a shield against the wickedness of Satan in this world and from Hell-fire in the world to come " ; and of the unitive state, when the mystic lives in and through God, a tradition ascribed to him relates that God has said, " My servant is always seeking to approach Me, so that I love him. And when I love him, I am his ear by which he hears, and I am his sight by which he

[1] Sha'rānī, *Ṭab.*, I., p. 21. *Cf.* R. A. Nicholson, *Literary History of the Arabs*, p. 225.

[2] Sarrāj, *Kitāb al-Luma'*, pp. 132, 133 ; Hujwīrī, *op. cit.*, p. 81.

[3] Sha'rānī, *Ṭab.*, I., p. 23.

[4] *Ibid.*, I., p. 22 ; *Tagh.*, I., p. 168. *Cf.* also *Ḥilya*, I., pp. 372 *ff.* (ed. Cairo).

sees, and I am his hands by which he grasps, and I am his feet by which he walks."[1]

Belonging also to this early group of authorities is one who may be considered a precursor of the later mystics, Ḥudayfa b. Ḥusayl al-Yamān (*ob.* 36/657), a native of Baṣra, an ascetic who rejoiced when he was told that his family had nothing, small or great, for he was then entirely dependent upon God. Among his sayings was one to the effect that a time was coming upon men when it would be said that what was most excellent was that which was best understood, combined with the weight of a grain of faith in the heart. He said also, " The best of you are not those who abandon this world for the next, but those who take from both."[2] Among his pupils was Khālid b. Rabī' al-'Absī al-Kūfī. These early authorities include 'Abdallah b. 'Amru b. al-'Āṣ (*ob.* 79/698), son of the governor of Egypt, famous for his traditions about Egypt and the characters of the Old Testament, and noted for his clear exposition and keenness of insight. It was said of him, by those who knew him, that his inner life corresponded to the outer.[3] Yet another of this generation cited by al-Muḥāsibī is Aḥnaf b. Qays Tamīmī (*ob.* 67/686), appointed to command the troops at Baṣra during the conflict between the Companions of the Prophet, whose allies included Ḥasan al-Baṣrī. The worst of maladies, Tamīmī held, was a base mind and a foul tongue, and the two virtues which could not be controverted were evenness of temper and avoidance of all that was vile.[4] Contemporary with him was Ṣafwān b. Maḥarriz al-Māzinī (*ob.* 74/693), who said that what he knew of good was of no use to him unless he acted in accordance with it, and added, " Would that I had known nothing !" It was related that he never went out of his house except for prayer and then returned in haste.[5]

To the next generation of authorities cited by al-Muḥāsibī belongs Abu'l-'Āliya (*ob.* 90/708), of whom it was said that

[1] *Mishkāt al-Maṣābīḥ*, X. iii. 1 ; VII. i. 1 ; IX. ii. 1.
[2] Sha'rānī, *Ṭab.*, I., p. 22. *Cf.* p. 10 above.
[3] Taghrībirdī, I., pp. 31, 73.
[4] Ibn Khallikān, I., pp. 635 *ff.*
[5] Sha'rānī, *op. cit.*, I., p. 30. Dhahabī, *Ṭab. al-Ḥuffāẓ*, p. 23. *Cf.* Abū Nu'aym, *op. cit.*, II., pp. 213 *ff.* (ed. Cairo).

he was averse to men dressing in wool (*ṣūf*),[1]—an indication that this custom was found among Muslim ascetics and devotees even at this early period—saying that the adornment of Muslims was dignity (*tajammul*) in their clothing. He loved solitude, and if more than four persons came to sit with him he would rise up and leave them, fearing vain conversation. Of knowledge he said that there was no greater sin than for a man to study the Qur'ān and then to be unmindful of it, and not to be vigilant because of his study.[2] Among the Followers of the same period cited is Sa'īd b. Musayyib (*ob.* 91/709 or 94/712), one of the seven great jurisconsults of Medina, a man of devout nature, who made a show of hypocrisy, according to the custom of the early Ṣūfīs, who sought to incur blame (*malāma*) in order to avoid self-conceit.[3] For thirty years the Mu'izzin never gave the call to prayer but Sa'īd b. Musayyib was already in his place in the mosque. He was ill-treated by the Umayyad Caliph 'Abd al-Malik b. Marwān (A.D. 685-705) and the people were debarred from coming to his assembly, but he was none the less greatly revered. Concerning things lawful and unlawful, he said, " The praise of God is altogether lawful, and the praise of aught else is altogether unlawful, for salvation lies in the former and perdition in the latter."[4] Another authority of the same generation is Ibrāhīm b. Taymī (*ob.* 92/710), who was imprisoned by Ḥajjāj, the viceroy of 'Abd al-Malik, having offered himself instead of another Ibrāhīm (Nakhā'ī), giving thus an early example of " preference " (*īthār*).[5] He died in prison from the effects of his sufferings.[6] Another victim of Ḥajjāj, included among al-Muḥāsibī's authorities, is Sa'īd b. Jubayr, who was also imprisoned, and when informed of the near approach of

[1] *Cf.* al-Muḥāsibī, " Masā'il fī a'mal," fols. 237-244; " Ri'āya," fol. 111*a*; Hujwīrī, pp. 15 *ff.* *Cf.* L. Massignon, *Essai*, pp. 131, 132.

[2] Sha'rāni, *Ṭab.*, I., p. 30. *Cf.* Abū Nu'aym, *op. cit.*, II., pp. 217 *ff.*, (ed. Cairo).

[3] *Cf.* Hujwīrī, *op. cit.*, pp. 62-69, and my *Studies in Early Mysticism*, p. 192.

[4] Hujwīrī, *op. cit.*, p. 87; Ibn Khallikān, I., p. 568; Sha'rānī, *Ṭab.*, I., p. 26. *Cf.* also Abū Nu'aym, *Ḥilya*, II., pp. 160 *ff.* (ed. Cairo).

[5] *Cf.* Hujwīrī, *op. cit.*, pp. 189 *ff.* *Cf.* p. 33 above.

[6] Sha'rānī, *Ṭab.*, I., p. 36.

his execution, he prevailed upon his gaolers to allow him to go out of the prison and prepare for death, saying that he would return in the morning. He did so and met his death on the executioner's carpet, praying that he might be the last of al-Ḥajjāj's victims, and his prayer was granted, for the tyrant died twenty-five days later.[1]

An authority of the second century after the Ḥijra is 'Abdallah b. Qays (*ob.* 103/721), a devotee who said that if the whole of this world were his, and God bade him cast it away, he would obey with a joyful heart. Love to God so absorbed him that he paid no heed to the advent of night or of day. He declared that since he had come to know God by direct experience, he had feared none but Him. He used to say, and al-Muḥāsibī later emphasised the statement, that it was folly on the part of a man to fear for others on account of their sins, and to feel secure about his own.[2] Two authorities of the same date were Abū Qulayb Jarmī (104/722), an orthodox legist of Baṣra, who was summoned to the office of Qāḍī, and to avoid it fled into Syria and remained there,[3] and Mujāhid b. Jubayr Makhzūmī (*ob.* 104/722), noted for his knowledge of the interpretation of the Qur'ān, who was editor of the *Tafsīr* of Ibn 'Abbās. He was evidently much admired by al-Muḥāsibī, who frequently refers to him.[4] Another of the Followers cited is Ṭāwwūs b. Kaysān al-Yamanī (*ob.* 105/723), of Persian descent, who used to say, "Would that you might acquire knowledge for yourself, for in truth faith, and action in accordance with knowledge, has departed from men," a fact which al-Muḥāsibī emphasises, as also the teaching of Ṭāwwūs that the most excellent service to God was that which was kept most secret, and his statement that if the hope and fear of the believer were weighed in the balance, they would be found to be equal.[5] One of the prayers of Ṭāwwūs, related by Sufyān al-Thawrī, runs thus: "O God, keep from us wealth and children, and give us as our provision faith and works."[6]

[1] Sha'rānī, *Ṭab.*, I., p. 36.
[2] Khaṭīb, X., p. 156; Sha'rānī, *op. cit.*, I., p. 24.
[3] Tagh, I., pp. 281, 282.
[4] Dhahabī, *Ṭab. al-Ḥuffāẓ*, p. 318.
[5] *Cf.* al-Muḥāsibī, Chapter X. below.
[6] Tagh, I., p. 289; Dhahabī, *op. cit.*, p. 314; Sulamī, "Ṭabaqāt," fol. 59*b*.

Ṭāwwūs was said to have gone on pilgrimage forty times, and it was related of his scrupulosity that he would not water his beast at a well which had been dug by order of the Government.[1]

To the same period belonged Bakr b. 'Abdallah al-Muzanī (*ob.* 108/726), whose sense of sin was such that he said, "If I were not one of them, I should hope that God would forgive all men." He said also that a man was not God-fearing until he was slow to covet and slow to wrath. Among his sayings also was one to the effect that, "If you meet with harsh treatment from your brethren because of sin that you have committed, then repent of it, unto God, and if you find increased love on their part because of your obedience to God, then give thanks to Him."[2] Another authority of this period was Muḥammad b. Sīrīn (*ob.* 110/728), a well-known Sunnite, a freedman of the Anṣār, who included Mālik b. Dīnār among his pupils, and was more of an ascetic than a mystic, given to silence and humility; if he heard anyone speak evil of another, he would find something good to say of that other. He said that if sin stank, none would be able to approach him for the greatness of his sins. When asked what form of discipline was the best means of approach to God, and of acceptance for the servant with Him, he said, "The understanding of His Lordship and action for His sake, and praise to God in times of happiness and patience in times of affliction."[3]

An important authority mentioned several times by al-Muḥāsibī is Abū 'Abdallah Wahb b. Munabbih al-Dimārī (*ob.* 110/728), a Yamanite of Persian descent, who had been a Jew before his conversion to Islām, who was at one time a Qadarite, and was an ascetic of the ascetics. It was said of him that for forty years no word of abuse of any living creature was heard from him; for forty years he never slept on a mat, and for twenty years he lived a life of chastity. He disapproved of poetry, and of logical reasoning (*qiyās*) in regard

[1] Tagh, I., p. 289.

[2] Sha'rānī, I., pp. 30, 31. *Cf.* also Abū Nu'aym, *Ḥilya*, II., pp. 224 *ff.* (ed. Cairo).

[3] Sarrāj, *op. cit.*, p. 142; Sha'rānī, *op. cit.*, p. 31; L. Massignon, *Essai*, pp. 175 *ff.*; Abū Nu'aym, *op. cit.*, II., pp. 263 *ff.*

to matters of religion. He used to say that there was sinful excess in knowledge as there was sinful excess in wealth. He was said to have stated that he had read more than ninety of the books of God, and in all of them he had found that he who depended upon himself in anything he did was an infidel. He related how God had declared to David that those would pass most quickly over Ṣirāṭ (the bridge as fine as a hair and sharper than the edge of a sword, leading over the fires of Hell, to Paradise), who were satisfied with His decrees and whose tongues were engaged in His worship. The greatest of sins, after polytheism, he considered to be contempt for other men. He held that faith was "naked" and was clothed upon with godliness and adorned by penitence. He wrote a *Zabūr* (Book of Psalms), the *Mubtadā'* (Introduction) and the *Isrā'īliyāt* (Legends of Israel), and his writings embody many Christian and Jewish legends, and appear to include free translations of Christian works.[1]

The greatest of these early authorities and the one most frequently cited by al-Muḥāsibī is the great ascetic and mystic Ḥasan al-Baṣrī (*ob.* 110/728), with whose teaching a native of Baṣra must early have been very familiar. Abū Sa'īd Ḥasan b. Abi'l-Ḥasan Maysanī al-Baṣrī was born at Medina and brought up at Baṣra. His teaching, given in the form of sermons and exegesis and discussion with his disciples, was transmitted, for the main part, as sayings or *Ḥadīth*, and it is in this form that al-Muḥāsibī employs it. al-Ḥasan taught a scrupulous abstinence and the complete renunciation of all things perishable. It was he who laid the foundation of the "science of hearts" (*'ilm al-qulūb*), so ably developed by al-Muḥāsibī. The only learned man (*faqīh*), al-Ḥasan held, is he who renounces this world, who is desirous of the next, who has discernment concerning his faith and who serves his Lord continuously. Ḥasan carried his asceticism so far as to say, "If God desires good for His servant, He removes his family by death and sets him apart for His service." Desire (*ṭama'*), he taught, was what corrupted the world, and hypocrisy, arising from desire, met with his condemnation, in whatever form it shewed itself. "He who wears wool out

[1] *Cf.* Wüstenfeld, *Geschichteschreiber der Araber*, pp. 4, 16; Sha'rānī, *op. cit.*, I., p. 34; L. Massignon, *Essai*, pp. 55, 143.

of humility towards God increases the illumination of his insight and his heart, but he who wears it out of pride and arrogance will be thrust down to Hell with the devils." Ḥasan sought to rouse his generation to a sense of sin and need. Verses of his have come down to us, which read as follows :

> " Not he who dies and is at rest is dead,
> He only is dead who is dead while yet alive."

Knowledge, he taught, was the first necessity and then conduct in accordance with that knowledge, based on the virtues of sincerity, patience and temperance. That one in whom the conditions of knowledge, conduct and virtue were perfectly fulfilled would not fail to have his part in the mercy of God Most High. To such a one, at the last, would be granted the Beatific Vision : " Men will look upon God on the Day of Resurrection according to His Will, with no veil between." " The lover," says Ḥasan, " is intoxicated by his love and is not awakened save by the vision of his Beloved." The study of al-Muḥāsibī's writings shews plainly how much he owes to both the ascetical and the mystical teaching of his great predecessor.[1]

Among the authorities cited by al-Muḥāsibī, who belong to the next half-century, is 'Aṭā' b. Abī Rabāḥ (*ob.* 115/733), the traditionist, an Abyssinian who had been a slave, of whom Aḥmad b. Ḥanbal said later that he was one of those on whom God had bestowed the treasures of knowledge because He loved him. He spent much of his life in Mecca and died there.[2] A great mystic disciple of Ḥasan al-Baṣrī, included among al-Muḥāsibī's authorities, is Mālik b. Dīnār (*ob.* 127/744), also of Baṣra, an ascetic who declared that he was not fit to wear wool (*ṣuf*) because it was the mark of purity (*ṣafā'*). His emphasis on sincerity in action—since sincerity bears the same relation to action as the spirit to the body—was reiterated by al-Muḥāsibī in many of his writings. Of the knowledge acquired by study Mālik says, " When the servant acquires knowledge in order to do good

[1] Sarrāj, *op. cit.*, p. 17; Sha'rānī, *op. cit.*, pp. 25, 26. *Cf.* L. Massignon, *Essai*, pp. 152 *ff.* Abū Nu'aym, *op. cit.*, II., pp. 131 *ff.*

[2] Sha'rānī, *op. cit.*, p. 34; Abū Nu'aym, *op. cit.*, III., pp. 310 *ff.*

works in accordance with it, his knowledge increases; but if he acquires it for any other purpose than to do good, he increases in wickedness and arrogance and contempt for the common folk."[1] Another of Ḥasan's mystic disciples who is cited is Thābit b. Asad al-Bunānī (*ob.* 127-744), who is reputed to have said, "When men assemble together to worship God, though their sins may be heavy as mountains upon them, yet they will rise up without one single sin weighing upon them." Prayer, he said, was the service of God on earth. "For twenty years," he said of himself, "I found it difficult to pray, and now for twenty years I have found pleasure in it." Of him it was said, "There are keys to good, and Thābit is one of the keys."[2] Other disciples of Ḥasan who are cited are Ayyūb al-Sikhtiyānī (*ob.* 131/748), one of the greatest of the Followers, a notable Sunnite traditionist, who lived at Baṣra and had a high reputation for legal learning and authenticity,[3] and Yūnus b. 'Ubayd Qaysī (*ob.* 139/756), who maintained the view that every good work was deficient in some respect, except the good work of restraining the tongue, and that was an unmixed good, because a man may increase his prayers and fasting and then break his fast in what is unlawful, and spend the night in prayer and be hypocritical in that and fall into vanity and false statements; but when a man guards his tongue, there is hope that his work will be wholly good. No man's tongue will be sincere, unless the rest of his works are sincere—teaching which al-Muḥāsibī took to heart.[4] To this period belongs Sulaymān b. Mihrān al-A'mash (*ob.* 148/765), to whose assembly kings and wealthy men used to forgather and were the humblest there, though he himself was so poor as to be in need of a loaf. He was reputed to have said, "If my self (*nafs*) were in my hand, I would cast it away on to the dung-heap."[5]

[1] Sha'rānī, *op. cit.*, p. 32; Hujwīrī, p. 89; Abū Nu'aym, *op. cit.*, II., pp. 357 *ff.*

[2] Sha'rānī, *op. cit.*, p. 31; Munawī, *op. cit.*, fol. 42*b*. *Cf.* Abū Nu'aym, *op. cit.*, II., pp. 318 *ff.*

[3] Ibn Khallikān, *op. cit.*, II., p. 588; Abū Nu'aym, *op. cit.*, III., pp. 3 *ff.*

[4] Sha'rānī, *op. cit.*, p. 55; Abū Nu'aym, *op. cit.*, III., pp. 15 *ff.*

[5] Tagh, I., p. 399.

A strictly Sunnite authority among the traditionists is 'Abdallah b. 'Awn b. Arṭabān (*ob.* 151/768), one of the founders of the group known as "People of the Sunna and the Congregation," of whom it is related that when he met people who were Qadarites, he would not salute them. He belonged to Baṣra and had a reputation for being reliable and scrupulous. Ibn Mahdī said that he had associated with 'Abdallah b. 'Awn for twenty-four years and did not know of a single sin which the angels could record against him. The greater part of his time he spent in his house in silence and meditation, and he never went out to the public bath. He was always unwilling that his works or his good qualities should be observed by others. Among his sayings was one to the effect that, "The servant has not attained to real satisfaction until his satisfaction with poverty is equal to his satisfaction with wealth." He said also, "As the eye of the bat cannot look at the light of the sun, the heart of him who loves this world cannot regard the light of wisdom."[1]

One of the earliest traditionists cited, who is known to have written down his traditions, is Ibn Jurayj al-Makkī (*ob.* 150/767), celebrated as a scholar, and he is noted as writing in Mecca, being the author of one of the first commentaries, at the time when the learned men of Islām began to write down traditions and to produce commentaries and treatises on jurisprudence. He considered that listening to music, the lawfulness of which was a question much debated among both the orthodox and the Ṣūfīs, was allowable, as being neither virtuous nor vicious, but merely a means of passing the time.[2] An authority cited, who was doing similar work in Syria, in writing down traditions and the canonical law, is 'Abd al-Raḥmān b. 'Amru al-Awzā'ī (*ob.* 157/773), who was born at Baalbek and died in Beyrout, a learned jurisconsult.[3] Another authority of this period is Abū 'Uthmān Wuhayb b. Ward al-Makkī (*ob.* 153/773), who

[1] Ibn Khallikān, II., p. 554; Sha'rānī, p. 55; Tagh, I., p. 407; Munāwī, *op. cit.*, fol. 62*a*. *Cf.* al-Ghazālī, *Iḥyā'*, IV., p. 275 (Cairo, A.H. 1272); Abū Nu'aym, *op. cit.*, III., pp. 37 *ff.*

[2] Tagh., I., pp. 387, 388; Sarrāj, *op. cit.*, p. 277; Ibn Khallikān, II., p. 116.

[3] Sha'rānī, *op. cit.*, p. 39.

was a teacher of the great Sufyān al-Thawrī, and was venerated as a great ascetic and saint, who observed abstinence (*wara'*) with great scrupulosity. Bishr al-Ḥāfī classed him with Ibrāhīm b. Adham, Yūsuf b. Asbāṭ and Muslim al-Khawwās, four whom God had exalted because of the fine quality of their spiritual teaching. Wuhayb b. Ward said that Paradise was to praise God and to know Him, and Hell was to commit sin and to indulge oneself in sensual desire. He also said, " Beware lest you be the friend of Iblīs in secret, while outwardly you shew him enmity."[1] Of the same period was 'Awn b. 'Abdallah b. 'Atba, a Sunnite Ṣūfī, who said, " Every man has a master who controls his actions, and that which rules my actions is the remembrance of God." Pride, he said, was the first sin by which God was disobeyed, and he warned men against thinking themselves superior to those beneath them, a line of teaching which al-Muḥāsibī developed in several of his writings. 'Awn b. 'Abdallah himself sometimes wore silk, lest the well-dressed should feel ashamed in his assembly, and sometimes wool, lest he should seem better dressed than the poor when they came. He held that association for worship was a means of polishing the mirror of the heart—*i.e.*, cleansing it from defilement —and the healing remedy for sickness of the soul.[2]

al-Muḥāsibī's authorities of this period include the great ascetic and Sunnite traditionist, Sufyān b. Sa'īd al-Thawrī (*ob.* 161/777), founder of the school of Ṣūfī tradition, who lived first at Kūfa and was exiled thence to Baṣra, who used to say, "If the divines ('*ulamā'*) are corrupt, who can restore them to soundness? Their corruption consists in their inclination towards worldliness, and if the physician is himself attracted by the sickness, how can he cure another?"—teaching which al-Muḥāsibī appropriated and developed. Among Sufyān's sayings on asceticism is one to the effect that, "when a dervish frequents the company of the rich and powerful, you may know that he is a hypocrite, and when he frequents the courts of kings, you may know that he is a thief." Again he says, " Praise be to that God Who slays

[1] Tagh, I., p. 412; L. Massignon, *Passion*, p. 697; Munāwī, *op. cit.*, fol. 86*a*.

[2] Sha'rānī, *op. cit.*, p. 36.

our children and takes away our wealth, and Whom yet we love."[1] It was to the school of mystic traditionists founded by Sufyān al-Thawrī that al-Muḥāsibī belonged, and his writings shew to what an extent he was indebted to this predecessor of his.[2]

A second great Ṣūfī, contemporary with Sufyān al-Thawrī, who is cited, is Ibrāhīm b. Adham (*ob.* 160/777), who exchanged a throne for the life of a dervish. Born at Balkh, he studied in 'Irāq, Mecca and Jerusalem, and lived a life of great asceticism, living on the work of his hands. He urged men to seek knowledge for the sake of doing good, for most men had gone astray, until their knowledge had become like the mountains and their good works like the atom. The mark of the true gnostic, he said, was that his chief concern was to do good and to serve God, and that his speech was chiefly the praise of God and His glorification. When asked what was the miraculous power granted by the favour of God (*karāma*) to the believer, he replied, " That he should say to the mountain, ' Be thou removed,' and it would be removed." Awzā'ī[3] wrote to him saying that he wished to bear him company, but Ibrāhīm replied that if a bird were to fly with one not of its genus, the bird would fly away and the other be left behind. His mystical teaching included the development of the ideas of meditation (*murāqaba*), of contrition (*kamad*), of the Divine friendship (*khulla*) and of gnosis (*ma'rifa*).[4]

Another of this group of Ṣūfīs referred to by al-Muḥāsibī is Rabāḥ al-Qaysī (*ob.* 180/796), an extreme ascetic who said that a man would not attain to the ranks of the righteous unless he left his wife in the position of a widow and his children as orphans, and betook himself to live with the dogs. Of the evils of worldliness he said, " As sight which is weak cannot look at the rays of the sun, so also the hearts of those who love this world do not contemplate the light of wisdom "; and again, " To remove the mountains from

[1] *Cf.* the saying of Ḥasan al-Baṣrī, p. 68 above.
[2] 'Aṭṭār, I., pp. 192, 193 ; Sha'rānī, p. 40 ; Tagh, I., p. 388.
[3] *Cf.* p. 71 above.
[4] Qushayrī, *Risāla*, p. 8 ; Sha'rānī, p. 59 ; Tagh, I., p. 428. *Cf.* L. Massignon, *Essai*, p. 226.

their place would be easier than to remove the love of domination when it is established in the soul." It was sufficient good for a man, he held, to attend assemblies for worship, and to think well of his Lord. This idea of "right thoughts" of God (*ḥusn al-ẓann*) as opposed to "evil thoughts" (*sū' al-ẓann*) was derived from the tradition that God had said, "I conform to what My servant thinks of Me. If he thinks what is good, then good is his; if he thinks what is evil, then evil is his."[1] al-Qaysī was also responsible for teaching on the mystical ideas of the revelation of the glory of God (*tajallī*) and of the Divine friendship (*khulla*).[2]

Included also in this group of early Ṣūfīs is Fuḍayl b. 'Iyāḍ (*ob.* 187/802), a disciple of Sufyān al-Thawrī, who lived at Kūfa and died in retreat at Mecca, known as one of the "beggars" (*ṣa'ālīk*) of Ṣūfism. He was said to have been a brigand, but of a chivalrous disposition, since he would not attack a caravan which included a woman, nor rob a poor traveller. It was related of him that he loved a certain maiden, and while climbing a wall to keep tryst with her, he heard someone reciting the verse, "Has not the time come for those who believe to submit their hearts to the admonition of God?" (Sūra 57: 15), and he repented and was converted. He who knows God as He ought to be known, he said, worships Him with all his might. His sayings on asceticism and the good life may well have formed the basis of much of al-Muḥāsibī's teaching. "To abandon action for the sake of men is polytheism," he said, and again, "He who loves to have his words heard when he speaks is not an ascetic. . . . When an enemy slanders you, he is of more profit to you than a friend, for each of his slanders is a kindness done to you." Asked whether asceticism (*zuhd*) or satisfaction (*riḍā'*—*i.e.*, complete resignation to the will of God) was better, he replied, "Satisfaction, for he who is satisfied desires no higher stage. There is a stage to be desired beyond renunciation, but none beyond satisfaction, and the sanctuary is superior to the gateway."[3]

Contemporary with Fuḍayl b. 'Iyāḍ was Abū 'Alī

[1] Nabhanī, *Jāmī'*, No. 30.
[2] Sha'rānī, p. 40; L. Massignon, *Essai*, pp. 195 *ff*.
[3] Qushayrī, *Risāla*, p. 9; Sha'rānī, p. 58; Hujwīrī, pp. 97, 98, 179.

Shaqīq al-Balkhī (*ob.* 194/809), who is said to have abandoned great wealth for a life of asceticism, an associate of Ibrāhīm b. Adham, whose teaching he systematised. He was one of the first in Khurāsān to hold regular discussions on Ṣūfism and the mystic "states." He said of himself that he studied the Qur'ān for twenty years until he was able to distinguish clearly between the material and temporal and the spiritual and eternal. He declared that a man's godliness (*taqwā*) was made known by three things, by what he accepted, by what he rejected, and by what he said. The ascetic (*zāhid*), he said, was the one who manifested renunciation by what he did, but the devout man was he who manifested renunciation by his tongue. Of the decadent state of morals in his time, Shaqīq said, "When the learned man is covetous and seeks to amass wealth, whom can the ignorant man imitate? And when the poor man (*faqīr*) is famed for his poverty, and is desirous of this world and its soft raiment and the pleasures of marriage, whom can the covetous man find to imitate, in order to escape from his greed? When the shepherd is the wolf, who will care for the sheep?" Shaqīq, in opposition to the views of the Mu'tazilites, extolled a rule of life involving a complete renunciation, a state of permanent acquiescence in the Will of God.[1] An ascetic of the same type was Yūsuf b. Asbāṭ (*ob.* 196/811), who spoke bitterly of the laxity of his day, and said that if a man were to renounce this world as did Abū Dharr and Abū Darda, he would not consider such a man an ascetic, for asceticism consists in adhering only to what is wholly lawful, and in his day there was nothing answering to this description to be found. The greatest humility, he said, was to go out of your house and to consider everyone you saw as being better than yourself.[2]

A well-known traditionist of this period, who is included among al-Muḥāsibī's authorities, is Sufyān b. 'Unayna al-Hilālī al-Kūfī (*ob.* 198/814), an ascetic who was said to have been content with a barley loaf as his daily provision of food for a period of sixty years. Much of his teaching, as revealed in his sayings, is reflected in the writings of al-

[1] Qushayrī, *op. cit.*, p. 13; Sha'rānī, *op. cit.*, p. 65; Tagh, I., p. 412.
[2] Jāmī, *Nafaḥāt al-Uns*, p. 32; Tagh, I., p. 413; Sha'rānī, *op. cit.*, p. 52.

Muḥāsibī—*e.g.*, " Nothing is more injurious than knowledge (of good) which is not acted upon "; and again, " Concealment of poverty is to be desired, for it is a good work and one which is hard to the soul." The Holy War for the sake of God (*jihād*), he said, consisted of ten parts, one of which was fighting against the enemy (of Islām) and nine parts were fighting against the self. Of prayer he said: " Let not anything that you know about yourself hinder you from prayer, for God may answer the prayer of the worst of His creatures, and He will answer the man who prays, saying, ' O God, veil me with Thy beauteous veil,' which means that, in His mercy, He will cast a veil over the sins of His servants in this world and the next."[1]

al-Muḥāsibī cites also the Imām Ibn Idrīs al-Shāfi'ī, whose pupil he was, according to one of his biographers.[2] Abu 'Abdallah M. b. Idrīs al-Shāfi'ī (*ob.* 204/820) was a pupil of the Imām Mālik and at first lived a secluded life, but later, as he gathered a group of adherents, he found himself unable to remain in retirement. He taught in Baghdad and afterwards went to Egypt. At first he was unfavourable to Ṣūfism, but later he was prepared to seek truth wherever it was to be found. He declared that no good thing was to be expected from a divine who concerned himself with plenary indulgences (*rukhaṣ*) attached to the performance of some act of devotion, for to seek such indulgences was to think lightly of God's commandment: divines should be lovers of God, and a lover does not think lightly of the command of his Beloved.[3]

Among the well-known Ṣūfīs of this period cited is Abū Sulaymān 'Abd al-Raḥmān al-Dārānī, who lived for some time in Baṣra, but later went to Dārāya, near Damascus, and died there in 215/830. He was known as the " Sweet Basil of Hearts " (*rayḥān-i dilha*) and was distinguished for his self-mortification and for his knowledge of spiritual ills and the temptations besetting the soul. He spoke of the need for watching over both heart and members—a favourite

[1] Sha'rānī, *op. cit.*, pp. 48, 49; Tagh, I., pp. 56 *ff*.

[2] *Cf.* Subkī, *Ṭabaqāt al-Shāfi'iyya*, II., p. 37.

[3] Hujwīrī, *op. cit.*, p. 116; Tagh, I., p. 588; Sha'rānī, *op. cit.*, I., p. 43.

theme of al-Muḥāsibī. He held that both hope and fear were necessary for the seeker after God. Hope he linked with contemplation (*mushāhada*) based on firm conviction (*i'tiqād*), while fear was linked with self-discipline (*mujāhada*), resulting from anxious uncertainty (*iḍṭirāb*).[1] Dārānī said of the *faqīr* that it was not fitting that the cleanliness of his garments should exceed the purity of his heart, but his outward appearance should resemble the state of his inward self. When asked about the best means of drawing near to God, he said, " Let your state be such that when God looks upon your heart, He will find that you desire nought in the two worlds save Him alone." There was nothing in either this world or the next, he said, of sufficient importance to keep men back from God ; everything which distracted a man from God, whether family or wealth or child, was to be regarded as a misfortune. The true knowledge of God was only to be obtained by obedience to the uttermost.[2]

In addition to this long list of earlier authorities and many others whom he cites, al-Muḥāsibī also refers by name to his contemporaries, and includes a considerable number of these among his sources. Such is Abū Muḥammad al-Fatḥ b. Sa'īd al-Mawṣilī (*ob.* 220/835), an associate of Bishr al-Ḥāfī and Sarī Saqaṭī, conspicuous for his abstinence and his intercourse (with God). Among his sayings was this, " The continual recollection of God in the heart produces joy in the Beloved, and upon him who prefers that recollection to his own lusts will God bestow His love. He who longs for God will renounce all save Him." The heart deprived of food and drink, he said, will die at the last, though it take long to do so.[3]

A mystic teacher to whom al-Muḥāsibī does not appear to refer by name is Abū 'Abdallah Aḥmad b. 'Asim al-Anṭākī, who is stated by a number of biographers to be the pupil of al-Muḥāsibī, but the evidence suggests that he was older than al-Muḥāsibī and was more probably his teacher. The date of his death is placed by a modern authority at 220/835.[4]

[1] Hujwīrī, *op. cit.*, pp. 112, 113.
[2] Sha'rānī, I., p. 68 ; Khaṭib, *op. cit.*, X., pp. 248, 249.
[3] Sha'rānī, *op. cit.*, I., p. 68.
[4] *Cf.* L. Massignon, *Essai*, pp. 201 *ff.*

He was a well-known writer, who edited the *Kitāb dawā dā' al-Nufūs* and the *Kitāb al-Shubahāt*.[1] It is certain that there is a close resemblance between his teaching and that of al-Muḥāsibī, though the latter's is much more developed. al-Anṭākī's statement that "Justice is of two kinds, the outward justice between yourself and the creature, and the inward justice between yourself and God," and that "the road of justice is the road of rectitude, but the road of grace is the road of perfection," is reproduced word for word in al-Muḥāsibī's teaching on the subject in his *Ādāb al-Nufūs* (fols. 65*a*, 65*b*). Many other sayings of Anṭākī shew a close resemblance to the teaching of al-Muḥāsibī—*e.g.*, "The most profitable part of the reason is that which makes known to you the grace of God towards you and helps you to give thanks for it and rises up to oppose sensuality" (*cf.* al-Muḥāsibī's *Kitāb al-'Aql*). Again he wrote, "Sincerity is to act without seeking the reward of your action from any save God—it is that which keeps you from hypocrisy and vainglory." "Assured faith," Anṭākī said, "is a gift which God places in the heart of a servant so that he may contemplate therewith the affairs of the next life and by its power may rend aside every veil between him and what is in the world to come, so that he gazes upon invisible things as if he saw them in very truth."[2] He advises men to be content and to avoid covetousness by preferring contentment, and to ensure the sweetness of asceticism by cutting short hope, and to destroy the motives to desire by despairing altogether of the creatures, to secure peace of mind by trust in God (*tafwīḍ*), to extinguish the fires of desire by the coldness of despair, to close the road to pride by the knowledge of assured faith (*yaqīn*), to seek peace of body through finding rest for the heart, to secure peace of mind through ceasing to contend and abandoning the search for one's own good, to acquire kindliness by continuous association with those worshippers of God who are also wise, and enlightenment by continuous contrition, the door to which is opened by

[1] *Cf.* Sprenger, *J.R.A.S. Bengal*, 1856.
[2] Sulamī, "Ṭabaqāt," fol. 29*b*. *Cf.* al-Muḥāsibī's teaching, Chapters VIII. and X. below.

long reflection, while the habit of reflection is to be acquired in solitary retreat. He says also, " The most harmful time for speech is when silence would be better for you, and the most harmful time for silence is when speech would be more fitting for you and more necessary." He says again, " That which brings you nearest to God is the abandonment of secret sins, because if you fail inwardly, both your outward and inward acts are made void."[1] It is Anṭākī's teaching on love which marks him out as a true mystic and may well have given al-Muḥāsibī inspiration for his own writings on mystic love. Asked whether he was longing for God, Anṭākī said, " No, for you long for one who is absent, but when that One is present, why should you long for Him?" Again he said that the signs of love include little exterior devotion, continual reflection and the taste for solitude and silence. When others look at the lover, he does not see them; when he is called, he does not hear; when misfortune comes upon him, he is not grieved; and when success looks him in the face, he does not rejoice. He fears no one and has hope of no one, and makes no request of anyone. Act then, Anṭākī says, as if there were no one on the earth but yourself and no one in Heaven but God. All actions, he teaches, are to be guided by knowledge, and true knowledge comes through the light of certainty by which God enlightens the heart of His servant, so that he beholds the things of the spiritual world, and by the power of that light all the veils between him and that world are removed until at last, by means of that radiance, he attains to contemplation of the Invisible.[2] al-Dārānī called him the " Explorer of Hearts " (*jāsūs al-qulūb*) because of the keenness of his insight.[3]

A very famous ascetic and mystic included among al-Muḥāsibī's contemporary sources is Abū Naṣr Bishr b. al-Ḥārith al-Ḥāfī—the Barefooted—(*ob.* 227/841), a pupil of Yūsuf b. Asbāṭ and an associate of al-Fuḍayl, who was born in Merv and lived a life of celibacy and of great asceticism in

[1] Abū Nu'aym, " Ḥilyat al-Awliyā," fols. 173*b*, 174*a*.
[2] 'Aṭṭār, II., pp. 1 *ff*. *Cf*. al-Muḥāsibī's teaching on Knowledge and Love, Chapters VI. and XII. below.
[3] Said also of Nūrī. *Cf*. p. 32 above.

Baghdad. Hunger, he said, purifies the heart and mortifies the lusts and gives rise to subtle knowledge. The *faqīr* in that age, he said, should count it good fortune to be neglected by men and to have his position concealed from them : when men contended for superiority (in regard to religious excellence) that meant ruin. He also had complaints to make of the divines of his time. " They should be characterised by three things," he said, " accuracy in speech, lawfulness in food and much asceticism in regard to worldly things. Today I do not know one among them who possesses a single one of these qualities—and how can such as these claim to have knowledge (of things Divine) ?" When asked about Ṣūfism, he said that its meaning was threefold ; it meant that the light of the Ṣūfī's gnosis did not obscure the light of his abstinence (*wara'*), that he did not assert about esoteric knowledge what was contrary to the exoteric knowledge of the Qur'ān and the Sunna, and that the gift of the power of working miracles (*karāmāt*) should not lead him to draw aside the veil from what God has made unlawful. Bishr al-Ḥāfī has left some written work.[1]

al-Muḥāsibī did not hesitate to quote the Imām Aḥmad b. Ḥanbal (*ob.* 241/855), who proved to be his bitter persecutor, after he himself had been persecuted, almost to the death, by the Mu'tazilites. Aḥmad b. Ḥanbal, though himself narrowly orthodox, associated with the great Ṣūfī Shaykhs, and while he was prepared to answer any question on religious practice on his own authority, he would refer any question on mystical doctrine (*ḥaqā'iq*) to Bishr al-Ḥāfī. al-Shāfi'ī, whose favourite pupil he was, when he himself set out for Egypt, said that he left behind him in Baghdad no more pious man or better jurisconsult than Ibn Ḥanbal.[2]

Through Ḥusayn b. Aḥmad al-Shāmī, al-Muḥāsibī cites the greatest of his mystical contemporaries, Abu'l-Fayḍ Dhu'l-Nūn al-Miṣrī (*ob.* 245/859), the first in Egypt to give teaching concerning the " states " (*aḥwāl*) and the " stations " (*maqāmāt*) of the seekers after God. He is too well known for any detailed account of his life and teaching to be needed

[1] Sha'rānī, I., p. 76. *Cf.* p. 39 above.
[2] Hujwīrī, pp. 117, 118. *Cf.* pp. 4, 14 *ff.* above.

here,[1] but it is to be noted that certain teaching of his, concerning the saints, bears a very close resemblance to al-Muḥāsibī's teaching on the same subject. It is related that the Caliph Mutawakkil was greatly attached to Dhu'l-Nūn and honoured him above all the pious and the ascetics, and on one occasion asked him to describe the saints, and Dhu'l-Nūn said : " O Commander of the Faithful, they are those whom God invested with the radiance of His love and adorned with the fair mantle of His grace, upon whose heads He set the crown of His joy, and He put love towards them into the hearts of His creatures. Then He brought them forth, having entrusted to their hearts the treasures of the Invisible, which depend upon union with the Beloved, and their hearts are turned towards Him and their eyes behold the greatness of His Majesty. Then He set them on the thrones of the search for a remedy, and He gave them knowledge of the places where the means of healing is to be found, and He caused their disciples to be abstinent and God-fearing, and to them He gave assurance of an answer to their prayers, and He said : ' O My saints, if there come to you one sick through separation from Me, heal him, or a fugitive from Me, seek him out . . . or afraid of Me, then reassure him, or desirous of union with me, then shew him favour, or seeking to approach Me, encourage him, or despairing of My grace, help him, or hoping for My loving-kindness, give him good news, or with right thoughts of Me, then welcome him, or shewing love to Me, shew friendship unto him, or seeking to know My attributes, guide him. Or if he be doing evil in despite of loving-kindness, then remonstrate with him, or forgetful of it, then remind him. If anyone who is injured asks help of you, give it to him, and to him who joins you in My name, shew friendship ; if he goes astray, search for him, but if he constrains you to sin, put him away from you. . . . O My saints, I have reasoned with you, and to you I have addressed Myself, towards you has been My desire and from you have I sought the fulfilment (of My Will), for upon you has My choice been laid, and you have I predestined for My work. You have I

[1] *Cf.* my *Studies in Early Mysticism*, pp. 191 *ff.*, 230 *ff.*, and L. Massignon, *Essai*, pp. 184 *ff.*

appointed for My service, and you have I chosen and made to be Mine elect. Not those who are proud do I seek to be My servants, nor do I desire the service of the covetous. To you have I given the most precious of rewards, the fairest of gifts, the greatest of graces. I am the Searcher of hearts, He Who knows the mysteries of the Invisible. . . . I am the Goal of your desire, I Who read the secrets of the heart. Let not the voice of any that is mighty, save Myself, make you to fear, nor any sovereign but Myself. . . . He who has shown you enmity is My enemy, and to him who was friendly towards you have I shewn friendship. Ye are My saints and ye are My beloved. Ye are Mine and I am yours.' "[1]

This list of authorities, long as it is, by no means exhausts the names cited by al-Muḥāsibī; but the list given represents those whose teaching shews most plainly on what he based his own writings, and he writes for the most part, as a modern scholar would, giving authority for his statements, usually in the form of a tradition, with the name of its immediate transmitter, and in some cases with the chain of authorities (*isnād*) by which it is traced back to the original traditionist, or the Prophet himself. Others of his writings represent the development of his own doctrines and original teaching, for which he has no sources to quote.

We have seen above that a certain proportion of al-Muḥāsibī's material is derived indirectly from Christian and Jewish sources through Islāmic traditions, but some may also have been derived directly, through conversation with individual Jews and Christians,[2] and through his own personal study of the Old and New Testaments and of Jewish and Christian mystical literature. The Mu'tazilite doctrines and method found a parallel in the development of less literal and more mystical interpretations of the Scriptures by the Jews, and during al-Muḥāsibī's lifetime the headship of the great Jewish academy of learning at Pumbeditha, in 'Irāq, was twice held by a Jewish mystic.[3] Much

[1] Khaṭīb, *op. cit.*, VIII., pp. 394 *ff*. *Cf*. al-Muḥāsibī's teaching, "Ḥilya," fol. 231*a* (MS. Leyden).

[2] *Cf*. Abū Nu'aym, "Ḥilya," fols. 209*a*, 240*b*, 248*a*.

[3] *Cf*. H. Graetz, *History of the Jews*, pp. 148 *ff*.

Jewish literature was produced at this time, and the Jews of Baṣra and Baghdad based their work on a study of the Talmudic and Midrashic writings, with their many mystical references and doctrines. These were Arabic-speaking Jews, and as early as the beginning of the eighth century an 'Irāqī Jew, Jawayh de Bassora, was translating from Syriac into Arabic, and it is evident that the Jews were writing, as well as speaking, Arabic at the time when al-Muḥāsibī was formulating his teaching.

al-Muḥāsibī's references to the New Testament—*e.g.*, his reproduction of the Parable of the Sower at the beginning of the " Ri'āya " (fols. 5*a ff.*), the separation of wheat from tares (" Ri'āya," fol. 54*a*), admonitions to trust in God combined with deprecation of anxiety for the morrow (*Masā'il fi'l-A'māl*, fol. 135*b*; *Ādāb al-Nufūs*, fol. 60*a*), the "inheritance" of the righteous (*Ri'āya*, fol. 125*a*), condemnation of the outward righteousness of prayer and fasting while the inward self is a " desolation " (*Kitāb al-'Ilm*, chapter vi.), and phrases and teaching derived from the Sermon on the Mount and also from the epistles of St. Paul—shew a knowledge of the phraseology of the Gospels and other writings of the New Testament which at least suggests, if it does not prove, an actual study of the Christian Scriptures on his part, which was possible, since before the ninth century A.D. an Arabic translation of the Gospels from the Syriac had been made for the use of Arabic-speaking Christians of the districts of the Near and Middle East,[1] and there was also an Arabic version of St. Paul's epistles and the book of Ecclesiasticus available at this period.[2]

Of Christian mystical literature there was a great store available in al-Muḥāsibī's time. Aphraates the Monk, by nationality a Persian, who lived in the fourth century A.D., wrote on the process of purification by asceticism, and has left teaching on the remembrance of death, which is very

[1] *Cf.* F. C. Burkitt, *Dictionary of the Bible*, p. 136.

[2] *Cf.* M. D. Gibson, *Studia Sinaitica*, No. II., pp. 5 *ff.* Ya'qūbī (Ibn Wāḍiḥ), writing in A.D. 872, was well acquainted with the Four Gospels and the Acts, and obviously uses a written source in his *Ta'rīkh*, I., pp. 73 *ff.* (ed. Houtsma).

similar to that which al-Muḥāsibī embodied in his ascetical teaching. Ephraim the Syrian, of the same period, was responsible for mystical teaching based on the need for penitence, self-discipline and purification, by means of which the " eye of the soul " is enabled to see the secret Light of God. The *Book of the Holy Hierotheos*, written probably at the end of the fifth century A.D., teaches that by purification and sanctification, the cleansing of the soul from defilement, followed by its adornment with all virtues, the seeker after God passes into fellowship with Him. Isaac of Nineveh, also, living in the seventh century A.D., in his *Mystic Treatises*, deals with the Way to God, and especially the stages by which the seeker, through asceticism, finds purification and illumination.[1] Another East Syrian mystical writer was Simon of Ṭaibūtheh, who died *c.* A.D. 680, a physician who sought to explain the different faculties of the soul in their relation to the body and to the practice of asceticism. He had acquired the knowledge of healing both body and soul, and his mystical teaching had much influence on later writers and on early Ṣūfism.[2] It is interesting to note that al-Muḥāsibī also uses the phraseology of medicine for the purposes of mystical teaching.[3] Another Christian ascetic, Dādīsho' Qaṭrāya, a monk who died about A.D. 690, wrote on " Solitude " and the asceticism, accompanied by meditation and contemplation, which would lead to " pure prayer."[4] Yet another East Syrian writer of this early period was Abraham bar Dāshandād, who flourished between A.D. 720 and 730, and wrote a mystical treatise which urges to meditation on the world to come, and contempt for this temporal world.[5]

These men wrote in Syriac, but Isaac's work, at least, was translated into Arabic, and there was so much intercourse between Christians and Muslims in the early centuries of the Islāmic era and up to al-Muḥāsibī's lifetime, that a

[1] For a more detailed treatment of these writers *cf.* my *Studies in Early Mysticism*, Chapter V.

[2] *Cf.* A. Mingana, *Early Christian Mystics*, pp. 1 *ff.*; Baumstark, *Geschichte der Syrischen Literatur*, pp. 209, 210; and pp. 236 *ff.* below.

[3] *Cf.* L. Massignon, *Passion*, p. 555.

[4] A. Mingana, *op. cit.*, pp. 70 *ff.*; Baumstark, *op. cit.*, p. 226.

[5] A. Mingana, *op. cit.*, pp. 185 *ff.*; Baumstark, *op. cit.*, p. 214.

knowledge of such literature and the mystical teaching which it contained might well have been available to al-Muḥāsibī, anxious as he was to discover truth wherever it was to be found.

Finally, the translation of Greek works into Arabic, an enterprise which received its chief impetus under the Caliph Ma'mūn, and was carried on with enthusiasm by the philosophic school of al-Kindī (*ob.* A.D. 860) at Baghdad, included the translation of one mystical work of the very first importance, the *Rubūbīya aw Uthūlūjiya Arisṭāṭālis* (the so-called "Theology of Aristotle"), which was actually a translation of Porphyry's lost commentary on the *Enneads* of Plotinus. An Arabic translation of this appeared in A.D. 840 and would probably have been in circulation during the last years of al-Muḥāsibī's life, and the contents may have been known earlier.[1] The Nestorian Ḥunayn b. Isḥāq al-'Ibādī (A.H. 803-73), who did most of his work at Baghdad, in addition to translating the *Magna Moralia* and other Aristotelian writings, translated the *Republic* and the *Timæus* of Plato, and these may have been available early enough for al-Muḥāsibī to be acquainted with them.[2]

al-Muḥāsibī, therefore, had a wide range of sources to draw upon, and much material from which to select what was appropriate to his purpose, on which he was able to base his own teaching, developing an ascetical and mystical doctrine, which shews itself to be the product of a profound and original thinker, one who had studied widely and reflected deeply, who had given himself to long years of meditation and contemplation, and in his writings we have also the fruits of his experience as ascetic and mystic, the experience of one who had trodden the mystic way and knew what it was to have attained to the goal.

[1] *Cf.* de Lacy O'Leary, *Arabic Thought and its Place in History*, pp. 116, 137 *ff*.

[2] *Cf.* A. Guillaume, *The Legacy of Islam*, pp. 250 *ff*. The *Timæus* had already been translated, in A.D. 815, by Ibn al-Batrīk.

CHAPTER VI

THE PSYCHOLOGICAL THEORY OF AL-MUḤĀSIBĪ

THE psychological theory of al-Muḥāsibī is based upon that of the Qur'ān, but is more clearly defined, especially in his analysis of the self and the means by which it comes into relation with the world of experience, whether that experience comes from without it or arises within it, whether the consciousness be invaded by the natural way of sensation and is limited to its interpretation, or whether it be the "supernatural" way, whereby the consciousness is invaded from within, apart from any sense-experience, and is offered thereby different opportunities of interpretation. In al-Muḥāsibī's view, as in that of other mystics, both aspects of reality can be apprehended as facts of experience, able to yield knowledge by interpretation, and for purposes of knowledge the region of the inner self (*al-bāṭin*) is as real as that of the outer world (*al-ẓāhir*), and of infinitely greater importance.

al-Muḥāsibī, basing his view on the Qur'anic teaching,[1] regards the heart (*qalb*) as the essence of the self, an immaterial principle which has the predominant control of the conscious life of man, by which reality is perceived and interpreted. Abu'l-Ḥasan 'Alī b. Sahl al-Isfahānī, a friend of al-Junayd, gives expression to the wide—and vague—sense in which the term was used, when he says, "From the time of Adam to the resurrection people cry, 'The heart, the heart,' and I wish that I might find someone to describe what the heart is or how it is, but I find none. What, then, is this heart, of which I hear only the name? That is to say, If I call intellect the heart, it is not the heart; and if I call spirit the heart, it is not the heart; and if I call knowledge the heart, it is not the heart. All the evidences of Truth exist in the heart, yet only the name of it is to be found."[2]

[1] *Cf.* Sūras 26 : 89; 15 : 12, 17; 67 : 3.
[2] Hujwīrī, *Kashf al-Maḥjūb*, p. 144.

al-Muḥāsibī's idea of the heart corresponds to the Hebrew conception of it, as representing the whole inner nature, intellectual, emotional and volitional,[1] and also the New Testament use of the word (καρδία), as the region of spiritual experience: "With the heart man believeth unto righteousness." "Sanctify the Lord God in your hearts."[2] So, too, the Christian mystic Isaac of Nineveh, using definitely psychological terms, writes, "The heart is the central organ of the inward senses";[3] while the chief textbook of Jewish mysticism, the *Zohar* (derived originally from very ancient sources), in a Commentary on the First Commandment, defines the "heart" as meaning "the good and evil inclinations."[4]

The "heart," in the sense in which al-Muḥāsibī and others of the Ṣūfīs use the term, really represents the whole human personality, man considered as a self-conscious being, in relation to this world and the world to come. It is the heart which constitutes the excellency of man, which distinguishes him from all other created beings, and enables him to know God and to accept or reject His commands, for it is the point of union between body and soul, where the spiritual is joined with the temporal. "God only desires their hearts from His servants," al-Muḥāsibī writes, "and their members will follow their hearts";[5] but while the "actions of the members" (*aʿmāl al-jawāriḥ*), the outward conduct, are under the ultimate control of the heart, which may direct them towards evil or good, there are also "actions of the heart" (*aʿmāl al-qulūb*), including the motives and sources of the outward actions, the cognitive, emotional and volitional processes, the exercise of the virtues and vices, the reception of the psychological "states" (*aḥwāl*) and the attainment of the mystic "stations" (*maqāmāt*). The heart has "hearing," by which it may listen to the Voice of God and also to the "whisperings" of Satan, and it has sight,

[1] *Cf.* Eccles. viii. 16, "I applied my heart to know wisdom and to see the business that is done upon the earth."

[2] Rom. x. 10; 1 Pet. iii. 15.

[3] *Mystic Treatises*, p. 20. So also Simon of Ṭaibūtheh, "The heart itself is the sense of senses" (*Early Christian Mystics*, p. 66).

[4] *Zohar*, IV., p. 61.

[5] "Riʿāya," fol. 110*a*.

the "eye" by which it has power to contemplate spiritual realities, when it is enlightened, and may be blind to them, when it is dimmed by the darkness of lust.[1]

The heart is the "beginning of all things." From the physical heart proceed the life and health of the body, according to the word of the Prophet—"Within man there is a fleshly fragment, and when it is corrupt the body is corrupt, and when it is sound the body is sound. Is it not the heart?"—while al-Muḥāsibī closes a list of the "members" of the body with the heart, saying, "It is the chief of the members, and upon it depend the purity of the body and its defilement." So it is also with the immaterial heart, as the Prophet also said, "When a man makes his inward self sound, God will make his outward conduct sound; when the secret life has been purified, God will purify the outward manifestation thereof."[2] And al-Muḥāsibī writes, "God has laid commands and prohibitions upon each member, which are binding upon it, and He ordained for the heart, after faith and repentance, single-mindedness of action towards God Most High, and fear of His chastisement, and satisfaction with His decrees, and hope in His grace."[3] From the heart, therefore, proceed both sins and righteousness, and according to its purity or impurity, so will a man attain to salvation or perdition, for "the corruption of religion," says al-Muḥāsibī, "lies in the corruption of the heart."[4] So also Simon of Taibūtheh had said, "When the tables of the heart are inscribed with good . . . it radiates light, peace and life. But when they are inscribed with evil, it radiates tumult, perturbation, darkness and the error of ignorance through its care for the desires of this world. It is through the latter that the heart is injured and darkened, and through the former that the mind, the memory and the understanding are purified and illuminated."[5] The heart is like a mirror, which serves its appointed purpose when it is brightly polished and has been freed from all

[1] *Cf.* "Muḥāsabat al-Nufūs," fol. 9; "Ri'āya," fol. 13*b*. *Cf.* St. Augustine, *Confessions*, VI. 10.

[2] "Muḥāsabat al-Nufūs," fol. 5.

[3] "Kitāb al-Mustarshid," fol. 5.

[4] *Ibid.*, fol. 4.

[5] *Early Christian Mystics*, p. 66.

defacement (*jalā' al-qalb*)[1], but when veiled or defaced by sin it can no longer reflect the Divine Glory. So Abū Hurayra, one of al-Muḥāsibī's authorities, had related in a tradition based upon the Qur'ān (Sūra 83: 14), " Verily, when a true believer commits a fault, a black spot is created in his heart, and if his sins are increased, the black spot increases, so that it takes possession of the whole heart,"[2] and so it may become spiritually dead, for if the hearts of men are veiled from God by their hardness, or defaced by the rust of sin, in this world, then their eyes will be veiled from the vision of Him in the world to come.[3] Therefore, knowledge of the heart and its qualities and its modes of action (*'ilm al-qulūb*) is the foundation of religion and the beginning of the road which leads the soul to God, and al-Muḥāsibī devotes much of his teaching to this subject.

The heart, then, while it has access to knowledge of the world to come (*al-ākhira*), has also access to the knowledge of this present world (*al-dunyā*). As al-Hujwīrī tells us, " When a man feels desire and passion, he turns to the heart, in order that it may guide him to the lower soul, which is the seat of falsehood, and when he finds the evidence of gnosis, he also turns to the heart, in order that it may guide him to the spirit, which is the source of truth and reality."[4] So there is warfare being waged continually within the heart, and that which urges it to enter by the gateway opening on to the spiritual world is the higher soul, the " spirit " of man (*rūḥ*, πνεῦμα), which is the Divine gift, one in nature with the Spirit of God, bestowed on Primal Man, at his creation, when God breathed upon him and man became a living soul.[5] Spirit is that which strives towards the higher life, controlled by reason, inspired by faith and love, by which the natural disposition is subordinated and transformed, by which the self is brought into subjection to the overruling claims of God. This is the abode of the hidden, inmost self,

[1] *Cf.* Palladius: " The mystic shall be worthy to see within his heart, even as in a polished mirror, the light of the revelation of God shining upon it " (*Paradise of the Fathers*, II., p. 320).

[2] *Mishkāt al-Maṣābīḥ*, X. iii. 2.

[3] " Ādāb al-Nufūs," fol. 93*a*; " Masā'il fī A'māl," fol. 139*a*.

[4] P. 277.

[5] Sūra 25: 29; 17: 87.

the conscience (*sirr*), which, being itself Divine in origin, can become conscious of the Divine. The *sirr* is the " ground " of the soul, the secret shrine of God Himself, wherein He knows man and man can know Him.[1] It is that bottommost depth of the soul, which lies hidden away, ineffable as God Himself, that of which an old German mystic says, " No human skill ever attains to know what the soul is in its bottommost depth. For that a supernatural skill is needed. It is what is without a name," of which, too, Heracleitus says, " Thou canst not discover the bounds of the soul, albeit thou pacest its every road, so deep is its foundation."[2]

But, on the other side, ever striving with the higher nature of man, urging the heart to enter and pass through the gateway opening on the world of sense, is the lower soul (*nafs*), the seat of the appetites and of passion, the " flesh " with its sinful lusts. It is the " law of the members " in conflict with the law of God and the leading of the spirit.[3] It is the " self " as opposed to goodness and to God, striving always for its own interests, regardless of what is pleasing to God or due to fellow-creatures, the self in its unregenerate state, that lower soul which commands to sin, which is headstrong to do evil (*al-nafs al-ammāra*). Of this appetitive self al-Muḥāsibī writes, " Place it where God Almighty placed it and describe it as He has described it and withstand it according to His command, for it is a greater enemy to you than Satan (*Iblīs*) himself, and Iblīs gains power over you only by means of it and your consent to it. You know to what it calls you and that it was created weak, though its nature is strong in greed and dissimulation, for it is self-confident, self-assertive, disobedient to God, untrustworthy. Its sincerity consists in lying, its claims are based on vanity; all that comes from it is deceitful, nothing that it does is praiseworthy. Be not deluded by the self and its hopes and its desires, for if you leave it alone, you are led astray, and if you give it what it desires, you will perish. If you neglect to examine it, you

[1] Sarrāj, *Kitab al-Luma'*, p. 231.

[2] *Cf.* R. Otto, *The Idea of the Holy*, pp. 200, 201.

[3] *Cf.* St. Paul: " The mind of the flesh is enmity against God, for it is not subject to the law of God, neither indeed can it be " (Rom. viii. 7).

will fall under its control, and if you weaken in your struggles against it, you will be overwhelmed, and if you follow it in its desires, you will go down into Hell. The truth is not in it, nor any tendency to good; it is the source of affliction and the origin of all evil and the treasure-house of Iblīs. None knows it save its Creator—what it displays as fear is really self-confidence, and what it displays as sincerity is only falsehood, and its claim to be single-minded in the service of God is pure hypocrisy." Satan and his myrmidons, and the self and its lusts, are in league in their desire to bring the soul of man to perdition.[1]

It is this lower soul which finds its pleasure and satisfaction in sin, which ceaselessly contends with the higher soul and is full of desire (*rāghiba*), always awake and attentive to that which means its own destruction in the world to come. Its chief joy is in what is abhorrent to its Lord, while that from which it turns with aversion is what He desires; the lightest of His commands is burdensome to it, and it flees from Him, rebelling against that which would lead it to eternal salvation.[2] This rebellious self al-Muḥāsibī compares to a beast of burden, and like an animal which is at first wild and untamed, it must be trained by constant discipline, in order to become of use to him who is its master, so that he, in his turn, may carry out the Will of that greater Master, his Lord, and since this discipline will mean the ultimate salvation of the self as part of the whole man, it is an act of compassion towards it.[3] Slowly and reluctantly the self may be brought under obedience, from time to time still struggling against the compulsion brought to bear upon it, and seeking the accomplishment of its own desires and rest from discipline, yet by degrees subdued by the constant pressure brought to bear while the higher soul gradually gains the upper hand, and it becomes the soul reproachful (*al-nafs al-lawwāma*), for therein the higher nature is waging an ever more successful war against the lower, until at last the victory is achieved and the struggle is over. Iblīs and his hosts have been routed and the lusts of the flesh no longer

[1] "Muḥāsabat al-Nufūs," fol. 5.
[2] "Bad' man anāb ila Allah," fols. 18*b*, 19*a*.
[3] "Muḥāsabat al-Nufūs," fol. 9.

make any appeal; the soul has become a captive, in complete submission to the Will of its Lord; it has attained to αταραξία and has become the "soul at rest" (*al-nafs al-muṭma'inna*).[1]

While earlier writers, and certain of his own contemporaries, held that the reason or intelligence (*'aql*, νοῦς) was to be identified with the heart (*qalb*) or the spirit (*rūḥ*), al-Muḥāsibī regarded the reason as something distinct, and concerning it he wrote a treatise, which became celebrated among those who discussed the subject of the intellect and its nature.[2] In this treatise al-Muḥāsibī defines the reason as a "natural disposition or instinct bestowed by God upon His creatures,"[3] which is invisible to them, both in themselves and in others, and can be neither touched nor tasted nor experienced. But God has made them to know Him by means of the reason, and through it they bear witness to Him, for through the intellect they recognise what is beneficial to them and what is injurious, and he who can distinguish between these two in things temporal knows that God has bestowed upon him reason, which has been withheld from the insane and the irresponsible and the weak-minded.[4] Like other Muslim writers, al-Muḥāsibī holds that the reason departs during sleep, as the spirits of men are said to do.[5] Through the actions of a man it can be seen whether he is possessed of reason, the power of discrimination between good and evil in material things, and reason used in this meaning corresponds to the quality of intelligence, or good sense. "The sign of it is the power to organise (*ḥusn al-tadbīr*) and to put things in their right place, whether in speech or in act, and the proof of that is the preference of the greater to the less."[6]

[1] "Ādāb al-Nufūs," fol. 79*a*; "Bad' man anāb ila Allah," fols. 21*a*, 21*b*. *Cf.* Sūra 89: 27: "O soul at rest, return unto thy Lord, well-satisfied, accepted." *Cf.* R. Otto, *Religious Essays*, pp. 7 *ff.*

[2] *Cf.* Subkī, *Ṭab. al-Shāfi'iyya*, II., pp. 39 *ff.*; Ghazālī, *Iḥyā*, I., p. 84.

[3] *Cf.* 'Amr b. 'Uthmān Makkī: "God imprisoned the *sirr* in the spirit, and the spirit in the soul, and the soul in the body: then He mingled the reason with them." Hujwīrī, *op. cit.*, p. 309.

[4] "Mā'iyyat al-'Aql wa ma'nāhu," fol. 104*b*.

[5] "Ri'āya," fol. 53*b*. *Cf.* Rūmī: "Each night Thou dost set free the spirit from the body's snare and dost erase the tablets of the mind" (*Mathnawī*, I. i. 388).

[6] "Ādāb al-Nufūs," fol. 91*a*.

The reason is also the means by which God speaks to the conscience of His servants, through promises and warnings, whereby they can discriminate also between what is morally good and evil, and know what may be beneficial in this world, but harmful in the next.[1] In dealing with this subject, al-Muḥāsibī takes into consideration the views of certain of the speculative thinkers, the scholastic theologians, who declared that the reason was the most excellent part of the spiritual (*rūḥ*), and asserted that the core of everything was its purest part, and therefore it was that the reason was called the mind (*lubb*=the core). Here the term *'aql* is used not only of the quality of intelligence, by which a man perceives, but of the percipient mind itself, and al-Muḥāsibī himself uses the term to cover both senses.[2] Others had asserted that the reason was a light, which God placed in the heart as a natural instinct, by which to perceive and comprehend, which increased in power as knowledge was acquired. Others, again, held that reason was the comprehending knowledge of God (*ma'rifa*) bestowed by Him upon His servant, that he might thereby increase in knowledge of good and evil.

al-Muḥāsibī's own view is that the reason is a natural instinct (*gharīza*), which makes use of experience, to acquire knowledge and to comprehend it. It is a gift which God has bestowed on man in order that he may understand the revelation sent down to him, and so may become a believer, God-fearing, abiding in the Divine commands. al-Muḥāsibī relates what tradition has to say of the creation by God of the reason or intellect, how it was given insight and the power to speak and be silent and to listen to the Divine message and to understand it, and how its Lord addressed it at the last, when its creation had been completed, saying, "By My Majesty and My Glory and My Greatness and My Power and My sovereignty over My creation, I have not created any being for which I have greater regard, or which is more precious to Me, than thyself, or more excellent in My sight than thou art in thy dignity, because through thee I am known and through thee I am worshipped, and by means of

[1] "Mā'iyyat al-'Aql," fol. 105*a*.

[2] *Cf.* al-Kindī's doctrine of Reason, de Boer, *History of Philosophy in Islam*, p. 102.

thee I am praised, and through thee I take and by thee I give, and by thee I requite. To thee I give My reward and upon thee comes My chastisement." So God has distinguished the reason by its excellence and has given it great power and has made the intelligent to hold the position which is highest and most honourable in this world and the next. al-Muḥāsibī urges his readers to have no companionship except with one who is intelligent and God-fearing, and not to associate with any save a learned man, possessed of insight.[1]

But no man can be said to have perfect understanding, through the reason, of God, for there is no limit to the knowledge of God, since He is Infinite and the true significance of His attributes is not to be encompassed by human knowledge: not even the angels, none but the All-High Himself can attain to such perfect knowledge.[2] At the same time, the reason enables the believer to understand the Unity of God (in the theological, though not the mystical sense of the term) and His power and sovereignty, and also the nature of sin and its consequences, and the sickness which afflicts the soul and how to seek the remedy thereof. The reason is that within man which is convinced by the presentation of facts and by proof concerning that which is not concrete, but abstract, material for thought. al-Muḥāsibī admits that the intellect, if it is weak, finds it difficult to prefer the service of God to sin, to choose knowledge rather than ignorance, and to prefer the following of the religious life to the pursuit of the pleasures of this life; but if rightly directed, it is one of the greatest gifts of God. There is no adornment like that of the reason, and no garment wherewith a man is clothed more fair than knowledge, for God Most High is not known except by means of the reason and is not obeyed

[1] "al-Waṣāyā (al-Naṣā'iḥ)," fol. 16*b*; "Kitāb al-Mustarshid," fol. 1.

[2] "Mā'iyyat al-'Aql," fols. 105 *ff.*, 108*a*. *Cf.* Barth: "Pure and exalted stands the power of God, not beside and not over, but on the other side of all conditioned—conditioning powers—the First and the Last and as such the Unknown, but nowhere and never a Magnitude amongst others in the medium known to us." *Cf.* also St. J. Chrysostom: "It is presumptuous to say that He who is beyond the apprehension of even the higher Powers can be compassed and comprised by the weak forces of our understanding" (*De Incomprehensibili*, III.).

except through knowledge. Every good and perfect gift, al-Muḥāsibī holds, comes from God; but it is for man to make the best possible use of such gifts, and he is to employ his reason in order to co-operate with the grace of God. "Know," he writes, "that the origin of every speech is action (*i.e.*, of the heart) and the origin of every action is knowledge, and the origin of all that is the grace of God (*tawfīq*), combined with the right use of the intelligence and much reflection."[1]

He quotes a tradition of the Prophet, who said, "God will not accept the prayers of a man or his fasting or his pilgrimages or his giving of alms or his warfare for the sake of God (*jihād*), or anything in the nature of good works, if he has not used his intelligence (in order to understand the true significance of these things)."[2] In accordance with this view was the statement made by one of the Companions, who declared that the increase of his intelligence by the amount of an atom each day was dearer to him than the taking up of the sword in the service of God and the sacrifice of himself and his goods, or the generous expenditure of his wealth on good works and in alms. al-Muḥāsibī, therefore, urges his readers to desire that gift of reason, that quality of intelligence, for it brings as its most excellent benefit the inclination to obey God in what He ordains for His servants and to avoid what is contrary to His law, and if that has been accomplished, the reason has brought good fortune (*naṣīb*). The man who is governed by reason is the most obedient to God, and disobedience to Him shews a lack of intelligence.[3] Of those of God's servants who obey Him and observe a scrupulous abstinence (*i.e.*, refrain from what is unlawful), that one who makes most use of his reason is most certain to choose what is well pleasing to God and is most acceptable to Him.[4]

The foregoing are the terms used to represent the means by which he the self-conscious ego comes into relation with the world of experience, and al-Muḥāsibī deals further with the equipment and working of those means. As the physical

[1] "Ādāb al-Nufūs," fol. 100*b*.
[2] "al-Waṣāyā (al-Naṣā'iḥ)," fol. 16*a*.
[3] *Ibid.*, fol. 16*b*.
[4] *Ibid.*, fol. 23*b*.

senses convey impressions from the outer world of sense-experience, so there are inner " senses " to deal with these impressions, the power of imagination, of reflection and of remembrance.[1] While the law of passivity means the reception of impressions from without, in the form of multiplicity, the law of activity, from within, reduces that multiplicity to a unity, and mind makes itself predominate over matter, by using its powers of perception and cognition and will. al-Muḥāsibī, in his rule of life, seeks to co-ordinate perception, by means of the memory, with reflection, through the intelligence, and with action, by means of the will.[2]

Of the psychological influence of the emotions, al-Muḥāsibī has much to say, and he makes full use of his knowledge of this influence in his appeals to those for whom he writes. The *Kitāb al-Tawahhum*, with its lurid pictures of the Hell destined for the unrepentant sinner, is calculated to rouse the emotion of fear to its highest pitch, while its picture of the joys of Paradise, set before the faithful believer as his goal, and that to which he may attain as his permanent abode, makes an equally strong appeal to hope (pleasure). " The danger is great," he writes, " and the body is weak, and death is nigh at hand, and the regard of God is upon you, and nothing that you do is hidden from Him, whether it be done openly or in secret. You cannot endure His wrath, and you have no strength to bear His chastisement, and you are unable to dispense with His presence ; therefore take care in regard to yourself before the time comes to meet with Him."[3] But for those who have held steadfastly to their faith, mindful always of that world to come, there will be the purification from all defilement, neither sorrow nor pain shall afflict them again, and death shall be no more, but everlasting joy shall be theirs. They shall stand in the presence of the Lord and, rejoicing in His good pleasure and His love, shall enter upon the life which is immortality.[4] With fear and hope thus filling and dominating their hearts, what can they do but refuse the evil and

[1] *Cf.* Simon of Ṭaibūtheh, *Early Christian Mystics*, p. 45.
[2] *Cf.* L. Massignon, *Passion*, pp. 480 *ff.*
[3] " Kitāb al-Tawahhum," fol. 161*a*. [4] *Ibid.*, fol. 168*a*

choose the good? That which breaks down the contumacy of man and opens his eyes to his errors and his sins is the power of fear and hope, directed towards his Lord, which work upon his mind and incite him to repentance while there is yet time, and make him willing to renounce what his heart desires and his carnal self longs after, which is abhorrent to God, so that he may be protected from the pains of Hell and become worthy of entrance into the presence of God.[1] "Fear," writes al-Muḥāsibī, "is indispensable to the heart, but it does not rise up until the desire to sin has wholly died within him, and faith has been established by the intensity of fear."[2] But the emotion of fear is not only the cruder type aroused by the possibility of physical pains and penalties, but the fear of doing what is contrary to the Divine Will. "What afflicts the servants of God is their fear of the loss of God's good pleasure, and His disapproval of them, and this is more to them and more painful to their hearts than the loss of Paradise and the fear of Hell." This is the fear of the servant, not the sinner, a fear inspired by the greatness of God, the sense of awe and reverence before the "mysterium tremendum" of the Transcendent God, the dread of the creature before the overwhelming Majesty of God the Creator, a fear which, because of the fascination also aroused by that mysterious Splendour, is mingled with the emotion of love.[3]

When asked about the nature of hope—that which is aroused by the prospect of pleasure, whether material or spiritual, al-Muḥāsibī said, "It is the desire for the grace of God and His mercy, and sincerity in right thoughts of Him at the approach of death."[4] He holds that hope is to be employed in three cases: firstly, to save men from despair when they have sinned and then repented, to enable them to hope that God will accept their repentance; secondly, to help men, when remembering their past sins, to do good works in the hope that these will be accepted in accordance

[1] "Ri'āyā," fols. 12*b*, 13*a*.
[2] Abū Nu'aym, "Ḥilya," fol. 232*a* (MS. Leyden).
[3] "Kitāb al-Zuhd," fol. 3*b*. *Cf.* also Chapter X. below.
[4] al-Sulamī, *op. cit.*, fol. 12*a*.

with His command not to despair of His mercy; thirdly, in doing any action, to hope that it will be well pleasing to Him and be found acceptable in His sight.[1]

Sorrow—that godly sorrow which worketh repentance—pride, humility and disgust are among the emotional states with which al-Muḥāsibī deals, shewing how they affect the minds of men and their actions in relation to God and their fellow-creatures.

As we have seen, the heart, including the reason, is the means by which reality is perceived and interpreted; it is the instrument of knowledge (*'ilm* and *ma'rifa*). All knowledge comes from God and is the gift of His grace,[2] but there are different types of knowledge, differing not only in respect of the subjects dealt with, but in the manner in which they come to the heart of man. There is knowledge concerning what is lawful and unlawful in relation to this world, and this is outward, external knowledge. There is also knowledge concerning what is lawful and unlawful in relation to the next world, including such duties as worship, and abstinence, and asceticism, and patience, and contentment, and resignation, and generosity of soul, and peace of mind, and the realisation of God's grace and strength of purpose and single-minded sincerity; these are the things which are lawful. On the other side are the fear of poverty, and discontent with what is decreed, and rancour, and secret hatred, and jealousy, and dishonesty, and the love of praise, and contempt, and love of domination, and desire, and avarice, and insolence, and petulance, and self-glorification, and many other things which are unlawful. And the knowledge which discerns between these two classes is a spiritual, inward knowledge.

These types of knowledge, necessary for all mankind, male and female, bond and free, can be acquired by accepting the tradition of others, who relate what was revealed by God to His prophets, or by the use of study and deduction, for the "gates" by which men come to knowledge of what is manifest and what is hidden are the gate of good counsel received from the wise, and the gate of a man's knowledge

[1] "Masā'il fī A'māl al-Qulūb," fol. 125*a*. *Cf.* Chapter X. below.

[2] "Ādāb al-Nufūs," fol. 100*b*; "Kitāb al-'Ilm," chapter viii.

of himself, so far as it can be attained by ordinary study.[1] This intellectual knowledge is acquired by a man's use of the reason in reflection (*tafakkur*), and consideration (*nazr*), and remembrance (*dhikr*), in order that he may continue to profit from experience (*i'tibār*) and exalt his virtue by adding to his knowledge. " He who reflects little," says al-Muḥāsibī, " learns little from experience, and he who learns little from experience gains little knowledge, and he who gains little knowledge increases in ignorance and does not attain to righteousness, nor the satisfaction of certainty, nor the spirit of wisdom. Nor can anyone acquire knowledge by mere repetition with the tongue."[2]

Reflection al-Muḥāsibī considers to be one of the most important " works of the heart." It is a form of inward service, by which God's servant is strengthened for outward service. In solitary reflection is found the key to wisdom, and thereby the servant advances from service to his goal—salvation.[3] al-Muḥāsibī goes so far as to say that reflection leads to all good, for reflection enables a man to know whether he is serving God or committing sin, and to know which of two duties comes first and to choose aright between them. Reflection for a single hour, he says, is better than service (by good works) for a whole year, because that reflection may turn a man from sin to obedience, and reflection brings knowledge both of what is obligatory and what is voluntary (*i.e.*, works of supererogation), and it leads to the glorification of God and love to Him, and whichever type of reflection it is, on what is to be avoided, or what is to be undertaken, it is the best means to employ, and a most excellent stage in the service of God.[4] But reflection is not an easy thing, because reflection upon the world to come turns aside the heart from its pleasure in the things of this world, and reflection on the Day of Resurrection and the Last Judgment is the cause of sorrow and grief and fear, which are distasteful, and reflection means, too, that as a result thereof the self will be cut off from what it desires, which is seen,

1 " Kitāb al-'Ilm," chapters iv., v.; " Ādāb al-Nufūs," fol. 83*a*.
2 " Mā'iyyat al-'Aql," fols. 111*b*, 112*a*.
3 " Kitāb al-Zuhd," fol. 3*b*.
4 " Ri'āya," fol. 14*a*; " Kitāb al-Zuhd," fol. 3*a*.

in the light of reflection, to be abhorrent to God, and, to the self-seeking, that which means seeking the will of God instead cannot be easy or acceptable. But reflection becomes possible and easy by the concentration of the thoughts and dependence upon God for His help, and such concentration of the mind is secured by cutting off the physical senses from what would be a cause of distraction from the outer world, and then by keeping the inner senses from consideration of any worldly affairs except those on which it is desirable to reflect. Then the thoughts are concentrated and the mind is attentive, and it becomes possible to reflect.[1]

Remembrance is linked up with reflection and is a part of it, for it includes the remembrance of what God has urged upon His servant and what He loves, and the remembrance of the power of the Adversary, and how the latter has been the cause of sin in the past, and it means, too, the remembrance of the regard of God upon His servant, of Him Who is the All-Seeing, the All-hearing, Whose knowledge penetrates to the very secrets of the heart, and such remembrance, combined with the shame it brings, will assuredly conduce to reflection, and reflection leads to certainty (*tathabbut*) about what is right and wrong.[2]

By these processes, then, knowledge is acquired, and of it al-Muḥāsibī says, " Knowledge is to the mind as a lamp to the eye, and as the light of the sun to the sight. Knowledge was given to man by God, so that his reason, making use thereof, might enable him to realise how the darkness of ignorance veils him from the remembrance of the next world and the regard of his Lord upon him. The reason is like the eye which seeks help from the lamp, knowing what is the result of darkness in the house, and so the wise servant strives with his intellect to make use of knowledge and to act in accordance with it, and so to ward off the sinful suggestions of the self and the Adversary.[3] al-Muḥāsibī further develops this theme of knowledge as light by the illustration of a man walking along a road in black darkness, afraid of being lost and of slipping in the heavy rain, and the possession of sight will not profit him without

[1] " Ri'āya," fols. 14*a ff.* [2] *Ibid.*, fol. 23*a*.
[3] *Ibid.*, fol. 49*a*.

a lantern, and a lantern will not profit him unless he has sound sight, and sight and the lantern together will not profit him if he does not direct his eyes to the spot where he places his feet, and so make sure of his footing, and if he looks up at the heavens, or turns round, even though his sight be sound and his lantern alight, if he does not direct his gaze towards the ground he is like a man who has no sight. Sound sight is like the reason and the lantern is like knowledge, and his gaze, directed towards his footing, is like the gaining of assurance by means of the reason and making every effort to understand what is presented to him. So, by the use of the reason, by the acquirement of knowledge, by the reflection and consideration which lead to assurance, a man can learn to distinguish between what is good and what is evil, and through the exercise of his will, thus informed by knowledge, can act rightly and in accordance with the Divine Law.[1]

But these types of knowledge received from others, or achieved by means of the processes of the reasoning intelligence, will only enable a man to know God indirectly and by external means; they do not represent that real and intimate comprehension of Him which is "as a fathomless sea," to which the intellect and its processes cannot attain, that gnosis (*ma'rifa*) which is the greatest of God's gifts, "before all things and the origin of all things,"[2] that inner intuition or insight which deals with reality—that is, with God—without the mediation of sense-experience or intellectual process, which is something mystical and supernatural. The soul, in the inmost depths of its hidden sanctuary (*sirr*), has a power of "divination," of knowing and recognising the Divine, when God shews Himself to the soul which has eyes to see Him, when the soul and God recognise each other, and can do so because they are in

[1] "Ri'āya," fol. 23*a*.

[2] "Ādāb al-Nufūs," fol. 93*b*. *Cf.* Hujwīrī, pp. 16 *ff.* *Cf.* also Simon of Ṭaibūtheh. "A part of knowledge is apprehended not by words, but through the inward silence of the mind . . . it lifts itself up towards the sublime ray of the hidden Godhead . . . it becomes a knowledge that is higher than all knowledge, for it has reached the Divine knowledge of the hidden Godhead, which is higher than all understanding" (*Early Christian Mystics*, p. 11).

truth akin, because man was made in the image of God and has therefore something of the Divine in the profoundest depth of his being, and this intuitive knowledge of God is the recognition, by the spirit of man, of the Divine Spirit, whence it came.

There is, then, another type of knowledge than that which comes through "natural" experience and its interpretation, and a mode of knowing other than that exercised by the intellect. It is derived from experience, indeed, but an experience which breaks in upon the soul from the Unseen, when and as God chooses, and this experience is apprehended, and knowledge of God attained, through the willing acceptance of the Divine grace by a soul which is receptive, ready, with eyes to see and ears to hear, and hands outstretched to receive that gift.[1] It is not by any processes of reason that this knowledge is gained, but by intuition, by direct contact with that which is presented to it. This power of direct apprehension of the Divine, this intuitive insight, is latent in every man; it is what raises him above all other creatures, and is inherent in his nature as being made in the image of God, but not every man is able to make use of it for the purpose for which it was given. When the eye of the heart is dimmed and its hearing dulled and the mirror is defaced by rust, then man cannot know God. But if the eye of the heart is no longer clouded by the darkness of lust, but enlightened by the removal of the veils between it and the vision presented to it, then it can contemplate the Divine Mystery.[2] If the ears, dulled by ignorance and unwillingness to hear, are enabled by knowledge (*'ilm*) and training to listen to the Voice of God, He will speak in such wise that they can hear and understand.[3] The revelation of God is pure grace on His part, the heart can only prepare itself to be ready when the hour comes, but since

[1] *Cf.* C. Sorley:

With parted lips and outstretched hands
And listening ears, Thy servant stands,
Call Thou early, call Thou late,
To Thy great service dedicate.

(*Expectans Expectavi.*)

[2] "Muḥāsabat al-Nufūs," fols. 9, 10.

[3] "Ri'āya," fols. *5a*, *5b*.

this understanding knowledge is necessary to perfection, the possession of it is the thing to be most sought after by the traveller on the road to God.

al-Muḥāsibī incites men to seek to prepare themselves to receive this gnosis, by shewing that it is indeed a pearl of great price (*fā'iqa*). "The best of men," he writes, "are those who live nearest to God, and those who are nearest to Him are those who know Him best. Men attain to excellence in proportion to their knowledge (*ma'rifa*). They serve God for His own sake alone, according to their knowledge of Him; they are convinced of the truth of His promises and humble themselves before Him, in proportion to their knowledge; and whether what they do and what they say is right depends upon their knowledge. They are satisfied with God and are acquiescent in His will and trust to Him in all their affairs according to their knowledge of Him. They thank God for His grace and place their hope in Him and fear Him, in accordance with what they know of Him. It is understanding knowledge which leads them to right thoughts of Him and gives them patience to obey Him and to refrain from disobeying Him, and to conceal their service to Him and to endure the afflictions which come upon them by His decree, which makes them love what is dear to Him and hate what is abhorrent to Him. If gnosis is lacking in a man, then he falls short in all these respects."[1]

This penetrating wisdom enables a man also to know himself thoroughly, for a knowledge of God is closely connected with a knowledge of self, and al-Muḥāsibī illustrates the effect of this knowledge by the parable of a basket placed in the road, containing flasks, which are full, with the necks fastened up. People pass by the basket and do not know what is in it, until a passer-by comes upon it and says, "I will uncover this basket and see what is in it." And he uncovers it and sees flasks which are full and he does not know what is in them, and he unfastens all the straps and there comes forth to him from one the scent of musk, and from another the scent of ambergris, and from this one the fragrance of frankincense and from that the perfume of saffron, and from others the scent of civet and

[1] "Ādāb al-Nufūs," fol. 100*b*. *Cf.* "Kitāb al-Mustarshid," fol. 4.

jasmine and other perfumes and ointments. From another flask comes the smell of naphtha, and from this the smell of tar and from that of sulphur, and the strong fetor of their smell is more than he can endure. People as a whole, al-Muḥāsibī says, are like the basket and the flasks, and they in their knowledge and qualities are as different as the flasks. But the individual is also like the basket, considered as a whole, and the flasks represent the individual's characteristics and moral qualities, and the sweet perfumes are the good qualities and desirable virtues, and the evil smells are the evil qualities and the vices. And the self, with all its qualities, can only be examined and tested by this understanding wisdom (*ma'rifa*).[1] It is, then, one of the greatest of good things and a means of approach to God. "Therefore," al-Muḥāsibī concludes, "seek it from Him Who is its King, in the spirit of one who is not worthy that it should be granted unto him."[2]

Only by means of this knowledge can men recognise the grace of God and become partakers thereof, otherwise they will pass it by unheeded, just as the beasts do not realise the fragrance of musk, even though their noses pass close to it, for they lack the power of discrimination.[3] So it is with the gifts of God: they must be recognised and appropriated if they are to bear fruit. "The hungry man," says al-Muḥāsibī, "desires bread and the thirsty man desires water, and if bread and water are placed before them it does not profit them to be aware that bread and water are there, and the proximity of bread and water is of no use to them unless they eat of the food and drink of the water. So also is it with you: your knowledge of good and its proximity to you does not benefit you, nor your desire for it, until it becomes a part of your very self and you become one of those who follow after it."[4] And, finally, it is only by gnosis that the believing soul can hope to attain to that immediate experience of the presence of God which al-Muḥāsibī calls "fellowship" (*uns*) with God, which issues in that unitive life which is the ultimate aim of the mystic.[5]

1 "Ādāb al-Nufūs," fols. 84*a*, 84*b*.
2 *Ibid.*, fol. 100*b*.
3 *Ibid.*, fol. 97*a*.
4 *Ibid.*, fol. 85*a*.
5 *Ibid.*, fol. 91*b*, 93*b*.

Since, then, God has appointed salvation to be by means of this gnosis, by which the will (*irāda*) is directed aright, it is for man to prepare himself by freeing the soul from all obstacles to the Divine gift; and al-Muḥāsibī's rule of life is directed towards this end, in order that all a man's capacities, his " members " and his senses, his outward conduct and his inward self, may be brought under control, until actions, feelings, intellect and will are brought into conformity with the Divine Will. " This effort of unification," writes a modern psychologist, " if inspired by a moral and religious ideal, will be an ascesis, a rectification of the desires and the will, crowned by a complete abandonment of self and all things to the transcendent Being, the sovereign Lord and sovereign God . . . the concentration of the soul, the simplification of its speculative content, beneath the urge of a single love, sustained by the firm hope of a correspondence on God's part."[1]

The very beginning of this process of ascetic preparation, the voluntary act of the heart, directed towards the attainment of gnosis, al-Muḥāsibī sees to be the Intention (*nīya*), for the intention, rightly directed and firmly maintained by continual, inward striving, will lead the novice onward in that difficult journey which many seek to undertake, in which but few persevere to the end.[2] One of the " gates " between God and man,[3] by which he is led into the knowledge of Divine things, is the " gate of the intention and its purification, which leads to the will to do good in secret and openly, in things great and small." The essential part of action is the intention, which must be free from all tinge of hypocrisy and all self-interested motives, otherwise the action is of no value. With his usual common sense, al-Muḥāsibī observes that it is of no use for the servant to know what he should do or refrain from doing, and not to know how to form his intention or how to be sincere in his purpose, as to what he will do or refrain from doing, since these precede action. Many a man lives his life and dies when his hour comes, without having realised the importance of this.[4] al-Muḥā-

[1] J. Maréchal, *Studies in the Psychology of the Mystics*, pp. 304, 316, 320.
[2] " Ādāb al-Nufūs," fol. 92*a*.
[3] *Cf.* p. 98 above.
[4] " Ādāb al-Nufūs," fols. 82*b*, 83*a*.

sibī defines the intention as, "The desire of the servant that he should act in one particular way, and when he wishes to do that act to that end, then that wish is an intention, directed either towards God Most High or towards another than Him . . . an intention is towards action in a certain way for the sake of this world or the world to come. As, for example, a man sets out on a warlike expedition and his intention in that is to gain a reward and fame, and so also he prays, intending to win the heavenly reward or the praise of men. But the intention of one who acts for the sake of God is to seek for His reward and no other. If you wish to be sincere and to pray and to obey God in all you do, and you have established your intention, and have put aside every sinful temptation, out of godly fear, then that wish is an intention directed towards God. But if you wish to fast, while intending to break your fast, and desire to pray but are too slothful, or interrupt your prayer through pre-occupation with this world, and wish to abandon sin out of godly fear but your soul will not bring itself to repent, then that desire on your part means love towards something other than God."[1] The preparation of the heart, then, depends primarily on the strength and direction of the desire which initiates it. So a modern writer points out, saying, "Recent psychology has emphasised the dependence of thought on desire. . . . Thought, desire and will are indissoluble elements in a single vital process ; yet conation seems prior in importance and, to a large extent, in time."[2]

al-Muḥāsibī deals with the case of that man who avoids formulating a good intention, either because his self shrinks from the sacrifice involved in carrying it out, or because he fears that his sincere intention may be frustrated by suggestions on the part of Iblīs, tempting him to hypocrisy, but this attitude al-Muḥāsibī judges to be weakness. Men are not called upon to change their nature, and since God allows the suggestions of Satan, He has also provided the means of repelling them, by giving to men the blessings of reason and knowledge. Men are tempted through their human nature, and God has commanded them to strive against temptation by using their reason and their

[1] "Ri'āya," fol. 66*a*.

[2] B. H. Streeter, *Reality*, p. 77.

knowledge. It is the duty of His servant to form a good intention and to deny to the self what it desires to do, to frustrate that intention. al-Muḥāsibī quotes a tradition in this connection from Wahb b. Munabbih,[1] who said, "Faith is the leader and reason is the driver and the self is the restive horse. If its leader is remiss, it turns aside from the road, and if its driver is neglectful, it is restive against its leader; but when both driver and leader are alert, then the self goes on its way, obediently, or unwillingly, as the case may be." So, when the self is given over to lust, lust can be driven back by the reason; but if the reins are loosened, then the self goes on its own way and leaves the road. No man can expect to get away from his own nature, according to which he was fashioned, or to be like the angels, whom their Lord created possessed of reason and insight (*baṣā'ir*) and also free from passion and sensual desires, and so they are not enticed by lust, and sensuality offers them no temptations. They serve God continually, and do not weary, for there is nothing to check or influence their service and continual devotion to God. Not to them is appointed the reward of the joys of Paradise, since they wage no war against passion and sensuality, nor do they endure pain or weariness or affliction. They are not subject to punishment, and they continue for ever in their devoted service of God.

At the other end of the scale are the beasts and the birds and the reptiles, whose nature is sensual, and to them is given instinct in accordance with what they need to fear and what they must seek for their sustenance, and they take care of themselves and their offspring. They have not been given reasoning powers, and cannot understand commands and prohibitions and the knowledge of consequences, and they are not liable to punishment for a sensuality which is forbidden to men and demons (*jinniyya*). But at the last they are turned again to their dust.[2]

[1] *Cf.* pp. 67, 68 above.

[2] *Cf.* a modern writer, F. P. Harton: "Animal behaviour is instinctive and unmoral . . . no animal is capable of abstract or speculative reasoning . . . he has no moral sense, nor is his will free in the sense that the human will is. Sin is impossible to the animal. It serves God by instinctively fulfilling the end for which it was created, and it cannot refuse that service" (*The Elements of the Spiritual Life*, p. 91).

But men and jinns are given reasoning powers as part of their natural endowment, and these are susceptible to commands and prohibitions, and they realise the consequences of what they do. By their nature they are attracted to what is suited to them, and also to what is not fitting for them, and God bids them strive through their reason against the temptations of their human nature, and for them He appoints the great reward and the bitter chastisement. Therefore al-Muḥāsibī urges men to form a good and sincere intention for all they undertake, and sincerity will have its reward.[1] But no action will prove to be good, if the intention is lacking or bad. " Do not strive for outward devotion " (*'ibāda*), he writes, " while your intention is corrupt and your will infirm, for your obedience will be changed altogether into disobedience, and punishment will come upon you in this world, together with chastisement in the world to come, with much weariness of the flesh and little profit and the loss of desires and delights, and you will perish in this world and the next. But adorn your service with piety and single-minded devotion and abstinence, and your intention with sincerity, and guard your desire by self-examination and concern yourself with the search for (a good) intention. Determine to seek sincerity in speech and in action and in all your states, in your service to God and in abandonment of sin, until you are as sure of your intention as of your action."[2] " Purify your intention," he says again, " for therein consists your well-being in the next life and in this also ; it is a covenant made with God, and you will attain to nothing except by means of it, and will be your salvation from all that makes for destruction. It is that which links you with God the All-Powerful, Who willed before you directed your intention. Determination lies in the intention, and no door is opened to you, nor does any spirit attain to God, nor is any gnosis of Him acquired, except by this means.

" Then take heed to your intention, for it is a secret bond between you and God, and in it resides single-mindedness and sincerity in speech and in action within the heart. Therefore do nothing without a rightly directed intention,

[1] " Ri'āya," fols. 66*a ff.* [2] " Muḥāsabat al-Nufūs," fol. 4.

and do not either eat or drink or speak or observe without a good purpose, and know that God has had mercy on you, when your intention is good and free from defect, and that there is with you an army that will not be routed and a watcher who will not sleep, and a guard who will not fail, and riches which cannot be touched. It is your wealth and your profit and the seal upon your purse, and therefore you must make it sure. Most of mankind have striven to do different kinds of service to God, without a rightly directed purpose, and intention can be directed only by knowledge, and knowledge can be attained only by the intention, and neither can dispense with the other. Therefore strive to direct your intention aright, for thereby you will attain to virtue and to single-mindedness, and it is the abode of awe and reverence and godly fear and caution and wariness and the love of God. So direct your intention that it may be pure from all defects and fair to behold, and thus you will attain to your goal."[1]

When a man knows the truth and is established in it, realising what is due from him to God, together with what is incumbent upon him, both outwardly and inwardly, which is the purification of the inward self and the right direction of the will, and the making of the intention sincere, and the careful scrutiny of the aspirations (*himma*), and the cleansing of the thoughts from all that is abhorrent to God, and adherence to contrition for all past actions of the heart and members which were contrary to the law of God, which God has appointed as a means of guarding the members from sin, then the outward life of the servant corresponds to his inner life, for what purifies and befits his inner life makes sound, and finds correspondence in, his outward life, and what is inimical to and corrupts his inner self finds its correspondence in his outward acts.[2]

[1] "Muḥāsabat al-Nufūs," fols. 8, 9. *Cf.* also "Waṣāyā (Naṣā'iḥ)," fol. 15*b*.

[2] "Ādāb al-Nufūs," fol. 61*a*. *Cf.* St. Mark: "For from within, out of the heart of men, proceed evil thoughts, adulteries, fornications, murders. . . . All these evil things come from within, and defile the man" (vii. 21, 23).

al-Muḥāsibī's rule of life is, then, an ascesis, directed towards the purification of the heart, beginning with a sincere intention towards that end, in order that the heart may be prepared to receive the Divine gift and to enter into a state of grace with God.

CHAPTER VII

THE ASCETIC THEOLOGY OF AL-MUḤĀSIBĪ: I. THE CREATOR AND THE CREATURE—HUMAN NATURE AND SIN—THE ENEMIES OF THE SOUL—TEMPTATION

THE ascesis which aims at a rectification of desires and will, with a view to the loss of the self, in order that it may find itself again in God, demands a right view of the relation of the human soul to God, and of the causes which have interfered with that relation as it was meant to be. Man was not created to be a dualism, but a unity, in which the lower animal nature should be united with the higher spiritual nature, and both should be united with God, but this ideal relation has remained unrealised. God has invested man, His highest creature, with a freedom of will which is not the perfect freedom of the Infinite Will, but does enable him, as distinct from both angels and beasts, to choose whether he will love and serve God or refuse that love and service where they are due, and, by making the sensual desires and the satisfaction of personal ends the chief end of life, become the bondslave of the " flesh " and the self.[1]

Therefore, in setting forth his rule of life, al-Muḥāsibī calls attention to the true relation between the human and the Divine, between the soul and God. " The first thing," he says, " is that you should know that you are a servant under authority, for whom there is no salvation except through fearing your Master and Lord, and no destruction for you if you do so. Therefore remember and reflect upon that for which you were created and the reason for which you were placed in this transient world, and know that you were not created for idle pleasure (*'abth*) and you were not abandoned to blindness (*i.e.*, not left without guidance), but you were created and placed in this world only by way of trial and experience, either to obey God or to disobey Him, and you will pass from this world into everlasting torment

[1] *Cf.* F. P. Harton, *Elements of the Spiritual Life*, pp. 92, 93.

or eternal bliss. If you know that you are a servant under authority, you will understand why you were created and to what you are exposed and to what you are inevitably taking your way. That is the very beginning of the purification of your self, for it cannot be purified unless it knows itself to be under authority and a creature, and then you will know that there can be no salvation for one who is but a creature and in a state of servantship, except through obedience to his Lord and Master, and the guide to that obedience is knowledge of His commands and prohibitions, for obedience is the road to salvation, and knowledge is the guide to the road, and the foundation of obedience is abstinence (*wara'*), and the foundation of abstinence is godliness (*taqwā*), and the foundation of that is self-examination (*muḥāsaba*), and self-examination is based on fear (*khawf*) and hope (*rajā'*), and that which guides to self-examination is the knowledge which enables God's creatures to serve Him with their hearts and members."[1]

Sin, therefore, in al-Muḥāsibī's view, is primarily disobedience on the part of the servant to his Lord, a rebellion of will which appears in moral and intellectual as well as in sensual and animal forms.[2] It is action, of the members or the heart, which is abhorrent to God (*makrūh*) which therefore mars the relation between the Creator and His creature, and, being the cause of separation between man and God, makes impossible that unification of purpose and will between the Divine and the human which man was created to realise. This frustration of the Divine purpose is due to the enemies of the soul, which seek to hinder it from the salvation for which it was created, and strive to compass its utter destruction.

There is, first, the enemy within, the lower self, dominated by concupiscence, the passion for its own satisfaction (*hawā*). Of passion a Ṣūfī writer says, "Man is commanded to resist it. It is of two kinds, desire of pleasure and lust, and desire of worldly honour and authority. He who follows pleasure and lust haunts taverns, and mankind are safe from his mischief; but he who desires honour and authority lives

[1] "Ri'āya," fols. 8*b ff*.

[2] *Cf.* 1 John iii. 4, "Sin is the transgression of the law."

in cells and monasteries, and not only has lost the way himself, but also leads others into error. One whose every act depends on passion, and who finds satisfaction in following it, is far from God, although he be with you in a mosque; but one who has renounced and abandoned it is near to God, although he be in a church" (and therefore no Muslim). And the same writer says, "Concupiscence is mingled as an ingredient in the clay of Adam; whoever renounces it becomes a prince and whoever follows it becomes a captive."[1] It may, then, take the form of yielding to the sensual desires (*shahawāt*), seeking pleasure through the senses, without any relation to the will of God. Or it may take the form of self-seeking in other directions than those of sensual pleasures, in the desire for what is futile and transient, for this world's goods, a preoccupation with the temporal to the exclusion of what is eternal. Or, again, it may take the form not only of self-seeking, but of preoccupation with the self, of self-satisfaction, self-sufficiency. The aim of the enemy within the soul is to make the self, in all its aspects, god in place of its Lord, and so bring it to perdition.

Of this enemy within the soul al-Muḥāsibī writes that a scrutiny of the self will shew its stratagems to avoid obedience to its Lord, and the extent to which it is enticed by what is abhorrent to Him, for the self is the source of all evil, and that which tempts to all affliction, headstrong to do wrong, and a follower after lust.[2] When the servant is concerned about the life of the world to come, and remembers it and reflects upon it, the self entices him to become absorbed in this world and its pleasures, and passion gets the better of reason, for the self is not controlled by any rational principle, and so the servant falls a victim to its blandishments, and the self, predominant, is an enemy against whom he needs to be always on his guard,[3] for "The self and concupiscence are two things which pollute the fruits of action, through their allurement."[4] It is the self which clings to wealth for its own use, and is opposed to the generous use of it for others, as it is the self which dislikes the bodily weariness involved in the service of God and craves for

[1] Hujwīrī, *op. cit.*, pp. 207, 208.
[2] "Riʿāya," fol. 91*a*.
[3] *Ibid.*, fol. 93*a*.
[4] "Ādāb al-Nufūs," fol. 89*b*.

rest. So obedience to the self will mean destruction in the Day of Resurrection and the conquest of the self will mean salvation, for in that day there will be no means of escape from death, and no retreat from the meeting with God, and no opportunity for returning to this world, and to offer as an excuse the weakness of the flesh will be manifest folly. Therefore it is in this life and in this world that this insidious enemy of the soul must be fought and overcome.[1]

Then there is the enemy without, the world (*al-dunyā*), all in the present order of things which appeals to the soul as an object of desire apart from, and in opposition to, God. It represents sinful and concupiscent humanity as a whole, society viewed as apart from God and controlled by selfish aims, in which even religion is practised for self-seeking ends. It is the world which tempts the self to intemperance, the opposite of *wara'*, and to impurity, to satisfy the desires of the flesh and the lust of the eyes, and to seek for vainglory, for selfish pomp and display, which allures by the attraction of its vanities. It is the sphere in which the law of God is ignored and the lawlessness of sin prevails in the mass. It is the place of trial and testing for the soul, where it experiences all manner of temptations and seductions. Of this enemy, ever battering at the fortress of the soul, al-Muḥāsibī writes, "I have found the origin of what is inimical to the spiritual life to come, the most far-reaching of the stratagems of Satan in corrupting the faithful and destroying the sanctions of religion, to be the love of this world and exaltation and glory therein. It is the root of evil and the chief of sins, and because of it God's creatures are remiss in what is due to Him, and go astray from His law, and neglect prayer and fasting and the rest of the ordinances, and, through love of wealth and reputation, they are enticed by the seductions of what is unlawful and sinful, and despise much of what is in accordance with the Divine command and purpose. For the sake of this world, they disobey God and fall into mortal sin, and bring themselves to perdition unawares, although the Prophet of God warned them of the seductions of this world, for he said, 'After my time worldliness shall come upon you, and it

[1] "Bad' man anāb ila Allāh," fol. 19*a*.

shall consume your faith, as fire consumes the fuel.' Also he said, 'There is nothing more abhorrent to God, after polytheism, than the love of this world.'"[1]

al-Muḥāsibī quotes also the tradition that God Most High said to Moses, "O Moses, renounce the love of this world, for there is no mortal sin which is committed against Me, which is graver than the love of this world." He refers also to a tradition of Jesus, that He said, "O ye who are My disciples, wealth is pleasing in this life and destructive of the next, for the rich are flattered by others in this world and are trampled under foot in the next. Verily, I say unto you, the rich shall not enter into the kingdom of heaven."[2] Again he gives the tradition, "Those who are concerned with the life of this world and its glory will have their reward for all they do, and they will suffer no loss in this world, but for them there will be nought but Hell-fire in the world to come, and all they have done here will be made void and of no profit, for it was vanity; such is the lot of those who love this world." And he adds, "May God preserve us and you from the love of it!"[3]

Not even the professedly pious and the learned are exempt from the attacks of this enemy, and such as these, if themselves corrupted, may be a source of corruption to others. The learned man who is intoxicated by the love of this world will, through his infatuation, make others to fall away from the love of God. Such men are "highway robbers," blocking the way of progress to the servants of God, who seek after Him. Of such, a wise man said, "He who increases his knowledge of God, and then increases his love of this world, increases his distance from God."[4]

al-Muḥāsibī gives another tradition, according to which Jesus said, "There are evil teachers (divines), who fast and pray and give alms, and fail to do what they command others to do, who teach and have no knowledge, and evil is that which they enjoin. They repent in word and wish, but

[1] "Waṣāyā (Naṣā'iḥ)," fol. 3*a*.

[2] *Ibid. Cf.* St. Matt. xix. 23, "Then said Jesus unto them, Verily I say unto you, That a rich man shall hardly enter into the kingdom of heaven."

[3] *Ibid.*, fol. 3*a*.

[4] *Ibid.*, fol. 4*a*.

act in accordance with their lusts; they will not be satisfied, nor let you go, until they have torn your garments from off you and have rent your hearts by their deceit. Verily, I say unto you, be not like unto the sieve, which lets the grain fall through and retains the chaff. So also ye bring forth wisdom from your mouths, while hatred remains within your breasts. O slaves of this world, how shall the world to come be attained by one whom lust does not keep from this world, and whose desires are not detached from it? Ye have done lip-service to this world and trodden knowledge under foot. Ye have corrupted your future life, and the good things of this world are dearer to you than the good things of the next, and what man is viler than you? Woe be unto you! Of what use is it to a darkened house, if the lamp is put upon the roof, while within it is deserted and in darkness? So also, what shall it profit you, if the light of knowledge is on your lips, while your inward parts are a desolation, dark and empty? O ye who are in bondage to this world, ye do not act as wise men, nor as slaves who shew reverence, nor as noble freemen. It is this world which will bring you speedily to destruction."[1]

So the world makes those whom it enslaves to be teachers of evil and "Satans" among men, who subordinate the claims of the true faith to those of this fleeting world. While in this life, they are a shame and a dishonour to their creation, and in the next they will be utterly destroyed, unless the All-Compassionate forgives them by His grace. Even the pleasures of this world, by which the soul is seduced, are deceitful, for they are speedily turned into vexation and anxiety, and the soul will find its joy exhausted and the world no longer a satisfaction, while its faith has been destroyed and through the love of this transitory world it is lost both in this life and the world to come.[2] "He who loves this world and its pleasures," writes al-Muḥāsibī, "casts out the fear of the next from his heart. While you rejoice in what you gain from this world, you have lost the fear of God Most High. Yes, and perhaps you are so satisfied with your life of worldliness that your care for spiritual things has grown

[1] "Waṣāyā (Naṣā'iḥ)," fols. *4a*, *4b*. *Cf. Logia et Agrapha*, No. 53.
[2] *Ibid.*, fol. *4b*.

weak, and it may be that the burden of your sins is lighter upon you than your affliction for worldly loss. Yes, and your fear of the diminution of your wealth is twice as great as your fear of committing sin. It may be that you give away to others what you have amassed by unlawful means, in order to obtain exaltation and reputation in this world, and perhaps you are satisfied with the creatures, when God is dissatisfied with them, in order that you may be reckoned good and gain position and advantage."[1] The desire of this world is corrupting to the soul, because it is so essentially self-seeking. When the soul seeks the goods of this world, it desires that none other than itself should control them, and it is provoked to jealousy, and the passions and the sensual desires are strengthened, and the soul seeks to refuse to others the good which it desires for itself, and instead desires evil for them, and it desires to set itself above others in the world, and to be esteemed more highly than they are, and to be praised by all men and blamed by none.[2]

The true servant of God should feel a stranger and a sojourner in this world, for his real abiding place is elsewhere. " What have you to do with delight in this world ?" asks al-Muḥāsibī. "It is the prison of the believer, and he does not rejoice in it, nor find pleasure in it, nor trust to it. This world is only an abode of affliction and temptation, a place of care and sorrow, and Adam, upon whom be peace, said, ' We were begotten of God, as the offspring of Heaven, and Iblīs has taken us captive through sin.' It is not fitting for us that we should rejoice, nor meet that we should do otherwise than weep and be grieved while we are in the abode of captivity, and continue so until we return to the abode from which we were taken captive.

"O my brothers, it is a shameful thing on the part of an intelligent being that he should rejoice in any of the goods of this world, and how should he rejoice in the praise of a man who is vain and deluded ? Then understand what I say to you, O servant of God, you who are so gratified by praise. Even though your pious works were to win for you the friendship of all the birds of the heavens, and the wild beasts and the cattle and the reptiles that creep upon the

[1] Waṣāyā (Naṣā'iḥ), fol. *6b*. [2] " Ādāb al-Nufūs," fol. *86b*.

earth, and though the angels were to praise you therefor, and men and jinns were all to rejoice in your company, and were to commend your actions in all circumstances, and praise you in what you did, and you became known thereby and your righteousness was commended, of what use is it to you or any other to rely upon that? For when you come to appear before God, then you will know the truth of the matter, and know whether God is pleased or displeased with you, and this alone is of consequence to you."[1]

The love of this world leads to the amassing of wealth, in order to obtain the pleasures of this world and its beautiful things and its lusts and its delights. Nothing is more likely to make a man's good works of no effect than a life of worldliness, enjoyed in oblivion of the fact that it means deprivation of the joys of the world to come, for it leads to concupiscence and sin. Wealth is attractive also to the self because it means the assumption of superiority to others and the gaining of reputation and honour and vainglory, but the favour of this world will mean the wrath of God in the world to come. In its anxiety not to miss any of the good things of this world, the soul forgets to prepare for the world to come. The world offers no more insidious temptation than the suggestion that wealth may be accumulated for lawful purposes, such as liberal generosity for the sake of God and for the purpose of doing good works; but this is merely a Satanic stratagem to lead the soul into sin under the guise of righteousness, by acquiring wealth obtained from doubtful sources, for the doubtful is but a short distance from the unlawful. "It is better," says one theologian, "to lose a dirham out of fear lest it was not lawfully obtained, than to give away a thousand dinars in alms, from doubtful sources, of which you do not know whether they are lawful for you or not."[2] Wealth may be the fruit of oppression, and the acquiring of it may mean the deprivation of widows and orphans, of the poor and the wayfaring. The business of acquiring it means being involved in the snares of this world and in methods of doubtful morality. Therefore it is

[1] "Waṣāyā (Naṣā'iḥ)," fol. 26*a*, *b*.

[2] *Ibid.*, fol. 7*a*.

hard for the rich to enter into the Kingdom of God. al-Muḥāsibī refers in this connection to the saying of the Prophet, " The beggars among the faithful will enter Paradise five hundred years before the rich," while the rich must expect to face the bondage and the thirst of Hell.[1] Those who are preoccupied with their wealth, like the Rich Fool, have not minds and hearts at leisure for the remembrance of the life to come, for the recollection of God and His purposes, for reflection and consideration upon the end for which they were created. The worship of God is of more account than the bestowal in alms of much wealth. Even in this life, that one who is content with a bare sufficiency is saved from the anxieties which wealth brings, and finds rest for his body, freedom from fatigue and tranquillity of mind.

This enemy from without, the world with its attractions and temptations and snares, can therefore beat down the defences of the soul and, by its corrupting influence, bring about its utter destruction. " Reflect, then," says al-Muḥāsibī, " on these things, and rest assured that happiness and salvation lie in avoiding this world."[2]

There is a third enemy of the soul who attacks both from without and from within, and it is this enemy whom al-Muḥāsibī regards pre-eminently as the Adversary (*al-'adū*), Iblīs (ὁ διάβολος), the principle of deliberate evil, once an angel of God and now fallen through disobedience, for he was commanded to worship Adam, the primal man, and refused, asserting that he would worship none save God Himself, and choosing thereby to disobey the Divine command, and to judge for himself what was right and wrong, for in his own view he was superior to Adam, since his origin was of fire and Adam's origin was of clay, and jealousy made him unwilling to obey, and he is therefore the type, to Muslims, of presumptuous disobedience.[3] He is the enemy of God, the prince of this world, with a host of myrmidons to assist him in his evil purpose of bringing the souls of men to perdition. al-Muḥāsibī, in quoting the Parable of the Sower, says, " The seed is like rightly directed words

[1] *Cf.* the story of Dives and Lazarus, St. Luke xvi. 19-26.
[2] " Waṣāyā," fols. 8*a ff.*
[3] *Cf.* Sūra 7 : 10 *ff.*; " Ri'āya," fol. 108*a*.

which the wise man speaks, and what fell upon the wayside is like the man who hears the word, but does not wish to listen to it, and before long Satan snatches it out of his heart and he forgets it."[1] He acts through the senses, stirring up passion and lust, and through the imagination, deceiving men with his delusions and infusing doubts of what is right and true, and through the mind, with false arguments. Satan has many wiles in regard to the ostentatious display of knowledge and good deeds, in order that they may be imitated, and so people, led astray by him, display their knowledge and make known their good deeds, coveting the rewards of those who lead others to good, and whose deeds are imitated, and they are ignorant of the fact that all this is due to the wiles of Satan.[2] He is the father of lies, and utters falsehood by the tongues of men, in order that they may be brought to destruction. Since he did not cease to tempt Adam and Eve until he had driven them out from the presence of their Lord, who, since that time, can reckon himself safe from the enemy of God, for he brought them to perdition in an abode in which there was only one trial (the forbidden tree), and how will it be with those who live in an abode which is full of affliction and trial and temptation and misfortunes ?[3]

Yet he is but a creature and cannot compel the surrender of the will nor destroy the soul unless it gives itself up to his temptations. As Hujwīrī writes, " The devil cannot enter a man's heart unless he desires to commit a sin ; but, when a certain amount of passion appears, the devil takes it and decks it out, and displays it to the man's heart ; this is called diabolic suggestion (*waswās*). It begins from passion, and in reference to this fact, God said to Iblīs, when he threatened to seduce all mankind, ' Verily, thou hast no power over My servants,' for the devil in reality is a man's lower soul and passion."[4] al-Muḥāsibī likewise states that the Adversary cannot obtain what he desires of the human soul except through the lusts of the lower self, and it is possible to refuse his seductions and to turn away from him.[5]

But he is an enemy who must be known and fought.

[1] " Ri'āya," fol. 5*a*.

[2] " Waṣāyā (Naṣā'iḥ)," fol. 24*a*.

[3] *Ibid*., fol. 4*b* ; " Ri'āya," fol. 51*b*.

[4] *Op. cit*., p. 208.

[5] " Ri'āya," fol. 91*a*.

"Knowledge of the enemy of God, Iblīs," writes al-Muḥāsibī, "means that you should know that the All-Glorious, may He be magnified and His Names sanctified, has commanded you to fight him, and to strive against him in secret and openly, in obedience and disobedience, for you know that he defied God in regard to His servant Adam, and opposes Him, in Adam's seed. You sleep, but he does not sleep; you are unmindful of him, but he is never unmindful of you; you are heedless, but he remains heedful. He is continually striving for your destruction, seeking to bring you to perdition when you sleep and in your waking hours, in your secret self and in your outward life, in obedience, for he renders it void, and in disobedience, for he makes you fall into it. He does not cease to practise against you trickery and treachery and deceit, and to employ his seductive and delightful snares, in your times of obedience and disobedience. Of these snares many of the creatures of God are ignorant, both of the devout, who are deceived and deluded thereby, and those many creatures of His who are neglectful, and he will not rest from making you fall into disobedience and hypocrisy and pride, for his desire is that you should return with him to his dwelling-place, and that is Hell." al-Muḥāsibī bids his readers, when they have recognised Iblīs by these characteristics and the place of his abode, to let their hearts adhere to the knowledge of him, in truth and in falsehood, without any neglect or remission, fighting stubbornly and striving with the greatest vigour, secretly and openly, outwardly and inwardly, taking care not to fall short, for the Adversary is always waiting to see whom he may devour.[1] "He is the enemy of God your Master," al-Muḥāsibī reminds his fellow-servants again, "and he was the first to disobey God Most Glorious, and he is the enemy of the saints of God from among the prophets, and the sincere and the pure of heart among His creatures. And know that you are engaged in a great combat, and if you weaken or turn aside from it you will perish, and you will give the enemy of God what he desires, and he will get the better of you, and his purpose for you will have its conclusion at last in infidelity to God. And he will drag you from bad

[1] "Muḥāsabat al-Nufūs," fol. 27*b*.

to worse, until God is wroth with you and leaves you to your fate and you will perish and fall into the fires of Hell. No creature has more power against you than Iblīs; therefore beware of following his road, for the end thereof is destruction, and salvation is by the grace of God and His mercy. May God protect us and you from Iblīs and his troops, for there is no strength or power save in God, the Exalted, the Mighty."[1]

Iblīs therefore attacks the soul from without, with the snares of sensual desire and of worldly attractions; but his more insidious attack is from within, by means of diabolical suggestions (*waswās*), which, by force of unwearied repetition, may eventually break down the power of resistance. Therefore the soul must always be on its guard, and against this strong enemy it must invoke the help of One Who is stronger still.

al-Muḥāsibī, then, is fully aware of the strength and the prevalence of the temptations which beset the soul from the lusts of the self which urge it to sin, from the enticing seductions of the world, and from the snares and assaults of Iblīs. He gives a vivid account of the state of mankind generally, as it appeared to him, which is true also of the individual soul. "I saw temptations (*fitan*) as thick clouds, and the wise man bewildered therein, and I saw lust predominant, and an Adversary full of rage, and souls possessed with the love of this evil, transient life, replete with sensual desires, united with its lusts, preferring this world to the next, loving position and glory and reputation, veiled from reflection, filled with hypocrisy, and blinded to what concerns the next life."[2]

But though these temptations, insinuated by the enemies of the soul, are so varied and so continuous, al-Muḥāsibī realises that they are only temptations, permitted by God as a means of testing and trying the soul, but having no power to overcome the soul, unless the soul of its own will surrenders to them. God has said, "We have made the earth and what is therein attractive, so that We may test them, in order to see which of them is foremost in knowledge,"[3]

[1] "Muḥāsabat al-Nufūs," fol. 27*b*.
[2] "Waṣāyā (Naṣā'iḥ)," fol. 2*b*. [3] Sūra 18 : 6.

to indicate that the enticements of this life and this world are for the sake of producing good, so that in spite of these temptations His servants need not be turned aside from His service, and by their resistance may indeed be strengthened for that service. The beauties and the delights of the earth are created only that they may be used in accordance with God's will, not as an end in themselves, or, if His will requires it, that they may be renounced for His sake.[1] al-Muḥāsibī writes elsewhere to the same effect: "Know that this world altogether, in little things and great, in its sweet things and its bitter things, in its beginning and its end, in all its circumstances, is a test from God for His servants, an experience intended to arouse in them two qualities, gratitude and patience, in respect of favours received and afflictions suffered."[2]

For those who have reason to fear their own weakness, the best way to resist temptation may be to avoid it altogether; and al-Muḥāsibī deprecates deliberate entry into temptation, where it can, and ought, to be avoided. He relates the tradition according to which the Prophet said, "Paradise is compassed about by what is abhorrent, and Hell is encompassed by what is desirable, and that which brings men to Hell is the effect of desire on the soul"; and he quotes Ibn Mas'ūd's comment on this tradition: "He who raises the veil falls into what is behind it—that is, he who follows his desires does what is unlawful, and falls into the flames of Hell—but for him who refrains from raising the veil, it forms a protection and a means of concealment, and so he does not enter into what is behind it, and he who refrains from penetrating the veil which is between him and Hell will, by the mercy of God, be granted Paradise as his abode."[3] When temptation is recognised to be such, it is well to keep at a safe distance from it; wilful entry into it may mean eternal damnation hereafter. Weakness can be strengthened and power gained by cutting off everything which is known to be a cause of sin, and every temptation except where it ought to be met with and resisted as part of the soul's service to God.

[1] "Ri'āya," fol. 91*a*. [2] "Ādāb al-Nufūs," fols. 67*b ff*.
[3] "Ri'āya," fol. 12*b*.

There is the temptation which comes through the "desire of the eyes" (*shahawāt al-'ayn*), looking upon that which is unlawful, which a man knows will take him by surprise if he sits in a public place, talking with his friends ; when he knows that he will be tempted and yield, then it is better for him to give up the habit of sitting there, and keep to his house and to the mosque, and so be deprived of the opportunity for temptation, and he may thereby become morally stronger, in spite of his weakness, than the strong man who exposes himself to temptation and succumbs to it because of his exposure.[1] Again, there is the temptation to spend time with others and enter into conversation which may involve danger to a man's religion—*e.g.*, if he finds himself prone to backbiting and unseemly jests and criticism of others, then, if necessity does not oblige him to go out, he should refrain from going and so entering into a temptation to which he knows that he is likely to succumb, for if he goes without any necessity to do so, and enters into undesirable conversation, he knows that he has stretched out his hand to destruction, of set purpose, despising the command of his Lord.[2]

Evil companionship, whether liable to lead to conversation on what is displeasing to God or to action which is contrary to His law, is to be avoided as an unnecessary temptation, and fellow-Muslims are not to be regarded as "brethren in God" if such is the effect of association with them. "How can he be a brother in God," al-Muḥāsibī asks, "and a companion in God, through whom, and on whose account, God is disobeyed? Who can be more injurious to your faith than he who is the cause of disobedience to God?" Such companions, even if called by the name of the faithful, are rather the enemies of God. The companion of an evil man was compared by the Prophet to the companion of the smith's bellows, who will be burned by the

[1] "Ri'āya," fol. 85*a* ; "Ādab al-Nufūs," fol. 68*b*.

[2] "Ri'āya," fol. 85*b*. *Cf.* L. Blosius: "If a servant of God takes delight in unnecessary intercourse with men: if he is intolerant of silence: if, without restraint, he desires to see this or that: if he eagerly inquires what is said and done, and willingly listens to idle reports and news, it is useless for him to propose to himself to rise to even the lowest degree of a more holy life" (*Spiritual Instruction*, cap. ii., sect. 3).

sparks which it blows upon him. Such temptation comes rather from a friend than from an enemy. Men can be divided into four classes: the man whom you do not know or with whom you do not associate, the man who is a heretic, the man who is a notorious evil-doer, and the man who is intimate with you and with whom you associate. With the heretic and the evil-doer you have no concern, and you will not engage in conversation with them. So also with those with whom you do not associate or do not know, you do not talk with them and are not tempted by them, for you ignore them. But with your friend, of your own type, who is your intimate, in whose company you take pleasure, with him you are heedless and you forget the claims of God and fall into sin because of his evil companionship, and this is one of the wiles of Iblīs, by which he tempts you to fall into his snares. Just as the hunter, when he sets snares to catch birds, does not attempt to deceive them by what is strange to them, but uses a decoy-bird who is one of themselves, and the birds, being accustomed to it, approach the snare, and through that bird are caught: so also Iblīs, knowing that a man avoids heretics and evil-doers, and is not intimate with people at large, moves a man's heart to associate and converse with his friends, so that caution may depart from him, and these companions, even when they are talking together of religion and the things of God, become heedless and fall into Satan's snare and are insensibly led on into what is sinful.[1]

For there is no evil companionship so dangerous as that of the friend who is given to the observance of ritual prayer and fasting, and the undertaking of warfare against the enemies of God, and going on pilgrimage, who yet does not fear God, for his conversation and his friendship are certain to lead to what is displeasing to God and unwholesome for his fellow. "He is like a friend of yours," says al-Muḥāsibī, "who is rich and wants for nothing, while you are poor and in need, and whenever he comes to you he consumes your food, while he does not use any of his wealth to shew hospitality to you. So also an evil companion takes your righteousness from you and gives you no good in exchange.

[1] "Ri'āya," fols. 85*b* *ff*.

The Adversary sees to it that, even if you begin by talking about what is pleasing to God, you end by discussing what is abhorrent to Him." So again al-Muḥāsibī urges the wisdom of avoiding temptation, for he who thinks he is strong, when temptation is presented, proves to be weaker than the weak man who is on his guard against temptation, and has abandoned all that would lead him into it. For those whose tongues lead them astray, who delight in talking, and who find conversation a temptation and a snare, al-Muḥāsibī counsels silence, unless the occasion calls for admonition for the sake of another, when silence would be ungenerous.[1]

But whether temptation is avoided, or whether it is unavoidable and must be faced, it calls for wariness (*ḥadhr*) and unceasing vigilance (*yayqaẓ*), and the soul needs to be constantly on its guard, lest it be taken by surprise and the suddenness of the attack should mean defeat. The temptation is, after all, only a suggestion (*waswās*), a thought which occurs to the mind (*khaṭra*), and the soul which is on its guard will repel it at this stage, for it comes from outside, and as such the soul has no responsibility for its occurrence. The suggestions of Satan have no significance in themselves, except that the acceptance of them is forbidden and they are to be avoided and rejected; and if these suggestions, which may lead to what is grave and of importance, are cut off while they are weak and ineffective, the man is saved from sin. What is from the enemy, but not accepted, can do no harm.[2] So also the Eastern Syrian monk and mystic Dādīsho' Qaṭrāya, in his book on "Solitude," writes, "Whenever the demons stir in your heart a thought of passion, wrath, vainglory or any other sinful feeling, do not yield to them, do not move with them, and do not allow them to enter into your heart and make it feel worldly pleasure; but while quickly remembering the delight prepared for you by our Lord, spit on that evanescent pleasure, and close the eyes of your mind, so that it may not look at that demoniacal thought. Coerce your soul to flee from sin, however much its pleasure attracts you, and move in your thought to-

[1] "Ri'āya," fol. 88*a*; "Masā'il fī A'māl," fol. 131*b*.
[2] "Ri'āya," fol. 48*b*.

wards your Lord and implore His help, which will give you victory."[1]

But, if temptation is not rejected at once, the self's natural propensity towards what is evil causes it to find the suggestion sweet and to respond to it. Even at this stage the soul which has the self well under control can cut short its pleasure and renounce the temptation, without being involved in sin. But when there is a conscious and willing acceptance of the temptation, then the soul has indeed fallen into sin, for the action of the will is under its own control. "Your pleasure in the sweetness of sweet food," says al-Muḥāsibī, "you find only in the eating of it. The pleasure of lust and sensuality is in the thought and pursuit of it, and the pleasure of hypocrisy is in the infection of the heart by it, therefore it is necessary to make the will sound and in all action to contemplate God alone."[2] It is possible to know whether temptation has been definitely rejected, or whether the soul is still dallying with it. If there is satisfaction and peace of mind in refusing to sin and renouncing the temptation, then the soul is sincere and free from desire and hypocrisy; but if the soul is averse to rejecting the temptation, then it has still a desire for it and is not safe from sin.[3]

But when the soul is continually on its guard to repel temptation as it arises, then temptation can strengthen the soul, humbling it and purifying it, and so become a means of spiritual progress. By refusing the enticements of the self and the temptations of the Adversary, the soul may be brought near to God, and so even the snares of Iblīs may serve the purposes of God. "You were preserved from him," al-Muḥāsibī writes, "because of your fear of God and your hope of His reward, and when your soul refused to adhere to this world, you approached nearer to God because of its enticements, for you were tested by means of this world and its vanities, and you did not cleave unto it, but you sought the world to come, and so you remained obedient in all to which you were tempted." To such a one temptations lose their power, he has attained to a pure heart, "which desires do not seduce, nor the delights of what is unlawful,

[1] *Early Christian Mystics*, p. 102. [2] "Ādāb al-Nufūs," fol. 89*b*.
[3] *Ibid.*, fol. 90*b*.

nor do sins pursue him, nor does blindness dull his heart, nor does hardness take possession of him; and the observance of what is due to God and abiding therein is easier for such a one, and temptation is lighter to him and the claims of the self are fewer and have less force, because his heart is pure." It is of such as these, who have come forth purified by temptation, that God speaks when He says, "Those who strive for Our sake, into Our ways We will guide"; and again, "Those who followed the right road, to them was guidance increased, and they were taught what to fear."[1] This is he who "keeps pace with his sins, taking refuge in the mercy of his Lord, striving to the utmost, seeking until he finds Him and is safe."[2]

[1] "Riʿāya," fols. 11*b ff.*; Sūras 29: 69; 47: 1.

[2] "Riʿāya," fol. 12*a*. *Cf.* St. Francis de Sales: "As soon as you feel within you any temptations, do as little children do when they see a wolf or a bear in the fields, for immediately they run to the arms of their father and mother, or at least call them to their help and assistance. Have recourse in like manner to God, entreating His mercy and His aid" (*Introduction to the Devout Life*, p. 252).

CHAPTER VIII

THE ASCETIC THEOLOGY OF AL-MUḤĀSIBĪ: II. SIN—MORTAL AND VENIAL SINS—THE CAPITAL SINS

SIN, then, in al-Muḥāsibī's view, is a deliberate thwarting of the Divine purpose, according to which man was created to serve God and to do His will, and the end of sin is separation from God and spiritual death. "Know, O my brother," he writes, "that sins produce heedlessness (*ghafla*)—that is, the sinner is forgetful of God and His law—and heedlessness produces hardness of heart, and hardness of heart leads to alienation from God, and alienation from God leads to Hell."[1] There is hardly a day in a man's life, he feels, in which he is not guilty of some sin of commission or omission, of the "members" or the heart, and outward piety is no proof of freedom from sin. "Most of the devout men of our time," he writes, "are heedless, self-deluded. We reckon ourselves among those who lead an austere and pious life, and it may be that in the sight of God we are among the wicked and the sinners. How can we believe that we are righteous, when not a day comes upon us but we purpose fresh sins, which we have not committed before, and we add them to our past sins, sins of the members and sins of the heart, pride and envy and malevolence and evil supposition and other sins beside? Every day of our lives we add new sins to the sins of yesterday, and increase our liability to judgment. The very first sin which we commit, consciously and deliberately, renders us guilty in the sight of God, and every sin committed thereafter increases our guilt. Then, O my brother, let godliness (*taqwā*) be your chief concern, for it is your capital stock, and works of supererogation beyond that represent your profit. There is no merchant so heedless, nor any man wise and sound in judgment, who reckons that he has made a profit, without having secured his capital."[2] Sin, then, is closely linked with

[1] "Kitāb al-Mustarshid," fol. 7.

[2] "Riʿāya," fol. 8*b*.

forgetfulness of what is due to God, while godly fear will help a man to continual remembrance of the Divine Will and avoidance of sin. Blessed are those who are anxious and concerned about the life to come; and blessed is the work of self-examination by one who reckons the hour which includes no anxiety or grief (on account of sin) or self-examination, to be wasted. With such a one, there is as little negligence as there is much sin in the case of another who ignores these things.[1]

al-Muḥāsibī, like other theologians, distinguishes between two classes of sins, that which is a conscious transgression of the Will of God in a grave matter, which is a cause of separation from God, and in the end, if not repented of, must lead to exclusion from His presence and being left in outer darkness, and this is Mortal Sin. There is also the type of sin which concerns more trivial matters, to which even the faithful believer is constantly tempted in his daily life, which involves guilt indeed, since it is entered upon by the conscious action of the will, but not separation from God, if repented of and not persisted in; this is Venial Sin. "All sins," writes al-Muḥāsibī, "are of two classes, small (*saghīra*) and great (*kabīra*). The great sins are of two types, those which are between you and God, without consequences to the creatures, and those which also affect your fellow-creatures, and the lesser sins are those on which the servant resolves and in which he abides (*i.e.*, when the temptation appears pleasant to him, he dallies with it, instead of repulsing it)."[2] Some Muslim theologians asserted that the mortal sins were seven in number, and others that they were seventy, and these included such sins as suicide and adultery and theft and destruction of the faith, disobedience to parents, the robbing of orphans, lying, the following after lust, and taking the name of God in vain, and despairing of His mercy. al-Muḥāsibī himself holds that all which God penalises with Hell is to be regarded as a mortal sin, but stubborn persistence in venial sin is itself a deadly sin,[3] and no sin is venial if it is combined with contumacy,

[1] "Ādāb al-Nufūs," fol. 83*b*.
[2] "Kitāb al-Tawba," fols. 13*b*, 14*b*.
[3] *Ibid*., fols. 15*b ff*.; "Waṣāyā (Naṣā'iḥ)," fol. 13*a*.

for obstinate persistence in sin is infidelity and rebellion against God. A man who ignores the importance of venial sins becomes involved in mortal sin. So also Thomas â Kempis notes, "He that escheweth not small faults, little and little shall slide into greater."[1] On the other hand, a grave sin ceases to be mortal if the sinner repents and prays for forgiveness. "He who commits mortal sin and then repents is nearer to forgiveness than he who stubbornly persists in venial sin."[2] Both types of sin involve guilt in the sight of God, and for both repentance is obligatory.

al-Muḥāsibī realises that sin may be in word and in deed, and includes sins of commission and omission, but he lays most stress on the secret sins of the heart, the sins of thought and imagination, which corrupt the intention and may result in wrong action, so defiling the man both inwardly and outwardly. Among the sins of the heart are not only the capital sins of hypocrisy and pride in all its forms, but also preference of the rich and deference towards them, and avoidance of the poor and their company, and the breaking of a compact, and treachery and fraud. Among the sins of the heart are jealousy, and secret hatred and contempt, and rejoicing in evil, and enmity, and evil suspicions, and a prying spirit, and lending countenance to lust, and opposition to what is right. The sins of the heart include also vanity and hardness of heart and lack of godliness, and greed and gluttony and covetousness and irreverence, and insolence and worldliness and ingratitude to God for His gifts.[3] "You will not attain (to the conquest of sin)," writes al-Muḥāsibī, "except by a sound purpose and a firm intention to combat desire, and by controlling your inward self, for if the servant controls his inward self, he dominates his members and he has knowledge of his own heart, and self-examination and other means of opposing the self in what she desires become easy to him, by the leave of God Most High; but if you lose control of your inward self, God's command will seem hard to you, and your members will go astray and your heart will be lost, and you will not be aware of it, and will find yourself unfit

[1] *De Imitatione*, I., cap. 25.
[2] "Waṣāyā (Naṣā'iḥ)," fols. 13*a*, 31*b*; "Kitāb al-Tawba," fol. 18*b*.
[3] "Waṣāyā (Naṣā'iḥ,)" fol. 31*a*.

for self-examination. Then keep to what is lawful, control your tongue except in what will aid you in approaching God Most High, guard also your hearing and your sight and consider in what you sin and for what you sin."[1] Again he says, " Fear the sins of the heart, and search out its hidden faults and the basic principles of its sins, and the evil of its inmost parts and the subtilties of its sensual desires and the secrets of its lusts, then strive to expel what is opposed to the good pleasure of God Most High from your hearts, for when you are delivered from the sins of the heart, then you are saved from the punishment of God Most High."[2]

al-Muḥāsibī deals in considerable detail with certain capital sins or root-principles, which give rise to sin in its various forms, sin which may be mortal or venial, according to the circumstances. Since the intention is the well-spring of action, and if that is defiled all that arises from it will be defiled also, he lays great stress on the capital sin of hypocrisy (*riyā'*), against which much of the teaching of the " Riʿāya " and of other works is directed. It is, of course, one of the " secret sins " of the heart, and often the sinner is self-deluded and hardly realises his hypocrisy. Hypocrisy means that the state of the heart, in its intention and desires, does not correspond to the virtue of the outward act; it is the desire for something beside God, in serving Him, and the desire to gain something from men by that service to God ; it is to do an action, outwardly for the glory of God, but with the intention of having glory of men. The Prophet had said, " The thing most to be feared for my community is hypocrisy and secret desire." If a man is not heedful of the direction of his secret desires, they will corrupt his service of God. As Wahb b. Munabbih said, " Secret desires in the heart are like a secret fire in the midst of a pile of aloes wood ; if the wood is perforated, the fire will be revealed, and if the wood is left untouched, the fire remains hidden. Hypocrisy, in its most open form, is falsehood, and in its most hidden form it is guile. It is hidden from him who is neglectful and is manifest to him who searches for it

[1] " Muḥāsabat al-Nufūs," fol. 5.
[2] " Waṣāyā (Naṣā'iḥ)," fol. 31*b*.

with understanding knowledge, and he who knows the gravity of his need of it cleaves to sincerity, out of fear of hypocrisy."

No action will be reckoned acceptable on the Day of Resurrection, if it was done with the desire for anything save the glory of God and the accomplishment of His Will. As no man will take bad money, which is liable to be rejected, when he goes on pilgrimage, but takes only what is current and valid, because he knows that it will be required for the needs of an arduous journey and for assistance to fellow-pilgrims, and he fears to find himself stranded without help, and he therefore rejects all that is spurious or doubtful, so also the wise man fears that death may come hastily upon him and he will be faced with the Day of Reckoning, and then his work may be made void through hypocrisy, and his evil deeds be found to outweigh the good, and so the fear of hypocrisy and the desire to avoid it will predominate in his heart.[1] Hypocrisy means that in carrying out the command of God the servant is really considering the wishes of men. It is a thing more difficult to discern than the creeping of the ant, and it takes varied forms. In one man, who reads much in the Word of God, it is the desire to have it said, "Such a one is learned." In another, who goes forth to battle for the sake of God, it is the wish that it should be said of him, "So and so is brave"; and in that one who gives away much in charity, the desire that men should say, "How generous he is!" It was of such hypocrites as these that the Prophet said, "They will be the first to enter Hell-fire." When the angels extol the work of such a servant, God will say, "This servant of Mine was not contemplating Me in what he did, his abode is in the seventh Hell."[2]

Hypocrisy is always due to desire, either the desire to please men, by what appears to be service to God, which is the worst form, or such a desire mingled also with the desire for the reward of God, and this latter represents polytheism in desire, for while the first type of hypocrite is at least single-minded in that he seeks men and not God, the second type is a polytheist in what he does, seeking both the praise of the creatures and the praise of God. Hypocrisy,

[1] "Riʿāya," fols. 40*a ff*. [2] *Ibid.*, fols. 42*a*, 46*a* (Broussa).

therefore, is a lesser form of polytheism, and, according to the Word of God, no good work will be accepted in which there is the weight of a grain of polytheism.[1]

What causes hypocrisy to arise in the heart is the love of praise and the fear of blame and abasement in this world, and the desire therein for the gifts of men, and the proof of such hypocrisy is the servant's discovery within himself that he likes the pious to know of his service to God, and that he loves to be praised and made much of, and hates to be blamed, and he does service to God, lest he should be blamed for his lack of desire for it.[2]

al-Muḥāsibī's illustrations of the various ways in which hypocrisy corrupts men's actions shew a shrewd knowledge of human nature, and may also be based upon his own personal experience of the insidious temptation to this form of sin. He speaks of the man who goes into battle, and when those braver than himself are placed in the front line and are sent forward to the attack, he knows that he will receive no praise, since he has not been selected for the post of danger, and he would like to withdraw altogether, since he has no taste for warfare that brings him no personal glory; but he fears lest men should say, "How cowardly he is!" and so he restrains himself and remains unwillingly, lest he should be blamed for cowardice, though in truth he has no desire to risk himself, and would like to escape.

So also the man who associates with the rich and generous. He has no desire to give alms himself, but he fears to be charged with avarice, and so gives as grudgingly as possible, to avoid being blamed for lack of generosity.

There is also the man who neglects the prescribed prayers by night and by day, who finds himself in company with one who is much more devout than he is, and he fears lest his companion should accuse him of sloth, so he prays two *rak'as* (inclinations in prayer) or several, because he does not want to be considered neglectful or to be blamed.

Another example is that of the man who has acquired a little knowledge of his religion, so that if he is asked about it he will not incur blame for ignorance, and his dread of blame drives him to lying, until he claims that he has written

[1] "Ri'āya," fol. 42*b*. [2] *Ibid.*, fol. 43*a*.

on theology what he has not written, and if he is asked about some problem he will give a decision (*fatwā*), without having any knowledge of the matter, and knowing that he is ignorant about it, and it would be more fitting for him to acknowledge that he does not know.[1]

There is the type of hypocrisy which leads those whom it affects to be men-pleasers, anxious that their good works should be seen by one from whom they hope for favour and reward, desiring that such a one may shew them kindness for the sake of their devotion to God, and may bestow on them gifts, and they know that such a one would be repelled by their sins if he knew of them, so they affect righteousness, in order to profit by it. Such a hypocrite will practise abstinence and restraint in speech, and be punctilious in fulfilling his agreements, in order that he may be approved and regarded as reliable, and so he may be selected for future favour. In such a case the capital sin of covetousness (*ṭamaʿ*) is joined with hypocrisy, and the man is doubly defiled.[2] Of the folly as well as the sinfulness of covetousness, al-Muḥāsibī observes that a man cannot obtain anything from the hands of his fellow-men which God has not decreed for him, and what he does obtain is what was ordained, and had he served his Lord with sincerity he would still have obtained it, but through his hypocrisy his service has been rendered void and he is exposed to the wrath of his Lord, and he has gained nothing either in this world or the world to come.[3]

al-Muḥāsibī has something to say also of those whose hypocrisy is shewn in the outward appearance, not only of action, but of clothing and physical aspect—*e.g.*, those who display hollow eyes and parched lips, and speak in low tones, to give an indication that they are fasting—and he quotes traditional words of Christ, " If one of you fasts, let him anoint his head and comb his hair and put collyrium on his eyes,"[4] lest he should appear unto men to fast. al-Muḥāsibī condemns equally those who wear rough clothing and patched shoes, appearing with dishevelled hair and disregard of convention, in order to display their devotion to

[1] " Riʿāya," fols. 43*b ff.*
[2] *Ibid.*, fol. 44*a*.
[3] *Ibid.*, fol. 45*a*.
[4] *Cf.* St. Matt. vi. 16-18.

the religious life, and on the other hand, those who profess to be religious, and wear rich garments, which they gird up after the manner of devotees, and expensive shoes such as are not commonly worn, who try to imitate both the religious and the worldlings and to win the commendation of both. Such, too, is the man who lengthens out his prayers, and prolongs his meditations and his genuflections and prostrations and the appearance of humility therein, who walks with bent head and downcast eyes, so long as he is seen of men, and who refrains from all this show of religion when he is alone.[1] al-Muḥāsibī declares that the one who may expect the severest reprobation at the Last Judgment will be he who dissembled with men, professing himself to be righteous, when there was no righteousness in him.[2]

A capital sin which is the cause of many others, and one which may lead to hypocrisy also, is pride, and with this al-Muḥāsibī deals at great length, and firstly in the form of self-esteem, conceit (*'ujb*), its most dangerous form, since it means giving to self the place which should be given to God, that inordinate love of self which leads the soul to rebellion against God, setting itself up in presumptuous defiance of His law, forgetting the relation of the creature to the Creator.[3] It is a form of corruption found in many pious men, which blinds them to their sins and makes sin and error attractive to them, for self-conceit blinds the heart, and makes it see what it desires as admirable when it is poisonous, and thinks that to be a cause

[1] "Ri'āya," fols. 46*b*, 47*a*. [2] "Waṣāyā (Naṣā'iḥ)," fol. 12*a*.

[3] *Cf.* J. Maréchal: "The 'proud Ego' is that which sets itself up as the absolute end of personal action . . . this pride is the precise negation of the creature's natural dependence, in its being and its end in relation to God . . . it is a meaningless claim to erect the finite and relative into an unconditioned and absolute . . . the 'proud Ego' turning the whole finality of its action back upon itself, arbitrarily restrains the becoming of the soul; the latter, indeed, must know no other limit to its fundamental striving than the possession of the unlimited Good and participation in the uncircumscribed Unity. The 'proud Ego' displaces the natural polarity of the mind in a downward direction" (*op. cit.*, p. 166). So also F. von Hügel: "The central, most heinous sin . . . is Pride and Self-sufficiency" (*The Life of Prayer*, p. 50).

of salvation when it is a cause of destruction, and productive of good fortune when it is a cause of sin. Pride destroys those whom it leads into error through their self-esteem, and they become puffed up, and those who are arrogant are insolent, and those who are deceived by pride deceive in their turn, and so it leads to the ruin not of one but of many.[1] When a man is proud, he pays little attention to his religion, and the only attention he pays to his sins is to make little of them, and he sees no need for repentance or fear, and so he abides in his sins and perishes therein. Pride makes him justify himself in what he desires and what he does, and therefore he ceases to oppose the lower self in its disobedience to the Will of God. Yet he supposes that he is one who does righteousness, when in the sight of God he is a wrongdoer and a sinner. 'Ā'isha, the wife of the Prophet, when asked, "When is a man a sinner?" replied, "When he supposes that he is righteous," and al-Muḥāsibī approves her answer.[2]

Spiritual pride—*i.e.*, pride in religion—he considers to be displayed in regard to action, knowledge, opinion and purpose, and the significance of it in the first three is one and the same thing, for good works, knowledge and right opinion are all from God, and are the gift of His grace, and these have their origin in Him. But pride leads to conceit and self-esteem on account of these things, and the servant is proud of them, and makes much of God's favour to him and His gifts bestowed on him, and so shews himself unworthy of God's grace, and cuts off from himself any claim to God's reward in the life to come. al-Muḥāsibī imagines that at this point he is asked by his disciple, "How is it possible that I should not attribute anything of this to myself, since that good work cannot be done apart from me, and if I did not know that I was the one who did it, I could not believe that it was by the grace of God nor hope for a reward from God?" And he replies that pride consists not in realising that he was the one who did or knew any particular thing, but in attributing to himself praise on that account, and forgetting that he was enabled to do it only by the Divine grace: if he remembered that, he would not be

[1] "Ri'āya," fol. 94*a*. [2] *Ibid.*, fol. 94*b*.

proud.[1] Moreover, thanks to his lack of goodwill, what he accomplishes is far less than he might do if his will were entirely surrendered to the Divine Will. How little reason, then, has man to be proud of his works. "Beware of pride in what you do," al-Muḥāsibī warns his reader, "and of making much of it before your Lord, for all your good works do not represent fitting gratitude for a single one of the benefits bestowed on you by your Lord. Moreover, the inspiration to your good works, such as they are, is a gift bestowed on you by God, and ever renewed by Him, and when are you sufficiently grateful for them? And, further, if you realised the greatness of God, and His might and His majesty, and of what He is worthy, you would feel ashamed to mention your works, for the good works of the whole creation are less than one of His gifts."[2]

David sinned through spiritual pride when he said, "O Lord, not an hour passes, of the night or of the day, but some worshipper of the house of David is serving Thee, either in prayer or fasting or in giving praise to Thee," and he attributed that to himself and took pride in it. But God said unto him, "O David, that has not come about except through Me, and but for My help you could not have attained to it, and therefore I will make you mean in your own sight." So David repented of his sin.[3] Such pride is presumption (*idlāl*), which makes a man think himself to be of great worth in the sight of God, and deserving of a reward for his good works. So a tradition relates that the prayer of the presumptuous does not rise higher than his own head. As for pride in opinion, it is sinful enough if it is pride in a right opinion, since it sets up the self above God; but pride in a wrong opinion is worse, for it leads to error and infidelity and falsehood against God Most High: it is the sin of the heretics, and if they had not been proud of their opinions, they would never have adhered to heresy. It was pride in a wrong opinion which brought to destruction most of the infidels and the heretics among the people of Islām.

There is also personal pride, vanity, which is pride in

[1] "Riʿāya," fols. 95*a*, 95*b*. [2] "Waṣāyā (Naṣāʾiḥ)," fol. 12*b*.
[3] "Riʿāya," fol. 96*a*.

beauty and good looks, and in the body, in its proportions and perfection and strength, and in the intellect, and in action, and in beauty of voice. It is self-satisfaction on account of these things, and forgetfulness of what is due of gratitude to God for His gift of these, forgetting for what purpose these were created and how they have been perverted, when beauty and good looks are employed for what is perishable and evil, and so the owner of them becomes proud and presumptuous, and through his beauty is exposed to evil and exalts himself over others.[1] So also pride in intellect and sagacity and power of perception leads to self-esteem on account of them, and forgetfulness of Him Who bestowed them, and so the servant abandons trust in God, neglects to ascertain the truth of the knowledge he acquires, and depends upon his own intellect, and this leads him to neglect the search for the gnosis which is the gift of God. Wahb b. Munabbih said, "Knowledge (*'ilm*) is like the rain, which descends from heaven, sweet and pure, and the trees absorb it by means of their roots, and change it according to the flavour of their fruits; if the fruit is bitter, it increases its bitterness, and if sweet, its sweetness, and so also knowledge, which men acquire and change according to their capacity for it and their desire for it. It increases the pride of the haughty man, for when he is ignorant, and then studies, he finds knowledge of which he is proud, and it increases his pride. But if a man is ignorant and God-fearing, and then gains knowledge, his fear of God is increased, and also his humility and submissiveness."[2] Such pride leads a man also to despise others, and especially those who serve God more faithfully, and he calls attention to their ignorance and folly and makes them appear to be asses, in comparison with his powers of perception and sagacity.[3]

Then there is pride of birth, which makes a man think highly of himself because of his forebears and his family, and he is proud because they were of noble birth and accounted honourable in this world, and he thinks much of himself on their account, and forgets that it was by the grace of his Lord that he was born of such a stock and not of the

[1] "Ri'āya," fol. 101*a*. [2] *Ibid.*, fol. 109*a*.

[3] *Ibid.*, fol. 101*b*.

common people. He magnifies himself to such an extent that he even believes, if his forebears were among the saints of God who served Him faithfully, that, on their account, he will be saved, without works, and be forgiven, though his sins are many and he has not repented of them. This pride of birth leads on to contempt of others, so that such a one regards others as slaves for his service, and he errs greatly in regard to God and is ignorant of His Will.[1]

Akin to this is pride in wealth, which makes much of it and relies upon it, and al-Muḥāsibī in this connection relates a tradition of Abū Dharr,[2] who said, "I was with the Prophet, and as he entered the mosque he said to me: 'O Abū Dharr, raise your head and see which you consider to be the man of most account in the mosque,' and I raised my head, and there was a man conspicuous by his fine clothes, and I said, 'This man.' Then he said, 'O Abū Dharr, bend your head and see who is the man of least account whom you see in the mosque,' and I looked, and there was a man wearing a threadbare garment, and I said, 'This man,' and the Prophet said, 'O Abū Dharr, this man, in the sight of God, is better than a whole world full of such as that other, for none is exalted in the sight of God, except through obedience, neither by wealth nor by anything.'" So none is justified in being proud of wealth or family, and therefore despising the poor. It was related also of the Prophet that he saw a rich man, who drew his garments round him, lest the garments of a poor man should touch him, and the Prophet said to him, "Were you afraid lest his poverty should shew hostility to your riches?"[3]

Pride in the form of arrogance (*kibr*) is a great defect, which leads to much evil and the wrath of God, for greatness, as al-Muḥāsibī reminds his readers, belongs by rights only to Him, and it is not fitting or good for any below Him, since everything except Him is a creature, under dominion, and He alone is the King, God Almighty, and this is a sin great in the sight of God, since greatness befits none save Him, and when the servant aspires to what is not fitting

[1] "Riʿāya," fols. 102*a*, 102*b*.
[2] A companion of the Prophet, famed for his asceticism.
[3] "Riʿāya," fols. 104*a ff*.

except for the Master, the Master is wroth with him. Did not God Most High say, "Greatness is My mantle, and majesty My veil, and he who snatches from Me either one of them will be cast into Hell"? And chastisement is well deserved by the arrogant man, for he has exceeded his place and arrogated to himself what was not fitting for him and not allowable for the creature.[1] It was related of Christ that He said, "The seed grows only in soft soil, it does not grow in rocky ground, so also wisdom dwells in the humble heart, and finds no abiding place in the heart of the proud."

"Will you not consider," asks al-Muḥāsibī, "that he who exalts his head to the ceiling cracks it, and he who bends it low protects and preserves it?" There was also a tradition related by Mālik b. Dīnār, to the effect that Solomon once said to the wind, "Carry us aloft," and it carried the king and his companions aloft until they heard the songs of the angels, singing "Holy, Holy, Holy." Then Solomon said to it, "Bear us down," and it wafted them down, until their feet touched the earth again, and lo, they heard the voice of a herald, who cried from Ḥeaven, "God has declared, 'If I knew that in the heart of your master was the weight of a grain of mustard-seed of arrogance, I would have flung him down farther than I raised him up.'"[2] This arrogance is seen under two aspects, the greater of which is that presumption displayed by the servant in relation to his Lord, and the other is that displayed by the servant towards his fellow-servants. The former disdains to bow his head in worship before Him Whom even the angels serve, and the latter despises and disdains his fellow-creatures, supposing himself to be better than his brother. But the claim to be better than his brother will involve him in the greater condemnation, for of him to whom much is given much will be required, and of him to whom little is given little will be required. The arrogant man should remember the man to whom it was said, "You are of worth, so long as you consider yourself worthless, but if you consider yourself to be of worth, then you are worthless in the sight of God"; and this is so because if a man is arrogant

[1] "Riʿāya," fols. 105*a*, 105*b*. Tradition of Abū Hurayra.
[2] *Ibid.*, fol. 106*b*.

God will humble him and bring him low, but when a man is humble, then he is precious in the sight of God.[1] Even towards heretics and infidels and polytheists, it is not well that a man should feel arrogance, on the ground that he is going to be saved and they will perish everlastingly, for he has no knowledge of what will come to pass, either for himself or for them. It may be that neither he nor the infidel will be forgiven and both will enter Gehenna together, or it may be that the arrogant man will pass in alone and the infidel will be forgiven by his Lord.

One of the evil products of pride is contention for superiority (*mubāhāt*). Of this sin al-Muḥāsibī notes that it may have reference to knowledge or action. That one who seeks for superiority in knowledge gives much time to study and to discussion, and is always ready to answer when questions are asked of himself or another. He loves to be proved to be right, so that he may be magnified, and his superiority may be known, and others may realise that he is more learned and more ready in recalling traditions, and if a friend of his relates a tradition he states that he also knows it, contending thus for superiority. In regard to action, he forgathers with others for the worship of God, or he undertakes the Holy War for the sake of God, or does some act of piety; and if another prays he rises up to pray also, anxious to be regarded as superior, and that his merit may be seen; and if he is praying with another he prolongs his own prayer, so that his companion may grow tired and become wearied and may cease to pray, and he himself will be seen to be superior, and be raised in status above his companion. So also in battle, he is anxious to take precedence of others, and that they should remain behind, so that he may be praised for his zeal in attacking the enemy, and so his superiority to others will be manifested; but it may be, comments al-Muḥāsibī, that he will be rejected on this account and his works rendered void, and he will not be safe from the wrath of God.[2]

Closely allied with this striving for superiority is boasting (*tafākhur*), which leads a man to decry the knowledge and learning of another and to boast of his own. So also he

[1] "Ri'āya," fol. 117*a*. [2] *Ibid.*, fol. 59*b*.

speaks with contempt of the poverty of others and their lack of property or profit, and glories in the fact that he is richer and more prosperous. In regard to warfare, he says, "You were not among the horsemen, nor among those who were foremost in the attack (as I was), you were faint-hearted and unwilling for the fight." He inquires from others how many of the traditions they have committed to memory, and how many of the great Shaykhs they have been privileged to meet, and how many theologians have they known, and to what extent were they marked out for distinction, and then he proceeds to recount the story of his own precedence in these respects, and sometimes he has not even any foundation for his statements about himself.[1]

These odious characteristics are the result not only of pride, but of envy (*ḥasad*), and al-Muḥāsibī deals also with this capital sin, which itself arises from greed, excessive desire (*ṭama'*). Emulation, al-Muḥāsibī considers, may be lawful in certain circumstances, while in other circumstances it becomes envy and is unlawful and a sin. The emulation (*munāfasa*) which seeks to equal others in what is good is commendable, as God commended those who competed with one another for His forgiveness for their sins.[2] So also two who serve an earthly master vie with one another in his presence, fearing lest one may gain more favour in his master's eyes, and the other fall short. So one strives to outstrip his fellow in prompt and acceptable service, in order that his master may look upon his service and he may find favour in his sight. So it is with those who seek to compete with one another in doing what is well pleasing in the sight of God, doing it only for His sake, without regard to the creatures. It is fitting, too, that the servant of God should emulate the blessed state of His saints, not grudging them the high station to which they have attained, but grieving because he himself falls short of it. The lack of such emulation in well-doing is indeed a sin of omission.[3]

But the envy which is jealousy, which involves the hatred of good for others, and the wish that they should be deprived of it, which leads to rejoicing in another's misfortune, is a

[1] "Ri'āya," fol. 60*a*. [2] Sūra 57 : 21. *Cf.* Sūra 83 : 26.
[3] "Ri'āya," fols. 138*a ff*.

capital sin against one's fellow-men. Through jealousy the son of Adam (Cain) slew his brother,[1] and jealousy was the first sin by which God was disobeyed in Heaven (*cf.* p. 119 above), and the first sin whereby He was disobeyed on earth, for Adam and Eve were jealous of that which belonged to the angels.[2] This, too, was the sin of Joseph's brethren. It may arise from arrogance, or self-conceit, or enmity, or hatred, or love of dignity and domination, and unwillingness that another should possess any good thing, whether material or spiritual, which the jealous do not themselves possess. So there is jealousy between believers; one is led to slander another lest he should be esteemed above himself, and he wishes that God would withdraw the veil from that other's sins, so that they would be manifest in the sight of men, and his reputation as a righteous man be destroyed. There is also jealousy in friendship, when two compete for the favours of a mutual friend, and one tries to poison his mind against the other, so that the coveted friendship shall be given to himself alone. So envy and jealousy lead to hatred and to joy in evil, and thence may come oppression and deprivation and even murder.

So, too, in trade and industry, jealousy leads one merchant or craftsman to compete for the business of another, and to undersell him or outbid him. And it is of their neighbours and those nearest to them that men are most jealous; a prophet is given no honour in his own country, but if a stranger with a reputation comes from afar, men are not jealous of him, because he does not compete with them nor compare with them. But jealousy injures the jealous man more than those of whom he is jealous, for it cannot transfer to him their good qualities, and it may bring about his own perdition; the injury that he seeks to do to another recoils upon himself, as when a man casts a stone at his enemy and the stone fails to reach his enemy, but rebounds and strikes him in the eye. Such a misfortune, al-Muḥāsibī observes, would be better for a man than that he should be possessed by jealousy, for the loss of an eye in this world matters

[1] *Cf.* 1 John iii. 12, "And wherefore slew he him? Because his own works were evil and his brother's righteous."

[2] Sūra 8 : 19.

nothing after death, but jealousy remains to bring upon him who harbours it the wrath of God, for it means that he grudges the grace of God given to another, and so sets himself in opposition to the Will of God.[1]

Avarice (*bukhl*) is another great sin, for the avaricious man withholds from God what is due to Him, or gives grudgingly, and the avaricious man will find himself thrust out from the presence of God, shut out from Paradise and in danger of Hell-fire. al-Muḥāsibī relates, in condemnation of this sin, a story of the Prophet, who was walking round the Ka'ba, when he saw a man clinging to its curtains and saying, "By the sanctity of this House, I implore Thee to forgive me." Muḥammad said to him, "What is your sin? Describe it to me," and the man answered, "It is greater than I can describe to you." The Prophet rejoined, "Wretched man, is your sin greater than the regions of the earth?" He said, "Yes, my sin is greater, O Apostle of God." He was asked again, "Is your sin greater than the mountains in magnitude?" The man replied, "My sin is greater." The Prophet said, "Is it greater than the extent of the ocean?" He said, "It is greater." The Prophet asked again, "Is your sin greater than the firmament of the heavens?" He replied as before, "Yes, it is greater than the heavens." Then Muḥammad said, "Is it greater than the Throne of God?" and he answered, "It is greater." The Prophet asked at length, "Is your sin greater than God Himself?" and the man said then, "Truly God is most Great and most Glorious." The Prophet said, "O wretched one, then describe it to me," and he said, "O Apostle of God, I am a man possessed of much wealth, and I shall be questioned concerning it, and I feel as if I were already meeting with the flames of Hell." Then the Prophet said, "Begone and do not burn me with your Hell-fire. By Him who sent me with guidance and grace, if you were to stand between the Black Stone and the Station of Abraham and pray for a thousand thousand years, until rivers of tears flowed from your eyes and the trees were watered thereby, and then you died and you had been guilty of the sin of avarice, God would send you forth into the flames of Hell.

[1] "Ri'āya," fols. 138*b* *ff*.

Woe be unto you, for you knew that avarice is infidelity (for it sets up Mammon in the place of God), and the abode of the infidel is Hell-fire." The greatest sinner of those upon whom God has bestowed great wealth is he who grudges it to the poor man seeking to borrow from him, and who is unwilling to give to his need. So al-Muḥāsibī adds, "May God preserve us and you from avarice."[1]

Among the great sins also al-Muḥāsibī classes sins of the tongue, which have their origin in the sins already mentioned. "Fear your tongue," he writes, "more than you fear wild beasts, and beware of ignoring it, for it is a wild beast and its first prey is its owner. Therefore close the door of speech to yourself and lock it, and do not open it except for what cannot be substituted for it, and when you open it, beware, and use only what speech is absolutely necessary for you, and then close the door, and beware of neglect in that matter, and of contentiousness in conversation, for if you speak overmuch your soul will perish."[2] al-Muḥāsibī quotes in this connection the sayings of the Prophet, who is related to have said, "The tongue is that which is most to be feared by its owner"; and again, "He who is silent is safe." So also Ibn Maʿsūd said, "There is nothing more worthy of prolonged imprisonment than the tongue. My tongue is a wild beast, and I fear that if I let it loose it will devour me." al-Muḥāsibī considers that of all the members it is the most prone to sin, and most of what a man will find recorded against him in the Day of Judgment will be the evil in which his tongue delighted.[3]

It is the tongue which gives expression to anger, which leads to bitter enmity and alienates a man from his fellow-men. It is the tongue which is responsible for backbiting (*ghība*), slandering others when they are absent, and for calumny (*namīma*), speaking evil to men of those they love, and so poisoning the mind of brother against brother. It is the tongue, too, which is responsible for speaking base things and for blasphemy and irreverence and unseemly ridicule, which deaden the heart and darken the countenances of men, and bring judgment upon the one who practises

[1] "Waṣāyā (Naṣā'iḥ)," fols. 11*a ff*.
[2] "Ādāb al-Nufūs," fol. 61*b*.
[3] *Ibid*., fol. 62*a*.

such things. Among the sins of the tongue, also, is the habit of complaining (*nawḥ*), the display of impatience in times of affliction or grief, and this is a sign of ignorance, for affliction is sent by God, and must be accepted by His servant as from His hand. The tongue sins also in betraying the confidence of another, which ought to be concealed, and a sin of the same type is the breaking of a promise, and failure to keep one's word, and the utterance of lies. In all these things the tongue is guilty of great sin, and the servant needs to be on his guard and to keep the tongue always under control.[1]

A sin which works great havoc, because it is difficult to detect and the sinner may be hardly aware of it, is self-deception (*ghirra*), which leads to continuance in sin and disobedience to God, for the sinner is deluded into thinking that that represents hope of His mercy, and his hope is false ; he deceives himself into expecting forgiveness, while he continues in sin. As Wahb b. Munabbih said, " Right thoughts of God mean the avoidance of delusion." Men are deluded in many different ways—*e.g.*, one section of the self-deluded are possessed with the idea of solitude (*khalwa*) apart from men, and seclusion, and are pretentious in fleeing from their society, and desire thereby to become illustrious, and their hearts take pleasure in being spoken of by the pious on this account, and so they display arrogance towards the common people, and are conceited about their own good deeds, while all the time they are self-deluded, blind to their own grievous sins, since they reckon themselves to be in fellowship with God, while alienated from His creatures.[2]

Some are deluded through their own knowledge, believing that because they are theologians and leaders among the pious, they will not be punished ; but such presumption is in itself ignorance, and by this means the learned man may be more deluded than the ignorant. Such a man is the theologian who deludes himself into thinking that no one knows more about the things of God than himself, and no one is better fitted to give a decision on the canon law, and he it is who upholds the community in its faith, and if it were not for him religion would be destroyed, and therefore he is beyond the reach of temptation and sin, and so

[1] " Kitāb al-Tawba," fols. 16*b ff.*

[2] " Ri'āya," fol. 135*a*.

through his self-delusion he ceases to fear God and to stand in awe of Him, and is blind to his own sins. Such a man is deluded because, while he has indeed a true knowledge of God, he does not realise that to possess the knowledge of good is not identical with being good, he knows what righteousness is and deludes himself into thinking that it is the same as being righteous. Others are deluded in supposing that the words they speak with their tongues, describing what is good, represent what they believe in their hearts, and likewise with good works and asceticism, they deceive themselves by thinking that the outward observance of religious duties can take the place of faith and purity of heart, and so they continue in delusion and in sin, counting themselves to be saved, when they are in reality far from salvation.[1]

These and many others are the sins to which men are tempted by the enemies of the soul, and to which too often they give way. "How many are justified in the eyes of men," exclaims al-Muḥāsibī, "who are not justified with God. How many a one who was diligent in the performance of outward acts of service has become fuel for the flames of Hell and his acts of service have become as dust strewn abroad, and the first of these is Iblīs. How many a servant has gone forth in the morning a believer, and has entered upon the evening an unbeliever and his faith has been taken from him and he is unaware of it. The wise man, fearing the loss of his faith, does not trust or rejoice in the praise of the vain and deluded man, and though there were to come to you a revelation that you were praised by the Lord of the Throne, yet it would behove you to cleave to fear and godliness, and to reflect upon the matter and to speak the truth concerning what you know to be praised in Heaven, for you were not worthy of it, and if you maintain that you have attained to it by your own efforts, and are worthy of it because of what you did, you have claimed a great thing, and you have denied the gifts of the grace of God, and if it were not for Him you would not be praised nor guided."[2]

So all these sins, having their root in self-seeking and in

[1] "Ri'āya," fols. 124*a ff*.
[2] "Waṣāyā (Naṣā'iḥ)," fol. 26*b*.

forgetfulness or denial of what is due to God and of the relation of the creature to his Lord, mar and hamper that relationship, and while the heart is defiled by them it cannot see or hear or be fitted to receive that gnosis which leads the soul to the end for which it was created, to glorify God and to enjoy Him for ever.

CHAPTER IX

THE ASCETIC THEOLOGY OF AL-MUḤĀSIBĪ : III. REPENTANCE—MORTIFICATION

MAN cannot be purified from sin except by the gift of God's grace, and the attitude of mind and heart which admits his guilt, his need of purification and his readiness to respond to the Divine mercy, and to accept the Divine gift of forgiveness, is repentance (*tawba*), which Hujwīrī calls " the first station of pilgrims on the way to the Truth,"[1] a turning away from sin and a turning towards God, which is conversion (*ināba*). Repentance from sin is an ordinance imposed by God Most High upon His servants, according to His Word, " Repent towards God, all of you, O believers, and it may be that ye will be saved."[2] The Apostle also said, " He who repents of sin is even as one who has no sin."[3] God is the Disposer towards repentance, and al-Muḥāsibī quotes the saying of a certain divine, " It is because of the wideness of God's mercy to His servants that He has ordained for them repentance as a means of escaping from sins, even though they be great and grievous and many, and that is the mercy of God towards His creatures and His compassion towards His servants, if that one who sins is not guilty of infidelity or wilful denial of the faith, sinning of set purpose or intention, for God will forgive all sins to him who abandons them and repents of them, and glory be to Him Who is pitiful and of great mercy towards His creatures, Who cares for His servants with unceasing care and never-failing loving-kindness, He Who has no need of the service of His creatures."[4] Repentance, then, is a Divine strengthening, though it rests with man to be receptive of it.

This world is the place of repentance and now is the time for it, for when death comes it will be too late for the soul to beg that it may return to relive its life ; it must rest during

[1] *Kashf al-Maḥjūb*, p. 294.
[2] Sūra 66 : 8.
[3] Hujwīrī, *op. cit.*, p. 294.
[4] " Kitāb al-Tawba," fols. 13*a ff*.

the period of waiting (Barzakh), until the time comes when it is called to the Resurrection. "The All-Blessed has warned us," writes al-Muḥāsibī, "that if we are neglectful in this world and do not seek to prepare for the meeting with Him, and death comes upon us suddenly, and we are summoned to a time of sorrow, then no complaint can be made, nor is any return (to this world) possible, and He urges us to take the right course while repentance is still accepted, and we can make our plaint, and our prayer can be answered, so that we may be prepared to meet Him, and be found watching when Death comes."[1] The servant who is ready to meet his Lord is the one who has repented, with sincere repentance, of his sins and iniquities, so that he finds in himself no sin of which he has not repented, which he needs to take into account, for if the soul departs in a state of impenitence, it is not fit to meet its Lord.

But, to al-Muḥāsibī, repentance is most necessary as the first step towards spiritual progress and the possibility of receiving that gnosis which is the goal of the seeker, and that which incites to repentance is compunction, godly sorrow (*ḥuzn*) and shame (*ḥayā'*). "The best of God's servants," said Sa'īd b. Jubayr, "is he who is afflicted by his sins, and when he remembers them he strives to overcome them." When reason prevails over the desires of the lower soul and knowledge overcomes ignorance, the sinner's heart will be the dwelling-place of fear and grief and anxiety, and sorrow will come upon him after long enjoyment of the pleasures of this world. Whenever he remembers the burden of his sins, fear rises up and his anxiety predominates, and his grief is prolonged.[2] It is the remembrance of the regard of God upon him, upon his inmost self and his outward acts, which brings shame.[3] This sorrow for sin, whereby the sinner is pricked in the heart, is caused by "the dart of God." "The beginning of that," al-Muḥāsibī writes in the *Book of the Beginning of Conversion to God*, "is that God All-Glorious brings back to the heart of His servant the recollection of Himself and the remembrance of the next world, and rouses him to reflection and the recol-

[1] "Ri'āya," fol. 34*b*. [2] *Ibid.*, fol. 12*a*.
[3] "Masā'il fī A'māl," fol. 138*a*.

lection of the greatness of the might of his Lord, and the worth of His satisfaction and the power of His wrath, and His promises and His warnings, and thereby his heart is kindled, and then God arouses him to a knowledge of Himself. He awakes him to the remembrance of the sins committed by himself in the past, the many iniquities which are recorded against him, which will not be obliterated until his Lord calls him to stand before Him, and asks him concerning all his sins, of what was written down against him and confirmed, and he will read it with deep shame and fear."[1] Of the shame which is an essential part of contrition (*nadāma*) al-Muḥāsibī declares that it is altogether good, it is a development of faith. The Prophet said, "God loves noble shame, and shame is the mark of a noble nature; God makes it to belong exclusively to those whom He wills among His creatures, and it is a means of profit to both the sinner and the obedient." Shame is a precious and a gracious thing, and it is shame that first rouses the sinner to realise what is the Will of God, and with shame is joined sincerity in seeking to obey that Will. But while man has reason to be ashamed before God, it is not fitting that he should be ashamed before any creature.[2] True shame is the fruit of a broken heart, for shame and contrition arise from the sense of having done wrong to the All-Merciful Lord, and having acted as His enemy and as a rebel against His will, rather than as a faithful and obedient servant.

Contrition is indeed a return unto the love of God, and therefore it gives rise to the confession of sins and to acknowledgment of unworthiness to receive His gifts. Such confession is necessary for him who seeks for the Divine forgiveness, and to sincere humility it will not be denied. God will not despise a broken and a contrite heart. "Among the signs of the penitent," al-Muḥāsibī says, "are emaciation of body and abstinence in food and weeping over himself, with much fear, and prolonged requests for forgiveness, and much prayer and fasting, for with humility he combines deprivation for his body. It is a sign of baseness and depravity to abandon weeping over himself and his many sins,

[1] "Bad' man anāb ila Allāh," fol. 19*a*.
[2] "Ri'āya," fol. 75*b ff*.

while the sign of sincerity is constant intercession for forgiveness by night and by day."[1] The penitent remembers the weakness of his soul and the strength of his Lord, and so he humbly approaches Him seeking His help for the fulfilling of what is due to Him and the observance of it, and the salvation to be found in Him, with a heart fearful and eager, saying, "I shall forget if Thou dost not make me to remember, and I am weak if Thou dost not strengthen me, and impatient if Thou dost not give me patience," and he continues in his search for help, depending on no power or might save that of his Lord, and he cuts off his hope from himself, and the direction of his hope is all of it towards his Creator and his Lord, and he will find God near and ready to answer, granting His grace and having compassion, for so He commanded him who turned towards God and resolved on obedience to Him.[2]

Repentance, says al-Muḥāsibī, is not made perfect except by breaking down the contumacy of the heart, by seeking forgiveness in contrition, by atoning for any sin done to others in offering satisfaction for the wrong inflicted, and by control of the members which lead into sin, in the future.[3] Therefore after contrition comes reparation (*radd*), the practical result of sincere repentance, which means the restoration to those who have been wronged of all that is due to them, and the retribution to which they are entitled. It may mean the acknowledgment of falsehood before witnesses, and repayment of what was lawfully due but withheld, or reconciliation with those from whom the penitent has become alienated through his sin. If he has killed any man, then he must buy slaves and set them free; if he has committed adultery, then he must arrange marriages for those who are poor, and endow them with his wealth; if he has sinned in drinking wine, then he must procure good and wholesome drink and give it away freely. If he has blamed anyone unjustly, he must praise that one and use gentle speech towards him and good words. So also if he has sold anyone into slavery or put anyone on bonds, on account of a debt owed to himself, it remains for him to be forbearing

[1] "Kitāb al-Tawba," fol. 13*a*. [2] "Ri'āya," fol. 18*b*.
[3] "Kitāb al-Mustarshid," fol. 5.

towards his debtor and to set him free.[1] When the one who was wronged has passed away, then restitution, so far as possible, should be made to his heirs. By offering such satisfaction for the wrong inflicted on others through his sins, the penitent will render reparation for sins committed, and can then hope for forgiveness.

The last, but by no means least essential, part of repentance is the resolve to amend and to lead a new life. The determination in the heart not to return to that sin nor to any other for ever is the characteristic, together with what has already been described, of the true penitent. So al-Muḥāsibī sums up the meaning of repentance: "It is the abandonment of sin, with the determination not to return to doing anything of the kind for ever, repenting of what is past, asking forgiveness of God Most High, making supplication of Him, seeking Him, taking refuge in prayer, longing for Him to accept your repentance and to forgive your sin, resolving to refrain from sin for what remains to you of life."[2]

Repentance, therefore, including the resolve to amend and the determination to lead a new life, leads inevitably to the purgative life, the search for purification by means of mortification (*mujāhada*) and self-discipline (*riyāḍa*). The *mujāhid* is the one who strives with all his might against himself for the sake of God. The Prophet is related to have said, "We have returned from the lesser warfare to the greater warfare, which is the struggle against oneself."[3] So a modern psychologist writes: "War must be proclaimed on the curiosity of the senses . . . war on over-keen passions, not only in so far as they are sources of sin, but in the measure in which their demands turn the soul aside, however little, from its effort after God; war on enjoyment and relaxing comfort; war, in a word, on everything that may loosen from below the ties of the interior life."[4]

Mortification is the act of man, but one to which he is encouraged by the joy which is set before him, "Man is guided to mortification," writes al-Hujwīrī, "by a flash of

[1] *Cf.* St. Matt. xviii. 23 *ff.* [2] "Kitāb al-Tawba," fol. 13*b*.
[3] Hujwīrī, *op. cit.*, p. 200.
[4] J. Maréchal, *Studies in the Psychology of the Mystics*, p. 163.

the Divine Beauty, and inasmuch as that flash is the cause of the existence of mortification, Divine guidance precedes mortification."[1] Only by mortification is it possible to attain to that detachment which is essential to the spiritual life, that cutting off (*inqiṭāʿ*) of all that distracts, all that hinders the progress of the soul in its struggle against sin and its striving towards purification. "Man was created to praise, reverence and serve God our Lord, and by that means to save his soul," wrote St. Ignatius. "Man should make use of the creatures in so far as they help him to attain his end, and in the same way he ought to withdraw himself from them in so far as they hinder him from it. . . . It is therefore necessary that we should be detached from all created things, desiring and choosing only those which most lead us to the end for which we were created."[2]

Of this detachment a modern director of souls[3] wrote that it demanded constant watchfulness, courage in dealing firmly with those things which impede spiritual progress. It includes detachment from things in order to secure a higher freedom, and the advance in knowledge of God which cannot be made until there is deliverance from the slavery which the love of the creatures imposes, and from the tyranny of circumstances. It means detachment from self, that the vision of God may not be blotted out by self-absorption, and therefore it is necessary to cut out interests and anxieties and become self-forgetful, that there may be room and leisure to grow up into God. It may mean detachment from affections, from natural antipathies and dislikes and from selfish love, detachment from friends and home and family, the renunciation of all, so that in losing all a man may find all, in fellowship with God Himself. It means detachment in the spiritual life, readiness to give up friends, opinions, thoughts, spiritual status. It is only by freeing itself from the distractions of the many that the heart can concentrate upon the One. "Let him who wishes to be near to God abandon all that alienates him from God," is al-Muḥāsibī's advice.[4]

[1] Hujwīrī, *op. cit.*, p. 203. [2] *Spiritual Exercises*, p. 12.
[3] Fr. East, of the Community of the Resurrection.
[4] "Ādāb al-Nufūs," fol. 97*b*.

Knowledge of a thing makes a man understand its true worth or lack of worth, and those who distinguish between the temporal and the eternal will set their hearts upon that which does not pass away. " He who knows this world is detached from it, and he who does not know it is attached to it, and he who knows the world to come is separated unto it, and he who does not know it is separated from it. The least of your desires for this world is the most injurious to you in the next, and the least of your desires for the world to come, which serves as a provision for you in this passing world, is what will be of most profit to you in the next."[1] al-Muḥāsibī quotes a tradition of Jesus, according to which He said, " The love of this world is the chief of all errors, and the best remedy for the believer in the matter of his faith is the detachment of his heart from the love of this world, and if he accomplishes that, the renunciation of this world seems a light thing to him, and the search for the world to come becomes easy to him; but he cannot attain to detachment, except by the right means, and I do not say that the right means consists in poverty and lack of possessions and much fasting and prayer and pilgrimage and warfare for the sake of God, but rather, in reflection and the cutting short of expectation, and returning to penitence and purification, and the abandonment of self-glorification by the heart and adherence to humility, and preoccupation with the fear of God, and continual sorrow and much concern with Him and the return to Him."[2]

The root-principle, which, if it is made sound, will affect all the branches, is " despair " of all the creatures—that is, detachment from them, so that it is possible to be indifferent to them and independent of them, whether they are injurious or beneficial, whether they give or withhold, whether they live or they die. What is of supreme importance is that the heart, detached from these, should cleave unto God, and if He is sought in all sincerity, if He is the real Object of the search, then the seeker will look beyond this present world to that which is eternal, and cut himself off from all earthly desire, and seek for detachment from the creatures, and make God his chief desire and strive to attain to Him, as one who

[1] " Ādāb al-Nufūs," fol. 97*a*. [2] *Ibid.*, fol. 86*b*.

has no need of this world, having indeed but one need alone, and he resolves to give himself unto God for the rest of life. Such detachment from the creatures, therefore, means the return unto God and the repose of the heart in Him, and when the heart finds its rest in Him, then it obeys His will and serves Him as His saints serve Him, and comes to know the true joy of service, and in self-abasement finds itself glorified.[1] Detachment from the things of this world and freedom from preoccupation with what it has to give will bring rest of body and mind, relief from anxiety and weariness, and result in happiness even in this world. Why, therefore, should the soul seek to preoccupy itself with what is of so little worth either now or hereafter, to the exclusion of what is of infinite worth now and for all time ?[2]

This detachment is to be not only from material things, but also from fellow-men, for they may be the greatest hindrance to the service of God. Intercourse with men (*mukhālaṭat al-nās*) leads to many transgressions and sins, for there are " Satans " among them, and he who is seeking God alone must detach himself from all save those whose companionship will further his aim, whether because they are better than he is and can help him on his way, or because through their need and its claims he can the better serve God. Solitude is essential for the seeker after God, though there are few who will accept the deprivation it involves, for to endure solitude, al-Muḥāsibī admits, is hard, and the power to do so is a grace which God gives to whom He wills. But it is necessary, while living at peace with men, and rendering them their due, to attain to detachment from them.[3] There is a close parallel to this in the recommendations of a spiritual director writing seven hundred years after al-Muḥāsibī. " The servant of God," he says, " must retire apart, therefore, and keep silence, in order to be able to progress in true virtue and to have an opportunity to apply his soul to Divine things. When, however, charity or any other reasonable cause exists, he may converse humbly

[1] " Ādāb al-Nufūs," fols. 79*a*, 79*b*.
[2] " Waṣāyā (Naṣā'iḥ)," fol. 9*a*; " Kitāb al-Zuhd," fol. 2*a*.
[3] " Waṣāyā (Naṣā'iḥ)," fol. 11*b*.

with men, shewing them a courteous kindness without excess, and keeping peace with all men as far as possible."[1]

He who is devoted to the service of God, al-Muḥāsibī observes, has detached himself from men, while he who is devoted to any other than God cannot do without them.[2] It was recorded of 'Umar that when he became Caliph he divorced his wife, though she was dearer to him than any-one else in the world, because he feared that his love for her would lead him to consider her before the duties of his office as the Vicegerent of God and the Leader of the Faith-ful. When he felt that God had so strengthened him that he could safely take her back, he sent for her that she might once more be his wife; but the messenger, when he arrived, found that she had passed from this world.[3]

Every preoccupation, with whatever it may be and how-ever good that thing may be, distracts from every other preoccupation because the heart is one, and cannot be pre-occupied with more than one thing, and it is only possible to attain to the single-minded service of God by detach-ment from all other preoccupations save that which serves this end. It is for you to direct your efforts towards advance, urges al-Muḥāsibī, looking towards God alone, for it is only the heart empty of all else which can be filled with the remembrance of God and devoted to His service only.[4] So also wrote a sixteenth-century Capuchin friar, "For as long as, being full of the love of earthly things, we let our under-standing, will and memory dissipate themselves upon ex-terior things, we shall never attain . . . that unity and sim-plicity of spirit which is the immediate disposition for the presence of God in our souls."[5]

This detachment and unification of the heart can only be attained by continuous mortification. "It means," says al-Muḥāsibī, "that you must exercise continuous vigilance (*tayaqquẓ*), and must find no place for heedlessness in your heart, in all activity on your part, as in every time of rest,

[1] L. Blosius, *Spiritual Instruction*, p. 22.
[2] "Ādāb al-Nufūs," fol. 64*b*.
[3] "Kitāb al-Makāsib wa'l-Wara'," fol. 40*a*.
[4] "Muḥāsabat al-Nufūs," fols. 67*b*, 69*a*; "Ri'āya," fol. 53*a*.
[5] C. Barbanson, *Secret Paths of Divine Love*, pp. 27, 28.

in silence and in speech, in your coming in and in your going out, in times of recreation, in love and in hatred, in laughter and in weeping, you must be exacting with yourself."[1] When the sickness of the heart has been prolonged, and its cure long neglected, then the remedy of mortification and self-discipline will need long and continuous application, "for the medicine, in a difficult case, does not cure the one who takes it, except by continued administration, and a garment, when it is very soiled, is not cleansed except by repeated washing."[2]

This unceasing mortification is, of course, a difficult thing, and requires much effort, but no more than is expended by men on things of much less moment. "Man finds it difficult to bring down the bird from the firmament of the heavens, and he brings it down; and he finds it difficult to bring forth the whale from the depths of the seas, and he brings it forth; and he finds it a hard thing to extract gold and silver from the bowels of the earth, and he does dig them out; and he finds it difficult to take the beasts of burden and the cattle and wild creatures, and fierce beasts from the wilderness and jungles, yet he takes them and tames them and forces them to work; and he finds it hard to capture vipers and snakes, but he does secure them. He finds it difficult to exorcise evil spirits, but he does get rid of them; and he finds it hard to get to know the stars of heaven, and the heavens themselves, and their movements and their rising and their setting; and it requires effort to understand the phases of the sun and moon and their orbits, and their rising and their setting, and he learns all that when he takes pains to do so. So also he takes pains in order to diagnose the sickness of one who is ill, and the remedy for it, and he gets to know it. He takes pains to learn the history of the kings of the past, of former ages, and writes it down and studies it, and all his effort is only the striving to take pains in the search for

[1] "Ādāb al-Nufūs," fols. 61*a*, 61*b*. *Cf.* Thomas à Kempis: "If thou desire to mount up to the height of perfection, thou must begin manly and set the axe to the root, that thou mayest root up and destroy all inordinate inclination to thyself and to all private and material good" (*De Imit.*, III., cap. 53).

[2] "Riʿāya," fol. 17*b*.

worldly gain; and in all this there is nothing which concerns his religion, over which he takes any pains. The setting in order of a single soul means effort, and he does not continue to keep it in order, and it is the self alone which corrupts him.

"There is nothing so difficult as purifying the corruption of his own self, and he has not persevered in purifying it from its corruption, and he is ignorant of part of what makes for its purification, and knows part, and that of which he is ignorant he takes no pains to learn, and what he knows of its corruption he neglects to remedy. No one takes pains to fast, or pray or give alms, or go on pilgrimage, or purify himself, or make ablution for anyone else; he takes the trouble for himself, not to purify another, but himself. Why does the wretched creature take such pains over knowledge of what is not really difficult, and take the greatest trouble over it, but in this question of his own soul he will take no trouble, and neglects to learn that concerning it of which he is ignorant?"[1]

Mortification is of greater importance to the spiritual life than the results attained by all these efforts made, and pains taken, for material gain or advantage. Its aim is the discipline of the soul and its purification, and the transference of what was used for evil ends to the pursuit of good, for the soul can be turned aside from its desire for this world, and become equally zealous in its desire for the world to come.[2] So Simon of Ṭaibūtheh had written, "Virtues as well as passions are born of the desire. . . . Passions are changed into virtues and virtues into passions by the will which acquiesces in them."[3] Mortification, therefore, means the destruction, not of anything good within the soul, or of

[1] "Ādāb al-Nufūs," fol. 78*b*. *Cf.* Thomas à Kempis: "One thing there is that hindereth many men from profiting and fervent amending: horror of difficulty, and labour of striving and of fighting. They above all other profiteth in virtues that enforceth themselves most manly to overcome those things that are most grievous and most contrary to them: for there man most profiteth and most ample grace deserveth, where he overcometh himself and mortifieth in spirit" (I., cap. 25).

[2] "Ādāb al-Nufūs," fol. 62*b*.

[3] *Early Christian Mystics*, p. 67.

the capacities given to it by God, but of its sinful tendencies.[1] It consists, firstly, of the avoidance of sin and temptation thereto, and especially the prevention of those sins to which any soul is especially exposed, either through circumstances or through its own especial weaknesses. al-Muḥāsibī, in the "Riʿāya," after dealing with specific sins and the causes which incite to these sins, devotes attention to that form of mortification which is best calculated to prevent them. Thus the preventive of hypocrisy, in word or deed, is the purification (*takhlīṣ*) of the motive and intention, making the action sincere and single-minded, entered upon, and carried out, for the sake of God alone. It is for the seeker to make every effort to attain to complete single-mindedness (*ikhlāṣ*), a quality which Bishr al-Ḥāfī defined as meaning "To escape from the cankers of one's actions," adding, to his questioner, "To let thine actions be free from ostentation and hypocrisy and self-interest."[2] This mortification at the very source of sin is like the action of a servant to whom his master delivers wheat-seed, bidding him to pass it through a sieve and make it free from darnel and barley, or silver which he bids him cast into the refinery, so that it may become pure silver, free from dross and alloy. If the servant obeys, then he separates the good from the evil, the true from the false, the pure from all that defiles it, and he throws away the tares and burns away the dross. So also the servant of God must mortify himself and repel evil suggestions and the temptation to hypocrisy, and must separate himself from it, as the silver is purified by separation from the dross, and the wheat by the casting out of the tares.[3] The servant mortifies these evil desires for the praise and favours of men, and repels the temptations of the self and Iblīs, and breaks the strength of his human nature, and so his thoughts are concentrated on the Will of his Lord, and his concern becomes one, he is doing all for the sake of his Lord, and is free from

[1] *Cf.* L. Blosius: "Pride, vainglory, self-complacency, desire of human favour and honour, motions of impatience, impulses of anger, the concupiscence of the flesh, the sting of lust, and in a word, all depraved passion and affections, with the powerful aid of the grace of God, he must diligently destroy and kill" (*Spiritual Instruction*, p. 22).

[2] Hujwīrī, *op. cit.*, p. 117.

[3] "Riʿāya," fol. 54*a*.

the dissipation of his interests through consideration of the creatures, and from the sin of hypocrisy and men-pleasing, because he knows that his relations with the creatures are of no real consequence, and that his relations with God are of the greatest significance in this world and the next.[1]

So also pride is to be mortified by the substitution of humility, for humility is opposed to self-seeking and pride, and especially to spiritual pride in knowledge of the truth and obedience in action; it is necessary to remember that these things are given by the grace of God, and but for His favour and His willingness to help in time of need, the soul would never attain to them. It is well that the believer should counteract the temptation to pride by the remembrance that he is one of the sons of Adam and he shares the human nature of his fellow-men; he is equally prone to sin and to weakness, and victory comes only through the help of God. So, too, pride in wealth or birth or natural gifts should be tempered by the reflection that of him to whom much is given much will be required, and the one who is entrusted with much less may make a better use of the little he has, and be reckoned of more worth in the sight of God.[2] Intellectual pride is to be mortified by the servant's realisation of his ignorance, in spite of what he has been given of knowledge, and of his remissness and neglect in regard to what little he does know by his intellect. If he has been granted wisdom and insight, it is for him to be grateful, and to remember that this will add to the proof against him (on the Day of Judgment), unless it strengthens his obedience,[3] and that he was given these gifts, in order that his intellect might be used for the comprehension of God and for preoccupation with Him, and that what has been given may be withdrawn if misused, and so he realises that he is but the recipient and God is the Giver, and he humbles himself accordingly.[4]

[1] "Ri'āya," fol. 46*a*. [2] *Ibid.*, fols. 98*a ff*.

[3] *Cf.* Thomas à Kempis: "The more and the better that thou canst, the more grievously thou shalt be judged, unless thou live the more holily. Be not lift up therefore for any craft or any learning, but rather dread for the knowledge that is given thee" (*De Imit.*, I., cap. 2).

[4] "Ri'āya," fol. 102*a*.

So, too, the pride which takes the form of arrogance (*kibr*) can be mortified through the realisation by the servant of his own worthlessness, when he remembers his creation from the dust of the earth, his birth in weakness, his state of ignorance before God gave him knowledge, his blindness before his eyes were opened to see and his mind to understand, his deafness before his ears were made to hear, and how it was God Who gave to him strength after weakness, Who made him rich after he was poor, Who satisfied his need when he was hungry, Who clothed his nakedness and brought him back to the right path when he had gone astray, Who raised him from abasement to exaltation. He was created in that first state of impotence, that his soul might realise its humiliation and its weakness and its lack of power and its need and its destitution, and that the knowledge of these things might restrain him from all arrogance and boasting and haughtiness and pride in himself, for he realises that he is in truth of small worth, and so he is humbled before his Lord. But God not only makes the self and its weakness known to him, He makes Himself known thereby to His servant, as the One Who has power to make his weakness strength, and the will and the loving-kindness to turn his darkness into light and to raise him from the dust unto the heavens, from abasement to exaltation, and by this knowledge the servant realises the might and the majesty of his Lord, and this, too, must make him humble in his own eyes.

As Luqmān the Wise said unto his son, "O my son, what has a creature of clay to do with pride?" for man was made of the earth which is trodden under foot, the lowest and meanest of all things.[1] This was the beginning of man, and he does not know what his end will be, only that he will return again in humility and weakness, and naked as he came forth from his mother's womb, and that he must stand before the judgment seat of God, there to give an account of all his works, knowing how he has neglected what was given him to do, and how he has wasted his life and dissipated his wealth. "Do you suppose," asks al-Muḥāsibī, "that he can fail to be humble about himself, or that his self-esteem will

[1] "Ri'āya," fols. 112*a ff*.

not depart from him?" Even if he had been created free from weakness and afflictions, and were not subject to death or punishment, arrogance on account of this freedom from trials and this purity would not befit him, because he is a servant, a slave, and the humiliation of a state of servitude is the opposite of arrogance, and arrogance is not fitting for the bondservant. So the most sincere of God's servants is the humblest, of no worth in his own sight, as he comes in submission and humility to lay his thanks at the feet of his Lord.[1] Humility is like the grain which bears seven ears, and in each ear a hundred grains, and though the earth be dry its roots are well established and its ears are not withered, and it gives to the creatures what they need for sustenance. So also humility, which is but a little thing with the ignorant man, is changed into a great thing when that man submits himself unto his Lord,[2] for he who is content in a state of humility in this fleeting world is counted as a prince in the sight of God.[3]

So likewise jealousy and envy are to be mortified by the servant's remembrance of what is due to his fellow-men, and of the fact that what has been given to them, over and above himself, was given by God, and since that which God wills to bestow on others can by no efforts of his be obtained for himself, apart from God's Will, this canker of the soul, which can bring him no benefit, but on the contrary corrupts his heart and is destructive of his happiness in this world and his salvation in the world to come, should be cut out, at whatever cost, so that the soul may be free from its poisonous grip, and this can be brought about by his willing acceptance of his Lord's choice for him and for others. Then, when this source of corruption has been destroyed, he advances to satisfaction with that for which he was made, and from that to a mind at rest.[4]

So, too, avarice may be mortified by the cutting off of desire, and the remembrance that God provides all that is needful and that to Him belongs the distribution of wealth or poverty, and when a man seeks to grasp wealth and amass it for himself or to hold what is given to him, for himself

[1] "Ri'āya," fols. 115*a ff.*
[2] "Kitāb al-Zuhd," fol. 7*b*.
[3] "Waṣāyā (Naṣā'iḥ), fol. 9*b*.
[4] "Ri'āya," fol. 32*a*.

alone, he is assuming that the control and choice lie with him, and he is ignoring Him to Whom the choice belongs, and is forgetting that wealth is bestowed on him to be used only in the service of God.[1] "Lock the door of covetousness," is al-Muḥāsibī's advice, "and open the door of contentment."

The tendency to sin through the tongue is to be mortified by silence except when speech is necessary or more excellent. "Laugh little," says al-Muḥāsibī, "avoid jesting, and restrain your complaints . . . do not talk overmuch with those who do not desire it."[2] Conversation on what does not concern the servant is to be avoided, while silence is to be sought for what does concern him, for reflection, whereby he may attain wisdom, for reflection is necessary to consider what is to be done and to choose what is in accordance with the Will of God.[3] Spiritual progress demands that the servant shall have recourse to silence, which means not only the avoidance of all temptation to the sins of anger, and slander, and reviling and falsehood, but also the opportunity to listen for the voice of God and, in quiet communion with Him, to receive the strength to resist such temptations when they return. "Silence produces beauty of adornment" (*cf.* 1 Peter iii. 1: "The ornament of a meek and quiet spirit") "and the manifestation of awe and the cessation of evil utterances and the graces of gratitude and praise to God—if it be right, the servant speaks, and if it be wrong, he betakes himself to something else, and therefore his speech is listened to and his comment followed," says al-Muḥāsibī; and again he says, "Silence is a safe refuge, and in quietness is peace."[4]

The evil of self-delusion can be mortified by self-investigation, and the realisation that what is spoken with the tongue and carried out in deeds must find its correspondence in the inner self, and if the servant finds the fear of God on his lips and not in his heart, and good deeds to his credit when his motives were insincere, and he preaches purity

[1] "Kitāb al-Zuhd," fol. 4*b*.
[2] "Kitāb al-Mustarshid," fol. 6.
[3] "Kitāb al-Zuhd," fol. 2*b*.
[4] *Ibid.*, fol. 3*a*. *Cf.* L. Blosius: "The servant of God should be given to a moderate silence, which is the mother of much good" (*op. cit.*, p. 19). "Kitāb al-Tawba," fol. 16*a*.

and is himself defiled by evil thoughts, then he must return unto himself, and see himself in all his vileness and impurity, and know himself for what he is, and realise that though God, in His mercy, may have veiled his sins from the knowledge of others, and to outward seeming all is fair, yet God Himself sees his deformity, and if his fellow-men knew of his depravity, they would turn aside from him and loathe him. So his self-delusion is destroyed, and, in humility and self-abasement, he seeks to amend his life and to bring his inward life into conformity with the outward, and combines contrition for the past with determination not to return to it.[1]

This mortification of particular sins leads on to the general mortification of the self and the members, for there are few days in a man's life when one or other of his members does not commit sin.[2] al-Muḥāsibī points out that every member is liable to misuse or excess in regard to its function—*e.g.*, the hearing may be neglectful or remiss in listening to what is profitable, but willing enough to hear what is evil; the eyes may fail to look on what is desirable, while they seek out what is unlawful; the tongue may give way to vain utterances and also to heretical speech; misuse of the taste may lead to gluttony and so on; the mortification of the outward senses is very necessary, and, moreover, control of the members is ordained by God; the abandonment of misuse (*fuḍūl*) is a virtue (*faḍīla*) which must be acquired. The misuse of the eyes for what they have no right to look upon may be prevented by the remembrance of the regard of God upon His servant, of Him Who is "too pure to behold iniquity," and so the servant withdraws his gaze from that which his eyes desired to see. So also in lending the ear to listen to what is displeasing to God, the servant remembers Him and refuses to hear, and abandons what his lower nature desires, out of his reverence for God. So, too, he checks his tongue when it is about to give way to false and uncharitable words, and he refrains from uttering what he meant to say. When his hand is stretched forth to do evil or his feet lead him into the ways of iniquity, he remembers that he is a servant of God, pledged to His service, and refuses to do that which is contrary to His Will. al-Muḥāsibī

[1] "Ri'āya," fols. 131*b ff.* [2] *Ibid.*, fol. 134*b*.

held that it was better for the servant that a member should be cut off, that an eye should be lost, in this world, than that he should enter the next world with two eyes to be blinded by the flames of Hell.[1]

He quotes the case of Ghazwān al-Raqāshī, who looked at what was unlawful, and forthwith plucked out his eye, and Fatḥ al-Mawṣilī, who said, "If my eye were to look upon sensuality, I should pluck it forth."[2] He who mortifies his senses al-Muḥāsibī likens also to one who has been attacked by disease in his foot, and it becomes serious and takes hold upon him, and he fears that if he does not cut it off it will spread to the whole of his body, and he bestows a part of his wealth on anyone who will remove it, and he is eager and pleased to cut it off, although it has been dear to him, and he had found it hard before now to have even a shaving cut off one of its nails, but when he sees the cause which he feels may lead to the destruction of his body, he is displeased with that, fearing lest it may come to something still worse.

So likewise he who contemplates his future life and sees the causes which may destroy him therein, within his heart and members, abandons them through magnanimity and love, and if he cannot do it except by giving away what he possesses, then he does so, like the man who gives his wealth, so that his foot may be cut off and cauterised with fire, and endures his fear of that, because of his greater fear of the consequences if he fails to do it. There is a difference between the two results: while the man who cuts off his foot has physical relief, what results for him who fears God Most High is the joy of rest in His presence.[3]

The two chief means by which the general mortification both of the self and the members is to be obtained are abstinence (*wara'*) and asceticism (*zuhd*), to which abstinence leads. In regard to *wara'*, the scrupulous abstinence which refrains from all that is unlawful and all that is doubtful, al-Muḥāsibī quotes the words of Ḥasan al-Baṣrī, who said, "Abstinence is the most excellent part of the service of

[1] "Kitāb al-Mustarshid," fol. 4; "Ri'āya," fol. 32*a*.
[2] "Kitāb al-Makāsib," fol. 48*a*. *Cf.* St. Matt. xviii. 19.
[3] "Bad' man anāb ila Allāh," fol. 21*a*.

God," and also, " The foundation of the faith is abstinence."[1] This abstinence involves the avoidance of everything which is displeasing to God, in the way of speech, or action on the part of the heart or the members, and the refusal of all that God disapproves in heart or members. This type of mortification is attained by self-examination (*muḥāsaba*), which means that, in all circumstances, before taking action, the servant must make sure that what he is about to do is right and in accordance with the Will of God, and must accept nothing in his heart and undertake no outward action, until it is quite clear to him what he is about; and if he realises that what he plans is contrary to the Divine Will, then he makes every effort to expel it from his heart, and to restrain his members from doing what God disapproves. Some things must be renounced because they are unlawful, from others it is well to abstain, lest the servant be thereby involved in what is doubtful. The things which must be renounced include all that God has forbidden, both wrong belief and wrong action; the things from which it is better to abstain are those about which the servant is doubtful, because he has no definite knowledge about them. It was related of the Prophet that he said, " He who renounces what is doubtful seeks to be free from defilement, for the sake of his faith and the judgment to come, for he who is involved in what is doubtful is liable to be involved in what is unlawful, and he who is liable to be involved in what is unlawful is like the one who grazes round about the prohibited pasture, he is about to enter into it."

It may be necessary, too, to abstain from what is right in itself, but may become the cause or occasion of what is wrong, as the Prophet said, " The servant will not become one of the godly until he abstains from what he is not afraid of, for fear of what he is afraid of "—for instance, he will abstain from certain forms of earning a livelihood because he cannot be sure that they will not involve him in wrongdoing, and he renounces the attempt to increase his wealth lest that should lead him to ignore what is due to God. So the servant abstains from what is likely to lead him astray,

[1] " Kitāb al-Makāsib," fol. 45*a*. *Cf.* 'Aṭṭār, *Tadhkirat al-Awliyā*, I., p. 27.

according to what one of the wise men said, " Refrain from swearing, even when the oath is true and is lawful to you, lest your tongue become accustomed to oaths and swear falsely, and refrain from taking revenge upon him who has wronged you, for fear lest you need an excuse for yourself."[1] God said, " Do not reckon what is good to be equal with what is evil," and forgiveness is good and taking revenge is evil. So the fear of God does not cease to stir the hearts of the God-fearing until they have renounced much of what is right, for fear of what is wrong.[2] But in this matter of abstinence al-Muḥāsibī holds that extremes are to be avoided ; what is wrong must be renounced without hesitation, whether it be in thought or word or deed, and much that is doubtful must be renounced, even if right in itself, because it may lead to wrong, but what is right and, as the result of investigation and self-examination, is seen to be in accordance with the Will of God, should not be renounced from mere scrupulosity, for such abstinence may lead to injury to health or reason and risk to life, and abstinence of this kind is itself unlawful and a sin against God.[3]

Closely connected with abstinence as a means of mortification is asceticism (*zuhd*), the renunciation of this world and its goods, of the pleasures of life, sensual and even spiritual, the preference of hunger to satiety, of wakefulness to sleep, of poverty to riches ; indeed, for the sake of God, the ascetic is prepared to renounce all save Him. " The believer who is seeking for godliness," writes al-Muḥāsibī, " renounces all that is destructive to him in this world and the next, and leanness is manifest in him, and mortification and solitude and separation from the companionship of the pious, and the appearance of grief and absence of joy, and he chooses all that, hating to indulge in pleasure which may incur the wrath of his Lord and make him worthy of His chastisement, and he hopes that his Lord will be well pleased with what he does, and that he will be saved from chastisement, and will be permitted to come into His presence and to taste of the joys of Paradise, unalloyed and unabated, and to abide

[1] *Cf.* St. Matt. xviii. 21-35, Parable of the Unjust Steward.
[2] " Kitāb al-Makāsib wa'l-Wara'," fols. 39*a ff*. *Cf.* Sūra 41 : 34.
[3] *Ibid.*, fol. 48*a*.

therein to eternity, enjoying the good pleasure of his Lord, the All-Gracious and All-Glorious."[1] Therefore, for the joy that is set before him, the seeker will renounce all that may hinder his spiritual progress, for in his renunciation he will have the continual aid of Him Who never withdraws His help from those who ask it, and continually has compassion on them, and to that one who practises asceticism with effort and struggle, in the search for what is pleasing to his Lord, who strives against the self and fights against his lusts for His sake, God will lighten the task and will mortify his lusts and will help him to go forward on his way.

al-Muḥāsibī compares the believer's state with the case of the servant of an earthly master, who is weak in body, and in approaching his master he falls from time to time on account of his weakness, then rises to his feet again, and that happens many times, and his master looks towards him, as he comes stumbling on his way in his weakness, falling on his face and rising again, but the master does nothing to prevent him from falling, as he advances towards him, seeking to come near to him and to do his good pleasure, and that master watches him suffer many times, though he himself possesses many beasts of burden; it would mean very little to him to have mercy and be pitiful enough to send him a beast to ride upon, so that he might be saved from falling and hasten on his way to meet his master. But God is kinder than that earthly master; when he sees His servant, the seeker, striving for His sake, near to perishing, yet not relinquishing the search for His good pleasure, contending against the self, grieved because he is checked in his progress, rather than because he suffers through falling. When his Lord sees him thus, He makes light to him the search to accomplish His good pleasure, and hastens his approach until he draws near to Him and reaches His side, He Who is unique in His generosity and grace, in His loving-kindness and compassion and tender mercy.[2]

[1] "Ri'āya," fol. 90*b*; Abū Nu'aym, "Ḥilyat al-Awliyā," fols. 234*a ff*. *Cf*. St. Clement of Alexandria on the Beatific Vision: "With loving hearts they feast eternally upon that never-ending sight, pure and radiantly clear, enjoying a delight that never cloys, unto unending ages" (*Strom*., VII. 3).

[2] "Ri'āya," fols. 90*b*, 91*a*.

Fasting is a type of asceticism which is enjoined by the law of God and is therefore incumbent upon the true believer. "Hunger breaks the power of the self," says al-Muḥāsibī, "and satiety increases insolence, and hunger strengthens concern and grief in concern, and concern and grief destroy sensual lusts and desire."[1] It is a means of mortifying the appetites and of preventing gluttony and excess in eating and drinking, for the one who is accustomed to fast has gained the mastery over his natural appetites; but, to al-Muḥāsibī, fasting from food and drink is of no value unless there is also abstinence from sin. "He who fasts," the Prophet said, "must guard against deceitful and lying speech and slander and calumny and ignorance and obscenity, and must take every care, and must walk with downcast eyes, and unless he does that God says concerning him that there is no need for him to abandon food and drink." The Prophet also said, "Even if you were to pray until you were (bent double) like the bow, and to fast until you were (as thin) as the bow-string, that would not be accepted from you, except through sincere abstinence."[2] Through such fasting, the heart is illuminated and the soul purified and the spirit is led into the presence of God.[3]

Poverty is also a form of asceticism to be sought after by the servant of God, and in this he has before him the example of the Prophet, who prayed, "O God, make me to live in poverty and make me to die in poverty, and raise me up at the Last Day among those who are poor and not among the rich." He said also, "What have I to do with this world, and what is my relation to it save that of a traveller on horseback, who seeks to rest under the shade of a tree, and then leaves it and goes on his way?" Preoccupation with the thought of God is more fitting for the seeker after Him than preoccupation with wealth, even though it is to be used for good works. Let God's servant, then, be content with sufficiency and renounce all beyond that, for he may rest assured that evil is bound up with seeking much of this world's goods. Let him follow in the steps of those who are now with the Blessed in Paradise, who, if they ate in the

[1] "Ādāb al-Nufūs," fols. 81*b*, 82*a*.

[2] "Waṣāyā (Naṣā'iḥ)," fol. 19*a*.

[3] Hujwīrī, *op. cit.*, p. 324.

morning, had nothing left for their evening meal, and if they sought a loan, found none to give it, who possessed no garment save that which covered their body, who had no means of enrichment, and yet morning and evening they were satisfied, acquiescent in the Will of their Lord.[1]

The best use that can be made of this world, al-Muḥāsibī concludes, is to renounce it and choose the next world, and if this is too high an ideal, then to renounce every attraction it offers to the self or the senses which is displeasing to God, and this is asceticism for the sake of God, and no one among the worldlings can injure one who has thus mortified his desires, nor tempt him to error or to sin, if his self does not respond to such a one, but repels him. So also with everyone who is hostile to God's servant, seeking to injure and ensnare him, if the servant does not sin against God in regard to such a one, and does not return evil for evil, that enemy cannot hurt him. In asceticism the servant will find relief from distress, when he has abandoned the pleasures of this world, and ceased to be anxious about provision for his journey through it. Then he has no weariness in the journey, and his soul is at rest, and he is saved from temptation and has no more need of contrition. He lives a praiseworthy life in this world, and when he dies, he dies a witness for God, having purified his heart from this world.[2]

The mortification of the senses, having its manifestation in the outward life, is only a part of what is necessary for the purification of the soul; there is also the more subtle interior mortification of the mind and heart, which is of greater importance and even more difficult. The first thing to be sought after, says al-Muḥāsibī, is that the inward self should be more excellent than the outward self; purification of feeling, thought and will is the preliminary to action, and its first foundation. This inner mortification means the laying of the foundations on which good is built up in

[1] "Waṣāyā (Naṣā'iḥ)," fols. *9a*, *9b*. *Cf.* fol. *6a*. *Cf.* also Thomas à Kempis: "They shall get liberty of mind that entereth into the strait life and taketh none heed of any worldly care. O the acceptable and jocund service of God, whereby a man is verily made free and holy" (*De Imit.*, III. 10).

[2] "Ri'āya," fol. *91a*; "Kitāb al-Zuhd," fol. *2a*, *2b*; "Ādāb al-Nufūs," fol. *64b*.

place of evil. It is possible for the building to fall and the foundation to remain, but it is not possible for the foundation to give way and for the building to remain; and if there is not this inner mortification before action, the inner evil will prevent the servant from gaining benefit from the outer good, and therefore to renounce the inner evil is the first thing for the servant, and afterwards let him seek to do good works, for the self, being stirred to grief by mortification, and impelled thereby, will betake itself to good. Knowledge of the way is necessary before walking therein, and when the good has been distinguished from the evil, the evil can be mortified, and what remains after that will be altogether good.[1]

So it comes back to self-examination again, in order that sin may be prevented at its source, and the intention and will mortified in so far as they seek what is contrary to the Divine Will. "O my brothers," writes al-Muḥāsibī, "search out your inmost selves and the secrets of your breasts, and purify them from malice and hatred and the tendency to rejoice in other's misfortunes, and from evil surmisings and enmity and loathing, which eat up good deeds. . . . It may be that some one of you is persevering in some sin and is unaware of it. Do you find in your hearts the love of this world and pleasure in its welcome of you, and enjoyment of its lusts? Do you sometimes find delight in being praised and made much of, and do you shrink from blame or feel exasperated by it, and do you dislike anything which is in opposition to your own wishes, and are you pleased with what is in agreement with them? And do you delight in regarding the creatures without taking any warning from them? Do you find within you the fear of poverty, and do you hate anything which God has decreed for you? For this and suchlike are sins of the heart and you are heedless of them. Is it not so? Then exert yourselves to mortify blameworthy habits (of thought), and do not underestimate them, for he who despises such sins has despised the warnings of God, to Whom be glory and praise."[2] al-Muḥāsibī in his *Book of Knowledge* speaks of those who are content with exterior mortification, renouncing the outward defects of hypocrisy

[1] "Ādāb al-Nufūs," fol. 66*a*. [2] "Waṣāyā (Naṣā'iḥ)," fol. 13*a*.

in word and deed, of polytheism, and the drinking of wine and lying and slander, and the use of charms, and oppression of others; who perform good works—*e.g.*, fasting and other works of righteousness—which are essentially outward, while they do not attain to inward righteousness and do not mortify these evil tendencies which lead to spiritual defects, with the result that such a one is outwardly mortified, pre-eminent in worship and prayer and fasting, while his inward parts are a desolation, and he approaches his Lord, deceived by his exterior mortification, while he is inwardly unmortified. With such a one, who has left the work of mortification incomplete and therefore stultified, al-Muḥāsibī compares that servant who by his efforts has renounced the outward defects and also guards against the inward faults, who advances against his self, which is headstrong to do evil, and mortifies it, that it may abandon its evil tendencies, and wages war against it until it submits, then he continues to strive against it until it is completely mortified, and then approaches his Lord, sanctified, made pure, repentant, free from defilement, both outward and inward.[1]

As craftsmen in this world have rest from their labours only when they have completed their work and have tested it and investigated it, before it is shewn to him who hired them, in order that it may be in accordance with what he desired, so also with those who serve God, when their service is offered to their Lord, if it is to be what He desired from them, and if they are to complete the work which He commanded them to do, then to outward mortification must be added the inward mortification, so that all the powers of soul and body may be collected into one and the purpose unified, that all the activities of members and of heart may be directed in single-mindedness towards God.[2]

The types of mortification considered have been active, but there is a further type which consists in the patient endurance of suffering, the acceptance of the afflictions and trials sent by God, and the endurance, too, of spiritual suffering. "If you are afflicted with trials and calamities," writes al-Muḥāsibī, "in that state urge yourselves to patience in adversity, for that is God's regard upon His servant.

[1] "Kitāb al-'Ilm," chapter vii. [2] "Ri'āya," fols. 9*b ff.*

And guard against complaint and lack of contentment with what is decreed, for we have heard that God says, ‘ He who is not satisfied with My decree, and is not patient in the adversity I send upon him, let him beware of sin,’ and He says also, ‘ He who is satisfied with My decree and My judgment and My ordinance is well pleasing in My sight, and when he comes before Me, I shall be satisfied with him, but he who is displeased with My decree and My judgment and My ordinance, is not well-pleasing to Me, and when he meets with Me, My wrath will be upon him.’ Therefore do not be grieved at God’s dealings with you. Know, rather, that your joy consists in suffering in this world, and to those who endure it with patience it is found a light thing, and thereby their sins are done away. We have heard that a certain divine said, ‘ Of him who does not rejoice in the suffering which saves him from the expiation of his sins, the angels say, “ We treated him with medicine and he is not cured.” ’ Who is more fitted for happiness through the sufferings of this world than he who is most assured of the choice of God for him,[1] and therefore he reckons them as of no account, and continues to rejoice in them? And who is more entitled to rejoice in afflictions than the one upon whom is the regard of God, whose sins are forgiven because of his sufferings, and he is requited for them, and enters into his reward, without being judged, and through them he is granted happiness for evermore?”[2] Therefore, when affliction and trials come, and apparent injustice and humiliation, then it is for the servant to mortify the self’s tendency to anger and a sense of injury, and its tendency to be grieved and displeased, and to practise patience and the acceptance with joy of these God-given trials, since their purpose is to strengthen and uplift the soul and to lead it into still closer fellowship with its Lord.[3]

[1] *Cf.* L. Blosius : “ He should turn the eyes of his soul . . . to God, Who allows him to be afflicted, and bear his trial with a meek and humble heart, considering that it comes only from the Lord. For when the knife cuts, it is not the knife, but the hand of the surgeon directing it that should be considered ” (*Spiritual Instruction*, p. 24).

[2] “ Waṣāyā (Naṣā’iḥ),” fols. 11*b*, 12*a*.

[3] *Cf.* the place of patience among the virtues, p. 194 below.

In his book on Self-Examination, al-Muḥāsibī summarises the effects of mortification, outward and inward, upon the soul of the seeker, who has "died unto sin," and won the victory over the flesh and its lusts and become a new man. When the servant is thus changed, God opens to him the gate of understanding, whereby to advance in faith and to attain to a higher station, and strengthens his determination and increases his insight, so that he can be a means of leading others also to perfection. He has his tongue under control, so that he has no further acquaintance with falsehood, and can reprove and persuade others to speak truth along with him. He is faithful in keeping his word and fulfilling all his obligations, and God deals bountifully with him in giving him the friendship of the righteous. He has detached himself from the creatures, and trusts in God's care for him, which will not fail. He does not desire evil to any creature, nor seek revenge for wrongs done to him, and even in this world he has his reward, for God grants unto him the love and friendship of His servants, by His favour and grace. He is merciful towards his fellow-men, and seeks no occasion against them, and this brings him near to the good pleasure of God and His mercy. It is an honourable and a gracious means of entrance into His presence, and leads the servant to look with charity upon all creatures, for they, with him, are the servants of the All-Compassionate. He controls his regard, both of the outward eyes and the eye of the heart, and withholds their gaze from that which is evil in the sight of God, remembering that He sees all things, even the secrets of men's breasts. He is content with what God has provided for him, and is dependent upon no creature; God is his sufficiency, on Him he relies, and in Him is his sure trust. In regard to all his desires and their satisfaction, he attains to perfect abstinence and asceticism, and this is the sign of those who are detached from all else, in order that they may be preoccupied with God.

al-Muḥāsibī gives a vivid picture of that soul which has undertaken the task of self-mortification and has persevered with it to the end. "This was his path, and God it was Who appointed it for the seeker, for the training of his soul. There is no asceticism on the part of the man who is ignorant of the high station of the seeker who is preoccupied with his Lord, who is seen to be thinking little of this world, humble, fearful, sorrowful, weeping, shewing a meek spirit, keeping far from the children of this world, suffering oppression, not seeking revenge, despoiled yet not desiring requital, dishevelled, dusty, shabby, thinking little of what he wears, wounded, alone, a stranger—but if the ignorant man were to look upon the heart of that seeker, and see how God has fulfilled in him what He promised of His favour, and what He gives him in exchange for that which he renounced of the vainglory of this world and its pleasure, he would desire to be in his place, and would realise that it is he, the seeker after God, who is truly rich and fair to look upon, who tastes delight, who is joyous, happy, for he has attained his desire, and has secured that which he sought from his Lord."[1]

So the glory of the servant increases greatly and his station is exalted, and he rides the steed of humility, but attains to glory and exaltation in the sight of God. He has power over the affairs of this world and the next,[2] and these things are attained by mortification, which is the foundation of all service to God, and leads to its development and its perfection. "These are the qualities produced by the fight waged against the self by those who practise self-examination, those who resolutely set themselves in opposition to the self and mortify it with the help of God. They attain to a high and honourable station, for all things depend upon strength of purpose, and to him who has strengthened his purpose the struggle against the lusts becomes easy, by the help of God Most High, and he will not have long to wait before the Divine grace is revealed within his heart."[3]

[1] "Bad' man anāb ila Allāh," fol. 23*b*.

[2] *Cf.* 1 Cor. iii. 21, 22: "For all things are yours, whether . . . the world or . . . things present or things to come: all are yours."

[3] "Muḥāsabat al-Nufūs," fol. 6 *ff*.

CHAPTER X

THE MORAL THEOLOGY OF AL-MUḤĀSIBĪ—GRACE AND THE VIRTUES

THE first stage, then, of the way by which the seeker advances towards the life in God is a preparation, beginning with repentance and conversion and leading to self-knowledge, that realisation of the creaturely status which is humility, "the only soil in which the spiritual life can germinate," which fits the soul for "the long process of pain and struggle needed if the demands of generous love are ever to be fufilled in it, and its many-levelled nature is to be purified and harmonised and develop all its powers."[1] That process of pain and struggle is mortification, from which the servant of God emerges with a tempered and efficacious will when the flesh has been made subservient to the spirit and the passions have been subdued to serve the purposes of God.

It is the way of purgation, the purification without which no man can hope to see God and to know Him as He is. This is the loss of self, in order that in the truest sense it may find itself, as it was created to be. It is dying, in order to live. "Can bread give strength unless it be broken, or the uncrushed grapes yield wine?" asked Rūmī.[2] "That which thou sowest," said St. Paul, "is not quickened unless it die."[3] Only the corn of wheat that falls into the ground and dies bears much fruit. So it is also that the mortified soul is reborn into new life. "When, therefore, a man forsakes his own will in all things, and casts away his own private self-love; when he renounces every gratification of spirit and nature; when he restrains inordinate desires; when he acknowledges that he is nothing and the vilest of all; when he promptly obeys God in his own soul and man in outward matters; when he ceases to entangle himself

[1] E. Underhill, *The Life of the Spirit and the Life of Today*, p. 168.
[2] *Mathnawī*, Book I., l. 2932.
[3] 1 Cor. xv. 36.

with unnecessary things and superfluous cares; when he allows the deeds and words of others to pass as they are, and yields to no rash judgment; when he is unduly moved neither by the praise nor the blame of men; when he bears sweetly and calmly for God's sake any injury, adversity or misery he may encounter within or without; when he indulges in not even a slight and passing complaint; when he entertains a certain common affection of charity for all men—then, without doubt, dead to the world, he lives to God."[1]

To such as these, who have willingly subdued themselves to the service of God, al-Muḥāsibī believes that the Divine grace will be revealed, and so they will enter on the next stage of their journey. "The grace of God," says Thomas à Kempis, "is a light supernatural, and a special gift of God, and a proper sign of the chosen children of God, and the earnest of everlasting health; for He lifteth up man from earthly things to love heavenly things, and him that is fleshly he maketh spiritual. Wherefore the more that nature is holden under and overcome, the more grace is poured in, and the inward man is every day renewed after the image of God with new visitations."[2] To al-Muḥāsibī also, the grace of God is a light supernatural (*nūr al-qulūb*), whereby the hearts of men are illuminated. "Nothing," he writes, "is more hard upon impurity than light, but the light is only an illumination to the heart if the servant is awake and alive to it, but when he is neglectful he dies and is in darkness, and his light is extinguished; and nothing is more pleasing to Iblīs than the darkness of the heart and its blackness and the extinction of its light. For nothing is more grievous to impurity than light and whiteness, and freedom from defilement, and purity, and evil can find no resting-place in the radiance of light."[3] Simon of Ṭaibūtheh (whose name signifies "of His grace" and who was so called because in

[1] L. Blosius, *Book of Spiritual Instruction*, pp. 32, 33.
[2] *De Imit.*, III., cap. 54.
[3] "Ādāb al-Nufūs," fol. 63*b*. *Cf.* St. John xiii. 20, 21: "Everyone that doeth evil hateth the light, neither cometh to the light, lest his deeds should be reproved. But he that doeth truth cometh to the light, that his deeds may be manifest, that they are wrought in God."

his teaching he laid great stress on the Divine grace) used the same image, " Blessed is the one who has kindled within himself his own lamp by the light of grace."[1] So the heart which has prepared itself for the enlightening grace of God will be granted that which strengthens it against all the forces of evil, and that against which they are powerless.

Grace not only directs the will aright, making it to correspond with the eternal Will of God, from which it had been turned aside by the lure of sin, but at the same time gives it the power to maintain itself aright. Wherever God is, there also is grace, for grace is the result of the contact of the spirit of man with the Divine Spirit, it is the Spirit of God Himself, working within, and influencing, the soul. al-Muḥāsibī writes advisedly that it is to the mortified soul that grace is "revealed," for the gracious influence of God is always there, but is not always operative in full measure except in the soul prepared to respond to it ; sin and self-centredness thwart it, the pride of the ego, making itself the final aim of its own action, restrains the progress of the soul ; only when these obstacles have been overcome, and the will has been freely surrendered to a higher Will, can grace have free course.[2] But to those who open their hearts to His grace, God gives freely of that which He is always ready to give. " When a man, by being offered spiritually," wrote Isaac of Nineveh, "dies to all dealings of this dwelling-place and trusts his life to the life after the resurrection, grace will dwell with him."[3] al-Muḥāsibī quotes a tradition from Abū Hurayra to the effect that God declared in His Word, "O son of Adam, if thou dost draw near to Me by half a span, I will approach thee by a span, and if thou dost approach Me by a span, I will approach thee by a cubit, and if thou dost approach Me by a cubit, I will approach thee by a fathom, and if thou dost come to Me walking, I will come to thee in haste "; and this,

[1] *Early Christian Mystics*, pp. 29, 49.

[2] *Cf.* Thomas à Kempis : " My grace is precious and suffereth not itself to be mingled with strange things nor earthly consolations. Wherefore it behoveth thee to cast away all impediments, if thou desire to receive the infusion thereof" (*De Imit.*, III., cap. 53).

[3] *Mystic Treatises*, p. 365.

adds al-Muḥāsibī, means the best of help and the most speedy answer (to prayer), and guidance into the straight road, and favour and protection, and defence against sin. The penitent, then, will not fail to hasten to that manner of life in which God will bestow upon him His grace.[1]

al-Muḥāsibī teaches that all good things, whether of action or thought or will, come from the grace of Him from Whom "all holy desires, all good counsels, and all just works do proceed." It is " that most blissful grace " that makes the poor in spirit rich in virtue, and those who are meek in heart rich in many goods, of which à Kempis wrote, " Thy grace sufficeth to me, other things that nature desireth not being obtained. If I be tempted and vexed with many tribulations, I shall not dread whilst that grace is with me. It is my strength, it giveth me counsel and help. It is more mighty than all enemies, it is wiser than all wise. It is mistress of truth, teacher of discipline, light of the heart, the solace of oppression, thrower down and driver away of sorrow, taker away of dread, nourisher of devotion, and bringer forth of tears. What am I without it but a dry tree and an unprofitable stock?"[2] Grace is God's loving kindness and mercy, and conversion, the beginning of the spiritual life, is itself the call of God. " The help given (*'ināya*) to enable us to return to Him is one of the greatest gifts of God,"[3] and sin is finally curable only by grace. " When God warns His servant and arouses him to caution, he realises that it is by the favour (*minna*) of God, and that his soul is thereby healed."[4] Those who strive to fulfil their responsibility as creatures to the Creator, and are determined to carry out that upon which they have resolved, will find that God, by His grace, establishes them in their purpose and makes them worthy to be called righteous.[5] It is by the grace of God that man is enabled to bear witness to His Unicity (*al-Waḥdāniya*), to be preoccupied with His service, to keep himself from sin, to get rid of self-pleasing, to withstand the wiles of Iblīs, to be armed against the lusts which lead to perdition, to be veiled from what is abomin-

[1] " Ri'āya," fol. 12*a*.
[2] *De Imit.*, III., cap. 55.
[3] " Ādāb al-Nufūs," fol. 72*a*.
[4] " Ri'āya," fol. 18*a*.
[5] *Ibid.*, fol. 19*b*.

able, while the beautiful is revealed to him, and to be protected from the deceit of what is praised by men. All that is worthy of praise and thanksgiving is bestowed by Him "Who secretly initiates what He openly crowns."[1]

The firstfruits of the Divine grace are the virtues, which are "infused," in that they are all the gift of God, but are "acquired," in the sense that man by his own striving and unceasing self-mortification lays himself open to the gift, and ceases to resist that "dominating, selective, searching, rescuing, forgiving, self-imparting grace of God."[2] The first and the greatest of the virtues, from which all others are developed, is Faith (*īmān*), based on the knowledge of God, which God Himself has given, by various means, through the creation itself, and His providence (*tadbīr*) in regard to His creatures, His care in providing them with sustenance (*rizq*), and His protection of them.[3] The knowledge which was revealed to man by the creation of the universe, with its evidence of a unified control, and of the action of a purposive Will, and the care of a loving Creator for His creatures, was confirmed and made clear by His Word and by the *Sunna* of His Prophet, that they might believe in Him and be saved.[4]

While faith is based on knowledge, it is a greater thing than knowledge, as the Christian mystic, Isaac of Nineveh, had written, "Knowledge is made perfect by faith, so that it acquires the power to ascend and to perceive that which is above perceptibility, and behold the splendour of Him that is not attained by the mind or the knowledge of the creatures."[5] "Faith," says al-Hujwīrī, "is really the act of

[1] "Waṣāyā (Naṣa'iḥ)," fols. 27*a*, 27*b*. *Cf.* von Hügel, *The Life of Prayer*, p. 24. *Cf.* also Simon of Ṭaibūtheh: "Every slip that occurs to us has its origin either in our negligence, or in our false suppositions, or in our scorning of our neighbours, or in our love of glory, or in our envy, or in our desire to assert our will, or in our natural inclination, or in our hatred. In all these, however, the (Divine) grace does not neglect us, and we do not fall into reprehensible slips, unless we tread on the voice of conscience and do not amend ourselves" (*op. cit.*, p. 31).

[2] *Cf.* R. Otto, *Religious Essays*, p. 15. *Cf.* also F. P. Harton, *op. cit.*, chapter iv.

[3] "Ādab al-Nufūs," fol. 93*b*.

[4] "Makāsib wa'l-Wara'," fol. 31*b*.

[5] *Mystic Treatises*, p. 246.

man joined to the guidance of God. . . . Inclination to believe is the guidance of God, while belief is the act of man. . . . In short, faith is the absorption of all human attributes in the search for God," and Muḥammad b. Khafīf, who regarded al-Muḥāsibī as his master, declared, "Faith is the belief of the heart in that knowledge which comes from the Unseen, because faith is that which is hidden, and it can be obtained only through Divine strengthening of one's certainty, which is the result of knowledge bestowed by God."[1] This is the faith of one "assured of God's Unicity, and that He is from everlasting and shall be unto eternity, by what was manifested through the vision of His Kingship (*malakūt*) and the evidences of His might, and the many witnesses to Him, and the signs which demonstrate His Divinity and His all-penetrating Will, and the establishment of the work of His hands, and the manifestation of His power over all His creation, and the beauty of His Providence. Are not all creatures His, and to Him all power belongs? Blessed be God, the Lord of the Worlds."[2]

But, for al-Muḥāsibī, faith does not subsist without works: it alone can give that deep conviction (*taṣdīq*) which will enable a man so to direct his will as to persevere in well-doing, for faith represents the relation of the heart to God at the springs of action, it means the entire abandonment of independence, which is self-dependence, and the substitution of self-committal, self-surrender—it is, indeed, the faculty of loving correspondence with God (*muwāfaqa*), since all life that is lived in faith is directed towards the one purpose of serving Him, and the will is strengthened to correspond moment by moment with that purpose. So the life of faith is also the life of righteousness: the grace which is in the believer supernaturalises the natural, for God, in calling men to serve Him, does not mean that they should cease from works, but He calls them to serve Him through works of obedience, and if their hearts are in harmony with God through faith, then their actions will also be in obedience to His will, and their human nature, the "flesh,"

[1] *Op. cit.*, pp. 289, 290. *Cf.* Sūra 6 : 125.
[2] "Ādāb al-Nufūs," fol. 59*b*.

cannot hinder them, because through faith it has been made subordinate to the spirit.

Faith, since it enables men to feel their need, and to take God at His Word, leads to reliance on Him (*thiqa*) and dependence on Him (*tawakkul*), for through assured faith doubts and suspicions are removed and certainty (*yaqīn*) is perfected, and the true meaning of action (*'amal*), *i.e.* as seen in the world around, is established, and it is that God is the Creator, the Provider, the Lord of life and death, the Giver, the Benefactor; He alone rules over all, and if this knowledge of Him is perfected in the hearts of men, then they will speak of these attributes with their tongues, and through the mention of them be led to return to Him, and to put their trust in Him, because He has declared that He will provide for them all they need, for body, mind and soul.[1] "Rely on Him, my brother," writes al-Muḥāsibī, "with the reliance of one who thinks rightly of Him, who has confidence in His promises and relies upon His fulfilment of them, whose heart has rest from anxiety, because he trusts in His word."[2]

But this dependence upon God, al-Muḥāsibī is careful to point out, does not mean the abandonment of work and the means of earning a livelihood. God provides His children with their daily bread, but He expects them to work for that which He provides. It was related of the Prophet that he said, "God has sent no prophet who was not a shepherd of sheep,"[3] and al-Muḥāsibī gives traditions of the prophets and saints who were required to make an effort for their livelihood. Even the Virgin Mother of Christ, when her Son was born, was required to shake the branch of the palm-tree, under which she lay, in order to bring down ripe dates for her sustenance.[4] Therefore dependence is not to be made an excuse for sloth, but it is to mean that those who depend

[1] "Makāsib wa'l-Wara'," fols. 32*a*, 32*b*. *Cf.* Abū Nu'aym, "Ḥilya," fols. 239*b*, 240*a*.

[2] "Ādāb al-Nufūs," fol 59*b*.

[3] Such were Abraham and Moses and David and Muḥammad himself in his youth. Perhaps too he, or the recorder of the tradition, had heard of Christ as the "Good Shepherd" (St. John xv.).

[4] *Cf.* Sūra 19 : 25.

upon God will not seek for more than they need, which He has promised as their portion.

But there is something which goes deeper than reliance on God's care for material needs, and dependence upon Him for daily bread, it is the heart-felt confidence and trust by which a man surrenders all that concerns him into the hands of God, and this is the trust (*tafwīḍ*) which brings him close to his Lord. This it is which completes his dependence upon God (*tawakkul*), through reliance upon Him and knowledge of His omnipotence and His mercy and His pity, and, like all the virtues, it is the gift of His grace. As 'Āmir b. 'Abdallah (*ob.* A.H. 103)[1] said to his sister, "Entrust your affairs to God and take your rest." The one who does this has ceased to be concerned with this world and to fear men and to desire what they possess; he has ceased to consider the snares of the self, and this means peace of mind and the freedom of the heart to occupy itself with God. It involves no trouble for heart or body, but instead means rest for both body and heart; why should that one who has entrusted his affairs to God feel any anxiety as to provision for the morrow, for he is concerned only with Him?[2] If men entrust their worldly affairs to others in order to secure rest for themselves, is it not more fitting that the believer should entrust all his affairs into the hands of the Exalted King, Who rules over all and disposes all things as seems to Him good? This trust means confiding to God all one's fears and hopes, placing no reliance on one's own strength and power or on that of the creatures, only on that of God, looking for no kindness or favour except from Him. The servant of God realises that he has no control nor strength nor power nor dominion of his own, which he needs to commit unto his Lord, for his Lord is overruling him and all his affairs; it means only that he willingly entrusts to his Lord that which He already controls, and says within himself that he will commit his affairs to his Lord, Who controls all things. He attains to this state of trust through reflection and recollection, and it means the cessation of all worldly anxieties and of hope

[1] *Cf.* Sha'rānī, *op. cit.* I., p. 24.
[2] *Cf.* St. Matt. vi. 34: "Seek ye first the kingdom of God and His righteousness, and all these things shall be added unto you."

and fear in regard to any creature, for he knows that his Lord will supply his needs and, remembering that all things are in His hand, he seeks no help from any creature, for his is the expectation of one who looks to his Lord and to no other. So trust (*tafwīḍ*) follows upon dependence (*tawakkul*), and dependence upon reliance (*thiqa*); because he relied on God's Word the servant depended upon Him, and because he depended upon Him, he trusted Him and committed to Him all his affairs, knowing that by Him all things are ordered aright.[1]

This trust means a confident hope, and hope is another of the gifts of the Divine grace arising out of faith, and, in the believer, it is not simply a temporary emotion affecting the soul,[2] but a continual attitude of mind, to be reckoned among the virtues. This virtue of hope is a movement of the will towards a desired good, and that object of hope is God Himself and fellowship with Him, that for which the soul was created. Hope sets the course of the soul towards God, and directs its desires towards its true goal, which is union with Him, and the will towards its real aim, which is the fulfilment of His Will. So the effect of hope is to produce a fruitful and purposeful activity in the will, and it is the source of that energy and courage and endurance without which advance and perseverance in the spiritual life would be impossible. It saves the novice on the road to God from despair, while for those who have advanced farther on the way it has become partial realisation, and complete confidence in regard to all that is to come. Hope is therefore the true "anchor of the soul," enabling it to hold fast to God.[3]

Of the hope which is the virtue of beginners on the Path, al-Muḥāsibī says that it means right thoughts of God, for God has granted it to those who have gone astray, to save them from the grievous sin of despairing of His mercy, and it is based upon the remembrance of His promises, for He

[1] "Masā'il fī A'māl," fols. 135*b* *ff*. *Cf.* also "Ādāb al-Nufūs," fol. 60*a*. *Cf.* 2 Tim. i. 12: "I know Him Whom I have believed, and am persuaded that He is able to keep that which I have committed unto Him."

[2] *Cf.* pp. 96 *ff*. above. [3] *Cf.* F. P. Harton, *op. cit.*, pp. 46 *ff*.

said, "Verily I will forgive him who has repented and believed and done righteously," and again, "Your Lord declared that He would be merciful unto him who did evil in ignorance, then afterwards repented of it and did good, to him will be forgiveness and mercy."[1] So when the repentant sinner is inclined to despair, he is reminded of the generosity and grace for which he may hope, through God's forgiveness and His favour and loving-kindness, which He has promised to those who repent and believe that He is a God of compassion, of great mercy, ready to pardon those who come to Him with contrite hearts. Hope can be continuous, for His mercy is unfailing, and from the repentant forgiveness will not be withheld. There would be little room for hope if men were judged for their first sin, or if repentance could be accepted only three or four times; but if the servant of God sins a thousand times, and a thousand times returns unto sin, but then repents in all sincerity unto God, God will forgive him, and knowing the wideness of His mercy, the repentant servant can always turn away from his sins with the hope of forgiveness and acceptance through His long-suffering mercy.[2]

But hope goes beyond this belief in God's mercy, in those who have advanced along the way, and, like faith, it must subsist along with works. "Hope, if sincere, is in proportion to the obedience of the servant" who repents and seeks henceforth to do the Will of his Lord. In all he does he looks only to God and serves only for His sake, hoping that what he does will be well pleasing in His sight, and this is the hope of the righteous man who is sincere in his service to God (*al-ṣādiq*).[3] It is set upon God and looks forward to the time when the servant shall enter into the joy of his Lord and shall be among the faithful, who inherit the Kingdom prepared for them, who dwell in the presence of their Lord and abide there for evermore.[4] So, with that hope set before him to urge him forward, the servant is

[1] "Ri'āya," fols. 124*a ff*. *Cf*. Sūra 20 : 84 ; 6 : 54.
[2] "Ri'āya," fol. 125*b*. [3] "Ādāb al-Nufūs," fol. 67*b*.
[4] "Ri'āya," fol. 125*a*. *Cf*. St. Matt. xxv. 34 : "Come, ye blessed . . . inherit the kingdom prepared for you from the foundation of the world."

encouraged to go steadily on his way, in a spirit of eager expectancy, striving to attain to that which he seeks.[1] It is hope which strengthens him for the quest, which is the inspiration of his earnest pressing forward towards the goal, the fellowship of his Lord, here and now in some measure, and in all its fullness in the life to come.[2]

But the one who is most hopeful is the one who fears most, and the emotion of fear which is instrumental in inciting the sinner to repentance, in the believer becomes the virtue of holy fear (*khawf*), which is a continual attitude of mind. "It is perpetual fear," said Ḥasan of Baṣra.[3] Fear and hope increase together in the heart, implanted there by the grace of God, "for it is He Who first aroused fear and hope in the heart, and these two are His two commanders (*i.e.*, those by whom He makes His Will known), to those to whom He sends them, and they act within the heart to drive away temptation, and by means of them God increases His fellowship with the believer and His joy in right thoughts of him."[4] This supernatural fear is given by the grace of God to that believing servant whose realisation of his sins and the punishment due to them has filled him with natural fear for himself, and because he seeks to have that grace bestowed on him, God has infused it into his heart as a free gift, without effort on his part, except that of preparing himself to receive it.[5] This supernatural fear casts out the natural fear, for it is written that upon the true servants of God "There shall come no fear."[6]

This holy fear is the awe (*wajal*) of the creature before his Creator, a recognition of His holiness and majesty, the reverent service due from the servant to his Lord and King.[7] It is the fear of Him "Who created mankind, unto Whom we return, in Whom lies our salvation, from Whom we have guidance thereto." It is the awe of one who has known what it is to draw near to Him and to realise the mighty power of Him Who is the Maker of Heaven and earth, of all things

1 "Bad' man anāb ila Allāh," fol. 21*b*; "Ri'āya," fol. 15*b*.
2 "Ādāb al-Nufūs," fol. 91*a*; "Kitāb al-Mustarshid," fol. 4.
3 "Ri'āya," fol. 13*b*.
4 "Bad' man anāb ila Allāh," fol. 23*a*.
5 "Ri'āya," fol. 14*a*.
6 Sūra 2 : 36.
7 *Cf.* pp. 10, 96, 97 above.

visible and invisible.[1] This holy fear includes the fear of sin, for sin mars the relation between the servant and his Lord, and is destructive to that whole-hearted service which he would fain offer to his King, so that this virtue is a preventive of sin before it attacks him and a means of arousing repentance after it has overtaken him, for the sincere servant fears greatly lest he should do or think what is contrary to the Will of his Lord, which will mean exposure to the Divine wrath and alienation from His love.[2] Holy fear, then, " this supernatural disposition of the soul," is firmly established within the believer, whose heart is cleaving unto his Lord, who is continually mindful of Him with unceasing awe. " And how should awe cease," asks al-Muḥāsibī, " from the heart of one who has received the Divine grace, towards whom mercy has been shewn by the Divine admonition, to whose heart has been brought near the reminder of how soon comes the meeting with his Lord ?" So it is that the faithful servants of God, conscious always of His nearness, are filled with continual awe and reverence as seeing Him Who is invisible.[3]

Closely linked with holy fear is godliness (*taqwā*), for, says al-Muḥāsibī, " the origin of godliness is the fear and dread of God Most High."[4] It is *pietas*, the reverential duty and obedience owed to God, which is the foundation of religion, the orientation of the whole life of the servant, outward and inward, towards God, so that all his actions, whether of the " members " or the heart, become acts of obedience (*ṭa'āt*), expressive of devotion towards God, and his life becomes one of service, God-directed, for godliness leads the servant ever to put himself into God's hands as a living instrument most ready to fulfil His good pleasure, and continually asking, " Lord, what wilt Thou have me to do ?"[5] al-Muḥāsibī defines godliness according to the description given by Ṭalq b. Ḥabīb,[6] who said, " Godliness is

[1] " Ādāb al-Nufūs," fol. 59*b*.

[2] " Ri'āya, fols. 125*b ff.*, 150*b*. *Cf.* R. Otto, *The Idea of the Holy*, pp. 16 *ff.*

[3] " Bad' man anāb ila Allāh," fol. 22*b* ; " Ri 'āya," fol. 13*a*.

[4] *Ibid.*, fol. 6*b*.

[5] *Cf.* L. Blosius, *op. cit.*, p. 74.

[6] Contemporary with the Prophet and one of the Godfearing. *Cf.* Sarrāj, *Kitāb al-Luma'*, p. 16.

action in obedience to God, according to the light received from God, in the hope of receiving His reward; it is the abandonment of disobedience to God, in accordance with the light received from Him, in fear of His chastisement. True godliness as regards the outward conduct is abiding in truth and abandoning disobedience, and true godliness as regards the inner life is the desire to fulfil all religious duties as unto God alone, in lowliness, with weeping and sorrow and prayer and fasting, and all the acts of devotion to which God invites His servants, without making them obligatory, because of His loving-kindness and tender mercy towards them, and what He invites them to is not found acceptable except through godliness, by which the desire therein is directed solely towards Him."[1]

Godliness, like the other virtues, is derived from faith in the Unicity of God, and hence its direction towards His service alone, and its avoidance of the sin which is contrary to the One Will which controls the universe. To the godly it is promised that in the Day of Resurrection, when all who have disobeyed God will bow their heads in humiliation and fear, they shall stand with heads uplifted, free from fear and grief, for they know Him in Whom they have believed, to Whose service they have devoted their lives, and they know that He is faithful Who has promised, and the Most Merciful of those who shew mercy, and He will not forsake His saints nor deliver them over to perdition, but will bring them into the abode of salvation.[2] The godly, therefore, make it their first aim, and their last, to fulfil what is due to God, and their hearts are not distracted by any thought of what is due to themselves, for they count themselves to have no rights in relation to Him; they fulfil all that He has laid upon them, and they complete their service by what goes beyond that, in voluntary acts of obedience, so that all may be well pleasing in His sight.[3]

Allied to godliness is charity, the spirit of compassionate service (*raḥma*) to others, and desire for their good, for the service of God involves service to fellow-men, in obedience to His law which enjoins it. al-Muḥāsibī condemns strongly the practice of judging others, and regarding their faults

[1] "Ri'āya," fol. 7*b*. [2] *Ibid.*, fol. 6*b*. [3] *Ibid.*, fol. 22*b*.

rather than one's own, "when the springs of compassion and kindness disappear from the heart and the rivers of hostility and hardness rise up, and men take pleasure in regarding others with disparagement and contempt."[1] The self-loss which means freedom from self-seeking, and the attitude of humility which is fitting for the servant in relation to his Lord, are to have their effect also upon the servant's attitude to his fellow-men. "It is required of you," says al-Muḥāsibī, "that you should seek good for others and not refuse it to them, and that you should not desire evil for them. Do you fall short of this, and are you content that men should desire good for you, while you seek evil for them? And it is required of you that you should not set yourself above others, whether (inwardly) in your heart or (outwardly) by your tongue, and it is required, too, that none should claim what is due from you to him, and be refused."[2] al-Muḥāsibī summarises the requirements of the virtue of charity in the Golden Rule, "Desire for others what you desire for yourself and avoid for them what you avoid for yourself."[3] Elsewhere he speaks of the virtue of fulfilling to others their due, while not requiring from them what is due to oneself, and serving them while not seeking any service from them.[4]

In accordance with this is his admonition to give with generosity to others, while concealing the gift, lest it should be known and some return, whether in praise or in kind, should be made to the giver. In this connection he relates the tradition of how the Prophet said, "When God created the earth and provided it with its inhabitants, and created the mountains, and established them that they should not be moved, and laid the foundations of the earth, the angels said, 'God has created nothing stronger than the mountains.' Then God created iron, and it cleft the mountains; then He created fire, and behold it cleft the iron; and God commanded the water, and it extinguished the fire; and He gave command to the wind, and it stilled the water. And the angels were of different opinions about this, and said, 'O Lord, which is the strongest of Thy creatures which Thou

[1] "Ādāb al-Nufūs," fol. 72*b*.
[2] *Ibid.*, fols. 86*a*, 91*a*.
[3] "Kitāb al-Mustarshid," fol. 5.
[4] "Ādāb al-Nufūs," fol. 65*a*.

hast created?' and He said, 'I have created nothing stronger than the son of Adam, when he gives alms with his right hand and conceals it from his left hand, and this is the strongest creature I have created.'" Charity, then, will lead the servant to do good to his fellow-servant, but to do it by stealth.[1]

This charity will embrace not only material but spiritual good; that which the servant has received of grace and mercy from God he will desire, as far as possible, to share with others. When that servant who is purified from sin, who has avoided hypocrisy and adhered to single-mindedness, who has subdued the self, who is resolute and strong, sees others who are suffering from sickness of the soul, dreading the wrath of God, bewildered, blind to the knowledge of God, spiritually dead, then compassion towards them takes possession of his heart, because he has the knowledge whereby God will open the eyes of their hearts, and that wherewith they will find healing for the sickness of their souls. He is like a man who has had much (bodily) affliction, which has kept him awake at night and tormented him by day, such as inflammation of the eyes or a cancer in the flesh, and he is cured by a remedy obtained without money and without cost, and he is freed from that evil, and he sleeps at night after long wakefulness, and has peace by day after long restlessness, and he makes progress towards health and fitness, and life becomes a pleasant thing therewith, and his enjoyment is complete. Then he begins to consider his fellows who suffer likewise, and pity for them rises up in his heart, and he has compassion on them, because of his knowledge of what he himself suffered and, knowing what is the remedy for their affliction, he bestows it on them. So it is also when the servant of God considers the spiritual sickness of his fellows, whose cure has become difficult, and he knows what will give them new life and raise them from their prostration and heal the sickness of their hearts, by the leave of God, and he resolves upon that and calls them to return unto God, realising that his own

[1] "Waṣāyā (Naṣā'iḥ)," fol. 24*b*. *Cf.* St. Matt. vi. 3: "When thou doest alms, let not thy left hand know what thy right hand doeth."

strength comes from God, and seeking in what he does only His glory. This is the greatest work of charity.[1]

Closely connected with charity in its regard for others is the virtue of justice (*'adl*, δικαιοσύνη). It is the "God-given love of right, which is in the last resort the Will of God as expressed in the constitution of the universe and the end for which it is created."[2] The just man fulfils what is due to God first, then what is due to his fellow-man, and considers himself last. Justice, says al-Muḥāsibī, is of two kinds, outward justice between the servant and his fellow-servants, and inward between the servant and his Lord. The road of justice is the direct road, along which it is obligatory for a man to travel. The just are characterised by knowledge of what is their duty, by action in accordance with that knowledge, and by patience. "The key to justice, and the beginning of it for the servant, is that he should know the worth of the self and that it should have no worth in his eyes, beyond its proper place, and that his inward self should correspond to his outward conduct." If there is that within him of which he would be ashamed if men could see it, it is for him to change his state to one of which he is not ashamed. The man who is farthest from justice is the one who is most neglectful of what is due to God, and the one least given to self-examination.[3] It is the mark of justice, al-Muḥāsibī notes, that there are not two rules in life, one for yourself and one for others, but one rule for yourself and others, and impartiality towards others on your part.[4] Justice is the virtue of order and discrimination—al-Hujwīrī defines it as "putting everything in its proper place." The intelligent man, with a sense of justice, says al-Muḥāsibī, opposes his desires and fights against his enemy and puts things in their right place, through his knowledge, and sees to it that affairs pursue their proper course. He is the man who considers, and perceives what is right, by the light of his knowledge, and discriminates accordingly.[5] Thereby he realises what is due to God and its causes and occasions and occur-

[1] "Ri'āya," fols. 150*b ff.* [2] *Cf.* F. P. Harton, *op. cit.*, p. 64.
[3] "Ādāb al-Nufūs," fol. 65*a*, 65*b*. [4] *Ibid.*, fol. 91*a*.
[5] *Kashf al-Maḥjūb*, p. 387; "Waṣāyā (Naṣā'iḥ)," fol. 15*b*; "Ri'āya," fol. 19*b*.

rences and aspects, in what these consist, and what is to be put first, in accordance with God's law for the universe, including man. The first thing which is due to God, and which justice requires should be rendered to Him, is worship, and then right action in accordance with the observance of His law. It is with the due observance of the rights of God, on the part of the servant, that al-Muḥāsibī's " Ri'āya," as its title indicates, is mainly concerned, and throughout that work he is insisting on that observance as a matter of right and justice between the servant and his Lord.[1]

Patience (*ṣabr*) is another of the virtues bestowed on the seeker by God, and Ḥasan al-Baṣrī stated that patience was of two types, patience in misfortune and affliction, and also patience to refrain from the things which God has commanded us to renounce and has forbidden us to pursue.[2] al-Muḥāsibī gives it high rank among the virtues, for he says that " the essence of reason is patience," and that it is a sign of strength, not weakness, for the weak man is not patient, but the strong man can dispense with what others think necessary of material things, and in times of affliction he can refrain from grief and can control himself, in proportion to his control over his emotions.[3] It is unfortunate that of al-Muḥāsibī's treatise on Patience and Satisfaction only a fragment is extant, and we have not therefore any adequate account of his teaching on a subject which he felt to be of sufficient importance to merit detailed treatment. Of it he says elsewhere, " Patience is a fair thing and leads, through fear, to gratitude, and thence to praise and joy."[4]

Patience, then, leads to gratitude (*shukr*), which is, in al-Muḥāsibī's view, a greater virtue, for patience represents the passive aspect of that attitude towards God, of which gratitude is the active aspect. Gratitude is the gift of God, as all good things are, and it is fitting that it should be considered after the other virtues which are the gifts of His grace, for it represents the vision of the Giver, not the gift.

[1] *Cf.* " Ri'āya," fol. 22*a ff.*

[2] Hujwīrī, *op. cit.*, p. 86. *Cf.* p. 174 above.

[3] " Bad' man anāb ila Allāh," fol. 24*b*. *Cf.* " Kitāb al-Ṣabr," and " Ādāb al-Nufūs," fol. 91*a*.

[4] " Ādāb al-Nufūs," fols. 64*a*, 64*b*.

Gratitude, says al-Muḥāsibī, recognises that every blessing comes from God and from no other. He is the Giver of all material and all spiritual good, and gratitude is due from the servant for affliction as much as for benefit, for he knows that to be a test of his gratitude (*i.e.*, his acknowledgment that all comes from God) or his infidelity (his denial that God alone controls all events), and every evil from which the servant is set free is also a cause for gratitude. All this is the lowest degree of gratitude, and to the highest none attains, for there is no limit to the grace of God, and none can give to Him fitting thanks for all His gifts.[1]

When the servant realises all this within his heart, then he praises God with his tongue, giving thanks to Him as the Giver of every good and perfect gift.[2] The grace of God bestowed upon the servant, says al-Muḥāsibī, is very great, and gratitude is incumbent upon him, mingled with fear lest this grace should be withdrawn from him. The only thing for which the servant is deserving of praise and commendation is for good works, and with these God has adorned him, and it is He Who bestows gifts and graces and benefits unceasingly, Who alone is worthy of praise and gratitude.[3] " Give thanks to Him, my brother," al-Muḥāsibī writes, " with the gratitude of one who knows His grace and the multitude of His benefits towards him and His goodness unto him, and who knows His grace shewn outwardly and inwardly, both to His elect and to mankind generally."[4] Again he says that men are neglectful of " the courtesy of gratitude," and he exhorts the servant to use every gift, with gratitude for its bestowal, and especially to use the tongue to offer praise and thanksgiving, and be ashamed to use it, being itself a gift from God, for evil purposes, while neglecting to use it for its proper end. He bids the servant

[1] *Cf.* Thomas à Kempis : " I know and acknowledge that I may not yield due thankings for the least point. I am less than all Thy goods given to me, and when I consider Thy noblesse, my spirit faileth for the greatness thereof. All that we have in body and in soul, and all that we have outward or inward, naturally or supernaturally, all are Thy benefits and commend Thee as a Benefactor, holy and good, of Whom we have received all things " (*De Imit.*, III., cap. 22).

[2] " Ādāb al-Nufūs," fol. 67*a*.

[3] " Waṣāyā (Naṣā'iḥ)," fol. 26*b*.

[4] " Ādāb al-Nufūs," fol. 59*b*.

give thanks to God for the gift of sight, whereby he looks unto God with reverence, giving thanks to Him, and fearing lest, by looking on what is unlawful, he should disobey Him through His own gift, as Adam did, in looking with covetous eyes upon the forbidden fruit. Then let the servant give thanks to God for the gift of hearing, whereby he is enabled to listen to His word and to His praises and to profitable discourses. So, then, let thanks be offered for gifts which can be exalted to such good uses, and let the servant be ashamed if they are degraded to evil uses. And let the servant be grateful for the gift of resolute endeavour, directed towards acts of obedience, fearing lest that same resolution should be directed towards evil purposes. Let praise be given to Him Who strengthens His servant against disobedience, and let no sin be committed against Him by misuse of His gifts. Let the servant thank Him for what He provides of clothing, to be worn out in doing what is well pleasing to Him, and fear to wear it out in what is abhorrent to Him Who clothes him, lest on the Day of Judgment his garments shall be of liquid pitch and his robe consist of shreds of fire. Let the servant also give thanks for wealth bestowed, to be spent for the sake of Him Who bestowed it, and let him fear to grudge it or spend it on what is displeasing to Him, thus sinning against God by means of His own gifts.

Above all these gifts of the senses and material goods are the spiritual gifts. Let the servant offer grateful thanks for the gift of faith, whereby he is enabled to strive to be well pleasing unto his Lord, and to attain to His good pleasure, fearing lest he should do what is unlawful and unfitting for the believer, and contrary to the true faith. Let the servant also give thanks for the gift of knowledge, whereby he may learn what is the Divine Will, and be saved from going astray. Let him thank God for His gift of the reason, and its use in reflection and deliberation and the establishment of a good intention, enabling the servant to profit by experience, and inspiring him with deep reverence and prolonged attrition in regard to all the members, and leading him to seek to live at peace with mankind at large, and to think upon what is well pleasing to God, and so to guard against sins and evil thoughts and the establishment of rancour and jealousy and enmity. Reason is a cause for gratitude also, because it enables the servant to praise God and glorify Him and honour Him, and to feel shame before Him, and to stand in awe of Him, and to reverence and obey Him, in accordance with what it has enabled him to understand of His might and His greatness and the magnitude of His power, to Whom praise is due. "I know of no gift, after knowledge," al-Muḥāsibī observes, "of greater worth than the gift of reason and the gift of will, gifts for which we cannot be sufficiently grateful, and the last of God's favours is the gift of a good end." The final cause for gratitude to God Most High is that He does not forgive in order to be thanked for His forgiveness, but He forgives, apart from that, whom He will.[1] Therefore al-Muḥāsibī prays that every servant may be led to offer his thanks to God for all His gifts, for He is the Benefactor, the All-Gracious Lord of the Worlds.

These virtues are acquired as the seeker passes on his way through the stations or stages (*maqāmāt*) which mark the journey to God.[2] The soul has to practise the virtues, with the aid of grace, and this life of the virtues is therefore predominantly active. "Station," says al-Hujwīrī, "belongs to the category of acts." But the self-mortification on which the reception of grace depends, and the complete self-control which the practice of the virtues produces, fit the soul to receive also the spiritual gifts called "states" (*aḥwāl*), which demand not effort and activity, but acquiescence, that attitude of complete self-surrender which allows the soul to be guided and controlled by the Divine Spirit. "State," says al-Hujwīrī again, "belongs to the category of gifts"; he that has a "state" is dead to self and stands by the state which God creates in him.[3] These are the distin-

[1] "Waṣāyā (Naṣā'iḥ)," fols. 22*b* *ff.*; "Kitāb al-Tawba," fol. 13*b*; "Ādāb al-Nufūs," fol. 93*b*. *Cf.* Isaac of Nineveh: "At first grace shews its help in manifest things, also in bodily ones, by its care of him. Grace instructs him also in hidden things. And it reveals to him the ambushes of thoughts and of deliberations difficult to understand. And grace provides him with insight, so that he understands what will happen" (*op. cit.*, p. 356).

[2] *Cf.* my *Rābi'a the Mystic*, chapters vii. to ix.

[3] *Op. cit.*, p. 181.

guishing marks of those who are advancing on the road to perfection, and are given by God to encourage them on their way. They are the gift of God alone and cannot be acquired; but the soul, with the aid of grace, may become increasingly susceptible to them, and this predisposition can be attained by the practice of meditation and recollection, which are the accompaniments of the life of prayer.

CHAPTER XI

THE DEVOTIONAL TEACHING OF AL-MUḤĀSIBĪ—THE LIFE OF PRAYER

THE life of prayer, says al-Hujwīrī, is the means by which the seeker finds the whole way to God,[1] and from the beginning to the end of that way prayer represents the closest association of the seeker with the Sought, for prayer, said Jeremy Taylor, " is of itself nothing but an ascent of the mind to God." al-Muḥāsibī quotes the words of the Prophet, who said that prayer was the basis and foundation of faith, and also the statement of one of the divines, who declared that prayer (*ṣalāt*) was so called because it was the link (*ṣila*) between the servant and his Lord. Those who enter upon prayer enter into His presence and stand before Him, in intimate converse (*munājāt*) with Him, humbling themselves before Him with submission and reverence, both of heart and members, making intercession, fearful yet desirous, with a heart free from all worldly concern, and thoughts concentrated upon the Majesty of God and His presence there, and the opportunity for familiar intercourse with Him. " For all that the servant does in the way of recitation and invocation and praise is intercourse with Him."[2]

The observance of the ritual or congregational prayer (*ṣalāt*), in which the prayers offered are not those of the individual only, but of a fellowship of believers, " an association of those who, animated by the same aspiration, concentrate themselves on a single object and open up their inner selves to the working of a single impulse,"[3] is an ordinance imposed by God upon His servants, which must be

[1] *Kashf al-Maḥjūb*, p. 301. " ' Life,' said St. Peter of Alcantara, ' must be a mingling of unceasing prayer and work : two feet are essential for us on this journey : the one work, the other prayer ' " (*Treatise on Prayer and Meditation*, p. 165).

[2] " Kitāb Fahm al-Ṣalāt," fol. 51*b*.

[3] M. Iqbal, *Reconstruction of Religious Thought in Islam*, p. 87.

fulfilled by all who reckon themselves among the faithful. In this formal congregational prayer, the posture of the body, and the other requirements of the ritual which are appointed for those who pray, are by no means unimportant, since they are a factor in determining the attitude of the mind. As a modern writer on psychology states, "The mind goes beyond the body only by first co-ordinating the latter with itself, whether by force or persuasion. Ritual and vocal prayer represent the method of persuasion." Certain ritual actions have a symbolical value and others produce a disposition of the body favourable to internal devotion—*e.g.*, kneeling, prostrations, the stillness of the body in prayer, the choice of the place and time for prayer, and are justifiable "because they bring about in us, on the mechanical and sensible plane, a harmony that is prerequisite for the life of the spirit." This is especially true of vocal prayer, which is the subtlest external symbol in religious observance and that which evokes its spiritual object most directly.[1]

al-Muḥāsibī considers the different requirements for the observance of ritual prayer and their symbolical meaning, with their religious value, as represented by the interior devotion by which these observances are inspired and which they, in their turn, maintain. With regard to the ceremonial ablutions he says, "When you take the water, you are glorifying God in your heart, in purifying yourself for His sake, and, if you are able, renew your penitence for your sins thereby, so that with purification may be combined repentance, because God desires that the two should be united, for God loves the penitent and those who purify themselves. . . . In bathing each member to ensure ceremonial purification, meditate upon the expiation required for the sins committed by the members. For it was related that he who declared his faith in God after performing his ablutions would have opened to him the gates of Paradise and could enter therein, by whichever he chose. Therefore say, 'O God make me to be one of the penitent and of those who are truly purified,' and then go to your prayers with reverence, glorifying Him in Whose Presence you desire to stand, and whisper your needs to Him, and

[1] *Cf.* J. Maréchal, *Studies in the Psychology of the Mystics*, p. 156.

make your petition and seek for His good pleasure and His forgiveness."[1]

This is the first of four things necessary in order to prepare for prayer, which are, the purification with water by the prescribed ablutions, the purification of the body and the garments and the place of prayer, the purpose and the resolve to pray, in hope of the Divine reward and in fear of the Divine punishment, and the desire to fulfil that which God has ordained. There are four other things which are to be observed when the worshipper actually enters upon prayer: he must find the direction of the *Qibla* and choose it, he must resolve to abandon what is not befitting prayer, of the activities of this world and the desire for worldly profit, he must raise his hands in supplication to God, and must utter the *Takbīr* (God is Most Great). So also he who prays must resolve to glorify God in all he does, remembering the exaltation of the position which is granted to him of standing in His presence to make supplication unto Him, and desiring that He will pour out upon him, when he prays, that which will make his faith a living thing, as he approaches in humility and longing, for the Prophet said, "If the servant prays, and his desire and his heart and his face are turned towards God, he goes to his prayer as a child to its mother."[2] al-Hujwīrī, in a passage so closely resembling this that it must surely be based upon it, says that prayer involves certain preliminary conditions—viz., "First, purification outwardly from filth and inwardly from lust; second, that one's outward garment should be clean and one's inner garment undefiled by anything unlawful; third, that the place where one purifies one's self should be outwardly free from contamination and inwardly free from corruptness and sin; fourth, turning towards the *Qibla*, the outward *qibla* being the Ka'ba, and the inward *qibla* being the Throne of God, by which is meant the mystery of Divine contemplation; fifth, standing outwardly in the state of power (*qudra*) and inwardly in the garden of proximity to God (*qurba*); sixth, sincere intention to approach unto God;

[1] "Fahm al-Ṣalāt," fols. 52*a*, 52*b*. *Cf.* Abū Nu'aym, *Ḥilya*, II., p. 222 (ed. Cairo).

[2] "Fahm al-Ṣalāt," fols. 52*b*, 53*a*.

seventh, saying the *takbīr* in the station of awe and annihilation, and standing in the abode of union and reciting the Qur'ān distinctly and reverently and bowing the head with humility, and prostrating oneself with abasement and making the profession of faith with concentration, and saluting with annihilation of one's attributes."[1]

al-Muḥāsibī bids those who prepare their bodies for prayer, and shew humility in their members, to let the attitude of their hearts correspond to that of their bodies. "Fear God and prepare your hearts with your bodies, and stand before God in the attitude of slaves before their masters, with humility and awe and submission and reverence, for you shew honour one to another and you listen in silence to the speech of your fellow-servants, out of respect or shame or hope or fear. O ye men, is not God, to Whom belong glory and majesty, more worthy of reverence, and is it not more fitting to feel shame before Him, Who is above all praise? O people, are ye ignorant of the grace of God towards His servants? Then why do ye not give greater honour to Him Who is Almighty than you give to His creatures? And there is no less need for you to listen in silence, unhappy that you are, to the Word of God, than to listen in silence to the words of His servants, lest the Lord be esteemed by you more lightly than His creatures. Then fear God, my brethren, and recognise the majesty of Him before Whom you stand and shew Him all reverence and awe."[2] Some of the truly devout, al-Muḥāsibī states, through the intensity of their prayer, were like an old garment, and some like a dried-up piece of wood; and some of them were twisted from much prayer, changed in aspect by standing in the presence of God; some unaware who was on their right hand or their left; and some, when they rose up for prayer, were as if naked, in their great humility. One of the Caliphs used to change colour, and at one moment was pale and at another flushed when he was making his ablutions for prayer; and when others remarked on this, he said, "I realise in Whose presence I stand." One of the Followers was equally affected and used to say, "Do you not

[1] *Op. cit.*, p. 300.
[2] "Waṣāyā (Naṣā'iḥ)," fol. 17*b*.

perceive in Whose presence I stand and with Whom I am conversing?"[1]

Prayer is in truth primarily worship. "Consider, O discerning man," said Simon of Ṭaibūtheh, "that you are the image of God and the bond of all the creation, both of the heavenly and the terrestrial beings, and whenever you bend your head to worship and glorify God, all the creatures, both heavenly and terrestrial, bow their heads with you and in you to worship God; and whenever you do not worship and glorify Him, all the creatures grieve over you and turn against you, and you fall from grace."[2] The first purpose of the one who prays is the glorification of God, and all prayer, whether congregational or purely individual, must begin with adoration on the part of the soul that recognises into Whose presence it has come. Of such a one al-Muḥāsibī writes, "What predominates in his heart while he is at prayer is his sense of the majesty of Him in Whose presence he stands, and the might of Him Whom he seeks, and the love of Him Who favours him with familiar intercourse with Himself, and he is conscious of that until he has finished praying, and he departs with a face so changed that his friends would not recognise him, because of the awe that he feels at the majesty of God, just as one who comes into the presence of some king, or someone for whom he yearns and whom he fears, stands in his presence with a different attitude from what was his before he entered, and goes out with an altered countenance. And how should it not be so with the Lord of the Worlds, the Eternal, Who has not ceased to be, nor will cease to be, He Who hath no equal?"[3]

Of the opening words of all ritual prayer, "In the Name of God," al-Muḥāsibī says that they should be uttered from the heart, with the realisation that it is the Name of Him to Whom Deity belongs, and Deity is supreme Perfection; everything which comes short of that is unfitting for Him, for nought is created except by the will of Him Who is the Compassionate, the Merciful, to Whom mercy belongs as an attribute, whereby He has compassion on those who seek this world, in their worldliness, and forgives them, and on

[1] "Waṣāyā (Naṣā'iḥ)," fol. 18*b*. [2] *Early Christian Mystics*, p. 23.
[3] "Masā'il fī A'māl," fol. 123*a*; "Fahm al-Ṣalāt," fol. 54*b*.

those who seek the world to come, whom He saves from chastisement and to whom He gives Paradise as their abode.[1]

But in addition to the ritual prayers appointed for the servant, there is personal prayer (*munājāt*), by which the servant approaches his Lord with his personal petitions and intercessions, and to these His ear is always open, and none need fear to come unto Him. "We have seen earthly kings," writes al-Muḥāsibī, "who do not give leave to men generally to enter into their presence, and it is not possible for all of those over whom they rule to speak with them, nor has anyone courage to seek that, except one who has great influence with them; but the King Supernal, by His grace, gives leave to all His servants, high and low, the sinner and the obedient, to converse with Him in private—indeed He bids them to do that and declares that He will be wroth with him who fails to do it. In the case of the disobedient servant, such a one as would despair of intimate converse with kings, who are themselves but creatures, it is only fitting that he should magnify the greatness of the grace bestowed upon him, since his Lord gives him leave to have confidential intercourse with Him, and indeed is not satisfied with giving leave, but goes so far as to lay it upon him as an obligation and to stir up his heart to that. He might have willed not to give leave to the sinner to enter into intimate converse with Him, except after repentance, nor to the obedient, unless he offered to Him a perfectly sincere prayer and gave thanks to Him for His grace in the matter, but He has willed to be gracious and merciful towards His creatures.

"And when one of those earthly kings gives leave to anyone who has influence with him to have a private audience with him, that one does not converse with him, except with great humility, and how much more will that be so if leave is given to one who comes to him guilty of sin and crime and evil deeds? Will not that one be wretched, fearing punishment, knowing that no regard will be paid to his humility and misery when he comes forward, because of his disobedience? How, then, will it be with the King of kings,

[1] "Masā'il fī A'māl," fol. 124*a*.

since all who pray to Him have neglected what is due to Him and have disobeyed His command, and all have need to fear and to stand in awe of that Almighty King, the Exalted, the Strong, to Whom the right of chastisement belongs ? The servant understands well the value of that to which God moves him, of prayer to Him, therefore let him be afraid on account of his sins, and be fearful and humble and occupied only with God in his heart, and let him shew humility with his outward members, and it may be that he will be forgiven for his long avoidance of Him and his frequent disobedience in times past."[1]

The very name of personal prayer (*munājāt*, lit. whispering in the ear) indicates the closeness of God's approach to His servants, for everyone with whom one enters into confidential and private conversation must be near at hand. God appointed this intimate converse to His servant and also appointed to him proximity to Him Who hears when His servant speaks. Everyone who has made his petition or called upon God has entered into that relation of intimacy with Him, because in doing that he was seeking God, and God was drawing near to Him, and was nearer to what he said than speech is to the tongue.[2]

al-Muḥāsibī sums up his teaching on the right approach to God in prayer by saying, " Then approach God with obedient hearts, wherein is knowledge of the greatness of God Most High and His might and His majesty and His power and the awe due to Him, feeling shame before Him, and let that which is His due be given unto Him. And draw near to Him with what is well pleasing to Him and avoidance of that which is abhorrent to Him, and come near to Him with intense love towards Him, loving what He loves and abhorring what He abhors, and come unto Him with a realisation of His good gifts and His grace, both manifest and hidden, and of His loving-kindness and His unfailing goodness, for, in spite of our many sins, He continues to

[1] " Fahm al-Ṣalāt," fol. 55*b*.

[2] " Masā'il fī A'māl," fol. 125*a*. So also Brother Lawrence : " If in this life we would enjoy the peace of Paradise, we must accustom ourselves to a familiar, humble, affectionate conversation with Him " (*Fourteenth Letter*).

bestow all kinds of gifts upon us. Are not these things so? Therefore approach God with fear lest His favours towards you should cease, and with keen shame lest you fall short in gratitude to Him. And draw near to God Most High with deep fear of Him and real hope in Him, and joy in the recollection of Him, and in your familiar intercourse with Him and your longing for Him and your desire for His presence. And approach Him with assured faith and dependence upon Him, and confidence in Him and peace of mind in regard to Him, and fellowship in Him and preoccupation with Him. Should this not be so? Then approach God with gravity of mien, with downcast eyes and humility, with reverence and submission, with meekness and patience, and restraint of passion and bitterness, with a quiet mind, and a desire for the good of the community and avoidance of any evil for them, with pity and compassion, and sympathy and a concern for your fellow-believers. And approach God with the desire to amend your life, and to deal faithfully with him who has dealt faithlessly with you, and to do good to him who has done evil to you, and to prefer others to yourself, though it be to your own loss. Draw near unto Him, choosing humility rather than exaltation, and preferring hardship for the sake of God rather than an easy life, and poverty to wealth and its acquirement. And approach unto Him, rejoicing in affliction in this world, and delighting in the regard of God upon you and in His choice of trial for you, whereby He brings you joy. And approach Him with the continuous remembrance of death and the resurrection and the bridge of Ṣirāṭ, which must be crossed. All these things are to be earnestly desired by all who came before God to make entreaty of Him."[1]

Prayer, then, is a personal act, by means of which the human personality comes into relation with the Divine Being, and there is giving and receiving, speech and answer, all that goes to make up a real and living fellowship. It is the means by which the human soul enters into co-operation with God and is enabled to share in the Divine action, "a unique process of discovery whereby the searching ego affirms itself in the very moment of self-negation and thus

[1] "Waṣāyā (Naṣā'iḥ)," fol. 32*a*.

discovers its own worth and justification as a dynamic factor in the life of the universe."[1] But if the soul is to receive, if it is to hear the answer to its beseeching, it must wait upon God and enter into the "heart of silence," where God is. The means by which it can be prepared for this close intercourse with God, and be freed from all distractions which might hinder or mar that intercourse, is meditation (*murāqaba*, lit. watchfulness, awareness), the orientation of the whole of the faculties, feeling, mind and will towards God. Not only must the members be stilled and the eyes closed, the attention of the mind fixed upon God, and the ear attentive to His voice,[2] but the heart and soul must be altogether "present" (*ḥāḍir*), preoccupied with God and with Him alone.

al-Muḥāsibī held that only by "absence" from self could the soul enter into "presence" with God, for "presence" was the fruit of "absence," and no light could be found in "absence" without "presence." The servant therefore must renounce heedlessness and distraction, in order that by absence from self he might attain to "presence," for of this a poet wrote:

"The 'absent' one is not he who is absent from his country,
But he who is absent from all desire.
The 'present' one is not he who hath no desire,
But he who hath no heart (thought of worldly things),
So that his desire is ever fixed on God."[3]

The means of attaining to "presence" is by the freedom from all other preoccupation, which is secured by meditation. "If you fear distraction, first cut off from yourself evil thought and then exercise and accustom your mind in meditation. As long as you are in the state of watchfulness, instruct your soul in meditation upon Divine things, so that when it flees against its will from the recitation (of your

[1] M. Iqbal, *op. cit.*, p. 87. *Cf.* also pp. 155 *ff.* above.
[2] *Cf.* "Riʿāya," fol. 5*a*.
[3] Hujwīrī, *op. cit.*, pp. 249, 250. *Cf.* also "Riʿāya," fol. 15*a*; "Waṣāyā," fol. 18*a*; and J. Maréchal: "The exercise of interior and personal prayer is one of the most powerful means of psychological unification" (*op. cit.*, p. 160).

prayers), it may by necessity wander in the spiritual things in which it was trained."[1]

On this subject of the concentration of the mind and heart, al-Muḥāsibī quotes the tradition of the Prophet, according to which he said, " For every human heart there are paths (diverse interests) leading out in all directions, and he whose heart follows those paths cannot give his mind to God. Whichever way he follows, he will perish and fall," and blessed is that servant whose heart is not preoccupied with anything save his Lord Most High, whose thoughts are concentrated on Him alone, in whom the flames of self-seeking desire have died down, and he has entered into that region where the soul is alone with God.[2] So a woman saint of a later age wrote, " Two things are necessary in all prayer, much thought of God and little thought of self."[3] al-Muḥāsibī would go farther and declare that the whole thought must be given to God and none at all to self. " In meditation," wrote Barbanson, " the mind must ascend to a simple and naked thought of Almighty God, into which all arrive who are truly introverted and experience the presence of God in their souls. . . . It is the placing of ourselves continually in His presence, directing to Him all our thoughts, intentions and desires, referring purely to His glory all that we are to do and to suffer. . . . Meditation will move the will and cause an affection for spiritual things and a forgetfulness of all things of the world."[4]

It is meditation upon God, says al-Muḥāsibī, which leads the soul to realise what it means to enter into friendship with Him (*khulla*), when the love of God supersedes all other attachment in the heart, and it is conscious that it is loved even as it loves, and enters into the joy of its Lord.[5]

[1] *Early Christian Mystics*, p. 25. *Cf.* L. Blosius : " Before prayer and during prayer the servant of God should free his mind, as far as he can, from all cares and from images of other things ; and thus attending calmly, reverently, simply and lovingly to God present within Him and putting himself present before God, he should pray to Him and adore Him in spirit and in truth " (*op. cit.*, p. 66).

[2] " Ri'āya," fol. 15*a*.

[3] St. Jeanne de Chantal, *Mystical Prayer*, p. 33.

[4] *The Secret Paths of Divine Love*, pp. 62, 64, 76.

[5] Abū Nu'aym, " Ḥilyat al-Awliyā," fol. 236*a* (MS. Leyden).

Those who give themselves to meditation are men of spiritual insight, whose thoughts dwell continually upon God, while they themselves are unknown, obscure among believers, serving God with a service which is hidden, for this practice of interior prayer is a "hidden manna that is not known or prized except by him who receives it, and by tasting it the desire comes of enjoying it the more." The servant who has realised this finds his rest in meditation upon God, which is a fair and most honourable "station," and his heart cleaves unto it, and if he is temporarily turned aside from it, he will return to it.[1] al-Muḥāsibī relates that when Ibn al-Mubārak (*ob.* A.H. 180) was asked for good counsel, he said, "Give yourself to meditation upon God"; and when the questioner asked what he meant by meditation, Ibn al-Mubārak replied, "Personal prayer and meditation are the result of laying your heart beneath the Throne of God and holding intimate converse with Him Who sits thereon, and the heart can be brought back to meditation by the thought of His regard upon you and the remembrance of His knowledge of you, for He knows what is hidden in the breasts of men."[2]

Meditation brings light to the soul. "When we abandon everything," wrote Isaac of Nineveh, "and our mind goes out to seek Him alone, there will be no thought in it of anything which screens its face from the aspect of the Lord of the Universe. The more the mind abandons the thought of visible things and the more it thinks of the future hope, in accordance with the degree of elevation above bodily things and intercourse with them, to the same extent it will be subtilised and become clear during prayer."[3] "Medita-

[1] "Ādāb al-Nufūs," fols. 62*a*, 63*b*. *Cf.* St. Jeanne de Chantal, *Works*, III., p. 527.

[2] "Ādāb al-Nufūs," fol. 64*a*. There is a curiously close parallel to the Muslim conception of the All-Seeing Penetration of God in C. Barbanson's statement: "God like a watchful sentinel (*raqīb*, one of the Muslim Names of God) observes us in every motion, thought and desire: noting where our heart is, where it comes, whither it goes, unto what it aspires, and what is the root of all our works and intentions" (*op. cit.*, p. 61).

[3] *Mystic Treatises*, p. 293. *Cf.* also St. Francis de Sales: "Inasmuch as prayer places our understanding in the clearness of the Divine Light

tion," writes al-Muḥāsibī, "is the gate of gnosis . . . though the servant were to serve God with outward acts of devotion for a thousand years, and a thousand years again, and then were not acquainted with the practice of meditation, all his service would but increase his distance from God, and increase the hardness of his heart and diminish his faith. Meditation is the chief possession of the gnostic, that whereby the sincere and the Godfearing make progress on the journey to God; it brings comfort to the sorrowing and rest to those who have renounced all for His sake. It is a strength to the godly and a means of exaltation to the devout." Therefore, al-Muḥāsibī advises those for whom he writes, practise meditation, for it leads to a knowledge of how to worship God and of the perfection of His governance, and to that understanding wisdom, *sapientia*, without which mere earthly knowledge is vain, and works are of no avail, and prayer cannot be directed aright.[1]

Meditation means that the soul consciously and deliberately gives itself up to the thought of God, in order to attain to that "lively and attentive apprehension of the omnipresence of God, which means that God is in everything and everywhere, and that there is not any place or thing in this world where He is not most assuredly present . . . and think that not only is God in the place where we are, but that He is in a very special manner in our heart and the depth of our spirit, which He quickens with His Divine presence."[2] "Meditate upon God," is al-Muḥāsibī's advice, "in all that concerns you, in all times of activity and in all times of rest. Things are made of more value by what goes before and what comes after. What precedes meditation and what makes it of more value is

---

and exposes our will to the warmth of heavenly love, there is nothing so purges our understanding of its ignorance and our will of its depraved inclinations; it is the water of benediction which, when our souls are watered therewith, makes the plants of our good desires revive and flourish, cleanses our souls of their imperfections and quenches the thirst caused by the passions of our hearts" (*Introduction to the Devout Life*, p. 53).

[1] "Muḥāsabat al-Nufūs," fols. 66*b*, 67*a* (MS. Br. Mus.).

[2] St. Francis de Sales, *Introduction to the Devout Life*, pp. 56, 57.

detachment, and what follows it is adherence to obedience, through meditation, both in secret and openly." This is the station of those who desire proximity and detachment to God, that communion with Him which means closer intimacy with Him than with the creatures, and he who knows His loving-kindness and His continual favour and goodness and grace will seek communion with Him, for how can the servant meditate on Him Whom he does not know, or preoccupy himself with One Whom he does not trust and with Whom he is not intimate?[1]

The purpose of meditation is to stir up the affections towards God and Divine things and to move the will to acts of devotion and surrender. This is the stage of affective prayer, when feeling is in the ascendant and prayer becomes more and more a state of loving converse between the soul and God. After the prayer of adoration, which is combined with a sense of deep humility on the part of the creature and penitence for its shortcomings, and after meditation upon the greatness of God and His goodness, the soul of the servant is stirred within him, and ardour is kindled in his heart, his mind is uplifted by the exaltation and the condescension of Him with Whom he holds intercourse, all weariness and all feeling of affliction passes from him, because of the realisation within his breast of the glory of God, and the awe and fascination aroused by that great Mystery. He feels that which captivates and transports him, in the ardour of his heart, for, says al-Muḥāsibī, "The glory of God has taken hold upon him, and awe of Him and longing for Him and love towards Him, and he strives, carried away by amazement and rapture, filled with yearning, stirred by strong emotion, beside himself with love, his heart cleaving unto his Lord, while the remembrance of Him is never absent from his heart, nor deep awe of Him."[2]

[1] "Ādāb al-Nufūs," fol. 95*a*. *Cf.* Simon of Ṭaibūtheh: "The end of all perfection for mutable men is that man should become intoxicated with communion with God and have a mind rapt from the world in such a way that he no longer knows himself. . . . This begins while one is still a novice, from a continual communion with God, which takes place in the meditation of the mind during prayer" (*op. cit.*, p. 51).

[2] "Bad' man anāb ila Allāh," fol. 22*b*.

It is in affective prayer that the heart is filled with holy aspiration (*himma*), which seeks to penetrate and surmount all things which lie between the soul and God. Such aspirations are "infused," Divine gifts granted to the soul so that it may ascend still higher on its upward path. These aspirations are "the inward exercise by which the soul stretches forth with ardent desire towards God in order to be united to Him, not indeed by sensible images, but in a certain supernatural way, which is incomparably better and superior."[1] Those to whom such aspirations are granted know the sweetness of prayer, their hearts are looking towards God and find their rest in Him.[2] At the beginning of meditation the reason takes precedence of the will, providing motives and inducements to stir up the latter to action. Then the will exercises itself in acts of devotion, inspired thereto by God, and grows stronger and stronger in order to transcend the other powers. Finally the will, vivified and strengthened, can withdraw itself from all external imaginations or internal speculations and enjoy a certain other presence, by a real infusion and communication which God affords of Himself. When the soul, says al-Muḥāsibī, enjoys this confidential intercourse with Him Whom it loves, then the sweetness of that inward converse pervades the whole mind, so that it is no longer cognisant of this world and what is therein.[3]

Having known the joy of such interior prayer, the soul seeks ever to return to it. There arises a desire for recollection (*dhikr*), which is the practice of the presence of God at all times, "a continual, loving attention to God," not prayer at stated intervals, though this is necessary also, but an attitude of unceasing prayer, so that the soul can at all times turn to its Lord and find itself alone with Him, for the recollected soul can find God in all things and all things in God. In all its daily occupations, in its contacts

[1] L. Blosius, *op. cit.*, p. 50.

[2] "Muḥāsabat al-Nufūs," fol. 70*b* (Br. Mus.); "Makāsib wa'l-wara," fol. 34*a*. *Cf.* Simon of Ṭaibūtheh: "The following is a true sign that the soul is making progress in our Lord: if Divine sweetness waxes strong in the soul" (*Early Christian Mystics*, p. 9).

[3] "Ḥilyat al-Awliyā," fol. 232*a*. *Cf.* C. Barbanson, *op. cit.*, p. 87.

with others and with the world, it looks beyond the immediate end to the Will of God and seeks to bring into relation with that Will all its own actions and desires and thoughts. It means, then, a continual remembrance of God, of His presence without and within, a state of unceasing awareness of Him and of surrender to His influence upon the soul.[1] Those who give themselves to recollection, says al-Muḥāsibī, begin with the aspiration and resolve in all their dealings with the affairs of this world or the next to be continually mindful in their hearts of God and what is well pleasing to Him, and to pray unceasingly to Him in the inmost sanctuary of their souls, being ever preoccupied with prayer unto their Lord, and with the realisation of His presence, concerned only with His Will; and from this recollection comes joy in His good pleasure, and hope of His regard, and absorption in converse with the Lord, and freedom from all sin against Him. Such a one is attentive to His Lord within his inmost soul, and chooses the love of Him in preference to the love of self, and is attached to God Most Glorious and detached from His creatures. Outwardly he appears to be like the people of this world, but inwardly he is as those who are exalted, full of awe before his Lord, for his outward state is like the first state of heedlessness on the part of his heart; but when his heart betook itself unto its Lord, it became preoccupied with the recollection of what was well pleasing unto Him, and had no more thought of what was pleasing to the creatures, giving to them the place which their Lord assigned to them as His bondservants, and he is no more concerned with them, but only with the Will of their Lord.[2] This is "introversion," the turning aside from what is outward, to enter the sanctuary within the soul.[3] "The servant of God," wrote Blosius,

[1] *Cf.* F. Harton, *op. cit.*, pp. 247 *ff.*; C. Barbanson, p. 91.
[2] "Masā'il fī A'māl," fols. 129*b*, 130*a*.
[3] *Cf.* E. Underhill, *Introversion*:

"What do you seek within?
I seek a life that shall never die,
Some haven to win
From mortality.

"should apply himself to introversion with unwearying energy. He must diligently recall his mind from all wanderings and strive to cultivate his spirit by holy thoughts and meditations. For never can he be perfectly joined to God so long as he, voluntarily, of set purpose and with pleasure, reflects on vain and idle matters."[1] This is also al-Muḥāsibī's teaching. "These are they," he writes, "who know that God answers their prayers, and their hearts have taken refuge in Him, and have abandoned all creaturely concerns and the consideration of all that is not according to His Will, and have escaped from the snare of self-interest and the slavery of those who are in bondage to this world, and they are apart with their Lord, Who directs them in all they do, and Who knows what is in the secret recesses of their inmost selves. They do not abate their efforts to remain in constant communion with Him, but keep in proximity to their Lord, and continuous preoccupation with Him is theirs, chosen by them in preference to preoccupation with any other, because of what was manifest of the excellence of conformity with His Will in that to which He calls them and which He bids them do. And their striving in that does not affect the serenity of their continuous recollection of Him, nor withdraw their hearts from that state of proximity to God which is theirs, or from their meditation, and their enjoyment of the stations granted by the Lord of grace, on which they had set their hope—these are the characteristics of the righteous and the saints as they go about their business in this world."[2]

The soul, then, that would attach itself to God through recollection must detach itself from all other preoccupation which would hinder it from its freedom to seek God at all times and, when it chooses, to find itself alone with Him. "The chief part of the recollection of God," said al-Mu-

---

"What do you find within?
I find great quiet where no noises come,
Without, the world's din:
Silence in my home."

[1] *Spiritual Instruction*, p. 34.
[2] "Makāsib wa'l-wara'," fols. 35*a*, 35*b*. *Cf.* "Ri'āya," fol. 149*a*.

ḥāsibī, "is keeping close to Him."[1] Again he writes, "He who is preoccupied with God is separated from the creatures, and those who are detached from the creatures have escaped to the regions of solitude and are alone with the sweetness of the recollection of God, and in proportion as the heart enters into communion with God, through recollection, it escapes from loneliness." al-Muḥāsibī refers to a certain divine, who used to say in his personal prayers, "O Thou Who hast brought me into communion with Thyself, through recollection, and hast separated me from Thy creatures, and through Thy mercy dost give me guidance in my inmost self." He refers also to the word of God Most High to David, when He said, "Enter into communion with Me and be detached from all save Me." One of the devotees, he states, was asked, "What did so and so do?" and he replied, "He was in fellowship (with God) and separated (from the creatures)." al-Muḥāsibī quotes also the words of Rābi'a al-'Adawiyya of Baṣra (*ob.* 185/801),[2] whom he may well have known in his youth, and whose fame must certainly have come to his ears, who was asked, "How did you attain to this station (of intimacy with God)?" and she replied, "By abandoning what did not concern me, and seeking fellowship with Him Who is Eternal." al-Muḥāsibī, in this connection, tells how Dhu'l-Nūn in one of his discourses prayed, "O Thou Who art the Beloved of everyone who is alone with the recollection of Thee, and the Companion of everyone who is preoccupied with the love of Thee."

[1] "Kitāb al-Mustarshid," fol. 2. "For the right practice of the presence of God, said Brother Lawrence, the heart must be empty of all other things, because God will possess the heart alone; and as He cannot possess it alone, without emptying it of all besides, so neither can He act there and do in it what He pleases, unless it be left vacant to Him" (*Third Letter*).

[2] For a full account of the life and teaching of this celebrated woman mystic *cf.* my *Rābi'a the Mystic and her Fellow-Saints in Islām*. It was she who said in regard to the practice of the presence of God:

> "I have made Thee the Companion of my heart,
> But my body is available for those who desire its company,
> And my body is friendly towards its guests,
> But the Beloved of my heart is the guest of my soul."

He gives also an account of a conversation between the Ṣūfī ascetic 'Abd al-Wāḥid b. Zayd (*ob.* 177/793) and a Christian monk, to whom he said, " O monk, thou hast been quick to embrace solitude," and the monk replied, " O young man, hadst thou tasted the sweetness of solitude, thou wouldst have separated thyself thereto of thine own accord. Solitude is the chief part of devotion (*'ibāda*), and reflection cannot realise it from afar." 'Abd al-Wāḥid said, " O monk, what is the least that the servant finds in solitude ?" and he said, " Rest from the artifices of men, and security from their evil-doing." 'Abd al-Wāḥid asked again, " O monk, when does the servant taste the sweetness of fellowship with God ?" He said, " When love is made pure and action is single-minded." " When is love made pure ?" asked 'Abd al-Wāḥid, and the monk answered, " When the purpose is unified and becomes one single purpose directed to the service of God."[1] It is significant, in view of this conversation, that 'Abd al-Wāḥid b. Zayd is known as the founder of one of the first Ṣūfī monasteries, which he established at 'Abbadān, near Baṣra.

Solitude and silence are essential for the practice of recollection, though it may be that they are found only within the soul of the seeker, while all around him in the outer world is the bustle of crowded streets and the noise of the business of life. But, for progress in the spiritual life, a place and time must be found where the soul can be alone with its Lord and, as in the ritual prayer, the outward circumstances influence the inward attitude, and therefore it is well for the seeker to find a retreat where he can at times be apart from his fellow-men, where he can practise introversion, with silence around him as well as within. " Loneliness," Isaac of Nineveh had taught, " serves the purpose that we should have a place where we can converse with God in solitude "; and again he said, " Everyone who loves God loves a solitary life. . . . If thou lovest truth, thou must love silence. This will make thee illuminated in God like the sun, and it will deliver thee from the idle thoughts of ignorance ; silence will unite thee with God."[2] " Take

[1] Abū Nu'aym, " Ḥilyat al-Awliyā," fol. 240*b*.
[2] *Mystic Treatises*, pp. 295, 299.

solitude for your portion," says al-Muḥāsibī, "and be occupied with the recollection of your Lord."[1] That one who is preoccupied with his Lord finds himself straitened by the companionship of the creatures and is wearied by them, and his heart's preference is for the sweetness of continuous recollection. Asked what was the outward sign that a servant was continually engaged in the practice of the presence of God, al-Muḥāsibī said, "He is alone when in company, and in company when alone, a stranger in his own abode, and at home when on a journey, an eyewitness when absent, absent when present." Asked to explain further what it meant to be alone in company and in company when alone, he said, "He is alone in recollection, occupied with the apprehension of what has taken possession of his heart, and concerned with his preoccupation, enjoying the sweetness of recollection and the exaltation thereof, and he is set apart by his preoccupation from those in whose company he is, while present with them in body."

It was related, according to Kumayl b. Ziyād, that 'Alī b. Abī Ṭālib said concerning those who gave themselves to recollection, "Knowledge of the Truth has broken in upon them and they have experienced the spirit of certainty. They find easy what the self-willed and disobedient find hard, and they find fellowship where the ignorant would feel lonely. They keep company with this world in their bodily presence, but their hearts are attached to the most exalted of stations, in the highest heaven, in the presence of the King Supernal, and this is the condition of that one who is alone when in company." When asked, "Who is he who is in company when alone?" al-Muḥāsibī said, "He who is in company with his own concern, for his concern has become simplified, and he has unified it and made it one single concern, and for him all types of knowledge (*'ulūm*) have been unified in the contemplation of the rational causes of things, and in profound reflection on the all-penetrative omnipotence of God, and he belongs to God as regards his intellect and his heart and his concern altogether, and all his members are directed as one towards the continual recollection of the existence of (His) penetrating vision and far-reaching perception and

[1] "Kitāb al-Mustarshid," fol. 7.

extensive favour, and no part of him is detached (*i.e.*, all his faculties are concentrated to this end), nor is he subject to any wandering thought, and this is the description of him who is in company when alone." The question was asked, "What is the meaning of 'absence' in 'presence'?" and he said, "Such a one is absent in thought (*i.e.*, his judgment and intellect have ceased to act), but present in heart, and the meaning of 'absent' is that he is absent to the eyes of those who behold, but present in his heart with the gnostics in spirit."[1]

In such times of recollection the heart is purged of the thought of everything except God, and though the soul cannot continuously withdraw itself from its fellows, it can frequently recollect itself in this inward realisation of God's presence. Such direct preoccupation with God alone means, as al-Muḥāsibī shews, the simplification and unification of thought, feeling and desire. Therefore should the servant "turn himself into his own soul and dwell there in his own heart, for there will he be able to find God." By recollection he realises that the invisible God is ever near him, nay, more, within him, and thus the servant can find God in himself whenever he recollects himself, so that his soul is filled with the sense of His presence. Now he can offer an unwandering and steadfast prayer to God, for, said Isaac of Nineveh, "the heart which is really dead to the world is wholly astir in God."

So the soul is led on to contemplation (*mushāhada*), for prayer, said Isaac again, is the seed and contemplation is the harvest.[2] The process of purification has done its work and the time for it is past, for "purgation," says al-Hujwīrī, "compared with contemplation is like a drop of water in the sea." Mortification, that process carried to its completion in meditation and recollection, when the heart becomes dead to all else, but alive in God, is but a stage for the seeker, which the adept has left behind. "Contemplation," says al-Hujwīrī again, "is the battlefield of men and mortification the playground of children."[3] The *summum bonum*, said the

[1] Abū Nu'aym, *op. cit.*, fol. 240*b*. *Cf.* p. 207 above.
[2] *Mystic Treatises*, pp. 113, 298. *Cf.* L. Blosius, pp. 36, 38.
[3] *Op. cit.*, pp. 77, 325.

Christian monk and mystic Dādīsho' Qaṭrāya, quoting the words of a wise man, "consists in that we should despise all perishable beauties in our desire for the Beauty of our Maker, and reject all corruptible wealth in our contemplation of the wealth of His knowledge, and tread underfoot all evanescent glories in our expectation of the glory which is prepared by Him for those who have accomplished His Will in wisdom, in the time of their sojourn on the earth."[1] Contemplation goes beyond the stage of meditation and recollection. Meditation is "striking the flint to secure a spark"; in contemplation the light is already lit and burns steadily; meditation is still seeking, contemplation has found, and when the end is secured, the means are no longer needed. In the perfect prayer of contemplation, he who prays is no longer conscious that he is praying, the door into the sanctuary has been opened; words and thought alike are stilled, for the "Master of the house" has come.[2] So Dhu'l-Nūn said, "Every intercessor is veiled by his intercessions from the contemplation of God . . . for when God is present and manifested, there is no need to make intercession. If He were absent, then should intercession be made to Him."[3]

"By contemplation," said al-Hujwīrī, "the Ṣūfīs mean spiritual vision of God in public and private, without asking how or in what manner. Contemplation in this world resembles the Vision of God in the next—since vision is possible hereafter, contemplation is possible here. Contemplation is an attribute of the heart and silence is a sign of contemplation."[4] So also al-Muḥāsibī teaches, "Action by the movements of the heart in the contemplation of invisible things is better than by the movement of the members."[5] This stage, when the soul looks unto God alone,

[1] *Early Christian Mystics*, p. 112.

[2] *Cf.* St. Peter of Alcantara, *Treatise on Prayer and Meditation*, p. 112, and Isaac of Nineveh, *op. cit.*, p. 112.

[3] al-Sulamī, *op. cit.*, fols. 7*b*, 8*a*.

[4] *Op cit.*, pp. 332, 333. *Cf.* St. Thomas Aquinas: "This contemplation will be perfect in the life to come . . . now the contemplation of the Divine Truth bestows on us a certain inchoate beatitude, which begins now and will be continued in the life to come" (Q. 180, Art. 4).

[5] Abū Nu'aym, *op. cit.*, fol. 241*a*.

can only be attained by cutting off every source of hope but God—emptying the heart of all else that it may receive God. The servant contemplates his Lord, having cut off his hope from all save Him, and he sees no place for his own choice, for God is sufficient for him, and in Him he has found the peace of certainty. No station is higher than that in which the soul dwells with God in perfect tranquillity, because God is enough for it, and it looks unto Him and away from the creatures, having lost nothing and gained all things. The contemplative no longer sees this world or what it contains, no longer regards himself, for the sole object of his contemplation is God. It is all one to him whether he sails upon the sea or walks upon dry land, whether he enjoys companionship or is alone, in his times of action and his times of rest, for God Most High is sufficient for him, and the life in Him preoccupies him from all else.[1] The Ṣūfī Abū Yazīd al-Bisṭāmī said that on his first pilgrimage to Mecca he saw only the temple (the Ka'ba); on his second visit he saw both the temple and the Lord of the temple; the third time he saw the Lord alone, and knew that what really mattered was not the earthly temple, but contemplation and "annihilation in the abode of friendship." For the sanctuary is where contemplation is, and when the servant has that Vision of God, the whole universe is his sanctuary.[2]

Contemplation is not a station to which man can attain by his own efforts, it is "a state in which one is kept by God, and man's actions do not begin to have value until God keeps him thus," for in contemplation the servant's will is merged in the Will of Him Whom he contemplates, and all that he does is done in and through Him.[3] For as the greatest joy of the people of Paradise is the contemplation of God face to face, so the greatest joy of the believer in this world is this relation to his Lord, of communion with Him in contemplation, after meditation upon Him and intercourse

[1] "Ādāb al-Nufūs," fols. 101*b ff.*

[2] al-Hujwīrī, *op. cit.*, p. 327.

[3] *Ibid.*, p. 205. *Cf.* St. Jeanne de Chantal: "Look on God and leave Him to act. That is all you have to do and the only exercise God requires of you, to which He alone has drawn you . . . one thing only is necessary, and that is, to have God" (*Works*, Vol. III., p. 287).

with Him in prayer, and service for His sake. Now he knows the sweetness of that service and is filled with love for it, for it is impossible for him who works to become intimate with his work, and not to become intimate with Him for Whom he works. So God has distinguished His saints with the beatitude of being preoccupied with Him, so that all the cares of this world have departed from their hearts, preoccupation with the world to come has taken possession of them, because of the joy, mingled with awe, with which they contemplate their Lord.[1] It was to such contemplation that the Prophet referred when he said, " Worship God as if you saw Him " ; and Ḥāritha, when he was granted a foretaste of the bliss to come, of the Vision of God which will be revealed in Paradise, when the saints look upon Him face to face, said of his experience, " It was as if I were looking upon the very Throne of God, made manifest to my eyes."[2]

The soul has passed through the stage of the purgative life, it has been granted the attainments and the encouragement of the illuminative life, and now it has entered upon the unitive way, the way of the lovers of God, who, by following it, attain to the perfection of the life of the saints in God.

[1] " Adāb al-Nufūs," fols. 101*a*, 101*b*. *Cf.* Gerlac Petersen : " By contemplation the whole being of the man is made conformable to the Will of God, so as to be able to look upon all things with an even mind, on the one hand never disturbed by unfavourable or painful circumstances, or on the other never rendered lax by prosperity " (*Divine Soliloquies*, p. 16).

[2] " Ādāb al-Nufūs," fol. 64*a*.

CHAPTER XII

THE MYSTICAL TEACHING OF AL-MUḤĀSIBĪ—THE UNITIVE WAY—GNOSIS—FELLOWSHIP—SATISFACTION—LOVE—THE BEATIFIC VISION—THE LIFE OF THE SAINTS IN GOD

THE seeker has entered upon the last stage of the quest, which means the attainment of the goal. The soul has passed through the period of strife and effort, when it was ever struggling against that Divine influence, which was felt to be in opposition to the human ego, until at last the rightly directed will asserted itself over the lower nature and the process of purification was accomplished. Then, ready to recognise and receive the gifts which God had been ever willing to bestow upon it, having become more and more receptive of that Divine influence, until its experience of God ceased to be objective and became subjective, it sought its Lord not without, but within, itself, and realised its own kinship with the Divine. Now the soul has merged its own will in that Eternal Will and is conscious that the human ego has become identified with a Being greater than itself yet one with itself. Now it has in truth become the " soul at rest " (*al-nafs al-muṭma'inna*), the servant has become the " friend " of God.

Of such a one al-Muḥāsibī writes that he finds rest in the peace of certainty (*rawḥ al-yaqīn*) and rejoices in a life in which he is independent of all save God, detached not only from dependence on others but free also from dependence on self.[1] "For in whatever creature the perfect shall be known," wrote an anonymous German mystic, " therein creature-nature, qualities, the I, the self and the like must all be lost and done away."[2] Yet this loss is felt to be pure gain, for the soul has come to " the valley of refreshment and joy and happiness, and enjoys in the fellowship of the saints the

[1] " Ḥilya," fol. 240*a* (MS. Leyden).
[2] *Theologia Germanica*, cap. I.

peace of assurance[1] in the recollection of God, and the beatitude of being apart in intimate communion with Him, and has tasted the sweetness of assured peace and the joy of satisfaction and the bliss of committing itself altogether into the hands of God (*tafwīḍ*)."[2] The soul has passed beyond the "stations" and the "states," the practice of the virtues has become habitual to it, it has entered into enjoyment of the spiritual gifts, and it has attained to assurance, to that which Hujwīrī calls *tamkīn* (lit. fixity), for now it lives the life which is "rooted and grounded" in God. "*Tamkīn*," he writes, "denotes the residence of spiritual adepts in the abode of perfection and in the highest grade. Those in stations can pass on from their stations, but it is impossible to pass beyond the grade of *tamkīn* because *maqām* (station) is the grade of beginners, whereas *tamkīn* is the resting-place of adepts, and 'stations' are stages on the way, whereas *tamkīn* is repose within the shrine."[3] To these, says al-Muḥāsibī, the name of saintship is applied, for they are the friends of God (*awliyā' Allāh*), who have attained to perfect faith (*yaqīn*), who have gained knowledge after ignorance, riches after poverty, fellowship after loneliness, rest after weariness, to whom have been been given the treasures of the Divine grace, who enter now into the joy of their Lord, for the righteousness of the perfect is theirs, their pilgrimage has prospered, and they have reached their goal.[4]

Those who experience this state of certainty, who enjoy the Divine friendship, have also attained to gnosis (*ma'rifa*),[5] for the saint is the true gnostic (*'ārif b'illāh*); that which he sought unwearyingly, that gift which he was preparing himself to receive throughout his quest, has been found and is his, by the grace of God bestowed on him. To him has been granted that supernatural wisdom by

[1] *Cf.* N. Söderblom: "One of the great problems of religion (is) how to gain *assurance*—assurance of Divine grace and of God's Will and work for the salvation of mankind" (*The Living God*, pp. 158, 163).

[2] "Ādāb al-Nufūs," fol. 80*a*.

[3] *Kashf al-Maḥjūb*, p. 371.

[4] "Ri'āya," fol. 52*a*; "Kitāb al-Mustarshid," fol. 4; "Muḥāsabat al-Nufūs," fol. 9.

[5] *Ibid.*, fol. 2.

which his understanding is enlightened, "a certain Divine light given to the soul whereby it both sees and tastes God and Divine things," that esoteric wisdom (*bāṭin-al-ḥikma*) which is the characteristic of God's elect, by which He has distinguished them.[1] "That which leads from the stage of patience—that is, the life of the virtues—to the stage of bliss (*darajat al-naʿīm*)," writes al-Muḥāsibī, "is the attainment of gnosis, which is the heart's recognition of its need of God, and its approach unto Him and to the invisible world and the vision thereof."[2] To action there is a limit, but to gnosis there is no limit, for it is directed towards perfection, the limitless perfection of the Supremely Perfect.[3] This is that supernatural knowledge which is concerned not with the earthly, but the spiritual. "When knowledge elevates itself above earthly things," Isaac of Nineveh had written, "and above the thought of service, and begins to try its impulses in things hidden from eyesight, and when it partly despises the recollection of (worldly) things, and when it stretches itself upward and clings to faith by thinking of the world to be and love of the promises and investigation concerning the hidden things . . . then faith swallows knowledge, gives a new birth to it, wholly spiritual. . . . Then it is able to direct its flight towards non-bodily places and to the depths of the inscrutable ocean of wonderful and Divine government which directs intelligible and apperceptible beings and to examine spiritual mysteries."[4]

By the light of this gnosis the spiritual eyes of the soul are

[1] "Makāsib wa'l-Waraʿ," fol. 35*b*. *Cf.* the Christian mystic Gerlac Petersen: "It is the Eternal Wisdom that goeth along with the soul, leading it and nobly strengthening it on the way, and it followeth it, fortifying it on every side in itself and bringing it happily to the end. By means of this Wisdom the soul taketh captive every thought, perception and affection unlike itself. To this Wisdom the soul turneth every conflict and hindrance. . . . By this Wisdom the soul often gathereth together all its powers, affections, senses both interior and exterior, presenting them whole and entire, not held back in any way by any other power (*cf.* p. 228 below) before the face of God Who changeth not, beyond time and place and every happening, and it placeth itself and all things there where the Eternal Truth places them" (*Divine Soliloquies*, pp. 89, 90).

[2] "Ādāb al-Nufūs," fol. 91*b*.

[3] *Ibid.*, fol. 95*b*.

[4] *Mystic Treatises*, p. 250.

shewn the hidden mysteries which are within itself and the secret riches of Divinity which are concealed from the eyes of fleshly men and are revealed spiritually.[1] This is " insight without sight," for the gnostic has within him that inner light (*baṣā'ir al-nūr*), whereby he sees and apprehends the spiritual meaning of things, and is conscious within himself that he has attained the Truth.[2] Dhū'l-Nūn al-Miṣrī, al-Muḥāsibī's contemporary, defines this supernatural knowledge in similar terms, saying, " Gnosis is in reality God's providential communication of the spiritual light to our inward hearts."[3]

It is not, therefore, a thing to which the servant, of himself, should make any pretensions, for it is only by a sudden working of Divine grace that it is unexpectedly revealed in the soul. " The Most High God," writes Hujwīrī, " as He pleases and by whatever means He pleases, shews His servant the way to Himself and opens to him the door of gnosis. . . . Therefore do not claim gnosis, lest thou perish in thy pretension, but cleave to the reality thereof, that thou mayst be saved."[4] al-Muḥāsibī also admonishes the servant of God to fear Him and not to claim knowledge of the gnosis of annihilation in God (*fanā'*)—the perception that all created things, including the self, are non-existent beside the subsistence of God—for he who asserts that it exists within himself is claiming to be among the heirs of the prophets and the elect of God, and it is for God to choose whom He will to be His saints. The true gnostic is he who recognises that all things are in the hands of God, and any assertion of self is agnosticism, for so long as there is room in the heart for anything save God, or the possibility of expressing aught but God,

[1] *Cf.* R. Otto : " The numinous issues from the deepest foundation of cognitive apprehension that the soul possesses and while at first interfused with the present world of sensuous experience it finally takes its stand in absolute contrast to it . . . the facts of the numinous consciousness point therefore to a hidden substantive source from which the religious ideas and feelings are formed, which lies in the mind independently of sense-experience, a 'pure reason' in the profoundest sense" (*The Idea of the Holy*, p. 117).

[2] " Kitāb al-Mustarshid," fol. 4. *Cf.* Sarrāj, *Kitāb al-Luma'*, p. 182.

[3] *Kashf al-Mahjūb*, p. 275.

[4] *Ibid.*, pp. 273, 274.

true gnosis has not been attained. He is no true gnostic who has not turned aside from all that is not God.[1]

Gnosis, then, is the characteristic of the elect, those whom God has chosen to be His saints, and al-Junayd related that he heard Ḥārith b. Asad (al-Muḥāsibī) say of the gnostics, "They are those who are worthy to apprehend the nature of the Divine Unity, to understand that all is God and all is His, worthy of being alone with the Alone, chosen unto Himself to be brought up under His eye (*'ala 'aynihi*), whom He has made to love Him, according to His word, 'I have chosen thee for Myself and to be brought up under My eye, and I have bestowed upon thee love from Myself.'"[2] It is the characteristic of those whom He has created for Himself, whom He has made to love Him, that they have passed beyond the sphere of merely human knowledge and its limitations, their power of understanding has been perfected and they are no more deceived, for all types of knowledge are laid open to them, and memory passes away, and they are amazed with a great amazement; but that which becomes clear to them is the love which takes possession of them through the knowledge which God has given to them of Himself.[3]

To the gnostic among those who believe is given that understanding faith which is capable of intimate converse, together with knowledge of the proximity of Him with Whom he converses, and he is not hindered by the knowledge of his own baseness, nor by the knowledge of His sublimity. These are regions in which knowledge is sought in inter-

[1] "Kitāb al-'Ilm," chapter viii. *Cf.* Hujwīrī, *op. cit.*, pp. 274 *ff.*, and Qushayrī, "In proportion to man's self-emptying is his attainment of gnosis" (*Risāla*, p. 141). *Cf.* also p. 222 above.

[2] Sūra 20 : 40 *ff.*

[3] Of this state Qushayrī says that the extreme degree of gnosis means amazement and ecstatic wonder: "He who has the most knowledge of God is most amazed at Him, and with those who have attained to Truth gnosis is contemplation mingled with amazement" (*Risāla*, pp. 171, 172). *Cf.* Schleiermacher: "It is to the devoted, contemplative spirit that the secret of the universe is revealed. Such a man will become aware of the eternal ideas, to him . . . the eternal will shine through the temporal; the infinite, which neither space nor time can comprehend, will be revealed in the finite forms of time and space" (*Religious Essays*, p. 79).

course with those who are near to God, and in preoccupation with learning the different roads which lead to the sphere of the purified, who have been deprived of their seclusion, set free from self-will, turned aside from what they desired, the winds of intelligence (*fiṭna*) have blown upon them and exposed them upon the seas of wisdom, and they have been submerged in the water of life. They take no steps to avoid misfortune, nor do they heed disaster. They shew no eagerness in the search for attainment of the end, for what are ends to others, for them are but beginnings. They are those who are manifested in what is hidden from mankind, and hidden in what is manifest to them, who are faithful to what God has revealed to them, preserving His secret, carrying out His command, and they act with gracious courtesy in what is laid upon them of what is due to Him. There is no good counsel given to them which they do not bestow on others, and no degree of proximity to their Lord to which they do not attain. They are magnanimous in devoting their very life-blood to the fulfilment of the first of His claims, in the search for a means of attaining unto Him, and they press forward without thought of consequences or reservation—indeed, their aim is to count all things but loss for His sake. The radiance of the Truth is given unto them as a light to guide them on their way, and knowledge of the Truth is made plain unto them. No blame attaches to them in any evil that befalls, nor does any fear oppress them in time of anxiety. In what they undertake they are not moved by desire, because of what they seek to maintain of God's Word, and they are witnesses thereto.[1]

The gnostics are those to whom God gives His guidance and His favour and His love, whom He preserves from sin, whom He veils with the veil of the sanctified (*al-aṣfiyā'*), who know Him and are known of Him.[2] Those who dwell on the mountain-heights, in communion with God, the prophets and the righteous and the elect among the faithful, are characterised by this gift of gnosis, whereby they are distinguished from others, by their greater knowledge of the All-Glorious, for they are the pure of heart, who adore Him without ceasing, and keep ever close to His side, seeking the

[1] "Ḥilya," fols. 240*b ff.* [2] "Muḥāsabat al-Nufūs," fol. 3.

Will of their Lord. These are the marks of the gnostics, who are no longer concerned with the demands of human desire and are oblivious to all that would claim them apart from Him, knowing no weariness in His service, eager to advance to more devoted service, cleaving to every means of approach to God. Devotion to Him has unified their desires and they see their way clear before them.[1] They know that at all times the help of their Lord is enough for them, and His secret loving-kindness, which will never be cut off from them, and they abide in this state and accomplish their work, and that for which they hope is brought to pass. The desires of the flesh have no longer any power over them, nor the Adversary, nor any false self-seeking hope, for through their knowledge of God they have slain their lusts and conquered their enemy and directed their activities towards one end, and are assured of their real concern. The favour of their Lord is always theirs, and His secret loving-kindness never fails them, and these are the marks of the gnostics in God, whose hearts God has illumined and kept from contamination, so that no creature has the worth of a mustard-seed in their hearts.[2] This is the gnosis of which Dhu'l-Nūn said that it meant "knowledge of the attributes of the Divine Unicity, which belongs to the saints of God, those who contemplate God in their hearts in such wise that He reveals unto them what He reveals to none other of His creatures."[3]

The gnostic who undergoes this spiritual experience, whereby he apprehends the true nature of God, enters into fellowship with Him (*uns*), for fellowship with God, said Dhu'l-Nūn, is a "shining light," it is knowledge of Him

[1] Isaac of Nineveh says of the unifying influence of gnosis, "Before the mind has been freed from manifold deliberations and has reached the unified simplicity of purity, it is not able to perceive spiritual things . . . if thou reachest purity . . . suddenly (gnosis) is found within thee, without inquiring after it" (*op. cit.*, p. 354).

[2] "Makāsib wa'l-wara'," fols. 34*a ff.* *Cf.* "Ḥilyā," fol. 236*b*, and Hujwīrī, p. 275.

[3] 'Aṭṭār, *op. cit.*, I., p. 127. *Cf.* R. Otto: "The clearer insight into the marvel comes in the experience as a burst of illumination . . . on the one hand an entry or penetration into consciousness of inspiration, sudden, unmeditated, once and for all achieved, and on the other hand a reminiscence of something that was a familiar possession even before the moment of insight" (*Idea of the Holy*, p. 200).

and proximity to Him.[1] It means separation from the creatures, says al-Muḥāsibī, in order to be in communion with Him, so that the heart is straitened when the claims of the creatures keep it from intercourse with its Lord, for the greatest joy in life is fellowship with God and the unification of all the powers (*ijtimāʿ al-himma*) in concentration upon the One, which is indeed the chief end of man.[2]

Those who are in fellowship with their Lord are no longer veiled from Him by the claims of this world and the afflictions of the worldlings, for they enjoy always the delight of being close to Him and the joy of having abandoned the visible for the things of the invisible world, the temporal for the eternal. Fellowship with the Creator makes them also compassionate to His creatures, whom they would fain bring into their own happy state, for they themselves have chosen that better part which shall not be taken away. They feel no envy of earthly kings, for unto them is appointed eternal glory in the presence of the King of kings, and though in the eyes of men they are despised, they are precious in His sight, and because now they count all things but loss for His sake, they shall in the world to come be exalted with Him in glory. How should he be a stranger who is in fellowship with His Lord, or why should separation and detachment from the conversation of men be grievous to the heart of him whose understanding and whose tongue are preoccupied in intercourse with God? There is nothing to be despised in him who has refused to lay up treasures on earth, in order that he may secure unto himself the treasure of entrance into the presence of His Lord in the life everlasting.[3]

Through fellowship with God the hearts of the gnostics are illumined and their souls exalted, and they are made independent of the creatures, and their fellowship leads them to

[1] "Ḥilya," fol. 201*b* (MS. Leyden).

[2] "Ḥilya," fols. 241*a*, *b*. *Cf.* p. 216 above; "Ādāb al-Nufūs," fol. 91*b*. So also R. Otto writes of "the achieved fellowship with the Holy, in knowing, feeling and willing" (*Idea of the Holy*, p. 181).

[3] "Bad' man anāb ila Allāh," fol. 24*a*. *Cf.* L. Blosius: "Such a man knows the Godhead better than many learned masters of theology who have never been admitted into the Holy of Holies and the secret chamber of the Eternal King and have never been illuminated in any extraordinary way with the light of grace" (*op. cit.*, p. 9).

strong yearning towards Him, and they are transported from toil to bliss in serving Him and rejoicing in His service. In His fellowship they know no loss or disappointment, for they are the most exalted of the creation, in soul, and the most enlightened, in heart, and the richest, since He is their sufficiency and life holds greater joys for them than for any others. Their grief is for what makes other men rejoice, and they rejoice in what causes grief to others; their search is for that which other men shun, and they flee from that which the heedless and neglectful desire. They find companionship where other men experience loneliness, since their fellowship is with God Most Glorious alone, for they seek to be made perfect through their intimacy with Him. Unto Him they confide their secrets and to Him they draw near with their needs, for in Him they find their protection and their refuge; they rely on Him and not on His creatures, and they are preoccupied with Him to the exclusion of all that would distract them from Him, for they are alone when men are in company, apart from the creatures and in fellowship with their Lord.[1]

al-Muḥāsibī quotes the words of a wise man who said in his prayers, "It is amazing that mankind should desire any other than Thyself, and I wonder that any should seek for fellowship apart from Thee. O Lord, Thou hast entered into fellowship with Thy friends among the saints and hast characterised them by the contentment of those who trust in Thee. Thou dost look upon their consciences and Thy regard is upon their inmost selves. There is no veil between Thee and me, and I know myself to be in Thy presence. When a sense of strangeness afflicts me, the recollection of Thee is my consolation, and when troubles overwhelm me, I return to seek Thine aid, O Lord of all creation."[2] The first step in fellowship, said Dhu'l-Nūn, is to meet with the Friend, and after that the thought of Him will never leave thee.[3] Such fellowship, said Sarrāj, leads of necessity to perfect tranquillity (*iṭma'inna*), that peace of God which passes all understanding.[4]

1 "Ri'āya," fol. 7*a*. *Cf.* Sarrāj, *op. cit.*, p. 65.
2 "Ḥilya," fol. 240*b*.
3 Sulamī, *op. cit.*, fol. 8*a*.
4 *Op. cit.*, p. 66.

This is the peace which is born of perfect concord (*muwāfaqa*) between God and the soul that has reached the state of Satisfaction (*riḍā'*), which is the essence of harmony, for it means, said Aḥmad b. Ḥanbal, to commit all one's affairs to God; but while it means the heart's acquiescence in the Will of God, it means also that God is well pleased with His servant.[1] On the servant's side, it is the perfection of the virtues of reliance on God (*thiqa*), dependence on Him (*tawakkul*), complete trust in Him (*tafwīḍ*), and patience (*ṣabr*), which have become second nature to the gnostic. al-Muhāsibī held that satisfaction was a "state," not a "station"; but, unlike some of the Ṣūfī Shaykhs, he maintained that such "states" were permanent and, in the gnostic, had become his attributes.[2] "Satisfaction," he said, "is the quiescence (*sukūn*) of the heart under the events which follow from the Divine decrees," and this is sound doctrine, Hujwīrī observes, supporting al-Muḥāsibī's contention that satisfaction is more than a "station," which is acquired by the co-operation of human effort with the Divine grace, for quiescence and tranquillity of heart are not qualities acquired by man, but are Divine gifts. Abu'l-'Abbās b. 'Aṭā had also defined satisfaction as the heart's acceptance of the eternal choice of God on behalf of His creature, so that in whatever befalls him he can recognise the eternal Will of God and His decree and accept it, not only without distress, but with joy.[3]

al-Muḥāsibī was asked how this state of satisfaction was attained, and he replied that it was through the knowledge of the heart that the Lord is just in all His decrees, without any doubt that the choice of God for His servant is better than his own. It comes when the understanding of men is enlightened and their hearts attain to certainty and their souls

[1] Hujwīrī, *op. cit.*, p. 177. *Cf.* my *Studies in Early Mysticism*, pp. 172 *ff*. So also the German mystic Johann von Kastl: "Therefore let the soul of its very necessity make the venture to trust wholly and completely in the Lord God. In this wise is the soul so pleasing to God, that He bestows His own grace upon it, and by that grace it comes to feel the true love and affection which drives away all doubt and all fear, and hopes confidently" (*De Adhærendo Deo*, chapter v.).

[2] *Cf.* pp. 185 *ff*. above.

[3] Hujwīrī, *op. cit.*, p. 180; 'Aṭṭār, I., p. 227.

to knowledge, and knowledge bears witness that God's Will is carried out, and they know that He does what is best for His servant in His choice for him and His love towards him, and the hearts of men know that He Who has no compeer is just in all He decrees, there is no doubt of His sovereignty, and the heart of His servant rejoices in accepting it.

al-Junayd relates that he heard al-Muḥāsibī say on this subject of Satisfaction, "Know that thou hast no concern with anything save God, and nothing is thine save what thou hast obtained from the good pleasure (*riḍwān*) of God, and if thou dost honour Him in what is due to Him, He will preserve thee from all evil."[1] al-Muḥāsibī was asked what was the reason of the affliction sent by God to believers, and he said that affliction was of three types: that which was sent to the worldlings (*mikhlaṭīn*, lit. busybodies) as a punishment and a torment, that which was sent to the novices (who had entered upon the journey to God) in order to purify them from their sins, and that which came upon the gnostics by way of favour because they were the chosen of God. When asked to describe the result of these afflictions, he said that the effect upon the worldlings was that impatience took possession of their hearts, and their heedlessness of what was due to God became a veil unto them and they fell into discontent and complained of their trials. But the novices who were seeking God maintained patience in the time of affliction until they were set free and escaped from it after toil and grief. Finally, the gnostics meet affliction with satisfaction, well pleased with all that comes from the hand of God Most Glorious, knowing that His decrees are just, and they rejoice in the occurrence of what is abhorrent, because of their knowledge of the ultimate result of God's choice for them. The gnostics profit by affliction, for they understand the word of God as if they heard Him speaking to them, and in the time of affliction they know Him to be nearer to them than their souls to their bodies, and they are aware of His regard upon them, and therefore they maintain patience and satisfaction in their time of trial, as being in the sight of God, and they cleave unto Him, and in His presence they cast aside all thought of saving themselves from affliction and

[1] "Ḥilya," fol. 235*a*.

give their bodies over unto death in the extremity of their devotion to Him, and therefore He removes their offences from them and saves them from the temptation to grow weary and to fail in loyalty to Him and to give way to complaint, and causes them to enter within the veil of His protection, where no enemy can attack them or make them to fear or deceive them by his claims to power.[1]

al-Hujwīrī, summarising and commenting on al-Muḥāsibī's views, perhaps with a fuller knowledge of them than we have,[2] quotes the saying of Ḥusayn b. 'Alī, " I say that whoever surveys the excellent choice made by God for him does not desire anything except what God has chosen for him," and continues, " When a man sees God's choice and abandons his own choice, he is delivered from all sorrow. This, however, does not hold good in absence from God (*ghayba*) ; it requires presence with God (*ḥuḍūr*), because ' satisfaction expels sorrows and cures heedlessness ' and purges the heart of thoughts relating to other than God and frees it from the bonds of tribulation : for it is characteristic of satisfaction to deliver. . . . Satisfaction is the acquiescence of one who knows that giving and withholding are in God's knowledge, and firmly believes that God sees him in all circumstances."[3] *Riḍā'*, then, is the gnostic's manifestation of his belief in the Divine Unity, for, as a Christian mystic expressed it, " He who findeth full satisfaction in God receiveth all his satisfaction from one source, and from one only, as One. And a man cannot find all satisfaction in God, unless all things are One to him and One is all, and something and nothing are alike."[4]

Gnosis, fellowship and satisfaction are the characteristics of the lovers of God, for " gnosis and love are spiritually identical, they teach the same truths in different language."[5] The will, says a modern writer on religion, when God-directed, appears indifferently as wisdom or as love : two names of the same power, the former more intelligential, the latter more spiritual.[6] The desire for fellowship arises from

[1] " Ḥilya," fols. 235*b ff.* (MS. Leyden). [2] *Cf.* p. 58 above.
[3] Hujwīrī, *op. cit.*, p. 178. [4] *Theologia Germanica*, p. 185.
[5] R. A. Nicholson, *The Mystics of Islam*, p. 101.
[6] Coleridge, *Lay Sermons*, p. 68. *Cf.* " Ādāb al-Nufūs," fol. 93*b*.

love, and fellowship in its turn increases love. "Have you seen any lover forgetful of his Beloved," asks al-Muḥāsibī, "or preferring himself to his love, or refraining from fellowship with Him, or seeking fellowship with any other? For if there is any impediment between the two, this is a denial of love. The lover is not sincere unless he loves the Unity (*i.e.*, realises there is none but the One), and if he ceases to love it, he has become an unbeliever."[1]

Perfect satisfaction is identical with love, for "those who are satisfied with being chosen by God are His lovers, whose existence is an illusion alike in His anger and His satisfaction: whose hearts dwell in the presence of purity and the garden of intimacy: who have no thought of created things and have escaped from the bonds of 'stations' and 'states' and have devoted themselves to the love of God. Their satisfaction involves no loss, for satisfaction with God is a manifest kingdom." Satisfaction may begin in acquisition and effort, the satisfaction of the novices on the Way, but it ends, for the adept gnostics, in love and rapture, for when all is accepted as coming from God, there is no room in the heart for any thought save that of the Beloved.[2]

al-Hujwīrī has some interesting theories to propound on the derivation of the term used to denote this Divine love (*maḥabba*). The word, he tells us, is said to be derived from *ḥibba*, seeds which fall to the earth in the desert, and their name was given to such seeds, because love is the source of life, as seeds are the origin of plants. Just as such seeds, when they have been scattered abroad and hidden in the earth, and the rain waters them and the sun shines upon them and heat and cold pass over them, are not corrupted by the changing seasons, but grow and bear flowers and give their fruit, so also love, when it finds a dwelling in the heart, is not corrupted by presence or absence, by pleasure or pain, by separation or union. Others have derived the name of love from *ḥabba*, the heart's core, in which love resides, and so love takes its name from its dwelling-place; others, again, derive it from *ḥabab*, a bubble of water and its effervescence,

1. "Riʿāya," fol. 131*a*.
2. *Kashf al-Maḥjūb*, pp. 178 *ff.*, 305.

because love is the effervescence of the heart in longing for union with its Beloved.[1]

Pure love to God is the mark of the perfect gnostic, of the traveller who has reached the goal, of the saints who are the friends of God. "Love," says al-Muḥāsibī, "is your whole-hearted inclination towards a thing, then your preference for it above yourself, above your welfare, material and spiritual, above all you possess, then your complete conformity (*muwāfaqa*) with it in secret and openly, and then your knowledge of your shortcomings in love towards it."[2] Only One is worthy of such love, and to this mystic love of God All-Glorious and an account of His lovers, al-Muḥāsibī devotes a whole book, containing the most beautiful expression of his mystical teaching which has come down to us, and giving to us the revelation of his own experience as mystic and lover.[3] Man's love of God arises from God's love for him,[4] and, in a commentary on al-Muḥāsibī's teaching on this subject, which is also the doctrine of al-Junayd and many of the Ṣūfī Shaykhs, Hujwīrī says that God's love of man is His goodwill towards him and His mercy shewn to him. Love is one of the names of His Will (*irāda*), and His Will is an eternal attribute whereby He wills His actions. God's love towards man, therefore, "consists in shewing much favour to him and giving him a recompense in this world and the next and making him secure from punishment and keeping him safe from sin, and bestowing on him lofty 'states' and exalted 'stations,' and causing him to turn his thoughts away from all that is other than God, and that specialisation of His Will is called love."

It is again al-Muḥāsibī's teaching which Hujwīrī reproduces in his explanation of man's love to God, describing it as "a quality which manifests itself in the heart of the pious believer in the form of veneration and magnification, so that he seeks to satisfy his Beloved and becomes impatient and restless in his desire for vision of Him, and can-

[1] *Kashf al-Maḥjūb*, pp. 305, 306. [2] Qushayrī, *Risāla*, p. 190.

[3] Transmitted by A. b. 'Abdallah b. Maymūn al-Khawwās in Abū Nu'aym's "Ḥilya," fols. 232 *ff*. *Cf*. pp. 57, 58 above.

[4] *Cf*. 1 St. John iv. 19: "We love Him, because He first loved us."

not rest in anyone except Him, and grows familiar with the remembrance of Him and abjures the remembrance of everything besides. Repose becomes unlawful to him and rest flees from him. He is cut off from all habits and associations and renounces sensual passion and turns towards the court of love and submits to the law of love and knows God by His attributes of perfection. . . . The lovers of God are those who devote themselves to death in nearness to Him, not those who seek (to know) His nature, because the seeker stands by himself, but he who devotes himself to death stands by his Beloved ; and the truest lovers are they who would fain die thus, and are overpowered, because a phenomenal being has no means of approaching the Eternal, save through the omnipotence of the Eternal. He who knows what is real love feels no more difficulties and all his doubts depart."[1]

The pure love of the saints for God is, then, His gift, which He gives to those whom He loves. It is God Who initiates this love, writes al-Muḥāsibī, by causing men to know Himself and leading them to obey Him and shewing love towards them, although He has no need of them. He deposited love for Himself in the hearts of His lovers and then clad them with light, shining forth in words inspired by the intensity of His love within their hearts. And when He had thus dealt with them, He shewed them unto His angels, rejoicing in them, and when they had aroused love in those whom He has chosen to dwell in the heavenly places, He spread their high renown among His creatures. Before creating them He praised them ; before they praised Him He thanked them, because He knew aforetime that He would inspire them with what had been written of them and announced concerning them. Then He brought them forth to His creatures, having appropriated their hearts unto Himself, and so He clothed the wise with their bodies and delivered them unto creation, having placed within their hearts the treasures of the Divine mysteries, which are inherent to their union with the Beloved.

Then, desiring that they, and mankind through them, should find life in Himself, He directed their intentions

[1] *Kashf al-Maḥjūb*, pp. 307 *ff*. *Cf*. p. 227 above.

aright and granted them the gift of gnosis (lit. made them to sit on the thrones of the gnostics). And from gnosis they derived the knowledge of (spiritual) remedies, and by the light of their gnosis they beheld whence healing comes. Then He instructed them in the cause of the malady (*i.e.*, the sickness of souls), and from whence they should seek help for the healing of their own hearts. Then He commanded them to bring relief to those who suffer, and bade them to make the requests of these sufferers their own, and promised to answer their prayers when making petition for such needs. Then He called upon them to concentrate their minds in listening to Him with all their hearts, when He said unto them, " O ye who are My witnesses, if any come to you sick, because he has lost Me, heal him, or fleeing from My service, bring him back again, or forgetful of My favours and My grace, remind him thereof, for I am the best Physician for you; I am gentle, and He who is gentle seeks those who are gentle to be His servants." He does not reveal His love to those who are unworthy of it, being loath to give unto them that which He has appropriated unto Himself, for it proceedeth from Him and exists through Him.[1]

The origin and source of love, therefore, is in God, not man;[2] this pure, disinterested love lies beyond the reach of humanity, limited to its own finite capacities, and if it is found in man it is a sign of God's favour and love. Love, by its very nature, is self-communicating, like light. Just as the light of gnosis must enlighten the heart to which it is given, so love, whether the Divine love of God Himself or the love of the mystic towards Him, to which it gives rise, must manifest itself; as the love of God manifests itself in all His loving-kindness towards His creatures, so love in their hearts must also be manifested not only in their passionate devotion to their Lord, but in an overflowing of love to their

[1] "Ḥilya," fol. 231*a*.

[2] *Cf.* 1 St. John iv. 7. The well-known ascetic Aḥmad b. Abi'l-Ḥawwārī (*ob.* A.H. 246) said also: " If God loves His servant, he loves Him, and the servant cannot love God until that love has been initiated by God's love to him, and that is when He knows that he is diligent in pleasing Him" ("Ḥilya," fol. 210*a*).

fellow-men. Those who have known the healing power of the Good Physician in their own souls must themselves become healers of men, for the sign of love to God, says al-Muḥāsibī, is love of all that He loves, and it must find its expression in doing what is acceptable to Him, and dealing with His creatures in that spirit of compassion in which He Himself deals with them.[1] "Love," said Dhu'l-Nūn also, "is to love what God loves and to hate what He hates and to do good always and to shun all that distracts from God."[2]

But as God has loved His own with an everlasting love, so also the love that is born of His love is indestructible. "Love to God," writes al-Muḥāsibī, "is love that is firmly established, indissoluble; it is the continual adoration of God with heart and tongue and the closest communion with Him and the severance of all ties that distract the heart from God, and the remembrance of His grace and favour, for he who knows the goodness and the grace and the loving-kindness of God is constrained to love Him, when he knows Him, for God has made him to know Himself and has guided him into the true faith. He has created nothing in the world which is not under His allegiance and on which He has not bestowed His favours. And when this knowledge has increased and is firmly established, godly fear is aroused and hope takes root." Abū 'Abdallah M. b. 'Abdallah b. Maymūn, with whom Muḥāsibī was discoursing on love, asked, "Fear of what and hope of what?" and Ḥārith answered, "Fear of what they have missed in past days of their heart's need, and over and above that, the fear that never leaves the hearts of lovers—the fear lest they should lose their bliss because of their lack of gratitude for all that He has done for them, and when fear has lingered in their hearts and they are on the point of despair, hope is aroused by the remembrance of the wideness of God's mercy, and

[1] "Ādāb al-Nufūs," fol. 90*b*. *Cf.* Dostoevsky: "Love a man even in his sin, for that love is a likeness of the Divine love and is the summit of love on earth. Love all God's creation, both the whole and the grain of sand. If thou love each thing, thou wilt perceive the mystery of God in all; and when once thou dost perceive this, thou wilt thenceforward grow every day to a fuller understanding of it" (*The Brothers Karamazof*, p. 339, ed. London, 1912).

[2] "Ḥilya," fol. 208*b*.

the hope of His lovers is certainty, and their approach to Him is that of affinity. They serve Him without weariness and, in all they do, they heed nought but his command, because of their knowledge concerning Him, that He has assured them of His loving regard upon them and His loving-kindness toward them." "Listen to the word of God," urges al-Muḥāsibī, "'The Lord is gracious unto His servants,' and all favours are included in His loving-kindness, which is manifest to His lovers above the rest of His creatures."[1]

This love begins in gratitude for God's love, but it ends in the love of God for His own sake, that pure, disinterested love which forgets the gift in contemplating the Giver, and the mystic carried away by love will sacrifice not only this world but the next, if only he may maintain his fellowship with the Beloved. The lover has chosen that better part which shall not be taken away. Sa'dī, himself deeply influenced by mysticism, wrote, of such self-abandoned lovers as these:

> "Lovers gambling all the goods away, of that world and of this,
> Are endowed with something precious that our sleek ascetics miss."[2]

So says one who had attained to certainty, "To love my Lord and to satisfy Him is better than Paradise";[3] and Abū Yazīd al-Bisṭāmī also said, "Paradise is of no consequence to the true lovers of God."[4] To such lovers Heaven would be Hell without the Beloved and Hell would be Heaven if He were there, and neither are of any worth in comparison with the presence of the Beloved and the lover's communion with Him. "When love is established in the heart of a servant," writes al-Muḥāsibī, "there is no place there for remembrance of men or demons, or of

[1] "Ḥilya," fol. 231*a*. *Cf.* C. Barbanson: "Divine Love makes all things light and sweet, taking away all bitterness, anguish and pain, and begetting a contempt for all lesser things" (*op. cit.*, p. 170).
[2] *Ṭayyibāt* No. 11 (ed. R. A. Nicholson).
[3] Abū Ṭālib, *Qut al-Qulūb*, I., p. 84.
[4] "Ḥilya," fols. 218*a*, *b*.

Paradise or of Hell, nor for anything except the remembrance of the Beloved and His grace."[1]

Elsewhere al-Muḥāsibī relates how Ḥasan (al-Baṣrī) justified himself for seeking the fellowship of God rather than of men, and for occupying himself with the remembrance of the Creator rather than the creatures by referring to the rank attained by Abraham (*khalīl*, the friend of God), to whom God said, "O Abraham, verily thou art My friend, and behold, in regarding thee I have found that thine heart has not been concerned with aught but Myself, and I choose for My friendship only that one who, if he were cast into Hell, while thinking of Me, would not feel pain at the touch of the flames; who, if Paradise were displayed to him in all its glory, adorned with its Ḥūrīs and all its delights, would not turn his eyes towards it, nor be distracted thereby from his preoccupation with Me. Such a one have I chosen upon whom to bestow My gifts, whom I have brought near unto Myself, to whom I have given My love, and he has entered into fellowship with Me, and what joy can equal that?"[2]

Asked who among the lovers of God was nearest to Him, al-Muḥāsibī in reply quoted the words of Abū Sulayman al-Dārānī, who said, "That one is nearest to God who examines his own heart and desires from this world and the next none but Him. This is the mark of the lover of God who approaches nearest to Him: all that he does, he does for the sake of God; he has attained to true godliness." In the lover all those qualities and virtues which were gained with so much effort by the novice and maintained with difficulty by the traveller on the Path have come to their perfection and fruition. Of the asceticism (*zuhd*) of lovers al-Muḥāsibī said that some maintained that the renunciation of the lover was of the whole world, what was lawful therein as well what was unlawful, because it counted for so little in his sight. Others said that the renunciation of the lover was of the next world as well as this, out of fear lest his Beloved should say to him, "O My lover, what hast thou abandoned for My sake?" and he would say, "I have abandoned this world for Thy sake," and He should say, "And of what worth is this world?" and then the lover would say, "O

[1] "Ḥilya," fol. 231*a*. [2] *Ibid.*, fol. 232*b*.

Lord, its value is no more than that of a gnat's wing, but Thou knowest that I do not serve Thee for the reward of Heaven; I seek none other but Thyself, and no thought of Paradise has been mingled with my thought of Thee." For the renunciation of the true lover is of this world and the world to come.[1]

It is interesting to note how the Christian mystics have expressed themselves in similar terms with regard to pure love. The fifteenth-century mystic St. Catherine of Genoa says, "Pure love loves God without any 'for' (*i.e.*, any further motive)"; and again she says, "I had given the keys of the house to Love, with ample permission to do all that was necessary and determined to have no consideration for soul or body, but to see that, of all the law of pure love required, there should not be wanting the slightest particle. And I stood so occupied in contemplating this work of love that if He had cast me, body and soul, into Hell, Hell itself would have appeared to me all love and consolation."[2] The Flemish mystic Ruysbroeck (*ob.* A.D. 1381) writes in the same strain: "While the soul does what it does for reward or gain, moved by fear of Hell or desire for Heaven, it is but a servant; but when this stage is past, the soul comes into a oneness of purpose with God and its deeds are no longer done from calculation but from sheer love, and this is pure love." "Lord, I am Thine," he writes elsewhere, "and should be Thine as gladly in Hell as in Heaven, if in that way I could advance Thy glory."[3] He uses almost the very words of al-Muḥāsibī's great predecessor and fellow-countrywoman, Rābi'a of Baṣra, a mystic who seemed to those who knew her "on fire with love and longing," who declared that she had served God not from fear of Hell or love of Paradise, like a servant, but only for love of Him and out of desire for Him;[4] and again in one of her prayers she prayed, "Whatever share of the next world Thou hast appointed to me, give it to Thy friends. Thou art enough for me."[5]

[1] "Ḥilya," fol. 233*b*.
[2] von Hügel, *The Mystical Element of Religion*, II., p. 268.
[3] Rufus Jones, *Studies in Mystical Religion*, pp. 310, 311.
[4] *Qūt al-Qulūb*, I., p. 57. [5] 'Aṭṭār, *Tadhkirat al-Awliyā*, I., p. 73.

The lover is filled at all times with yearning (*shawq*) for the Beloved, " the soul being so on fire with love of God that she is ever thirsting after His presence " ;[1] and of this all-absorbing love al-Muḥāsibī wrote, " Love to God is intensity of longing, because longing, in its essence, is the heart's remembrance of the contemplation of the one longed for." Some of the divines, he said, defined longing as " the heart's expectation of the crowning joy of union with the Beloved," and he himself had asked a man whom he met in the assembly of Walīd b. Shaja' about longing and when a man could claim that he had really experienced it, and the man replied, " When he has kept himself pure, out of his fear of the evil of the times and the sinful desires of the self " ; and al-Muḥāsibī thought that wise man spoke truly in what he said, for if those who were filled with longing did not force upon themselves exhaustion and humility, they would be deprived of the sweet influences which God bestows upon the hearts of His lovers. al-Muḥāsibī was asked what was his view of longing, and he replied, " Longing, in my view, is a lamp kindled from the light of original love (*al-maḥabbat al-aṣliyya*), but greater than the light of original love." Asked what was " original love," he said, " The love (born of) faith, for God has borne witness that the faithful love Him, saying, ' Those who believed were the strongest in love to God,'[2] and the light of passionate longing is derived from the light of love, and that which makes it exceed that light comes from the love which is attachment (*ḥubb al-wadād*, *i.e.*, that which is based on experience, not merely faith), and longing arises in the heart only from the light of this love which is attachment. And when God lights that lamp in the heart of one of His servants, there is no radiance kindled in the heart which is not derived from it, and that lamp is not extinguished except by looking upon one's actions with the eye of self-confidence, which turns the lover aside from the love of God."[3]

al-Muḥāsibī refers to a woman devotee, who said,

[1] *Cf.* " Bad' man anāb ila Allāh," fol. 22*a*; C. Barbanson, *op. cit.*, p. 47; and my *Studies in Early Mysticism*, p. 204.

[2] Sūra 2 : 160.

[3] " Ḥilya," fol. 231*b*. *Cf.* St. Augustine, " Love is faith in action."

"Verily, God has granted to those who long to meet Him a state such that if it were taken from them, they would be deprived of eternal bliss." She was asked, "What is that state?" and answered, "Of their own accord they have counted what was gain to them as loss." And they wondered how she had become the shrine of the Divine grace (*fawā'id*), being such as she was. al-Muḥāsibī concludes that love is identical with longing, since longing is one of the developments of original love.[1]

"The love of God in its essence," writes al-Muḥāsibī, "is really the illumination of the heart by joy, because of its nearness to the Beloved; and when the heart is filled with that radiant joy, it finds its delight in being alone with the recollection of its Beloved, for love, in solitude, rises up triumphant, and the heart of the lover is possessed by the sense of its fellowship with Him; and when solitude is combined with secret intercourse with the Beloved, the joy of that intercourse overwhelms the mind, so that it is no longer concerned with this world and what is therein." It was in reference to such intercourse that Daygham the devotee expressed his wonder that mankind should seek enlightenment for their hearts from the recollection of anything but their Lord.[2] "He who desires to enter into the glory of love to God must separate himself from those he loves and enter into that sanctuary where he is alone with the Lord of lords." Ibrāhīm b. Adham, that great ascetic who abandoned an earthly throne out of love for the Supreme King, said to one of his brethren in God, "If you desire to be the friend of God and to be amongst His lovers, turn your back on this world and the next, and do not covet either, but rather free yourself from both, and concern yourself with God alone, and He will concern Himself with you and bestow His loving-kindness upon you."[3]

Such all-absorbing love leaves its mark upon those for whom God has "poured out the cup of His love"; they are emaciated, for they content themselves with a bare sufficiency of this world's goods, being free from all fleshly desire, deaf to the temptations of the Adversary, blind to all attractions save those of the Beloved; all that they desire is com-

[1] "Ḥilya," fol. 231*b*. [2] *Ibid.*, fol. 231*b*. [3] *Ibid.*, fol. 232*b*.

munion with Him.[1] So also Ibn 'Abd al-Ṣamad[2] declared, " Love it is which makes blind and deaf, for it makes the lover blind to all save the Beloved, nor does he hear the claims of any save Him."[3] We find the Christian mystic Blosius describing the friends of God in similar terms: " These souls, since they are constantly occupied within themselves with the things of God and constantly cleave close to Him, remain in their outward life blind, although they see; deaf, although they hear; and dumb, although they speak."[4] Of such a lover al-Muḥāsibī writes that he knows that the service of God means preoccupation from the service of all others; God has clothed him with the mantle of knowledge of Himself and has set him free from slavery to this world, and he glories in the glory of the All-Glorious, Who has glorified him with a glory not of this world, and enriched him with heavenly treasures, and made him dear to others than his own kin, a spring whence wisdom flows forth and is spread abroad through his acts, and his aspirations mount heavenward, and he attains in spirit to the goal of his desire, and mounts ever higher until he is set free from all that could hamper or check his ascent. Such a one, devoted to God and detached from the creatures, outwardly is like the creatures of this world, but inwardly like those to whom God has revealed Himself, who reverence their Lord, for such a one has given up his heart to his Lord and is concerned only with what is well pleasing in His sight, having turned aside from what is well pleasing to men, and he lives the good life in this world, yet undefiled by it, for his heart is filled with the love of the All-Compassionate and the longing to draw near unto Him and to look upon His face.[5]

Love, then, means the Vision of God (*ru'ya*)—" He who possesses the more love," said St. Thomas Aquinas, " will see God the more perfectly and will be the more beatified "[6] —that contemplation in full measure, which begins in

[1] " Ḥilya," fol. 233*a*.

[2] *Cf.* L. Massignon, *Passion*, p. 220.

[3] Kalābādhī, *Kitāb al-Ta'arruf*, p. 80.

[4] *Spiritual Instruction*, p. 11.

[5] " Ḥilya," fol. 233*b ff*. *Cf.* C. Barbanson, *op. cit.*, p. 230.

[6] *Summa Theologica*, Q. 12, Art. 6.

prayer. Contemplation is of two kinds, says Hujwīrī, one which is the result of perfect faith, and the contemplation which is the result of rapturous love, "for in the rapture of love a man attains to such a degree that his whole being is absorbed in the thought of his Beloved and he sees nothing else. One sees the act with his bodily eye, and, as he looks, beholds the Agent with his spiritual eye; another is rapt by love of the Agent from all things, so that he sees only the Agent. The one method is demonstrative, the other is ecstatic. In the former case a manifest proof is derived from the evidences, in the latter case the seer is enraptured and transported by desire: evidences and verities are a veil to him, because he who knows a thing does not reverence aught besides, and he who loves a thing does not regard aught besides. . . . When the lover turns his eye away from created things, he will inevitably see the Creator with his heart. . . . He does not see the act, but the Agent only and entirely, just as when one looks at the picture and sees only the painter." It is the distinction between the one who meditates upon the Divine acts and the one who is amazed at the Divine majesty;[1] the one is a follower of friendship, the other is a companion of love.[2]

This is the station of those who have travelled along the road to God, having attained to quiet and peace of mind in Him, satisfied because they know none but Him, and "when you have come to this stage," says al-Muḥāsibī, writing from his own inner experience of the contemplation of love, "His majesty and His glory have taken possession of your heart." These are they whom God has chosen to dwell in peace and

[1] So also St. Francis de Sales: "The desire we have to obtain Divine love makes us meditate, but love obtained makes us contemplate" (*The Love of God*, p. 240).

[2] *Op. cit.*, pp. 330, 91, 373. *Cf.* St. Thomas Aquinas: "There is delight in the contemplative life, not only by reason of the contemplation itself, but also by reason of the Divine love. In both respects the delight thereof surpasses all human delight both because spiritual delight is greater than carnal pleasure . . . and the love whereby God is loved surpasses all love. This is the ultimate perfection of the contemplative life, namely that the Divine Truth be not only seen, but loved" (*Summa Theologica*, Q. 180, Art. 7). *Cf.* the Catholic conception of ordinary and extraordinary contemplation, A. Poulain, *Les Grâces d'Oraison*, chapter iv., and L. Blosius, *Spiritual Instruction*, Introd., pp. x *ff*.

has veiled all affliction from them, and they contemplate God in that upon which they have set their hope, and their hearts have been veiled from all save Him.[1]

Contemplation is the perfection of love, for as Abū Ya'qūb al-Sūsī the Ṣūfī (*ob.* A.H. 330) said, "Love is not perfected until it passes out from the vision of love to the vision of the Beloved."[2] For lovers the vision is a necessity, for love, says al-Hujwīrī, "subsists through vision of the Beloved"; and elsewhere he writes, "God sustains His lovers with perpetual contemplation and keeps them alive with the life of love." This is the stage of the spiritual adept, whose "every look becomes an act of contemplation."[3] Of such a one, whose heart has been purified by love, Isaac of Nineveh had written, "What no eye hath seen and no ear has heard, and what has not entered into the heart of man to ask in prayer, is revealed to him by purity, which during no moment ceases from mysteries and spiritual visions."[4] The lover of God has attained to the summit of contemplation, that which by Catholic theologians is called "extraordinary" contemplation, which goes beyond the contemplation attained by the devotee; it is "a singular and miraculous union of mind with God, by simple intuition, accompanied by most ardent love."[5] Now, writes the Christian Ruysbroeck, "our powers become simplified in love, silent and bowed down in the presence of God. There the soul must abide, simple, pure, spotless, empty of self, raised to an imageless nakedness, and it is in this state of complete emptiness that God shews His Divine brightness, the Incomprehensible Light . . . this is the contemplative life."[6]

The lovers of God, therefore, are continually in contemplation of the Beloved. "It is the custom of God," says Sarī al-Saqatī, "to let the hearts of those who love Him have vision of Him always, in order that the delight thereof may enable them to endure tribulation, for they say, 'We deem

[1] "Ādāb al-Nufūs," fol. 102*b*. [2] Sarrāj, *Kitāb al-Luma'*, p. 59.

[3] *Op. cit.*, pp. 306, 332, 275.

[4] *Op. cit.*, p. 349. *Cf.* Ruysbroeck: "They contemplate God in all things without distinction, by a simple gaze, in the Divine brightness" (*Adornment of the Spiritual Marriage*, III., cap. 3).

[5] B. A. Wilberforce, *Book of Spiritual Instruction*, Introd., p. ix.

[6] *Book of the Sparkling Stone*, cap. 7.

all torments more desirable than to be veiled from Thyself. When Thy beauty is revealed to our hearts, we take no thought of affliction.' "[1] To that one whom God has placed in the rank of His lovers, writes al-Muḥāsibī, He gives the vision of Himself, for He has sworn, saying, " By my glory, I will shew him My face and I will heal his soul by the Vision of Myself."[2]

These lovers have found the object of their desire, for " finding " (*wujūd*) is a grace bestowed by the Beloved on the lover, it is the thrill of ecstasy which is experienced in the contemplation of the Divine Vision.[3] al-Muḥāsibī was asked what were the signs that the lover had attained to this state of ecstasy (*'alāmat wujūd qalbihi*), and he said to the young man who had questioned him, " The hearts of such lovers are held captive in the hidden shrine of the Divine loving-kindness, they are marked out by their knowledge of the revelation of the Divine Majesty (*mukāshafa*), being transformed by the joy of the Vision, in contemplation of the Invisible, and the enveloping Glory of God, and from them all hindrances are removed, for they tread the path of friendship with God, and are transported into the Garden of Vision and their hearts dwell in that region, where they see without eyes, and are in the company of the Beloved without looking upon Him, and converse with an unseen Friend. This is the description of the lovers of God, who do righteousness, who are gifted with heavenly wisdom, who are on their guard both night and day, pure in all their thoughts, those whom God has prepared for His service, whom He has preserved by His care, whom He has invested with His own authority. They are continually serving Him to Whom belong the heavens and the earth ; they are completely satisfied, for they live the good life, their bliss is eternal, and their joy is made perfect, and they possess an everlasting treasure within their hearts, for it is as if they contemplated with the eye of the heart the glory that is invisible, and God is the Object and Goal of their aspirations."[4]

To them is given a foretaste in this life of the joy which is to be theirs for evermore in the life hereafter, for the true

[1] Hujwīrī, *op. cit.*, p. 111.
[2] " Ḥilya," fol. 232*b*.
[3] *Cf.* Hujwīrī, *op. cit.*, pp. 413 *ff*.
[4] " Ḥilya," fols. 238*a ff*.

beatitude of Paradise consists in the light of the revelation of God and the contemplation of His face; He has promised that those who love Him in this world shall be close to Him in the next, and He will invite them to sit down with Him, that they may for ever gaze upon their Beloved. al-Muḥāsibī quotes on this subject the words of Dhu'l-Nūn, who said, "I have read in the *Tawra* that the righteous who believe, who walk in the Way of their Lord, in obedience to Him, will be rapt away to contemplate the face of the All-Glorious, for the goal of the true lover's desire is to look upon the face of God, and when they meet with Him, He bestows upon them no greater grace than the vision of His countenance."[1] Here and now, then, the lovers of God attain to intuitive knowledge of the Beatific Vision, which is the chief joy of Paradise, which here is granted only to the saints.[2]

When this stage of contemplation is attained, the contemplative soul has realised its oneness with Him Whom it contemplates. "In that gaze," said the Christian mystic Gerlac Petersen, "there is no confusion, no narrowness, no doubt nor any fear: for in it the mind perceiveth that it is made perfect in Him Who is One, and seeth that she is one spirit with Him, the I am, and that she is one with the Selfsame Who is God."[3] This is the contemplation which is the violence of love, which leads to the absorption of the human attributes in the realisation of the Vision of God, and their annihilation by the everlastingness of God.[4] Now, says al-Muḥāsibī, the servant has reached the station of revelation (*mukāshafa*), when the veil is drawn aside from the invisible things of God. In this stage of contemplation there is no

[1] "Ḥilya," fols. 232*a*, 233*a*.

[2] For an illuminating study of the Vision of God and its place in Christian thought *cf.* K. E. Kirk, *The Vision of God*.

[3] *Divine Soliloquies*, p. 14.

[4] Hujwīrī, *op. cit.*, p. 165. *Cf.* J. Maréchal's statement that contemplation enriches and also simplifies, since the contemplative fixes his inner gaze on God, the Absolute Unity, Who has, by the previous ascesis, become the centre of equilibrium and the vital impulses of his whole psychological being, and it leads to the abandonment even of all consciousness of the fundamental dualism of the Ego and the non-Ego (*op. cit.*, pp. 175 *ff.*).

distinction between this world and the next, for the soul has drawn so near to God, and to the world to come, that it looks upon both, as if with the eye, face to face. This is the contemplation in the degree of love, which is perfect union, for there is now no barrier between the lover and the Beloved.[1] "It is love that unites us to God, Who is the last end of the human mind," wrote St. Thomas Aquinas.[2] The consciousness of His love at work in the soul, and of its love responding to His, is evidence of His presence therein, of the Divine indwelling. "Union," writes an unknown Christian mystic, "belongeth to such as are perfect and is brought to pass by pureness and singleness of heart, by love and by the contemplation of God, the Creator of all things. . . . Where a man forsaketh and cometh out of himself and his own things, there God entereth in with His own—that is, with Himself. . . . He who is imbued with or illuminated by the Eternal or Divine love, he is a Godlike man and a partaker of the Divine nature."[3]

al-Muḥāsibī also teaches that the lover of God becomes Godlike through the contemplation of the Beloved. When the heart is enlightened by the Light of God, it becomes the shrine of the Divine Spirit, according to the Word of God revealed to David, when He said, "O David, if love to Me is found within My creatures, they become spiritualised (*ruḥāniyīn*=πνευματικοὶ), and the mark of the spiritually minded is that they no longer walk in darkness, for I am the Light of their hearts."[4] This is no borrowed light from without, but a radiance which is kindled from within; that spiritualisation, that illumination, come from the union of the lover with the Beloved. By love, writes a German mystic, "we are turned to God and are made one with God, so that we are one spirit with Him and share His blessedness.

[1] "Ādāb al-Nufūs," fols. 95*b*, 91*b*; "Ḥilya," fol. 238*a*; Hujwīrī, *op. cit.*, pp. 165, 333.

[2] *Summa Theologica*, Q. 180, Art. 7.

[3] *Theologia Germanica*, pp. 47, 82, 155.

[4] "Ḥilya," fol. 232*a*. *Cf.* R. Otto: "The Divine (is) experienced as 'light,' 'fire,' 'spirit' . . . it is a penetrating glow and illumination, fulfilment, transfiguration—most of all where it is experienced as 'Life,' or (what is but the intensification of all this) as very 'Being'" (*The Idea of the Holy*, p. 207).

He indeed who cleaves to God dwells in light—it is man's more exalted perfection in this life to be so united to God that the whole soul, with all its faculties and all its forces, is unified in its Lord and becomes one spirit with Him."[1]

This glory is the inheritance of the saints, and theirs is a kingdom which no earthly king possesses. al-Muḥāsibī was asked when the saints would enter into their kingdom, and he answered, "When the All-Glorious shall dwell in them and take them wholly as His own, because of their love to Him."[2] "He who has met with Me and is My lover," said God to David, "him have I brought into My Paradise."[3] These have entered upon the unitive state and their lives give evidence that now they live in God. Such lovers, says al-Muḥāsibī, are continually in union with their Lord, and when God unites them with Himself, they manifest Divine gifts in such wise that all know them as those who love God. Love has no figure nor likeness nor form nor adornment by which to be recognised; but the lover is known by his characteristics, for his words are guided and inspired by the light of God. "The sign of love to God," says al-Muḥāsibī, "is the indwelling of the Divine grace (*ḥulūl al-fawā'id*) in the heart of him whom God has chosen to be His lover, as a certain divine recited :

'He has chosen ones, those who are His own, inspired by love of Him,
Whom He chose in times long past.
He chose them before they took created forms,
By His promises and His Divine gifts and His revelation to them.' "[4]

Now it is God who controls the aspirations of the lover, and in all his states he acts according to His choice, for

[1] J. von Kastl, *De Adhærendo Deo*, cap. 12.
[2] "Ḥilya," fol. 233*a*. [3] *Ibid.*, fol. 232*a*.
[4] *Ibid. Cf.* Abū Sa'īd b. Abi'l-Khayr: "God created the souls four thousand years before He created their bodies and placed them near to Himself and there He shed His light upon them" (M. b. al-Munawwar *Asrār al-Tawḥīd*, p. 399).

God is overruling all he does. In the unitive life there is no thought or glance or suggestion or wish or movement, whether outward or inward, no look, nor anything within the heart, but God is there, and His grace is in action, controlling the heart, the motive source of all.[1] al-Muḥāsibī relates the tradition that the Word of God came to Yaḥya b. Zachariyā (John the Baptist), saying, "O Yaḥya, I have laid it upon Myself that when any servant loves Me, I become his hearing by which he hears, and his sight whereby he sees, and his tongue wherewith he speaks, and his heart whereby he understands; and when that is so, I make distasteful to him preoccupation with any save Myself and I take possession of his thoughts. O Yaḥya, I am the companion of his heart and the goal of his desire and his hope, and I give Myself to him every day and every hour."[2] The Christian mystic Gerlac Petersen uses similar language of the soul that has attained to union. "Thus the soul worketh all its works in God; nay, thus doth God work His own work in it, so that it is not so much the soul who worketh, as that the soul itself is the work of God. . . . And thus in truth it knoweth that God seeth by the eyes of the body, speaketh by its mouth, heareth by its ears, and through other senses it stretcheth forth towards all things with a pure heart."[3] al-Hujwīrī seems to have al-Muḥāsibī's teaching in his mind when he says of the unitive state, "It is man's glory that he should escape by God's goodness from the imperfections of his own actions and should find them to be absorbed in the bounties of God, so that he depends entirely on God and commits all his attributes to His charge and refers all his actions to Him and none to himself. . . . When the Divine omnipotence manifests its dominion over humanity, it transports a man out of his own being, so that his speech becomes the speech of God."[4]

So the mystic becomes a partaker of the Divine life here and now, for God has entered in and dwells with him and acts through him. "Whoso knows God," says al-Muḥā-

[1] "Ḥilya," fol. 238*a*; "Muḥāsabat al-Nufūs," fol. 67*b*.
[2] "Ḥilya," fol. 232*b*.
[3] *Divine Soliloquies*, p. 14.
[4] *Op. cit.*, p. 254.

sibī, "loves Him, and whoso loves Him He makes to dwell with Him, and whom He makes to dwell with Him, in whom He dwells, blessed is he, yea blessed."[1]

[1] "Ḥilya," fol. 232*b*. So also the *Zohar*: "Ye supernal saints, the Glory of God is within you and your faces reflect that Divine Radiance. Blessed are ye" (IV., p. 65).

CHAPTER XIII

SUMMARY OF AL-MUḤĀSIBĪ'S TEACHING—HIS INFLUENCE UPON HIS CONTEMPORARIES—HIS CRITICS—HIS DISCIPLES—HIS EFFECT UPON LATER WRITERS

AL-MUḤĀSIBĪ, therefore, while making use of the teachers who had preceded him, develops a mystical doctrine of his own, which is based on his personal experience. He realises that all outward conduct, good or bad, depends upon the state of the heart, and therefore his teaching is directed primarily towards the inner purification of the believer. He shews that by a moral ascesis, a rule of life, according to which the inner state and the outward conduct will correspond to one another, the soul, advancing from one station to another, and becoming more and more receptive of the "states" which God is prepared to bestow, can grow in purity and grace until, having passed from the stage of the novice to that of the traveller on the path, the seeker may at last become the adept, the gnostic, who is the lover of God, worthy to be of the number of His saints and to enter into the unitive life with Him.

This rule of life, he shews, will mean a simplification and unification of all the faculties, and especially the reason, which controls them, in order that the will may be directed towards this one end, and when human effort has reached its limits, the seeker may feel assured that the Divine grace will complete the work. The whole journey to God involves the willing and whole-hearted co-operation of the human with the Divine, resulting in a growing receptivity dependent on an ever-increasing degree of self-surrender and self-emptying which begins with the servant's acceptance of his duty to serve and to worship one Master only, and ends with the state in which, being no longer servant but friend, his will is one with the Divine Will, his soul the dwelling-place of the Beloved, himself the instrument and means through which God works, by which He manifests Himself to His creatures. Perfect sincerity,[1] the disinterested love of God, action which is always in complete harmony with the Will of God, and unfailing charity towards His servants, are the distinguishing marks of the saints of God, those who have attained to their full stature and are spiritually perfect.[2]

In his ascetical teaching al-Muḥāsibī follows a *via media*; he condemns rigorism, while making no concessions to self-centred desires, and the result is a well-balanced but searching rule of life. In his theological teaching he is precise and definite, making use of an exact terminology. Above all, he realises that religion is a matter of personal experience; it is the response of the human soul to the Divine love which it finds within itself. al-Muḥāsibī may be reckoned as the one who really assured to orthodox mysticism its place in Islām, preceding, as he did, those who wrote systematic treatises on Ṣūfism, and for most of these treatises it would appear that his teaching formed the ultimate basis.

Such a fully developed doctrine of the religious life, marking a great advance on the mystic thinkers who had preceded him, could not fail to have a profound influence during the lifetime of its author and after his death. While it succeeded in attracting a considerable group of the most influential Ṣūfīs of the day, who became his disciples and, in due course, the transmitters of his teaching, it also attracted the attention and the active hostility of those who were opposed to his doctrines, who criticised the methods which he employed to support them.

The basis of the charges brought against him by his enemies is stated impartially and in judicial terms by Shahrastānī (*ob.* 548/1153), who classes Ḥārith al-Muḥāsibī together

[1] "Sincerity (*ṣidq*)," said Dhu'l-Nūn, "is the sword of God on earth; it cuts everything that it touches," and a sincere will cuts off all secondary causes and severs all ties of relationship, so that nothing remains except God (*Kashf al-Maḥjūb*, p. 101).

[2] "The mystical union," says A. Poulain, "is a tree the seed of which is first concealed in the earth, and the roots that are secretly put forth in darkness constitute the night of sense. From these a frail stem springs up into the light, and this is spiritual quiet. The tree grows and becomes full union and ecstasy. Finally in spiritual marriage it attains the end of its development and then it bears flowers and fruit" (*Cath. Encyc.*, p. 327).

with Mālik b. Anas, Aḥmad b. Ḥanbal himself, Sufyān al-Thawrī, Da'ūd al-Isfahānī, 'Abd Allah b. Sa'īd al-Kilābī and Abū'l-'Abbās al-Qalānisī among the Imāms who did not have recourse to interpretation (*ta'wīl*) nor allegory (*tashbīh*) in regard to the Qur'ān; but he notes that al-Muḥāsibī, with the last two mentioned, employed scholastic methods (*kalām*) and sought to establish the religious principles laid down by the earliest Imāms, by means of logical proofs derived from dialectic and arguments based on first principles. Shahrastānī reckons them all as *Ṣifatiyya*, holding orthodox views on the Divine attributes (*ṣifāt*).[1] The orthodox traditionists, represented by the Ḥanbalites, held that the Word of God was to be interpreted literally and to be regarded as uncreated, and that left no room for the use of reason, while the Mu'tazilites (*cf.* p. 4 above) held that the Qur'ān was created and that it was to be interpreted in the light of reason. They also denied the existence of the Divine attributes as being a denial of the Unity. al-Muḥāsibī, therefore, by his preference of reason to dogma, is to be ranked among the scholastic theologians as well as among the Ṣufīs, and on account of his methods of discussion, in addition to the subjects which he discussed, laid himself open to the charge of unorthodoxy, if not actually of heresy (since to the Ḥanbalites every innovation was heresy) and of leanings towards Mu'tazilitism.

The most hostile of his contemporary critics, as we have seen, was Aḥmad b. Ḥanbal, whose bitter enmity towards the Mu'tazilites, and all who diverged in any way from the narrowest type of Sunnite orthodoxy, led him to denounce al-Muḥāsibī for employing the weapons of logic and dialectic, albeit they were used as much in refutation of the Mu'tazilites, and other heretics as in support of his own mystical teaching.[2] When Aḥmad b. Ḥanbal reproached him for his writings directed against the Mu'tazilites, al-Muḥāsibī justified himself by stating that the refutation of heresy was an obligation laid upon the faithful. Aḥmad said, "Yes, but you have first demonstrated what is heretical in their teaching, and then you have refuted it, and are you sure that he

[1] Shahrastānī, *Kitāb al-Milal wa'l-Niḥal*, p. 65.
[2] *Cf.* Sam'ānī, *Ansāb*, fol. 509*b*.

who considers what is heretical will pay attention to your refutation? One of two things will happen: your statement of their heresies will be the thing that will remain in his mind while your refutation of it is ignored, or if he does pay attention to your refutation, he will not understand it properly."[1] It was related also of Aḥmad b. Ḥanbal that he said, "Beware of al-Ḥārith, beware, for he is at the root of the trouble (*i.e.*, the prevalence of speculation). He is like a lion which is chained up; be on the lookout for the day when he will spring upon men."[2]

After Aḥmad b. Ḥanbal, his disciple Abū Zur'a Rāzī (*ob.* A.H. 264/878) made a further attack on Muḥāsibī's writings, bidding one who questioned him about them to beware of these books, for they were heretical and liable to lead men astray.[3] "Your business," said Abū Zur'a, "is with the traditions and in them you will find what will make you independent of these books." The questioner proceeded to justify himself by saying, "There is a direct admonition to the conscience (*'ibra*) in these books, to which Abū Zur'a replied, "He who finds no admonition in the Word of God will find none in these books. Have you heard that Mālik b. Anas and Sufyān al-Thawrī and al-Awzā'ī and the chief of the Imāms wrote books like these on the subject of passing thoughts (*khaṭarāt*) and diabolical suggestions and such things? But these (*Ṣūfīs*) are people who differ from the orthodox theologians: at one time they bring to our notice Ḥarith al-Muḥāsibī and at another 'Abd al-Raḥīm al-Dubaylī,[4] and sometimes it is Ḥātim al-Aṣamm (*ob.* A.H. 237) and sometimes Shaqīq (Balkhī)." Then Abū Zur'a added, "How swift men are to turn to heresy!"[5]

Another of al-Muḥāsibī's contemporaries who condemned his mystical teaching, because of the method he advocated of attaining to such knowledge, was Sarī Saqaṭī,[6] who deprecated a doctrine of Ṣūfism which to him did not

[1] *Munkidh*, p. 15. [2] Ibn al-Jawzī, *Talbīs Iblīs*, p. 178.
[3] *Cf.* Ḥājjī Khalīfa, *Kashf al-Ẓunūn*, III., p. 471.
[4] A disciple of Abū Yazīd al-Bisṭāmī.
[5] Khaṭīb, *op. cit.*, VIII., p. 215; Dhahabī, *Mīzān al-I'tidāl*, I., p. 173; Ibn al-Jawzī, *Talbīs Iblīs*, p. 177.
[6] *Cf.* pp. 39 *ff.* above.

seem to be based on orthodox tradition, and said to his nephew al-Junayd, " If you begin by acquiring a knowledge of the traditions and comprehending the fundamental principles of the faith and the Sunna, and then become an ascetic and a devotee, you may hope to become an adept in the knowledge of Ṣūfism and to become a Ṣūfi gnostic; but if you begin with devotion and godliness (*taqwā*) and ecstasy, you will become preoccupied with them to the exclusion of theology and the Sunna, and you will end by becoming an ecstatic (*shāṭiḥ*) or by going astray because of your ignorance of the fundamental principles of the faith and the Sunna, and the best thing for you is to return to exoteric knowledge (*'ilm al- ẓāhir*) and the books of traditions, for they form the root of which devotion and knowledge of God are the branches, and you have strengthened the branches before establishing the root, and it has been said that some were hindered from attainment (*wuṣūl*) simply by neglecting what is fundamental—that is, the books of the traditions and the knowledge that has been handed down to us, and the Sunna—and if you have to return to the rudiments, it means that you have been degraded from the station of those who are adepts, and you have had to descend from the ranks of the gnostics, and you have failed to attain to certainty and assured faith."[1] al-Junayd seems to have taken his uncle's warning to heart, for he also ranged himself among al-Muḥāsibī's critics, in respect especially of his critical works on the Mu'tazilites, observing that the least danger of speculation on matters of dogmatic theology is that the heart loses its reverence for the Lord Most High, and when the heart loses its reverence it also loses its faith.[2]

After al-Muḥāsibī's death, the criticisms of the orthodox traditionists, and especially of the Ḥanbalites, continued to be directed against his writings and his disciples. Leo Africanus (al-Fāsī) mentions briefly that al-Muḥāsibī's followers were condemned by the Muslim lawyers,[3] and the comparative lack of references to his teaching points to continued hostility on the part of the orthodox and the with-

[1] Abū Ṭālib, *Qūt al-Qulūb*, I., p. 158.
[2] *Taghrībirdī*, *op. cit.*, II., p. 178.
[3] *Descrittione dell' Africa*, III., par. 143.

drawal of his works from circulation. One of the most outstanding of these critics was Ibn al-Jawzī of Baghdad (*ob.* 597/1200), a bigoted Ḥanbalite, who quotes with approval Aḥmad b. Ḥanbal's attitude towards Muḥāsibī, and also that of Abu Zur'a, and adds that Abū 'Abd al-Raḥmān al-Sulamī (*ob.* 412/1021) of Nīshāpūr stated that the first of the mystics to discuss the states and stations of the Ṣūfī Path in his country were Dhu'l-Nūn al-Miṣrī and Sulaymān al-Dārānī and Aḥmad b. Abi'-l Ḥawwārī and Abū Yazīd and Sahl (Tustarī), and these, Ibn al-Jawzī notes, were all heretics, who were rejected and driven into exile, and so, too, al-Sulamī stated that because Ḥarīth al-Muḥāsibī discussed questions of *kalām* and the Divine attributes, he was driven out by Aḥmad b. Ḥanbal and forced to remain in retirement until his death. Ibn al-Jawzī further criticises al-Muḥāsibī for his teaching on the superiority of poverty to wealth and for his view that 'Abd al-Raḥmān b. 'Awf, a wealthy Companion of the Prophet, would be hindered by his wealth from hastening to Paradise in the hereafter. Ibn al-Jawzī considers that this view of wealth and its drawbacks is contrary to the Shari'a and is unreasonable, shewing a lack of knowledge on al-Muḥāsibī's part, and, being also opposed to the teaching of the Prophet and Ibn Ḥanbal, it comes near to being sinful. Ibn al-Jawzī expresses astonishment that al-Ghazālī should have commended it. He proceeds to question the authenticity of the traditions on which al-Muḥāsibī bases his Ṣūfī teachings, and himself quotes the example of Abraham and Sufyān al-Thawrī, who were possessors of wealth. Ibn al-Jawzī's criticisms of the Ṣūfīs generally also contain statements which may well be directed against al-Muḥāsibī among others—*e.g.*, what he has to say of *Ḥulūl*, the indwelling the human by the Divine (*cf.* p. 250 above) which suggested the Christian doctrine of the Incarnation, and of the contemplation of God in this life.[1]

Among the critics of al-Muḥāsibī was also Ibn Taymiya (*ob.* 728/1328), another devoted follower of Ibn Ḥanbal, and an intolerant opponent of both Ṣūfism and scholasticism,

[1] *Talbīs Iblīs* (*Nāmūs*), pp. 177 *ff.*, 187 *ff.*, 282 *ff.* *Cf.* pp. 244 *ff.* above.

who aimed at freeing Islām from all heresies and forms of corruption.[1]

The great historian Muḥammad b. Qāymāz al-Dhahabī (*ob.* 748/1348), himself a Shāfi'ite, though he gives a full account of the criticisms made by Ibn Ḥanbal and Abū Zur'a, does not hesitate to quote the account of al-Muḥāsibī given by Ibn al-'Arābī (*ob.* 341/855) in the *Ṭabaqāt al-Nussāk* (Classes of Ascetics), where the author states that al-Muḥāsibī was recognised as an authority on tradition and jurisprudence and the history of the ascetics; but Dhahabī notes that al-Muḥāsibī discussed questions of "pronunciation" (*lafẓ*)[2] and faith (*īmān*) (*cf.* pp. 182 *ff* above) and whether God speaks "with a voice" (*kalām Allah biṣawt*), in accordance with the tradition "When God spoke by way of revelation, the inhabitants of Paradise heard His voice."[3] Writing elsewhere, Dhahabī definitely takes the side of al-Muḥāsibī. After referring to the criticism of Abū Zur'a, he says, "Where is the like of al-Ḥārith to be found? What if Abū Zur'a had seen the works of the later (Ṣūfī) writers such as the *Qūt* (*al-Qulūb*) of Abū Ṭālib (al-Makkī, *ob.* 386/996), and what book is to be compared with the *Qūt*? What if he had seen the *Bahjat al-Asrār* of Ibn Jahḍam (*ob.* 404/1023) and the *Ḥaqā'iq al-Tafsīr* of al-Sulamī and the many references (to al-Muḥāsibī) in the *Iḥyā'*? What if he had seen the *Ghurriyat* (*li ṭālibī ṭarīq al-Ḥaqq*) of 'Abd al-Qādir al-Kilānī (*ob.* 561/1166)?[4] What if he had seen the *Fuṣūṣ al-Ḥikam* and the *Futūḥāt al-Makkiya*? Yes, when Ḥarīth was the tongue of the people, at that time, there were contemporary with him a thousand Imāms in Ḥadith, amongst them the equals of Aḥmad b. Ḥanbal and Ibn Rāhwiya, and in the time of traditionists such as Ibn al-Dakhmasī and Abū Shaḥāna, al-Muḥāsibī was the *Quṭb* of the gnostics, as much as the author of the *Fuṣūṣ* and Ibn Sab'īn (*ob.* 668/1269). We ask God for forgiveness and pardon," is Dhahabī's conclusion, perhaps

[1] *Cf.* O'Leary, *Arabic Thought and its Place in History*, p. 206.

[2] Ibn Ḥanbal asserted that the very pronunciation of the Qur'ān was uncreated, and al-Muḥāsibī opposed this view.

[3] "Ta'rīkh," fol. 24*a*. al-Muḥāsibī developed his views on this subject in his "Tawahhum," fol. 170*a*.

[4] The *Bezels of Philosophy* and *Meccan Revelations* of Ibn al-'Arabī (*ob.* 838/1240).

because of his hardihood in constituting himself a critic of the critics.[1]

In the fourteenth century we find 'Abd al-Raḥīm b. Ḥusayn 'Irāqī (*ob.* 806/1404) attacking al-Muḥāsibī through an anonymous supporter of his who opposed Abū Zur'a's criticisms of his works. 'Irāqī admits that there is much good in Ibn Asad's books and that he cites many authentic traditions concerning the law of God, but he ventured to look into these matters according to that way (*ṭarīqa*) which could only be apprehended by those of penetrating insight, possessed of genius, with the gift of originality, and so fitted for the consideration of the inner reality of things, and this sent him back to the consideration of the traditions to which his understanding enabled him to attain. Commenting on Abū Zur'a's answer that those who could not find admonition in the Word of God would find none in al-Muḥāsibī's books, 'Irāqī adds that this would be because such a one would lack insight and his understanding would come short of attaining its object, for the Word of God, he said, " watches over " every book, and it is by its light that a man can distinguish truth from falsehood, and he who has not gained insight by the study of God's Word will not be able to discriminate between what is wrong and what is right, and will not find any helpful admonition anywhere else. 'Irāqī gives examples of the lessons to be drawn from the Word of God, and goes on to state that in all matters relating to the faith, insight is gained only by this clear light derived from the sacred Book, and it is by accepting its moral warnings and admonitions that men pass from destruction to salvation in all the varied circumstances of life. " There is no doubt," 'Irāqī states, " that all things necessary to salvation are found in the Word of God, either set forth plainly or by implication, for him who applies his heart to it and who listens thereto, and it is a sufficient witness for him who has no other source of guidance, to be found either in the books of Ibn Asad or of anyone else." 'Irāqī guards himself against the suggestion that he is hereby condemning other books of jurisprudence and tradition, by stating that if they are orthodox, *i.e.* based entirely on the Qur'ān, then they are

[1] *Mīzān al-I'tidāl*, I., p. 172.

to be praised. As for Abū Zur'a's remark that men were eager to pursue what was heretical, he obviously wished to deter the man who was upholding al-Muḥāsibī's teaching from looking into these books, lest he should apply himself to what Ḥārith adduced of the sayings of the heretics in order to contradict and refute them, for he who considered these sayings might come to agree with them, through his lack of understanding, and so fall into heresy and error. He felt that Abū Zur'a's words on the subject of Sufyān and Mālik involved no commendation of the books of al-Muḥāsibī, but of theirs, nor was Abu Zur'a seeking to criticise the early theologians for the paucity of their writings, for those who lived nearest to the radiant light of revelation and the time of the Prophet felt less need for committing the Shari'a to writing than those who came later and felt that it must be preserved by being written down. Now all this, observes 'Irāqī, does not mean that any other meaning is to be given to Abū Zur'a's words than that which they appear to mean, nor to read into them more than was in his mind, and any person whose heart is sound will see, he thinks, that the matter is as he himself has stated it to be.

'Irāqī proceeds to criticise Dhahabī for asking in his *Mizān*, " Where is the equal of Ḥārith ?" and for quoting in connection with his teaching the Proof of Islām, Abū Ḥāmid al-Ghazālī, and the Shaykh of Islām 'Abd al-Qādir al-Kīlānī and then the saints as a whole and the gnostics generally, which he indicates by saying that Ḥārith was the tongue of the people and the Quṭb of the gnostics, as Ibn al-'Arabī was. Would that I knew, says 'Iraqī bitterly, what (this) Quṭb of the gnostics did that was like the author of the *Fuṣūṣ* and Ibn Sab'īn, for indeed he would have judged them both to be infidels and sinners, and it may be that both were infidels (as he would have thought) and that all the gnostics sinned. Perhaps, he reflects, Dhahabī was speaking in contempt, but none the less he thought fit to ask God for forgiveness and pardon, and 'Irāqī hopes that Dhahabī may indeed be forgiven for what he said, and that he himself may be pardoned for what he has related and for enduring this speech from Dhahabī.[1]

[1] " al-Ba'ith 'ala-l-Khalāṣ," fol. 18*b ff.*

But al-Muḥāsibī's personality was great enough to withstand the attacks of his critics, and his works survived in spite of the condemnation of the orthodox theologians; they continued to be read and were sufficiently well known to be much quoted by later writers. His teaching was carried on by his pupils and disciples, many of whom became famous and influential teachers (*cf.* Chapter III. above). al-Junayd, in particular, of whom Hujwīrī says that "all Ṣūfīs unanimously acknowledge his leadership," though his orthodoxy led him to condemn al-Muḥāsibī's dialectical methods, was responsible for transmitting much of his mystical teaching to later generations of Ṣūfīs, and, through al-Junayd, al-Muḥāsibī exercised a considerable influence on Junayd's pupil and disciple, the great mystic Ḥusayn b. Mansūr al-Ḥallāj (*ob.* 309/932), who accepted certain of his semi-Mu'tazilite views, made use of his methods and modelled his style on that of al-Muḥāsibī. He accepts al-Muḥāsibī's views of knowledge as coming through tradition and reflection, and of that supernatural knowledge which is the gift of God and confirms, while it goes far beyond, the natural knowledge which can be acquired by human effort.[1] He also lays stress, like al-Muḥāsibī, on sincerity (*ṣidq*) as the final test of goodness,[2] and he uses *ghurba* in the same sense as al-Muḥāsibī, representing the station of that one who is a stranger to this world and the next, becoming dissociated from phenomenal existence more and more completely as he enters into more intimate communion with the Divine.[3] The use of the term *ḥulūl* to signify the infusion of the grace of God, the interpenetration of the human with the Divine, for which al-Ḥallāj was criticised, had already been employed by al-Muḥāsibī with the same significance, as we have seen. al-Ḥallāj carried the doctrine so far as to hold that when the union between God and the soul was accomplished, the saint had the right to identify himself with God, since he knew himself to be deified by the Divine Spirit and to be the witness chosen by God to represent Him to the world,

[1] *Ṭawāsīn*, X., p. 23. *Cf. La Passion d'al-Hallāj*, pp. 852 *ff*.

[2] *Ṭawāsīn*, V., p. 21; *Passion*, pp. 685 *ff*.

[3] "Waṣāyā (Naṣā'iḥ)," fol. 3*a*; *Ṭawāsīn*, III., pp. 1, 3, VI., p. 20. *Cf* "Ḥilyā," fol. 240*b*.

and so he declared to his generation, "If you do not recognise God, at least recognise His signs. I am that sign, I am the Creative Truth (*ana al-Ḥaqq*)."[1]

A reconciliation between the claims of tradition and reason was effected by Abu'l-Ḥasan al-Ash'arī (*ob.* 324/935), who was a Mu'tazilite for the first half of his life and then, like al-Muḥāsibī before him, used the dialectic of the Mu'tazilites to oppose their teaching, and established a scholastic theology which, while rigidly orthodox in most respects, rejected both the extreme literalism of the Ḥanbalites and the pure rationalism of the Mu'tazilites, and so attained to a more reasonable faith. In this he was so plainly following in the steps of al-Muḥāsibī and his school that Shahrastānī says that the Ṣifatiyya, among whom, as we have seen, he reckoned al-Muḥāsibī, were later called the Ash'ariyya.[2] The Ash'arites themselves considered al-Muḥāsibī to be their forerunner in this choice of the *via media*, and Abū 'Abdallah b. Khafīf, himself an Ash'arite theologian and mystic, contemporary with al-Ḥallāj, and founder of the Khafīfiyya order,[3] instructed his followers to accept the teaching of five Shaykhs and to disregard all others, and those five were Ḥārith al-Muḥāsibī, al-Junayd, Abū Muḥammad Ruwaym (*ob.* 303/915), Abu'l-'Abbās b. 'Aṭā (*ob.* 310/922) and 'Amr. b. 'Uthmān al-Makkī (*ob.* 297/909), for their teaching was a combination of orthodox and mystical theology (*'ilm wa ḥaqā'iq*), and they taught the observance of both the Ṣūfī Way and the Sharī'a. All five were worthy of acceptance and imitation, and 'Aṭṭār adds that the great Ṣūfīs reckoned Ibn Khafīf himself as the sixth.[4] The Khafīfīs were later reorganised by al-Kāzarūnī (*ob.* 426/1034), and he accepted the teaching of three Shaykhs, Ibn Khafīf, Ḥārith al-Muḥāsibī and Abū 'Amr b. 'Alī.[5]

[1] *Cf.* *Ṭawāsīn*, p. 134 and p. 250 above. For a complete account of the teaching of al-Ḥallāj and its relation to that of al-Muḥāsibī *cf.* L. Massignon, *La Passion d'al-Ḥallāj*, chapters xi. and xii.

[2] Shahrastānī, *op. cit.*, pp. 64, 65. *Cf.* D. B. Macdonald, *The Development of Muslim Theology, Jurisprudence and Constitutional Theory*, p. 293.

[3] Hujwīrī, *op. cit.*, pp. 247 *ff*. *Cf.* E. Blochet, *Études sur l'ésotérisme*, p. 175.

[4] Qushayrī, *Risāla*, p. 15; 'Aṭṭār, *op. cit.*, I., p. 225.

[5] *Ibid.*, II., pp. 291 *ff*.

The Ash'arite 'Abd al-Qāhir al-Baghdadī (*ob.* 429/1037) includes al-Muḥāsibī in a list of the orthodox scholastics, which comprises also 'Abd Allah b. Sa'id, 'Abd al-'Azīz al-Makkī, Karābisī and Qalānisī, who held the view that if a man believed, though he neglected the intellectual methods on which the foundations of the faith were based, he might hope for forgiveness, and this, too, was al-Baghdadī's opinion.[1]

The writers on Ṣūfism who came after him, and the biographers of the saints, were deeply impressed by al-Muḥāsibī's personality and his teaching. Among the earliest of these writers was Abū 'Abd al-Raḥmān al-Sulamī, a mystic of Nīshāpūr, who esteemed al-Muḥāsibī highly as author and teacher, and quotes many of his sayings, and as al-Sulamī himself held high rank as a biographer of the Ṣūfīs, his opinions were accepted as authoritative by later writers.[2]

There is much in the writings of the philosopher and mystic Ibn Sīnā (Avicenna) (*ob.* 428/1037) which suggests the influence of al-Muḥāsibī, for he distinguishes the ascetic (*zāhid*), who renounces all connection with this present world, from the devotee (*'ābid*), who observes all the exterior requirements of religion, and the gnostic (*'ārif*), who gives himself up wholly to meditation upon the Kingdom of God, seeking the illumination of his soul by the Divine Light. So too, Ibn Sīnā holds that the first stage on the road to God is that of will (*irāda*), the stage of right intention; the second is that of self-discipline, in order to subordinate the carnal soul to the rational soul, so that the imagination and intelligence shall be attracted to the higher and not to the lower. Then comes the stage of the entire surrender of the soul to spiritual love, whence it passes to the continual contemplation of the Divine and to that intuitive knowledge which leads to union.[3] In his *Qaṣīda on the Soul*, Ibn Sīnā takes the view set forth by al-Muḥāsibī that the soul is a prisoner in this world, to which it has descended from its home in the world above. It is held captive, he says, by thick nets and a strong cage which keeps it, while in this world, from

[1] *Uṣūl*, pp. 254 *ff*. *Cf*. A. Wensinck, *The Muslim Creed*, p. 135.
[2] "Ṭabaqāt al-Ṣufiyya," fols. 11*b ff*.
[3] *Fī maqāmāt al-'ārifīn*.

seeking its true heavenly sphere. Here it weeps in grief, but when at last the veil is raised and it looks upon things hidden from mortal eyes, it is filled with joy, for the gnosis of that which is invisible has been granted to it and it can return again whence it came. It is for discipline, hard but purposive, that God sends it into this world, so that, having been purified by what it suffers here, it may be fit to return again to Him.[1]

The traditionist Abū Bakr al-Khaṭīb al-Baghdadī (*ob.* 463/1071) mentions al-Muḥāsibī with approval and commends his books as very profitable, including those directed against the Mu'tazilites and other heretics.[2] Of the Ṣūfī writers, the great Persian mystical author Abu'l-Ḥasan al-Jullabī al-Hujwīrī (*ob.* 446/1074), a native of Ghazna in Afghanistan, who travelled widely and met many of the Ṣūfī Shaykhs, not only quotes al-Muḥāsibī's teaching very frequently and bases much of his own upon it, but also reckons his followers, the Muḥāsibīs, as forming one of the ten approved sects of Ṣūfism known in his time, all of whom, he stated, asserted the truth and belonged to the mass of orthodox Muslims. al-Muḥāsibī he describes as "a man of approved spiritual influence and mortified passions, versed in theology, jurisprudence and mysticism. He discoursed on detachment from the world and unification, while his outward and inward dealings (with God) were beyond reproach."[3] Hujwīrī's contemporary 'Abd al-Karīm al-Qushayrī (*ob.* 465/1075), a Shāfi'ite mystic of Nīshāpūr and a disciple of Sulamī, in his carefully conceived and carefully worked out treatise on the principles of Ṣūfism, frequently cites al-Muḥāsibī's teaching and bases his own upon it.[4]

Another great writer on Ṣūfism, Shihāb al-Dīn Abū Ḥafṣ Suhrawardī (*ob.* 632/1234), regarded as the founder of the Suhrawardiyya order, who was for some time the chief Shaykh of the Ṣūfīs at Baghdad, in his chief work, dealing with the life of the mystic, elaborates a psychological theory

[1] Ibn Khallikān, I., p. 443; Ẓiyā Bey, *Kharābāt*, I., pp. 283, 284. *Cf.* al-Muḥāsibī, p. 117, and pp. 122 *ff.* above.

[2] *Ta'rikh Baghdād*, VIII., p. 211. [3] *Kashf al-Maḥjūb*, pp. 176 *ff.*

[4] *Risāla*, pp. 46, 61, 101, 102, 167, etc.

very similar to that of al-Muḥāsibī, whose views on reason he incorporates, regarding it as a "natural light whereby good and evil are distinguished," in accordance with al-Muḥāsibī's definition, and he also admits its limitations, and draws the same distinction between *'ilm* and *ma'rifa*. He holds the same views on the lower soul (*nafs*) and the need for training it until it becomes subordinate to the higher soul (*rūḥ*).[1] He deals with the capital sins and the remedies for them, with prayer and the need for listening (*istimā'*) for the voice of God, and for a correspondence between the outward and the inward attitude of him who prays: "In body a man should look towards the *qibla*, in heart towards the Lord of the *qibla*," and the speech of the tongue should be in harmony with the feeling of the heart.[2] He gives teaching also on "presence" and "absence," on the safety to be found in silence, of the need for meditation and self-examination, on the "stations" and the "states," on trust and satisfaction and the close relation between satisfaction and love, in connection with which he quotes al-Muḥāsibī by name, and he also regards longing (*shawq*) as a "branch" of which the root is love.[3] A study of Suhrawardī's writings shews plainly that it is on al-Muḥāsibī's teaching that he has based a great part of his own rule of life for the ascetics and mystics of Islām.

In the thirteenth century was founded the order of the Shādhiliyya, by Abu'l-Ḥasan al-Shādhilī (*ob.* 656/1258), a Ṣūfī who accepted the doctrines of al-Junayd and Nūrī and taught his disciples to devote their lives wholly to the service of God and to follow in the steps of the early Ṣūfīs. Among his followers were Tāj al-Dīn b. 'Aṭā Allah (*ob.* 709/1309), the author of the *Ḥikam al-'Aṭā'iyya*, and Abu'l-'Abbās al-Mursī (*ob.* 686/1287), and it is evident that al-Muḥāsibī's writings were known and approved by them, for Shar'ānī (Shar'āwī) related that Ibn 'Aṭā Allah was one day reading the book of the *Ri'āya* to Shaykh Abu'l-'Abbās, and the latter said the book could be summed up in two phrases, "Serve God according to knowledge, and never

[1] *'Awārif al-Ma'ārif* (margin *Iḥyā'*), IV., pp. 171 *ff.*, 208 *ff.*, 213.

[2] *Ibid.*, III., pp. 169 *ff.*

[3] *Ibid.*, IV., pp. 245, 321 *ff.*, 326, 331, 356 *ff.*

be satisfied with yourself."[1] It was a member of this order, 'Abd al-'Azīz b. 'Abd al-Salām al-Sulamī (Maqdīsī) (*ob.* 660/1262), who wrote a summary of it called *Ḥall Maqāṣid al-Ri'āya*,[2] and other later members of this order who recommended the use of the *Ri'āya* were Ibn 'Abbād Rundi (*ob.* 796/1394) and Zarrūq Burnūsī (*ob.* 899/1494).

In the fourteenth century 'Afīf al-Dīn al-Yāfi'ī (*ob.* 768/1367), a Shāfi'ite scholar, interested in history and literature as well as philosophy and mystical theology, refers to al-Muḥāsibī as " a fount of wisdom, a leader of the Ṣūfī Path, the tongue of Truth," and elsewhere quotes his teaching on otherworldliness and the preference of poverty to wealth, giving it at considerable length.[3]

We find also the Shāfi'ite lawyer of Damascus, Tāj al-Dīn al-Subkī (*ob.* 771/1370), stating that most of the Ṣifatiyya scholastic theologians (*mutakallimūn*) traced their origin to al-Muḥāsibī or derived their teaching from him, and he himself expresses the opinion that his books are very profitable. al-Subkī discusses the question of Ibn Ḥanbal's hostility to al-Muḥāsibī and observes that no doubt it is better to refrain from speculation when there is no need for it, since unnecessary speculation is liable to lead to heresy, but states his own opinion that Ḥārith indulged in *kalām* only where it was necessary for his purpose. al-Subkī also refers to the comments of the Imām al-Ḥaramayn, Abū'l-Ma'ālī al-Juwaynī (478/1085), the Ash'arite theologian of Nīshāpūr, who, in discussing the nature of the reason, stated that no one of the theologians had gone so carefully into the matter as Ḥārith al-Muḥāsibī, and quoted his definition of reason. The Imām accepted al-Muḥāsibī's statement of the matter as being sound and in accordance with the facts. al-Subkī insists that such approval on the part of the Imām al-Ḥaramayn did not commit him to any statement of naturalist philosophy (*ṭabā'i'*) or any of the assertions of the philosophers, his idea was only to gain some enlightenment for his *Book of Demonstration*. al-Subkī considers the most authentic account of

[1] *Ṭabaqāt al-Kubra*, II., p. 18.

[2] Subkī, *Ṭab. al-Shāfi'iyya*, V., p. 103 ; Berlin 2812.

[3] " Mir'āt al-Janān," fol. 143*a* ; *Nashr al-Maḥāsin*, II., pp. 382 *ff.* ; *Rawḍ al-Riyāḥīn*, p. 15. *Cf.* " Naṣā'iḥ," fol. 4*b*.

Ḥārith's view to be that he considered the reason to be the light of a natural quality which is strengthened and increased by godliness, not light in the sense in which philosophers use the term.[1]

Ibn Ḥajar al-'Asqalānī (*ob.* 852/1449) includes al-Muḥāsibī in his great biography of traditionists, and the inclusion indicates his acceptance of al-Muḥāsibī's orthodoxy. Commenting on Ibn Ḥanbal's advice to one of al-Muḥāsibī's friends, Isma'īl b. Isḥāq al-Sarrāj (*cf.* pp. 14 *ff.* above), not to associate with him, Ibn Ḥajar suggests that the reason for this prohibition was that Ibn Ḥanbal knew that Ibn Isḥāq came short of the station of al-Muḥāsibī and his disciples, for al-Muḥāsibī was in a rank to which not everyone could attain, and men should fear to aspire to a state the obligations of which they might be unable to fulfil. Ibn Ḥajar, therefore, refuses to accept the view that Ibn Ḥanbal meant any condemnation of al-Muḥāsibī by his advice, and suggests that, on the contrary, he was thereby acknowledging the high degree of sanctity to which al-Muḥāsibī had attained.[2]

[1] *Ṭabaqāt al-Shāfi'iyya*, II., pp. 39 *ff.*
[2] *Tahdhīb al-Tahdhīb*, II., p. 136.

CHAPTER XIV

AL-MUḤĀSIBĪ'S INFLUENCE ON AL-GHAZĀLĪ, BARHEBRÆUS, THE SPANISH MYSTICS, JEWISH MYSTICISM AND CHRISTIAN SCHOLASTICISM

By far the greatest of those who were influenced by al-Muḥāsibī, and the one upon whom he had the greatest influence, was Abū Ḥāmid Muḥammad al-Ṭūsī al-Ghazālī (*ob.* 505/1111), known as the Proof of Islām and the Ornament of the Faith, a pupil of the Imām al-Ḥaramayn.[1] Highly esteemed by his contemporaries as a scholar, teacher and theologian, he became the dominant influence in Muslim scholastic, and he is still, at the present time, one of the most widely read of Muslim authors, as evidenced by the fact that his works are constantly being edited or reissued. Ghazālī, in his chief work, the great *Iḥyā' 'Ulūm al-Dīn* (The Revivification of the Religious Sciences), and in others of his writings, was concerned to combine a modified and orthodox Ṣūfism with Sunni theology, as al-Muḥāsibī had done before him, and his works bear witness to the profound influence of al-Muḥāsibī upon his doctrines. He himself admits his indebtedness to al-Muḥāsibī, whose writings he studied, together with those of Abū Ṭālib al-Makkī, al-Junayd, Shibli and Abū Yazīd Bisṭāmī, as representing the real doctrines of Ṣūfism.[2] Elsewhere he states that al-Muḥāsibī was the savant (*ḥabr*) of the nation in his knowledge of religious practice and excelled all others in his teaching on the errors of the self, and on sins of action and delusions in regard to good works, and his words, Ghazālī notes, were worthy of attention, because what he said was based upon his own experience.[3]

Ghazālī's eschatological teaching, as set forth in his *al-*

[1] For a full account of his life and writings *cf.* Subkī, *Ṭab. al-Shāfi'iyya*, IV., pp. 101-182; A. Palacios, *Algazel dogmatica, moral, ascetica*; H. Gösche, *Über Ghazzālī's Leben und Werke*; Sayyid Murtāḍa, *Ithāf al-Sāda.*

[2] *Munkidh min al-Ḍalāl*, p. 20.

[3] *Iḥyā'*, III., p. 229.

Durrat al-Fākhira, shews a close resemblance to that of al-Muḥāsibī in the *Ba'th wa'l-Nushūr* and the *Kitāb al-Tawahhum*, and passage after passage appears to have been based on the former work.[1]

In the account which he gives of his own religious experience, Ghazālī says of himself that he began by noting how mankind differ in regard to their faith and the religious sects into which they are divided, and how the distinctions of these different systems are like a deep sea in which many are submerged and few escape, and each sect asserts that it is the means by which men are led to salvation. From his youth up, Ghazālī says that he has questioned the beliefs of each sect and scrutinised the details of each doctrine, in order to distinguish truth from error and to separate what is orthodox from what is heretical. Having considered the different classes of thinkers, he found few who were sincere among them, and it appeared to him that what he most desired of the bliss of the hereafter could be attained only by godliness (*taqwā*) and restraint of self-will, and that the fundamental principle on which this way of life was based was detachment of the earth from this world. In the Ṣūfīs he found the rightly guided leaders on the road to God, those to whom light had been given, whose manner of life had been based on that of the Prophet.[2] It is clear that al-Muḥāsibī's account of his conversion (*cf.* pp. 18 *ff.* above) has formed the model for Ghazālī, who has employed the same phrases to describe his own spiritual difficulties and experiences. In his teaching on the religious life, ascetical, devotional and mystical, Ghazālī again bases his doctrines on those of al-Muḥāsibī, while developing, and expanding what was only suggested by al-Muḥāsibī, into a much fuller system of mystical theology.

His psychological ideas correspond closely to those of al-Muḥāsibī. It is the heart which enables man to attain to

[1] *Cf. al-Durrat al-Fākhira*, pp. 40, 41, 55, 56, 57, 59-63, 67, 68, 71 *ff.*, 79, 81, 91, 98 *ff.*, 105, with "al-Ba'th wa'l-Nushūr," fols. 196*b*, 197*b*, 198*b*, 199*b*, 200*b*, 201*a*, 202*a*, and "Kitāb al-Tawwahum," fols. 154*a*, 156*a*.

[2] *Munkidh*, pp. 1 *ff.* This work shews that Ghazālī had made a close study of al-Muḥāsibī's "Naṣā'iḥ."

knowledge of God and to draw near to Him. It is the heart which rejoices in proximity to God and, when purified, brings spiritual health to man and, when defiled and corrupted, brings him to misery. "Comprehending knowledge of the heart and of the real nature of its qualities is the root of religion and the foundation of the Way of those who seek God."[1] Elsewhere, Ghazālī, after relating a legend given by al-Muḥāsibī in this connection, quotes his statement that "God only requires their hearts from His servants."[2] He also writes of the "eye" of the heart.[3] Of the origin of the Reason Ghazālī gives the tradition related by al-Muḥāsibī, and also his definition of it.[4] Reason, he says elsewhere, is the guide of the individual believer to enable him to know the truth, that which is in conformity with the Qur'ān and the Sunna. Reason is the sense of sight by which man can secure assurance, but he emphasises the fact, as al-Muḥāsibī had done, that reason alone cannot lead the believer to God or form the foundation of a real knowledge of Him.[5] Ghazālī's theory of knowledge, while more fully developed than that of al-Muḥāsibī, resembles it very closely in its essentials. He also distinguishes between types of knowledge—the knowledge which comes from the revelation made by God to the prophets, which is found in the Sharī'a, and that which comes through the use of the reason—and he lays the same stress as his predecessor on the use of reflection, and quotes the same tradition to the effect that to reflect for one hour is better than to perform acts of piety for sixty years.[6] But he teaches also that there is a knowledge of God which comes not from the revelation given aforetime to the prophets and given by them to others, but is a direct enlightening of the heart of the saints, those who have been purified to receive it. "When God controls

[1] *Iḥyā'*, III., p. 2. *Cf.* also *Munkidh*, pp. 26, 27. *Cf.* pp. 87, 89 above.

[2] *Mukāshafat al-Qulūb*, p. 134. *Cf.* "Ri'āya," fol. 110*a* and p. 87 above.

[3] *Risālat al-Ladunniyya*, p. 12.

[4] *Iḥyā'*, III., p. 4; I., pp. 74, 75. *Cf.* "Naṣā'iḥ," fol. 16*b*; "Mustarshid," fol. 1. *Cf.* p. 93 above.

[5] *Kitāb al-Iqtiṣād*, p. 23. *Minhāj*, chapter ii.; *Munkidh*, p. 27. *Cf.* "Ri'āya," fol. 23*a*; "Ādāb al-Nufūs," fol. 100*b* and pp. 94 *ff.* above.

[6] *Risālat al-Ladunniyya*, chapter iii.; *Iḥyā'*, IV., p. 361. *Cf.* pp. 99 *ff.* above. *Iḥyā'*, III., p. 14. *Cf.* "Kitāb al-'Ilm," chapters iv., v.

the heart of His servant, He bestows His mercy upon him and his heart is enlightened and his breast is filled with joy and the mysteries of the invisible world are revealed to him, and the veil of heedlessness, by the loving-kindness of God, is taken from his heart and the inner meaning of the Divine Truth is made perfect therein."[1]

The different divisions of the *Iḥyā'* set forth a rule of life which begins with a statement of what is due to God, in accordance with what He has ordained, and teaching in regard to traditional customs, which represent the "actions of the members," and in this Ghazālī quotes and upholds al-Muḥāsibī's views, and goes on to the "actions of the heart," those which are pernicious and require ascetic discipline as their antidote, and those which are wholesome, representing the virtues acquired by the help of God, which make the soul fit to receive the mystic states and to attain the rank of the saints, and, to Ghazālī also, these are the lovers of God who enter into fellowship and union with Him. Practically all these subjects are dealt with by al-Muḥāsibī in the "Ri'āya" and his other works, and Ghazālī follows his predecessor's treatment of them to a great extent. He also divides sins into those of the servant against God alone and those which offend against his fellow-servants, and he classifies sins generally as either mortal or venial. He holds, like al-Muḥāsibī, that a venial sin may become mortal, and the chief causes of this are contumacy and stubborn persistence, and states that there is no venial sin combined with contumacy and no mortal sin if forgiveness is asked for it.[2] There is a considerable resemblance between al-Muḥāsibī's classification of sins and Ghazālī's enumeration of the veils between God and man, in the *Mishkāt al-Anwār*.[3]

Of temptation, and especially the temptations which come from Satan, Ghazālī says that first there is the idea entering into the mind (*khāṭir*) because the heart has been off its guard, the idea produces a desire for the thing suggested, desire leads to the decision of the heart in favour of what is

[1] *Iḥyā'*, III., p. 16; *Jawāhir*, p. 14; *Mīzān*, p. 43. *Cf.* "Ādāb al-Nufūs," fol. 93*b* and pp. 102 *ff.* above.

[2] *Iḥyā'*, IV., pp. 14, 15. *Cf.* pp. 130 *ff.* above.

[3] *Mishkāt al-Anwār*, pp. 48 *ff.*, 28 *ff.* *Cf.* pp. 131 *ff.* above.

suggested, and this leads to the intention and purpose to do the thing, and finally the thing is done ; the original suggestion is what leads to evil, and this can be checked at the start, and the occurrence of it is not sin in itself if it is not allowed to proceed as far as action.[1]

Ghazālī's list of capital sins includes lust and hypocrisy as the chief sources of the sins of the "members" and the heart, and he goes on to deal with anger, hatred, jealousy, sins of the tongue, worldliness, love of wealth, avarice, pride and self-conceit and self-delusion. Hypocrisy he considers to be the hidden lust of the self, more harmful than the lusts of the body ;[2] it is a form of polytheism, and he also compares it to the creeping of the ant in its insidiousness, and repeats much of al-Muḥāsibī's teaching, referring to him by name.[3] The cure for hypocrisy which Ghazālī advocates is single-mindedness towards God. "It is," he said, "that all your works be done for the sake of God Most High, your heart not resting content with the praise of people nor despairing on account of their censure. Know that hypocrisy arises from exalting mankind, and the remedy is that you should regard them as forced to labour under the decree of God, and reckon them as inanimate objects in their inability to attain to satisfaction or misery, so that you may escape from hypocrisy on their account."[4]

Ghazālī deals at considerable length with pride in its different forms, including self-conceit (*'ujb*), in connection with which he quotes the tradition of 'Ā'isha quoted also by al-Muḥāsibī, and reproduces his teaching on the evil effects of this sin and speaks in the same way of its different types —spiritual pride, for which he gives the same tradition of David as an example, pride in the body and pride in the intellect. Pride of birth and pride in possessions is included, and Ghazālī gives the same story of Abū Dharr and the Prophet.[5] Speaking of pride in the form of arrogance (*kibr*),

[1] *Iḥyā'* III., p. 23. *Cf.* p. 126 above.

[2] *Cf.* al-Muḥāsibī's teaching that hypocrisy is always desire, "Ri'āya," fol. 42*b*.

[3] *Iḥyā'*, III., pp. 264, 265, 275 *ff*. *Cf.* pp. 132 *ff*. above.

[4] *Ayyuha'l-Walad*, p. 68. *Cf. Iḥyā'*, III., pp. 237, 268 and pp. 161 *ff*. above.

[5] *Iḥyā'*, III., pp. 318 *ff*. *Cf.* pp. 136 *ff*. above.

Ghazālī relates the tradition of Abū Hurayra, on the exclusive claim of God to greatness and majesty, and also the tradition of the words ascribed to Christ that " as the seed grows in soft soil, so wisdom dwells in the humble heart." Ghazālī, like al-Muḥāsibī, teaches that arrogance may be directed towards God or one's fellow-creatures, and that the arrogant man is lacking in true knowledge of his relation to his Lord. Here Ghazālī gives Wahb's parable of the rain, and shews how knowledge strengthens the qualities a man already possesses, and, if he is prone to pride, knowledge will make him prouder still. Ghazālī's remedies for pride are also those of al-Muḥāsibī, and he gives the story of the Outcast of Israel, called by this name for his many sins, who passed by a pious man wearing a turban, and the outcast, hoping to gain merit by the proximity of the pious man, sat down beside him only to be rudely repulsed, whereupon the Lord sent a message by His prophet to say that He had forgiven the sins of the outcast and had rejected the works of the righteous man. According to one account the turban was transferred to the head of the outcast, a legend given also by al-Muḥāsibī in this connection. This whole section on the different forms of pride is derived from al-Muḥāsibī's teaching on these sins and their remedies.[1]

In regard to envy and jealousy Ghazālī also points out this sin was responsible for the first sin in Heaven, that of Iblīs, and the first on earth, that of Adam, and for the sin of his son (Cain). Dealing with emulation, Ghazālī holds that it may be directed towards good when its motive is the love of God, and towards evil when it is actuated by love of this world.[2] In condemnation of avarice (*bukhl*) Ghazālī quotes the same story of the man clinging to the curtains of the Ka'ba and his conversation with the Prophet. It is interesting to note that the commentator 'Irāqī regards this tradition as unauthentic.[3] In condemning love of wealth and asserting the superiority of poverty, Ghazālī frankly admits his indebtedness to al-Muḥāsibī and inserts a long section

[1] *Iḥyā'*, III., pp. 290 *ff.*, 300 *ff.*; *Munkidh*, p. 34. *Cf.* " Ri'āya," fols. 109*b*, 110*a*.

[2] *Iḥyā'*, III., pp. 63 *ff.*, 167 *ff.* *Cf.* pp. 144 *ff.* above.

[3] *Ibid.*, p. 221. *Cf.* " Waṣāyā (Naṣā'iḥ)," fols. 11*a* *ff.*

from his "Waṣāyā (Naṣā'iḥ)," and it is to this part of Ghazālī's teaching and his acceptance of al-Muḥāsibī's views that Ibn al-Jawzī takes exception. Ghazalī maintains al-Muḥāsibī's view that poverty is always better than wealth, whatever may be the motive for amassing wealth, and whatever the manner in which it is spent.[1]

Ghazālī follows al-Muḥāsibī in his view of the sins of the tongue, and, like him, states that of all the members of the body it is most prone to sin. He quotes the same traditions of the Prophet in regard to the danger of the tongue and the safety of silence, and of Ibn Mas'ūd, and gives much the same list of sins for which the tongue is responsible.[2] Ghazālī finally treats of the sin of self-delusion, which attacks the self-righteous and those who mistake the outward observance of religion for the inward reality.[3]

When he turns to these things which make for salvation from these sins, the way of purgation and illumination which will lead ultimately to the unitive life, Ghazālī begins with repentance as the first step on the way and enforces his teaching with the same traditions as al-Muḥāsibī. Repentance is due to the conviction that sin is dangerous to the salvation of the soul, and it gives rise to contrition over what is past, and the purpose to abandon sin in the present, to offer expiation for evil done and to amend life in the future, and this means a minute examination of the past life and a survey of the inner life from day to day.[4] In regard to the mortification of sins in general and of particular sins, Ghazālī advocates the same remedies as al-Muḥāsibī and lays special stress on asceticism and poverty and the Prophet's preference of poverty. The true ascetic is he who abandons the lesser good for the sake of the greater.[5] Like al-Muḥāsibī, Ghazālī advocates the virtues of dependence on God and trust in Him, which arise from faith, for, like al-Muḥāsibī, Ghazālī holds that faith must bear fruit in action, and faith in God as the Sole Cause and Provider, on Whose

[1] *Iḥyā'*, III. pp. 229 *ff*. *Cf*. "Waṣāyā," fols. 4*b ff*.
[2] *Ibid*., II., pp. 93 *ff*. *Cf*. pp. 146 *ff*. above.
[3] *Ibid*., III., pp. 334 *ff*. *Cf*. "Ri'āya," fols. 122*b ff*.
[4] *Ibid*., IV., pp. 11, 12. *Cf*. pp. 151 *ff*. above.
[5] *Ibid*., pp. 187 *ff*. *Cf*. pp. 171 *ff*. above.

power all things depend, will lead to complete reliance on Him and abandonment of the personal will to His Will, which is complete trust (*tafwīḍ*).[1]

Of the virtue of hope, which arises from trust, Ghazālī notes that in the traveller it has become a "station" and is established.[2] With hope Ghazālī joins fear, for he who knows most of himself and his relation to his Lord fears most; it is only godly fear that can burn up desire and lead the servant to those higher realms of the life lived close to his Lord, where there will be no place for either hope or fear, for these have reference to the future, and the believer, in communion with his Lord, has passed beyond both.[3] Ghazālī also includes among the virtues patience, necessary in a world which is a place of trial, and trial greatest for the devoted soul, for it is God's training whereby it may be perfected.[4] Gratitude Ghazālī finds to be the complement of patience, the same quality displayed towards God's benefits, the recognition of the Giver in His gifts. Ghazālī gives a long account of the gifts of God and points out, like al-Muḥāsibī, that gratitude includes not only praise to God for His favours, but the right use of them.[5]

Ghazālī's teaching, on the devotional side, also shews a close resemblance to that of his great predecessor. He begins his section on Prayer with the statement, "God differs from (earthly) kings for all His unique majesty and greatness, in inspiring His creatures to ask and make their plea to Him, and He differs from the sultans (of this world) in opening the door and lifting the veil and giving leave to His servants to enter into confidential intercourse . . . and He does not limit Himself to permission, but He shews His kindness by inspiring desire for this and calling (His servant) to Him. And others, kings who are but creatures, do not freely grant a private audience except after the offer of gifts and bribery."[6] A comparison with al-Muḥāsibī's teaching on personal

[1] *Iḥyā'*, IV., pp. 211 *ff.*, 223 *ff.* *Cf.* pp. 185 *ff.* above.
[2] *Ibid.*, p. 123. *Cf.* p. 186 above.
[3] *Ibid.*, p. 135. *Cf.* pp. 188 *ff.* above.
[4] *Ibid.*, pp. 55 *ff.*, 60 *ff.* *Cf.* pp. 174, 175 above.
[5] *Ibid.*, pp. 71, 72, 73. *Cf.* pp. 194 *ff.* above.
[6] *Ibid.*, I., p. 169.

prayer (*cf.* p. 204 above) can leave little doubt of the origin of this passage.

In his section on the Excellence of Humility, Ghazālī gives the same example of awe and reverence on the part of those who were about to enter upon prayer.[1] Again Ghazālī says, " Worship (*'ibāda*) is an outward form, which is prescribed by the Law, and we show our devotion to God by observing it, but its spirit and inner life are humility and intention and presence of the heart and single-minded sincerity (*ikhlāṣ*) "; and he goes on to describe the conditions necessary for these inward " acts " of the heart. " The presence of the heart," writes Ghazālī, " is the essence of prayer," and by the presence of the heart he means its freedom from all else except attention to that in which it is engaged; and again, " Your heart is present when you come before some great man, who has no (real) power to harm or benefit you. So when it is not present during your communion with the King of kings, in Whose hand are the Kingdom and the Power, with Whom it rests to send prosperity or adversity, do not imagine that the cause is anything but the weakness of your faith."[2] " Presence " of the heart is secured by cutting off all distractions and all thought save of Him Who is worshipped, " for he who loves anything is constantly remembering it, and inevitably the remembrance of what is loved takes possession of the heart, and therefore you see that a man whose love is set on another than God has no prayer free from idle thoughts."[3] " Let the face of your heart," says Ghazālī, " be with the face of your body, and remember that as the face does not turn towards the direction of the House (the Ka'ba) except by turning away from everything else, so the heart does not turn towards God unless it has been emptied of all else."[4] " But when you can say," he adds, " that my worship and my devotion, my living and my dying, belong to God, know that this is the state of one lost to himself and found unto his Lord."[5]

[1] *Iḥyā'*, I., pp. 134, 135.
[2] *Ibid.*, pp. 142, 145, 157. *Cf.* p. 202 above.
[3] *Ibid.*, p. 145. *Cf.* p. 207 above.
[4] *Ibid.*, p. 148. *Cf.* p. 201 above.
[5] *Ibid.*, p. 149. *Cf.* p. 211 above.

To Ghazālī, too, the sincerity of the intention is all-important, if the will is to be rightly directed in regard to the actions of the members or the heart, and he quotes al-Muḥāsibī by name in this connection. He also defines intention as a desire for action for the sake of God or for the sake of this world ; it is, he says, the soul of action, while sincerity (*ṣidq*) is that which guides a man to righteousness, and righteousness guides him to Paradise.[1]

To the soul which has reached this stage, Ghazālī teaches that gnosis is granted as the outflowing of the grace of God, for it has become purely receptive, not desirous, and God can now do all.[2] It is the stage of the lover of God, and to Ghazālī also, God's love precedes that of His servant, for it is God's love for him that draws his servant near to Himself, so that his qualities may be changed and he may become Godlike.[3] Of the signs of the servant's love to his Lord, Ghazālī says that the lover abandons what he desires for that which the Beloved desires and he finds no joy in aught but Him.[4] He notes, too, that he whose heart is possessed by the love of God loves all that He has created (*cf.* p. 238 above). It is the mark of love to God that the lover seeks the fellowship (*uns*) of his Lord and intimate intercourse alone with the Beloved, and here Ghazālī follows closely the teaching of al-Muḥāsibī given in the *Ḥilya*, concerning the fellowship with God which means detachment from men, using al-Muḥāsibī's very words and phrases, and employing the same illustrations and quoting the same authorities—*e.g.*, Ibrāhīm b. Adham, the prophet David, Rābi'a al-'Adawiyya, 'Abd al-Wāḥid b. Zayd and the Christian monk—and giving as his own al-Muḥāsibī's definition of fellowship (*cf.* pp. 228 *ff.* above).[5]

Included among the signs of love is satisfaction (*riḍā'*), and on this subject Ghazālī also states that God sends affliction to those whom He loves, and if they bear it patiently they

[1] *Iḥyā'*, IV., pp. 309 *ff.*, 326, 330. *Cf.* pp. 106 *ff.* above and "Ḥilya," fols. 235*a*, 238*a*.
[2] *Mishkāt al-Anwār*, pp. 55, 56 ; *Iḥyā'*, IV., pp. 267, 275, 276.
[3] *Iḥyā'*, IV., pp. 271, 282. *Cf.* pp. 236, 249 *ff.* above.
[4] *Ibid.*, p. 284. *Cf.* p. 238 above.
[5] *Ibid.*, p. 291. *Cf.* "Ḥilya," fols. 241*b ff.*

are favoured, but if they meet it with satisfaction they are singled out as the chosen of God (*cf.* p. 232 above). The true lover's will is the Will of the Beloved, and even though he be cast into Hell-fire, if that be God's Will, he is satisfied therein.[1] Love and fellowship mean contemplation, for God lifts the veil from the heart of His lover, so that he may contemplate Him in his heart and may rejoice in the Vision of his Lord, for to contemplate God is the desire of His saints in this world and the next, and fellowship is the rejoicing of the heart in the contemplation of the Divine Beauty, and satisfaction is the cause of continual contemplation.[2]

It is to these lovers that union is granted, and again Ghazālī brings forward al-Muḥāsibī's teaching on the subject and repeats the tradition of the Word of God to David concerning those who are " spiritualised."[3] They are those, he says, whom God has cleansed from all defilement, so that nothing may remain in them but Himself, those whom He indwells completely, that they may adore none but Him.[4] They are those who have attained, the *wāṣilūn*, who lose themselves in God and are conscious that they are one with Him ;[5] and of those who are living the unitive life in God Ghazālī writes, " Praise be to God Who hath consumed the hearts of His saints in the fire of His love and hath taken captive their thoughts and their spirits in longing to meet with Him and to look upon Him and hath fixed their sight and their insight upon the Vision of the beauty of His presence, until by the inbreathing of the spirit of union, they have been rapt beyond themselves . . . and they see nought like unto Him among things visible or invisible, and they are mindful of nought in the two worlds save Him alone. Their longing is only for that which is to be found in His presence, and their going to and from is round about Him alone. For from Him is all that they hear, and it is to Him that they give heed, since He hath closed their eyes to all but Him and hath made them deaf to all words save His. These are they whom

[1] *Iḥyā'*, IV., pp. 297, 299. *Cf.* pp. 239 *ff.* above.
[2] *Ibid.*, pp. 281, 294. *Cf.* pp. 244 *ff.* above.
[3] *Ibid.*, p. 295. *Cf.* p. 249 above.
[4] *Munkidh*, p. 34. [5] *Mishkāt al-Anwār*, p. 56.

God hath called to be His saints, who are His and His alone."[1]

It was al-Muḥāsibī who laid the foundations on which Ghazālī has built up the mighty structure of his teaching, al-Muḥāsibī who originated, while Ghazālī, out of his own genius and greater knowledge, has developed and added, and so brought to perfection his own doctrine of the religious life, lived Godward and manward.

Through Ghazālī, whose influence has been coextensive with the world of Islām, whose books have been read and studied from West Africa to Oceania, the doctrines which al-Muḥāsibī had set forth before him, out of which he developed his own, had a far-reaching effect, both in East and West. Barhebræus (*ob.* A.D. 1286), a Jacobite Christian of Jewish origin, one of the most eminent men of his Church and nation, who wrote widely on many subjects, turned to mysticism, as al-Muḥāsibī and Ghazālī had done before him, and of his two mystical works, the *Ethikon* and the *Book of the Dove*, the former appears to be in the main modelled on Ghazālī's *Iḥyā'*, in regard to both the arrangement of the contents and the actual contents themselves;[2] but the doctrines in which the teaching of Barhebræus most closely resembles Ghazālī are those which the latter had, in his turn, derived from al-Muḥāsibī, and since Barhebræus was as proficient in Arabic as in Syriac and visited Baghdad several times, there is no reason why he should not have read al-Muḥāsibī's works for himself, in addition to those of Ghazālī. In his classification of sins, on the causes which make venial sins mortal, in his teaching on repentance and the remedies for sins, for he also takes al-Muḥāsibī's view that sin is due to the sickness of the soul, for which a "medicine" can be found, the *Ethikon* follows much of the teaching of al-Muḥāsibī,[3] as also in the emphasis laid on sins of the tongue and the value of silence.[4] What Barhebræus has to say of the types of natural knowledge, and that supernatural knowledge which is gnosis, is very similar to al-

[1] *Iḥyā'*, II., p. 236. *Cf.* IV., p. 281 and pp. 243 *ff.* above.
[2] *Cf.* Barhebræus, *Book of the Dove*, Introduction.
[3] *Ethikon*, IV., p. 4; IV., pp. 4, 5; IV., pp. 4, 3.
[4] *Ibid.*, III., p. 15; *Book of the Dove*, III., p. 1.

Muḥāsibī's teaching, though very probably derived through Ghazālī, where he says, *e.g.*, " No man whose mind has been captivated by the desire of his Lord can further be captivated by the desire of anything in this world. For nobody who has found God will not wholly forget this world."[1]

To Barhebræus, also, knowledge is synonymous with love; He Who is known is the Beloved.[2] " The love of God," writes Barhebræus, " is augmented in the soul when man is strengthened in his state of abstention (*wara'*), when he meditates upon the wonderful works of the Creator, when his mind beholds the Divine power that penetrates the universe . . . hating every desire, seeking and desiring the Good One alone . . . purifying its inner heart from all beside Him."[3] And this turning away of the heart includes the renunciation of Paradise and its rewards; the renunciation of lovers is of those who, because they seek the Beloved alone, turn away their faces from all beside Him, for love is the fulfilment of the will of the Beloved.[4] Barhebræus follows al-Muḥāsibī in his teaching on longing, which, he says, necessarily follows love, and he uses almost the same words as al-Muḥāsibī, when he says, " When the Beloved is absent and the lover remembers the image of His beauty, he longs to see Him "; and again he writes, " The friend of God thirsts to see Him, longing after the time when he shall come and see His face."[5] In his view, too, love leads to that contemplation which is the heart's vision of the Beloved; and it comes about by closing the avenues of the senses, by opening up the heart to the Divine influence and withdrawing the veil from the inner senses.[6] The lover who is thus in contemplation of his Lord, says Barhebræus, is blind to all the beauties of the creatures and deaf to all human sounds (*cf.* p. 243 above), for he has entered into union with the Beloved. " When the mind becomes united with the

[1] *Book of the Dove*, III., p. 6. *Cf.* al-Muḥāsibī, pp. 227 *ff.* above.
[2] *Op. cit.*, Sentences 53, 96.
[3] *Book of the Dove*, III., p. 7. *Cf.* al-Muḥāsibī, p. 238 above.
[4] *Ibid.*, I., p. 3; II., p. 9, IV., p. 15. *Cf.* al-Muḥāsibī, pp. 346 *ff.* above.
[5] *Ibid.*, IV. p. 9; III., p. 6. *Cf.* al-Muḥāsibī, pp. 242 *ff.* above.
[6] Sentence 11. *Cf.* pp. 244 *ff.* above.

good, it ascends from glory to glory, forgetting not only the things of this world, but also itself, and in the light it sees itself in the likeness of God," and then the mercy of the mystic is poured out over all, like the mercy of God.[1]

Through Ghazālī also, al-Muḥāsibī's works most probably had an effect on Western mysticism, and his influence might also have been exerted there by the direct study of his books, for there is evidence that his work was known in North Africa. Leo Africanus (al-Fāsī, *ob.* A.D. 1494), the traveller, relates that in Fez he found certain learned men, "calling themselves moral philosophers, reverenced by the common people as gods." These people, he says, appeared eighty years after the Prophet, under the leadership of al-Ḥasan b. Abū'l-Ḥasan of Baṣra (Ḥasan al-Baṣrī), and a hundred years later al-Ḥārith Ibn Asad was known as a doctor of this sect: he belonged to Baghdad and left volumes of writings, and afterwards those who were found to be his followers were condemned by the Muslim jurisconsults. But eighty years later the sect began to revive under a certain famous professor (Ḥusayn b. Manṣūr al-Ḥallāj), who secured many disciples to whom he taught his doctrine, and was condemned with his followers to death. He wrote to the "patriarch," adds Leo Africanus, and asked leave to dispute with the lawyers, and on his request being granted, put them to silence. The "patriarch" revoked the sentence and caused many colleges and monasteries to be erected (presumably for the teaching and practice of Ṣūfism). The sect, he says, flourished for about a hundred years, till the coming of the Mongols caused some to flee to Cairo and some to Arabia, and they were dispersed for twenty years, until Niẓām al-Mulk (*ob.* 485/1092), who was addicted to the sect, so restored, erected and confirmed the same that, with the help of al-Ghazālī, he reconciled the lawyers with the disciples of this sect, on condition that the lawyers should be called Conservers of the Prophet and the sectaries Reformers of the same.[2]

This statement by Leo Africanus in regard to the history

[1] *Book of the Dove*, III., p. 4. *Cf.* al-Muḥāsibī, pp. 248 *ff.* above.

[2] *Descrittione dell' Africa*, III., p. 43 (Hakluyt Series, I., pp. 92, 93, 94).

of the Ṣūfīs is a proof that al-Muḥāsibī and his works were well known in North Africa, and this is confirmed by the fact that several of the extant copies of al-Muḥāsibī's works are in the Maghabī script.[1] The expedition which conquered Spain for Islām started from North Africa, and for long Andalusia was regarded as a province of North Africa and at first ruled from there, and later by Berber dynasties who were devoted adherents of religion and much given to the cult of the saints. Spain produced some great Ṣūfī writers, and al-Muḥāsibī's teaching, derived from a study of his own works or through Ghazālī's writings, may well have had an influence upon the mystics of Spain. The greatest of these Spanish Ṣūfīs, Muḥyī al-Dīn Ibn al-'Arabī (638/1240),[2] makes the same distinction as al-Muḥāsibī between the rational type of knowledge, which is the result of consideration, and the knowledge of hidden mysteries, which is above the sphere of reason, a knowledge which is the inbreathing of the Divine Spirit, given only to the prophets and the saints, whereby they attain to all knowledge.[3] He also teaches that when a man cleanses his heart, then the manifestations of God become clearer and more abundant in him, and the servant becomes nearer to God than others and God becomes his hearing and his sight. "When thou seest all thine actions to be His actions, and all His attributes to be thine attributes, and thine essence to be His essence, then, whithersoever ye turn, there is the Face of God."[4] Ibn al-'Arabī, however, developed a theosophic theory of Being which was very far removed from al-Muḥāsibī's simple doctrine of the relation between creature and Creator. Yet Ibn al-'Arabī, like that earlier Spanish mystic Abū Bakr Ibn Tufayl (*ob.* 581/1185), held, with al-Muḥāsibī, that the contemplative life must be translated into action, the mystic must give himself to a life

[1] "Waṣāyā," London, Or. 7900; "Murāqaba," "Tawba" and "Naṣā'iḥ," Cairo, *Taṣ.*, Shīn 3.

[2] For a full account of his life and teaching *cf.* von Kremer, *Gesch, der herr. Ideen*, pp. 102 *ff.* *Cf.* also R. A. Nicholson, *Studies in Islamic Mysticism*, pp. 77-142, and D. B. Macdonald, *Muslim Theology*, pp. 261 *ff.*

[3] *Commentary on the Iḥyā'*, VII., p. 245.

[4] *Kitāb al-Ajwiba* (J.R.A.S., 1901), p. 809. *Cf.* al-Muḥāsibī, pp. 103, 224, 251 above.

of active good, in relation both to God and man; he taught that "actions of the heart" must lead to, and direct aright, the "actions of the members." It is possible, too, that Ibn al-'Arabī's eschatological writings may have owed something to al-Muḥāsibī's works on the same subjects. It is to be noted that Dhahabī places Ibn al-'Arabī and his fellow-townsman Ibn Sab'īn (*ob.* 667/1269) side by side with al-Muḥāsibī in a list of representative Ṣūfī writers, evidently considering that the latter had handed the torch on to the former.[1]

Muslim mysticism in Spain, at this period, was closely bound up with Jewish mysticism, and both affected it and was affected by it, for Jewish scholars in the East were influenced by the mystical writings of the Ṣūfī teachers there and, in their turn, brought Muslim and Jewish learning from Baghdad to Spain, where it had its influence not only upon the Jewish mystics, but upon Muslim mystics as well. al-Muḥāsibī's teaching, reinforced as it was by his frequent references to Jewish traditions and sources, no doubt was included in the Muslim writings which, for a period of some centuries, affected Jewish mysticism in the West. The Jewish philosopher Ibn Gabīrōl (Avicebron, *ob.* A.D. 1058), in his *Fons Vitæ*, taught the doctrine of a knowledge of the principle behind all phenomena, which was hidden from the ignorant and foolish, and revealed to that one who meditated on the Divine mysteries an illuminative wisdom, that which al-Muḥāsibī conceived of as *ma'rifa*. Ibn Gabīrōl taught also that the traveller must be inspired by a great and ardent love if he was to attain to that mystic gnosis.[2]

There is much also in the teaching of Moses Maimonides of Cordova (*ob.* A.D. 1205), who had made a considerable study of Muslim learning, which is reminiscent of al-Muḥāsibī's teaching—*e.g.*, "It must be man's aim, after having acquired the knowledge of God, to deliver himself up to Him, and to have his heart constantly filled with longing after Him. He accomplishes this generally by seclusion and retirement."[3] Again he writes, "If we pray with the motion of our lips and our face toward the wall and at the same time think of our business, if we read the Law with

[1] *Mīzān al-'Itidāl*, p. 173. [2] *Op. cit.*, V., pp. 40-43.
[3] *Guide for the Perplexed*, pp. 386, 387.

our tongue and do not think of what we are reading," it is of no profit. Of the practice of the presence of God Maimonides writes, "When we have acquired a true knowledge of God and rejoice in that knowledge in such a manner that whilst speaking with others or attending to our own needs, our mind is all that time with God; when we are with our heart constantly near God, even whilst our body is in the society of men—that is the state of the prophets."[1] And of gnosis he writes, "Those who possess the knowledge of God and have their thoughts entirely directed to that knowledge are, as it were, always in the light. When a man obtains a knowledge of God and rejoices in it, it is impossible that any kind of evil should befall him while he is with God and God with him. Those who have God dwelling in their hearts are not touched by any evil whatever." Of the reverence due to God he writes, "We do not sit, move and occupy ourselves when we are alone and at home in the same manner as we do in the presence of a great king—if we therefore desire to attain human perfection and to be truly men of God, we must bear in mind that the great King that is over us and is always joined to us, is greater than any earthly king." Of the contemplation which comes through gnosis he says, "We look upon God by means of the light which He sends down to us."[2]

It is the *Zohar*, the chief textbook of Jewish mysticism, compiled from many sources in the thirteenth century, which shews most plainly the influence of the Muslim mystics, and in this there are many striking reflections of al-Muḥāsibī's teaching—*e.g.*, on the relation of heart and members, "When a man wills to serve his Master, his desire is first generated in the heart, which is the basis and the active principle of the whole body. From thence the desire is diffused through all the members of the body, so that the desire of the rest of the members of the body and the desire of the heart unite into one whole and draw upon themselves the resplendence of the Divine Glory (the *Shekinah*) to reside with them. Such a man becomes himself, as it were, a portion of the Holy One. . . . Whosoever is of a willing heart may

[1] *Op. cit.*, p. 387. *Cf.* pp. 215 *ff.* above.
[2] *Op. cit.*, pp. 389, 391.

draw unto himself the Divine Glory."[1] There is a reminder of al-Muḥāsibī's teaching in the Zoharic admonition to the sinner, "Repent of thy sins. Reflect on these things and return to thy Master . . . reflect whether thou canst rely on the merits of thy forebears to protect thee."[2] There is also the idea in the *Zohar* that a man's soul departs during sleep. "Every night the Supreme Point absorbs in itself the souls of the righteous . . . for in the night man's soul mounts up into heaven to gaze upon the mystery of the Divine Glory, each one according to its merits . . . and a man has then a foretaste of death."[3] The *Zohar* teaches that it is through resistance to temptation and to the suggestions of the Evil One that the seeker attains to strength and righteousness. "If it were not for this Accuser, the righteous would not possess the supernal treasures of the world to come. Happy, therefore, are they who, coming into conflict with the Tempter, prevail against him, for through him will they attain bliss and all the good and desirable possessions of the world to come, and continually gain strength from the Holy King."[4] The place of godly fear in worship is emphasised by the *Zohar*, "Worship from fear is to be highly prized . . . but we should combine fear with love. After fear comes love, for he who worships out of love attaches himself to the holiness of the world to come."[5]

The Zoharic teaching on prayer and the contemplative life which leads to gnosis and union with the One is very similar to that of al-Muḥāsibī. "Happy is the portion of whoever can penetrate into the mysteries of his Master and become absorbed unto Him . . . especially does a man achieve this when he offers up his prayer to his Master in intense devotion, his will then becoming as the flame inseparable from the coal. Whilst a man's mouth and lips are moving, his heart and will must soar to the height of heights, so as to acknowledge the unity of the whole in virtue of the mystery of mysteries in which all ideas, all wills,

[1] *Zohar*, IV., p. 171. *Cf.* pp. 87 *ff.* above.
[2] *Op. cit.*, p. 174. *Cf.* p. 139 above; "Riʿāya," fols. 102*a ff.*
[3] *Op. cit.*, pp. 225, 232. *Cf.* p. 92 above.
[4] *Op. cit.*, p. 63. *Cf.* al-Muḥāsibī, pp. 127, 128 above.
[5] *Op. cit.*, IV., p. 234; I., p. 48. *Cf.* pp. 188 *ff.*, 238 *ff.* above.

and all thoughts find their goal, to wit, the mystery of the One, the Infinite" (*En-Sōf*).[1] According to the Zoharic teaching, also, there is provision made in Paradise for the children who have died before their time, and for the purification of sinful souls by passing through the "river of fire," which corresponds to the fiery waves which al-Muḥāsibī describes as being below the bridge of Ṣirāt; and in the *Zohar*, too, the destroying angels are there. In the Zoharic judgment, also, a man's deeds are weighed, and if the evil exceed the good he is condemned to torment.[2]

Through Ghazālī and possibly through Ibn al-'Arabī, al-Muḥāsibī may well have had an indirect influence upon the Christian mystics, and in this respect, also, Jewish scholars acted as a link, for the Spanish and Provençal rabbis contributed to introduce the works of Muslim writers to the Christian West. It was especially in Lower Italy and Spain that the two came into contact. At Palermo, when, after a hundred and thirty years of Muslim rule, Sicily fell into Norman hands in A.D. 1091, Arabic works were studied and translated by Christian scholars, while Toledo, in Spain, continued to be a centre of Muslim learning, even after the Christian conquest of A.D. 1085; the rich libraries of Arab culture became the resort of Western scholars, and Raymond, Archbishop of Toledo (A.D. 1130-1150), founded a school of translators there to translate from Arabic to Latin. Here, too, was founded the first European School of Oriental Studies in 1250, and within the next sixty years Arabic was being studied at Miramar, Paris, Louvain and Salamanca.

St. Thomas Aquinas (*ob.* A.D. 1274) made it his business to study the Arabic writers, and some of his devotional and mystical teaching bears the closest resemblance to that of al-Muḥāsibī, though it is most probable that al-Muḥāsibī's doctrines reached him by way of Ghazālī. Of worship and prayer St. Thomas writes, "We offer God a spiritual adora-

[1] *Op. cit.*, IV., pp. 224, 225. *Cf.* al-Muḥāsibī, pp. 203 *ff.*

[2] *Op. cit.*, IV., pp. 119, 174. *Cf.* al-Muḥāsibī, *Ba'th al-Nushūr*, "Kitāb al-Tawahhum." For a detailed study of the relation between Jewish and Islamic Mysticism *cf.* A. Bension, *The Zohar in Moslem and Christian Spain.*

tion, consisting in the internal devotion of the mind, and a bodily adoration, which consists in an exterior humbling of the body. In all acts of worship (*latria*) that which is without is referred to that which is within as being of greater import; it follows that exterior adoration is offered on account of interior adoration, in other words we exhibit signs of humility in our bodies in order to incite our affection to submit to God—proceeding from the sensible to the intelligible."[1] Of man's need of the Divine grace if he is to attain to gnosis and the love of God which will bring him to the *summum bonum*, of the Vision of God, and of the limitations of the natural reason in its efforts to attain to spiritual truth, St. Thomas says, "It is impossible for any created intellect to comprehend God"; and again, "We have a more perfect knowledge of God by grace than by natural reason."[2] It is by the assistance of sanctifying grace also that man is enabled to love God, for sanctifying grace, he holds, is an effect in man of the Divine love, and it leads to the transformation and illumination of the natural reason by the Divine light, whereby the soul may look upon God. "To so sublime a vision," he writes, "the created intellect needs to be raised by some kind of outpouring of the Divine grace. . . . The disposition by which the created intellect is raised to the Vision of the Divine is rightly called the Light of glory."[3] This supernatural light means that the soul becomes a participator in the light of God, and is enabled to know and judge all things. "This light is a likeness of the Divine intellect—those who contemplate God (thereby) see all things and have all knowledge."[4] In this contemplation man finds his ultimate happiness, for as to al-Muḥāsibī, so also to St. Thomas, contemplation means union, for in that vision the will of the lover has become one with the Will of the Beloved. "The last end," writes St. Thomas, "to which a man is conducted by the assistance of the Divine grace is the Vision of God—and man cannot attain to this unless he be united to God by conformity of the will." But now,

[1] *Summa Theologica*, Q. 84, Art. 2. *Cf.* al-Muḥāsibī, pp. 200 *ff.* above.
[2] *Ibid.*, Q. 12, Arts. 7, 13. *Cf.* al-Muḥāsibī, Chapter VI. above.
[3] *Summa contra Gentiles*, cap. LIII. *Cf.* pp. 103, 249 *ff.* above.
[4] *Ibid.*, cap. LIX., *Sum. Theol.*, Q. 12, Art. 5. *Cf.* p. 226 above.

says St. Thomas, the rational creature is made " deiform," for that vision is of the things which are within the soul, and therefore it means that " God is in the souls of the blessed." No creature can come nearer to God than the one who contemplates Him, and " by the Vision man is made a partaker of eternal life."[1]

Raymond Lull (*ob.* A.D. 1314) of Catalonia, the " Illuminated Doctor," was among the Christian mystics of Spain who owed much to the inspiration of Arab writers, and he founded a school of Oriental Languages at Rome, for the study, among other things, of Arabic and Islām. Of him a modern writer says, " He became like a living flame urging man on towards God, towards contemplation and especially towards action." Much of his teaching, too, might well have been founded upon al-Muḥāsibī's writings, though in this case also it may have been derived through later writers. Of the self-examination of the penitent, Raymond Lull says that " he must take counsel with his understanding and will and memory and imagination in respect of all the bodily senses, and examine himself upon the sins which he has committed, as to sight, hearing, smell, taste and touch, in speech and imagination, remembrance and understanding, love and hate."[2] In his recapitulation of sins and their remedies there is a re-echo of the ascetical teaching of al-Muḥāsibī. " If through pride thou hast sunk to the depths of sin, rise thou again with love to the heights of diligence, remembering that after death no repentance, neither calling for mercy avails thee (*cf.* p. 150 above). If thou sink to the sin of envy, let thy love rise to the heights of charity. If thou sink to the sin of wrath, let thy love rise to patience and abstinence, and consider how easily death may come to thee."[3]

Of gnosis he writes that the infused knowledge (*ma'rifa*) comes from the will, from prayer and devotion, and acquired knowledge (*'ilm*) from study and understanding, which is almost identical with what al-Muḥāsibī regards as

[1] *Sum. Theol.*, Q. 12, Art. 11; *Sum. con. Gen.*, cap. LIX. *Cf.* pp. 247 *ff.* above.

[2] *The Tree of Love*, p. 46. *Cf.* pp. 113, 158, 173 above.

[3] *Ibid.*, p. 80. *Cf.* pp. 160 *ff.* above.

the preparation for the reception of the Divine gift, as distinct from mere human knowledge.[1]

Of the place of hope and fear in the religious life, as qualities of the lover of God, Raymond Lull says, "Between Hope and Fear, Love made her home"; and of the marks of the lover he makes the lover himself say, "My hope is in my remembrance, understanding and love of the justice and mercy of my Beloved. My charity lies in this, that I love my Beloved more than myself or than any beside. My patience is in my fear and love of my Beloved. My strength of mind is with my remembrance, understanding and love of the evil things that come to me through my Beloved. I am in my Beloved; I go to my Beloved; I come from my Beloved; and in my remembrance, honour, service, love and understanding of Him is my treasure." Again the lover says, "I distinguish not between the trials that Thou sendest me and the joys." What Lull has to say of solitude and fellowship in relation to the lover is also very reminiscent of al-Muḥāsibī. "Solitude," he writes, "is solace and companionship between lover and Beloved, for solace and companionship are the solitude of the lover's heart when he remembers nought save his Beloved." Love is that which bids you ever love, "in walking and sitting, in sleeping and waking, in buying and selling, in weeping and in laughter, in speech and in silence, in gain and in loss."[2]

There is much in Dante which recalls the teaching of Islamic mysticism, and it is now generally recognised that the *Divina Commedia* was influenced by the Muslim conception of Heaven and Hell, and especially the conception set forth by the Ṣūfīs, and while Dante probably owes most to Ibn al-'Arabī, there are also traces of earlier teaching, and al-Muḥāsibī must have been one of the earliest to elaborate the eschatological teaching set forth in the traditions and to combine it with a more mystical doctrine of Paradise. He also had the conception of purgatory, of a purifying punishment, which is that of Hell, but temporary, not eternal (*cf.* p. 50 above). The reward of the righteous who died re-

[1] *Book of the Lover and the Beloved*, p. 74. *Cf.* pp. 103 *ff.* above.

[2] *Tree of Love*, pp. 105, 104; *Book of the Lover and the Beloved*, pp. 26, 76, 39. *Cf.* al-Muḥāsibī, pp. 28, 96 *ff.*, 243 *ff.* above.

pentant was to be that of the bliss of Paradise, but to the saints and to the elect was promised the supreme joy of looking upon the very face of God, and of hearing the voice of the Beloved. To Dante, also, the supreme bliss of the sanctified was to look upon that Divine Light which was Truth itself, and so to enter for ever into the life in God, " for in that Light man becometh such that to turn thence to any other sight becomes no longer possible, for the Good, which is the object of his will, is therein wholly gathered, and that which outside it is defective, within is perfect."[1] It may well be that al-Muḥāsibī's conception of the Beatific Vision, transmitted by other writers, if not conveyed directly, had some share in influencing Dante's idea of that Vision of God which was the final reward of the Blessed.

So we may feel that al-Muḥāsibī's influence, whether direct or indirect, upon the mystics who came after him, Muslim, Jewish and Christian, was far-reaching. Not without reason has he been called the Thomas à Kempis of his people and his time, and it was he who first most clearly defined the mystic Path which had as its goal the realisation by the soul of its oneness with the Divine, and he who made plain the way for the many who followed him.

[1] *Paradiso*, 54, 100-105. *Cf.* pp. 49, 51 above. For a full discussion of the relation between Dante's vision and the Islamic legends, *cf.* M. Asin (Palacios), *Islam and the Divine Comedy*.

BIBLIOGRAPHY

I.—ARABIC, PERSIAN, HEBREW AND SYRIAC

Leo Africanus (al-Fāsī). *Descrittione dell' Africa.* Hakluyt Series, I.

M. al-D. Ibn al-'Arabī. *Kitāb al-Ajwiba.* J.R.A.S., 1901.

Abū Ṣāliḥ al-Armān. *Churches and Monasteries of Egypt.* (Arabic Text.) Oxford, a.d. 1895.

Abu'l-'Aṭāhiya. *Diwān.* Beyrout, a.d. 1886.

F. al-D. 'Aṭṭār. *Tadhkirat al-Awliyā.* (Ed. R. A. Nicholson.) London, a.d. 1905.

Ibn Sīnā (Avicenna). *Fī maqāmāt al-'Ārifīn.* (Ed. M. A. F. Mehren.) Leyden, a.d. 1889.

'A. al-Q. al-Baghdādī. *Kitāb Uṣūl al-Dīn.* Stambul, a.d. 1928.

Abū Bakr b. Khayr. *Bibliotheca Arabico-Hispana.* (Ed. F. Codera and J. Ribera.) a.d. 1894.

Abu'l-Faraj Barhebræus. *Book of the Dove.* (Tr. A. J. Wensinck.) Leyden, a.d. 1919.

Abu'l-Faraj Barhebræus. *Ethikon.* (Ed. P. Bedjan.) Paris, a.d. 1898.

S. al-D. al-Dhahabī. *Mizān al-I'tidāl.* Lucknow, a.d. 1884.

S. al-D. al-Dhahabī. *Ṭabaqāt al-Ḥuffāẓ.* (Ed. H. F. Wüstenfeld.) Göttingen, a.d. 1833-34.

S. al-D. al-Dhahabī. "Ta'rīkh al-Islām." MS. Leyden 843.

M. b. M. al-Ghazālī. *Ayyuha'l-Walad.* (Ed. G. Scherer.) Beyrout.

M. b. M. al-Ghazālī. *al-Durrat al-Fākhira.* (Ed. L. Gautier.) Paris, a.d. 1878.

M. b. M. al-Ghazālī. *Iḥyā' 'Ulūm al-Dīn.* Cairo, a.h. 1272 (reprint 1340).

M. b. M. al-Ghazālī. *Kitāb al-Iqtiṣād.* Cairo, a.h. 1327.

M. b. M. al-Ghazālī. *Jawāhir.* Cairo, a.h. 1329.

M. b. M. al-Ghazālī. *al-Risālat al-Laduniyya.* Cairo, a.h. 1328.

M. b. M. al-Ghazālī. *Minhāj.* Cairo, a.h. 1313.

M. b. M. al-Ghazālī. *Mishkāt al-Anwār.* Cairo, a.h. 1322.

M. b. M. al-Ghazālī. *Mizān al-'amal.* Cairo, a.h. 1328.

M. b. M. al-Ghazālī. *Mukāshafat al-Qulūb.* Cairo, a.d. 1883.

M. b. M. al-Ghazālī. *al-Munkidh min al-Ḍalāl.* Cairo, a.h. 1309.

Ibn Ḥajar al-'Asqalānī. *Tahdhīb al-Tahdhīb.* Hyderabad, a.h. 1325.

Ḥajjī Khalīfa. *Kashf al-Zunūn*. (Ed. G. Flügel.) Leipzig, A.D. 1835-58.

A. b. 'U. al-Jullabī al-Hujwīrī. *Kashf al-Maḥjūb*. (Tr. R. A. Nicholson.) London, A.D. 1911.

S. b. 'A. al-'A. al-Ḥurayfīsh. *al-Rawḍ al-Fā'iq*. Cairo, A.H. 1279.

'A. al-R. b. Ḥ. 'Irāqī. "al-Ba'ith 'ala'l-Khalāṣ." MS. Br. Mus., Or. 4275.

Isaac of Nineveh. *Mystic Treatises*. (Tr. A. J. Wensinck.) Amsterdam, A.D. 1923.

'A. al-R. al-Jāmī. *Nafaḥāt al-Uns*. (Ed. W. N. Lees.) Calcutta, A.D. 1850.

J. al-D. Ibn al-Jawzī. *al-Nāmūs fī Talbīs*. Cairo, A.H. 1340.

M. b. I. al-Kalābādhī. *Kitāb al-Ta'arruf*. (Ed. A. J. Arberry.) Cairo, A.D. 1934.

Ibn Khallikān. *Biographical Dictionary*. (Tr. de Slane.) Paris, A.D. 1842.

M. b. 'A. al-Khaṭīb. *Mishkāt al-Maṣābīḥ*. Lucknow, A.H. 1319.

A. b. 'A. al-Khaṭīb al-Baghdādī. *Ta'rīkh Baghdād*. Cairo, A.D. 1931.

'A. al-M. al-Kindī. *Risālat al-Hāshimī ila al-Kindī*. London, A.D. 1885.

M. Maimonides. *Guide for the Perplexed*. (Tr. M. Friedlander.) London, A.D. 1904.

Abu Ṭālib al-Makkī. *Qūt al-Qulūb*. Cairo, A.H. 1310.

Ḥ. b. A. al-Muḥāsibī. "Faṣl fī'l-Maḥabba." MS. Leyden, Or. 311*a*, fols. 231 *ff*.; MS. Damas., Zah. Taṣ. 117 (XI.), fols. 4*a ff*.

Ḥ. b. A. al-Muḥāsibī. "Kitāb al-Ba'th wa'l-Nushūr." MS. Paris, 1913.

Ḥ. b. A. al-Muḥāsibī. "Kitāb bad' man anāb ila Allāh." MS. Stambul, Jārallāh.

Ḥ. b. A. al-Muḥāsibī. "Kitāb Fahm al-Ṣalāt." MS. Stambul, Jārallāh.

Ḥ. b. A. al-Muḥāsibī. "Masā'il fī a'māl al-Qulūb." MS. Stambul, Jārallāh.

Ḥ. b. A. al-Muḥāsibī. "Risālat Ādāb al-Nufūs." MS. Stambul, Jārallāh.

Ḥ. b. A. al-Muḥāsibī. "Risālat al-'Azama." MS. Stambul, Jārallāh.

Ḥ. b. A. al-Muḥāsibī. "Risālat al-Makāsib wa'l-Wara'." MS. Stambul, Jārallāh.

Ḥ. b. A. al-Muḥāsibī. "Risālat Ma'iyyat al-'Aql." MS. Stambul, Jārallāh.

Ḥ. b. A. al-Muḥāsibī. "Riṣālat al-Tanbīh." MS. Stambul, Jārallāh.

Ḥ. b. A. al-Muḥāsibī. "Kitāb fī Zuhd." MS. Stambul, Jārallāh.

Ḥ. b. A. al-Muḥāsibī. "Kitāb Iḥkām al-Tawba." MS. Cairo, Taṣ. Sh. 3.

Ḥ. b. A. al-Muḥāsibī. "Kitāb al-'Ilm." MS. Milan, Am. 460.

Ḥ. b. A. al-Muḥāsibī. "Kitāb al-Mustarshid." MS. Cairo, Taṣ. Sh. 3.

Ḥ. b. A. al-Muḥāsibī. "Kitāb al-Ṣabr." MS. Bankipore 105.

Ḥ. b. A. al-Muḥāsibī. "Kitāb al-Ri'āya." MS. Oxford, Hunt. 611; Broussa, Jāmi' Kabīr 1534; Angora, Diy. Is. Riyāséti 403.

Ḥ. b. A. al-Muḥāsibī. "Sharḥ al-Ma'rifa (Muḥāsabat al-Nufūs)." MS. Cairo, Taṣ. Sh. 3; Berlin 2815; Br. Mus., Or. 4026.

Ḥ. b. A. al-Muḥāsibī. "Kitāb al-Tawahhum." MS. Oxford, Hunt. 611.

Ḥ. b. A. al-Muḥāsibī. "Kitāb al-Waṣāyā (Naṣā'iḥ)." Cairo, Taṣ. 1416; Br. Mus., Or. 7900; Stambul, Baghdādī Wehbi 614.

'A. al-R. al-Munāwī. "al-Kawākib al-Durriya." MS. Br. Mus., Add. 23369.

M. b. al-Munawwar. *Asrār al-Tawḥīd.* (Ed. V. A. Zhukovski.) Petrograd, A.D. 1899.

M. b. Isḥāq al-Nadīm. *Fihrist.* (Ed. G. Flügel.) Leipzig, A.D. 1871-72.

Abū Nu'aym al-Isfahānī. "Ḥilyāt al-Awliyā." MS. Leyden, Or. 311*a*; Damas., Zah. Taṣ. 117.

Abū Nu'aym al-Isfahānī. *Ḥilyat al-Awliyā.* Cairo, A.D. 1932.

Abu'l-Q. al-Qushayrī. *Risāla.* Cairo, A.D. 1867.

J. al-Dīn Rūmī. *Mathnawī.* (Ed. R. A. Nicholson.) London, A.D. 1925.

M. al-Dīn Sa'dī. *Ṭayyibāt.* (Ed. L. White King.) London, A.D. 1926.

'A. al-K. Sam'ānī. *Kitāb al-Ansāb.* Leyden, A.D. 1919.

Abū Nasr al-Sarrāj. *Kitāb al-Luma'.* (Ed. R. A. Nicholson.) London, A.D. 1914.

'A. al-W. Sha'rānī (Sha'rāwī). *al-Ṭabaqāt al-Kubrā* (*Lawaqih*). Cairo, A.D. 1299.

Abu'l-Fatḥ, Shahrastānī. *Kitāb al-Milal wa'l-Nihal.* (Ed. W. Cureton.) London, A.D. 1842.

Ṣibt Ibn al-Jawzī. "Mir'āt al-Zamān." MS. Br. Mus., Add. 23277.

T. al-D. al-Subkī. *al-Ṭabaqāt al-Shāfi'iyya.* Cairo, A.H. 1324.

Sh. al-D. Abū Ḥafṣ Suhrawardī. *'Awārif al-Ma'ārif* (on margin of Ghazali's *Iḥyā'*). Cairo, A.H. 1272.

'A. al-R. al-Sulamī. "Ṭabaqāt al-Ṣūfiyya." MS. Br. Mus., Add. 18520.

'A. b. Rabban al-Ṭabarī. *Kitāb al-Dīn wa'l-Dawlat.* (Ed. A. J. Mingana.) A.D. 1922.

Abu'l-Maḥāsin b. Taghrībirdī. *al-Nujūm al-Zāhira.* Leyden, A.D. 1855-61.

Yāfi'ī al-Sh. al-Tamīmī. "Mir'āt al-Janān." MS. Br. Mus., Or. 1511 (Sup. 473).

Yāfi'ī al-Sh. al-Tamīmī. *Nashr al-Maḥsin.* Cairo.

Yāfi'ī al-Sh. al-Tamīmī. *Rawḍ al-Riyāḥīn.* Cairo, A.H. 1286.

Ibn Wāḍiḥ al-Ya'qūbī. *Ta'rīkh.* (Ed. Th. Houtsma.) Leyden, A.D. 1883.

J. Zaydān. *Hist. of Islamic Civilisation.* (Tr. D. S. Margoliouth.) London, A.D. 1907.

Ẓiya Bey. *Kharābāt.* Stambul, A.H. 1291.

The *Zohar*, I.-IV. (Tr. H. Sperling and M. Simon.) London, A.D. 1931-34.

II.—GENERAL

T. Arnold and A. Guillaume. *The Legacy of Islam.* Oxford, 1931.

M. Asin. *See* Palacios.

St. Augustine. *Confessions.* London, 1886.

C. Barbanson. *The Secret Paths of Divine Love.* (Tr. Dom J. McCann.) London, 1927.

A. Baumstark. *Geschichte der Syrischen Literatur.* Bonn, 1922.

A. Bension. *The Zohar in Moslem and Christian Spain.* London, 1932.

E. Blochet. *Études sur l'ésotérisme.* J.As., 1902.

L. Blosius. *A Book of Spiritual Instruction.* (Tr. B. A. Wilberforce.) London, 1925.

T. J. de Boer. *History of Philosophy in Islam.* (Tr. E. R. Jones.) London, 1903.

A. C. Bouquet. *Religious Experience: Its Nature, Types and Validity.* Cambridge, 1932.

E. G. Browne. *Literary History of Persia.* Cambridge, 1928.

E. E. Calverly. *Worship in Islam.* Madras, 1925.

Carra de Vaux. *Les Penseurs de l'Islam.* Paris, 1923.

St. Chrysostom. *De Incomprehensibili.* Patrologiæ. Paris, 1858-62.

St. Clement. *Stromateis.* (Ed. Hort and Mayor.) 1902.

St. Clement. *Writings.* (Ed. Migne.) Patrologia Græca, VIII., IX.

S. Coleridge. *Lay Sermons.* London, 1852.

Dante. *La Divina Commedia.* London, 1900.

O. Depont and X. Coppolani. *Les Confréries religieuses musulmanes.* Algiers, 1897.

St. Francis de Sales. *Introduction to the Devout Life.* (Tr. A. Ross.) London, 1930.

St. Francis de Sales. *Treatise on the Love of God.* (Tr. H. B. Mackey.) London, 1884.

M. D. Gibson. *Studia Sinaitica.* London, 1894.

I. Goldziher. *Muhammedanische Studien.* Halle, 1889.

H. Gösche. *Über Ghazzali's Leben und Werke.* Berlin, 1858.

H. GRAETZ. *History of the Jews.* (Tr. B. Löwy.) London, 1891.
A. GUILLAUME. *The Traditions of Islam.* Oxford, 1924.
F. P. HARTON. *The Elements of the Spiritual Life.* London, 1932.
M. HORTEN. *Indische Strömungen in der Islamischen Mystik.* Heidelberg, 1927.
F. VON HÜGEL. *The Mystical Element of Religion.* London, 1923.
F. VON HÜGEL. *The Life of Prayer.* London, 1929.
ST. IGNATIUS. *Spiritual Exercises.* London, 1923.
M. IQBAL. *Reconstruction of Religious Thought in Islam.* Oxford, 1934.
ST. JEANNE DE CHANTAL. *Mystical Prayer.* London, 1929.
RUFUS JONES. *Studies in Mystical Religion.* London, 1909.
J. VON KASTL. *De Adhærendo Deo.*
T. À KEMPIS. *De Imitatione Christi.* Paris, 1886.
T. À KEMPIS. *The Imitation of Christ.* London, 1924.
K. E. KIRK. *The Vision of God.* London, 1931.
A. VON KREMER, *Geschichte der herrschenden Ideen des Islams.* Leipzig, 1868.
H. LAMMENS. *L'Islam, croyances et institutions.* Beyrout, 1926.
BROTHER LAWRENCE. *The Practice of the Presence of God.* London, 1906.
R. LEVY. *A Baghdad Chronicle.* Cambridge, 1929.
RAYMOND LULL. *Book of the Lover and the Beloved.* London, 1923.
RAYMOND LULL. *The Tree of Love.* London, 1926.
D. B. MACDONALD. *The Development of Muslim Theology, Jurisprudence and Constitutional Theory.* London, 1903.
D. B. MACDONALD. *The Religious Attitude and Life in Islam.* Chicago, 1909.
J. MARÉCHAL. *Studies in the Psychology of the Mystics.* (Tr. A. Thorold.) London, 1927.
D. S. MARGOLIOUTH. *The Early Development of Mohammedanism.* London, 1914.
L. MASSIGNON. *Essai sur les Origines du Lexique Technique de la Mystique Musulmane.* Paris, 1922.
L. MASSIGNON. *La Passion d'al-Hallāj.* Paris, 1922.
L. MASSIGNON. *Recueil de Textes Inédits.* Paris, 1930.
S. MUNK. *Mélanges de Philosophie Juive et Arabe.* Paris, 1859.
R. A. NICHOLSON. *Eastern Poetry and Prose.* Cambridge, 1922.
R. A. NICHOLSON. *The Idea of Personality in Ṣūfism.* Cambridge, 1923.
R. A. NICHOLSON. *The Mystics of Islam.* London, 1914.
R. A. NICHOLSON. *A Literary History of the Arabs.* Cambridge, 1930.
R. A. NICHOLSON. *Studies in Islamic Mysticism.* Cambridge, 1921.
T. NÖLDEKE. *Sketches from Eastern History.* (Tr. J. S. Black.) London, 1892.

de L. O'Leary. *Arabic Thought and its Place in History.* London, 1922.

R. Otto. *The Idea of the Holy.* (Tr. J. W. Harvey.) Oxford, 1931.

R. Otto. *Religious Essays.* (Tr. B. Lunn.) Oxford, 1931.

M. Asin Palacios. *Logia et Agrapha.* Patriologia. Paris, 1926.

M. Asin Palacios. *Algazel dogmatica, moral, ascetica.*

M. Asin Palacios. *La Mystique d'al-Ghazali.* (Mélanges de l'Université St. Joseph.) Beyrout, 1921.

Palladius. *Paradise of the Fathers.* (Tr. E. A. Budge.) London, 1907.

St. Peter of Alcantara. *Treatise on Prayer and Meditation.* London, 1926.

Gerlac Petersen. *Divine Soliloquies.* London, 1920.

A. Poulain. *Les Grâces d'Oraison.* Paris, 1909.

J. Ruysbroeck. *Adornment of the Spiritual Marriage.* (Tr. C. A. Wynschenk Dom.) London, 1916.

J. Ruysbroeck. *Book of the Sparkling Stone.* (Tr. C. A. Wynschenk Dom.) London, 1916.

A. Schmölders. *Essai sur les Écoles Philosophiques chez les Arabes.* Paris, 1842.

M. Smith. *Rābi'a the Mystic and her Fellow-Saints in Islām.* Cambridge, 1928.

M. Smith. *Studies in Early Mysticism in the Near and Middle East.* London, 1931.

N. Söderblom. *The Living God.* Oxford, 1933.

B. H. Streeter. *Reality.* London, 1926.

B. H. Streeter. *The Spirit.* London, 1921.

G. le Strange. *Baghdad during the Abbasid Caliphate.* Oxford, 1900.

Theologica Germanica. (Tr. S. Winkworth.) London, 1924.

St. Thomas Aquinas. *Summa Theologica.*

St. Thomas Aquinas. *Summa contra Gentiles.* London, 1928.

E. Underhill. *The Life of the Spirit and the Life of Today.* London, 1923.

A. J. Wensinck. *The Muslim Creed.* Cambridge, 1932.

F. Wüstenfeld. *Die Geschichteschreiber der Araber und ihre Werke.* Göttingen, 1882.

INDEX

I.—GENERAL

Arabic names to which the definite article al- is prefixed will be found under their initial letter. Titles of books, etc., are printed in italics.

World, this present, 89, 109, 113, 114 *ff.*, 123, 127, 150, 156 *ff.*, 172, 174, 203, 244, 264, 273, 276, 281. *See* dunyā
Worship, 34, 46, 56, 72, 74, 98, 277, 287, 288
Wuhayb b. Ward al-Makkī, 71
Wüstenfeld, F., 68

Yaman, 62
Yāfi'ī, 'Afīf al-Dīn, 267
Yaḥya b. Zachariyā, 251
Yazīd b. Hārūn, 39, 61
Yūnus b. 'Ubayd Qaysī, 70
Yūsuf b. Asbāṭ, 72, 75, 79

Zabūr, 68
Zanjānī, M. b. A., 38
Zaydan, J., 2, 4
Ẓiyā Bey, 265
Żohar, the, 87, 252, 285 *ff.*
Zoroastrianism, 2

II.—TECHNICAL TERMS, Etc.

'ābid, 264
'abth, 111
ādāb, 27
'adl, 4, 193 *ff.*
'adū, 119
ahl al-ṣuffa, 63
aḥwāl, 7, 80, 87, 197
-ākhira, 89
'amal, 189
a'māl, al-jawāriḥ, 87
a'māl, al-qulūb, 87
Amīr al-Kāfirīn, 5
'aql, 7, 56, 78, 92 *ff.*
'ārif, 17, 25, 223, 264
aṣfiyā', 227
awliyā', 223
awtād, 34

baṣā'ir, 107, 225
bāṭin, 7, 86, 224
bayt al-ḥikma, 3, 4
bukhl, 145, 274

darajat al-na'īm, 224
dhikr, 30, 99, 212
dunyā, 89, 114

fapīla, 166
fā'iqa, 103
fanā', 28, 225
faqīh, 68
faqīr, 34, 75, 77, 80
farā'iḍ, 19
fatwā, 135
fawā'id, 243, 250
fikra, 21
firāsa, 61
fitan, 122
fiṭna, 227
fuḍūl, 166

ghafla, 129
gharīẓa, 93
ghayba, 59, 233
ghība, 146
ghirra, 45, 147
ghurba, 262

ḥabr, 268
ḥadhr, 126
ḥadīth, 3, 7, 60, 62, 68
ḥalāl, 62
ḥaqā'iq, 15, 80, 263
Ḥaqq, 263
ḥarām, 62
ḥasad, 143
hawā, 112
ḥayā', 151
himma, 30, 109, 212, 229
ḥudūd, 19, 46
ḥuḍūr, 233
ḥulūl, 30, 250, 258, 262
ḥusn al-ẓann, 74
ḥuẓn, 151